A. W. N. Pugin, from recollection, by Joseph Nash

Recollections of
A. W. N. PUGIN
and his father
AUGUSTUS PUGIN

BENJAMIN FERREY

with an appendix by E. Sheridan Purcell
and an introduction and index by
Clive and Jane Wainwright

LONDON
THE SCOLAR PRESS
1978

The Recollections of A. N. W. Pugin, and his father,
Augustus Pugin

First published in 1861 by Edward Stamford, London.
This edition, with introduction and index by
Clive and Jane Wainwright, first published in 1978 by
The Scolar Press Limited
39 Great Russell Street London WC1B 3PH
ISBN 0 85967 358 8

Introduction and index copyright
© Clive and Jane Wainwright, 1978

Printed in England by The Scolar Press Limited
Ilkley Yorkshire LS29 8JP

PREFACE TO 1978 EDITION

Few would disagree with the statement that A. W. N. Pugin was the most talented and influential architect, theorist and decorative designer of the early Victorian Gothic Revival. His life and works have already been dealt with in several books. The best is *Pugin, a Mediaeval Victorian* by Michael Trappes-Lomax (1932). An especially important group of buildings designed for one of Pugin's major patrons is fascinatingly discussed and placed in the context of the Catholic Revival by D. Gwynn in *Lord Shrewsbury, Pugin, and The Catholic Revival* (1946). The most recent ˌbook is *Pugin* (1971) by Phoebe Stanton, which though it gives a short and adequate account of his life and works is marred by the inadequacy of its references to the sources used. It is however remarkable that we still lack a full biography of Pugin, one of Europe's greatest nineteenth-century architects.

Ferrey's biography is still a standard source which, though it requires amending and correcting, will never be superseded. Pugin died at forty, leaving notebooks, diaries and hundreds of letters. He left no autobiography beyond some short notes on his early life which are now in the Victoria and Albert Museum Library with his diaries. But the next best thing to an autobiography is a biography written by a close friend. In the Introduction to this edition I will attempt to give perspective to Ferrey's text by writing about Pugin in the light of modern research. I shall not include a bibliography but almost all the important sources for the study of Pugin and his works will be found in my notes.

Two publications will however shortly revolutionize the study of Pugin's architecture and design. They are both catalogues of collections of Pugin's letters, manuscripts and drawings. That of the RIBA Drawings Collection's holdings will probably appear before this volume. The other catalogue is of the holdings of Pugin material in the Victoria and Albert Museum. They will both be the work

of Alexandra Wedgwood and will contain, besides the
entries concerning each drawing, a mass of fascinating
information on Pugin and his works. I am indebted to
Alexandra Wedgwood for allowing me to read the proofs
of the RIBA Catalogue.

I wish to thank Mrs Joan Howkins for giving me free
access to those of her family papers which relate to Pugin.
I must also pay tribute to the way in which the late
Charles Handley-Read encouraged my early interest in
Pugin and gave generously of his time and knowledge to
this end. Most of all I must thank my wife Jane for undertaking the time-consuming and tedious task of compiling
the index, which will I am sure be the most useful adjunct
to Ferrey's original text which this book contains.

Clive Wainwright
London W.C.1
March 1977

CONTENTS

Appendix: in which the writings and character
of Augustus Welby Northmore Pugin are considered
in their Catholic aspect.

EDMUND SHERIDAN PURCELL

JANE WAINWRIGHT

ILLUSTRATIONS

INTRODUCTION

CLIVE WAINWRIGHT

Benjamin Ferrey (1810–80) was almost an exact contemporary of A. W. N. Pugin (1812–52) and deserves study
as an architect in his own right. His entry in the *Dictionary
of National Biography* states that 'In 1845 he designed for
the Baroness (then Miss) Burdett Coutts the church of St
Stephen, Rochester Row, Westminster. . . . During the
next twenty years he was one of the best employed and
best liked architects of his day.' Two of his obituaries give
not only a great deal more information concerning his
career but also a lengthy list of his buildings[1]. He designed
a wide range of buildings and also carried out a considerable number of church restorations.

He held the post of Diocesan Architect of Bath and
Wells and in this capacity he extensively restored both
the Cathedral and the Bishop's Palace at Wells. His
scholarly restoration of St Mary Magdalene, Taunton,
Somerset set a very high standard and was much discussed
by his contemporaries[2]. He also designed a number of
new churches in this diocese, the most important being
at Buckland St Mary in Somerset.

His friendship with A. W. N. Pugin grew from their
contact as fellow pupils in the studio of A. C. Pugin.
Ferrey amusingly describes the strict regimen which
prevailed in the Pugin household (pp. 26–8). It is not clear
when he started work there, but he was certainly thus
employed by July 1826 (p. 36). The pupils accompanied
the elder Pugin on his frequent visits to mediaeval buildings in both England and France. These visits were made
for the illustrations of Pugin's architectural publications.
Ferrey relates an amusing anecdote in connection with
one such trip to Normandy in August 1825 (pp. 19–21)
which seems to indicate that he was already in Pugin's
studio by that date.

On 21 September 1829 A. W. N. Pugin recorded in his
diary 'Went to Hatfield House with my friend Ferrey to

make sketches'[3]. This friendship continued during the period 1829–31 when A. W. N. Pugin was himself in business as a manufacturer of carvings and furniture. Early in 1831, for instance, Pugin's firm made a splendid oak communion table which Pugin had designed for presentation to Christchurch Priory in Hampshire[4]. Ferrey had in fact been born and brought up in Christchurch and he relates the details of Pugin's involvement with the town (pp. 69–72). Ferrey, in collaboration with William Brayley, published in 1834 *The Antiquities of the Priory Church of Christchurch, Hants.*, which illustrates the table *in situ*.

In 1832 or 1833 Ferrey moved to the office of the arch neo-classicist William Wilkins. Whether Ferrey went to Wilkins's office immediately after the death of A. C. Pugin on 19 December 1832 is unclear. Wilkins's work on the National Gallery started in 1832 and 'Mr Ferrey entered the office of Mr Wilkins for a short while as assistant and worked on the detail drawings of the New National Gallery. To this association perhaps may be attributed the fact that Mr Ferrey, though originally brought up in a Gothic School, and known as one of the early workers in the Gothic Revival, was never bigoted as regards the Classic styles with which his pencil was always familiar. . . . Mr Ferrey commenced his practice in Great Russell Street Bloomsbury [in 1834]'[5].

A careful examination of the plates of *Examples of Gothic Architecture*, Volume II, by A. C. and A. W. N. Pugin, throws some light upon this phase of the lives of both Ferrey and A. W. N. Pugin. This volume was started in 1831 by the two Pugins helped by the various pupils including Ferrey, and it was delayed by the sudden death of A. C. Pugin in 1832. But Ferrey continued to work on the illustrations and on plate I of the Deanery, Wells we find 'Sketched & measured by A. N. W. Pugin; Drawn by B. Ferrey: London Published Sept 1833 by A. W. Pugin 105 Great Russell Street, Bloomsbury'. Plate VIII, though bearing as before the names of Ferrey and Pugin, also states '. . . Published June 1834 for A. N. W. Pugin by

Messrs Walker & Ferrey at their office 105 Great Russell Street'. The frontispiece, which was designed by Pugin in 1834, bears the same legend but the title page of 1836 states that the book was 'Sold by Thomas L. Walker, Architect . . . at his office 106 Great Russell Street'.

It would therefore seem that either Ferrey only worked for Wilkins for a short time between September 1833 and June 1834 or that he went to work for him after A. C. Pugin's death in 1832 but at the same time worked with A. W. N. Pugin on *Examples*. By June 1834 he was in partnership with Thomas Larkins Walker, another of A. C. Pugin's pupils, and they were sharing the old Pugin house at 105 Great Russell Street with A. W. N. Pugin himself. But by 1836 Walker had moved next door to 106, Pugin already having moved away to his new house in Wiltshire. How long Ferrey continued at 105 I have not established, but the street directories for 1838 give his address as 85 Great Russell Street, stating that T. L. Walker was still at 106. I have dealt with this complicated period after A. C. Pugin's death because it throws light not only on Ferrey's career but on A. W. N. Pugin's also.

From 1836 Ferrey and Pugin were both much involved in their separate careers and to what extent they were able to continue their close friendship is unclear. But Pugin's almost exclusive employment in building Roman Catholic churches during the next few years and that of Ferrey in building Anglican ones must have created a certain tension between them. Pugin's uncomprising and fanatical hatred of non-Catholic art was certainly a trial to his Anglican friends, though they naturally appreciated his genius as an architect and author. Ferrey (p. 113) says 'Still to conclude that none but Roman Catholic artists can produce works of merit and feeling, even in a religious sense is a lamentable mistake, of which Pugin himself must have been convinced before his death'. They however certainly met on occasions. 'When travelling from Derby [August 1844] a short time before his wife's death the author met him at the railway station in a state of the greatest agitation. . . . In conversation during the journey he constantly expressed his belief that he should find his wife dead' (pp. 175–6). It would seem from the tone of this quotation that Pugin and Ferrey remained on friendly terms well into the 1840s. But the bias of this biography towards Pugin's early life must be partly due to the fact that Ferrey had more first-hand knowledge of this phase of Pugin's life. There is also the reason he himself gives (p. xli) 'cut off before he reached his prime, more importance is attached to the early period in which Pugin's talents were developed; and the writer's intimacy with him commencing from boyhood he had peculiar opportunities of watching his whole career'.

A. C. PUGIN

The career of Augustus Charles Pugin is not only of interest in its own right, but also for the insights which any study of it gives us into the complex structure of the architectural and artistic world of Regency London. This was the period when the scholarly illustrated publications which were essential to the progress of the Gothic Revival were starting to be published. A. C. Pugin's friendship with architects such as Wyattville and Nash and with publishers such as Britton and Ackerman led him into architecture itself and also architectural publication. 'In 1821 his work on *Gothic Specimens* made its appearance thereby forming an epoch both in the life of the author and in the study of that branch of art it was so well calculated to promote. . . . It has been justly remarked too that he has performed for Gothic architecture services similar to those which Stuart and his fellow labourers effected for that of Greece.'[6]

His several architectural publications gave architects for the first time access to the type of accurate measured drawings which were of direct use in their work. During the later eighteenth century architects such as Soane, Adam and Wyatt made frequent use of books such as Dugdale's *St Pauls*, Dart's *Westminster* or Murphy's *Bathala*. By the 1820s John Britton's publications such as *Cathedral Antiquities* (1814–32) and *Architectural Antiquities* (1805–14) had made available accurate and beautifully engraved perspectives of both the interiors and exteriors of mediaeval buildings. Pugin and Britton in fact co-operated over the publication of several books. But A. C. Pugin's books went an important stage further than Britton's—they included accurate measured drawings of the buildings and the details of the ornament. Thus architects now had just the measured drawings which they required to enable them to build convincing mediaeval-style buildings.

A. C. Pugin's work as an architect has yet to be properly studied. Ferrey enigmatically states that (pp. 50–51) 'The superior knowledge of Gothic architecture which the elder Pugin was known to possess, led many architects whose acquaintance with mediaeval art was superficial, to apply to him for aid. This he was always ready to afford and through the help of his son and his pupils he assisted others in carrying out their works. Many buildings might in strictness claim him as their author instead of the architect to whom they are publicly ascribed.' We also know that he was 'employed [as an architect] . . . by the Earl of Essex and the Marquis of Downshire. He also erected several private houses; and with Mr Morgan, constructed the Diorama [in Park Square East] in the Regent's Park.'[7]

As we saw above, the question of Pugin's pupils is an important one[8]. They included Ferrey and Walker, other architects like F. T. Dolman and Talbot Bury, painters like Joseph Nash and E. W. Cooke, and even the comedian Charles Mathews. Ferrey states (p. 28) 'Pugin's office was in great repute and always filled with pupils. It is remarkable, however, that of the many youths who were articled to him very few followed the profession of architects in after life. Some died, others changed their pursuits or succeeded to independent property; but to use one of Pugin's quaint expressions none *sunk into filth or perished on the scaffold.*' Pugin was very keen to further the career of his pupils. To this end he allowed them individually to place their names on any plate engraved for his publications for which they had executed the original drawing. Thus a careful study of the names which appear on the plates of these publications will establish how long each pupil stayed in Pugin's studio.

A. C. Pugin was a watercolourist of some importance. He exhibited in the Royal Academy exhibitions and was an active member of the Old Water Colour Society[9]. He certainly moved in artistic as well as architectural circles. He knew Turner, with whom he collaborated on one occasion. A number of his pupils became painters, the best-known instances perhaps being E. W. Cooke and Joseph Nash.

A. W. N. PUGIN

Early Life

Though Ferrey stresses the importance of Pugin's early life he leaves a number of questions unanswered. Pugin's exact role for instance in the design of furniture for Windsor Castle (pp. 52–53), or in the supply of architectural carvings to Scotland and Ireland by his own firm (64–65), is not fully explained. His remarkable success in designing furniture in the Gothic Revival style for Windsor while still only fifteen years old established him as a major furniture designer[10]. The involvement of his short-lived firm in Ireland remains obscure, but the importance of its Scottish work has recently been established. One of its first jobs was to supply wood carvings for Murthly Castle in Perthshire. This castle was designed by the notable Scottish architect James Gillespie Graham. 'In the cash book for the house Pugin's name first appears on 10th October 1829 when he was paid £162 12s 0d for oak carvings.'[11] Pugin's connection with Graham

is an interesting one; Ferrey (pp. 62–63) tells us of the
dramatic circumstances which led to their first meeting
and gives the date as 1830. It would seem likely however
that they knew each other before this date and that
they met in London in August 1829, the meeting being
to discuss the work at Murthly[12].

Pugin's involvement with Gillespie Graham seems to
have continued in to the later 1830s, though Ferrey makes
no mention of this. No documentation exists but he was
almost certainly involved with Graham in the design of
several of the interiors at Taymouth Castle. James
Macaulay very sensibly compares the Banner Hall at
Taymouth with Pugin's work at the New Palace of
Westminster[13]. I am convinced that on stylistic grounds
alone this work can safely be attributed to Pugin.

This early period of Pugin's life, which includes his work
at Windsor in 1827, the foundation and bankruptcy of his
own firm in 1829–31, and his first involvement with
Charles Barry in Birmingham in 1835, is of great interest
and importance. He was also very involved at this period
in designing stage sets for theatrical production. It must
be stressed that he did not become an architect until 1835,
his formative years being spent as a designer of furniture,
metalwork, Gothic ornament and stage sets and in book
illustration. I have dealt with this part of his career elsewhere[14]. In Birmingham he worked for Charles Barry on
the design of furniture and fittings as well as architectural
details for King Edward's Grammar School. Several
pieces of the furniture which he designed for this school
still exist[15], as do a number of his drawings for both
furniture and Gothic detail. This relationship with Barry
naturally led to his involvement with his scheme for the
design of the New Palace of Westminster.

Antiquary and Collector

This aspect of Pugin's life has been somewhat neglected
by his biographers. He grew up surrounded by the old
books and antiquities which his father had collected. He

A. W. N. Pugin, aged about thirty: the only photograph of Pugin known to exist.

was forced to sell his father's quite considerable collection in 1833 because of his own insecure financial position and the death of his father[16]. But before this date Pugin himself had started to collect both books and antiquities. Ferrey tells us (p. 62) of his 'Schooner in which he generally managed to bring over many interesting carvings and other antiquities purchased in the old stores of Holland and Flanders. Thus he used these excursions as subservient to the object of forming a museum, which in later life offered him the greatest pleasure and became one of the chief attractions of his residence at Ramsgate.' He not only bought antiquities for himself but also for use in the houses and churches which he was restoring or building. Scarisbrick, Oxbrugh and Oscott were all enhanced in the later 1830s by the ancient pieces of carved woodwork which Pugin incorporated into his schemes for the decoration of their interiors.

By collecting antiquities and using them in his buildings Pugin was following the eighteenth-century tradition which had encouraged Neo-Classical architects to incorporate ancient Greek and Roman carvings into their buildings. Many of Pugin's contemporaries such as Willement, Cottingham and Buckler used ancient fragments in this creative way. Interestingly, however, the architects of the next generation such as Bodley, Seddon or Street were very rarely given to this practice. Only Burges of this later generation had the same approach to the use of antiquities as Pugin.

One large collection of antiquities which was collected by Pugin still survives at St Mary's College, Oscott, near Birmingham. During the later 1830s Pugin was 'Architect and Professor of Ecclesiastical Antiquities' at Oscott. To help instruct his pupils concerning mediaeval art and architecture he collected together ancient carvings, encaustic tiles, church plate and vestments. These objects were housed in a special museum, which still survives. Pugin designed the interior decoration of a chapel at Oscott into which he incorporated old woodwork. He was also very actively collecting both mediaeval carvings and plaster casts in the early 1840s for the instruction of the carvers working at the New Palace of Westminster. They were housed in a building near to the site of the Palace itself and grew eventually to several thousand in number. As we have seen, some of these antiquities were purchased on the continent by Pugin himself; others he purchased from the leading London antique dealers of the day. Several of these dealers were close friends of his, Edward Hull and John Webb being perhaps the most important. Webb was later to turn to cabinet-making and in this capacity he made to Pugin's design some of the most notable pieces of furniture in the House of Lords.

Pugin did not confine his collecting activities to antiquities. He was also an avid collector of rare books. 'Had he now reserved but a moderate share of his annual income he would have left a handsome fortune behind him, but Pugin's love of all that was interesting and useful in connection with his art was so strong that he never could resist the temptation of purchasing ancient works of art and literature' (p. 147). Shortly after his death this splendid collection was sold at auction by his son, just as Pugin had sold his father's collection twenty years before[17].

Salisbury and Ramsgate

Pugin's first real architectural work was the house which he built in 1835 for himself, his second wife and his two children. It is called St Marie's Grange and is situated in a valley a little south of Salisbury in Wiltshire. Ferrey illustrates it and says (p. 72) that it had 'all the peculiar arrangements common to domestic dwellings of the 15th century. The structure was principally of brick . . . and undoubtedly formed a striking contrast to the class of modern suburban houses generally erected.' Ferrey's illustration however bears only a vague resemblance to the actual house and may well be taken from an early design; he had presumably either never seen the actual house or had forgotten its actual form by the time he was writing.

The house as it survives today was fully illustrated and discussed some years ago[18]. It was sold by Pugin in 1841 (p. 96) when he moved back to London. It was altered at some point in the 1840s or 1850s in an attempt to make it a more practical dwelling and it is possible that this work was carried out to Pugin's own designs before he sold it[19]. Its importance as a source for Gothic Revival domestic architecture of the high Victorian period has not been sufficiently appreciated by modern commentators. Its influence on the domestic work of Webb, Butterfield and Street during the 1840s and 1850s was probably quite considerable.

In 1843 he started to build his last house, and next to it his own church. They were the Grange and Church of St Augustine at Ramsgate in Kent, which Ferrey describes and illustrates (pp. 173–5). They still exist and have often been described[20]. It was at Ramsgate that Pugin spent his last years and his body lies buried in the church itself. Ferrey describes his life at Ramsgate (pp. 177–83) as 'of almost monastic regularity . . . in his private chapel at six o'clock . . . in his library until half past seven . . . morning prayers . . . breakfast which seldom lasted more than seven minutes . . . he then worked until one o'clock . . . this meal lasted but a quarter of an hour . . . he resumed his work . . . until ten when compline was sung in his own private chapel. The last hour of this busy day was devoted to the study of historical and theological works.' Thus was Pugin able to create so much in so short a career.

The New Palace of Westminster

Ferrey devotes Chapter XVIII to the re-building of this Palace and speaks thus of the destruction of the old Palace by fire in October 1834 (p. 240) 'an opportunity soon presented itself of showing the capabilities of mediaeval architecture which had hitherto never occurred in this or any other country in modern times'. It is difficult to overestimate the importance of this building; both its architecture and its splendidly decorated interiors must form a crucial part of any study of the Victorian phase of the Gothic Revival. There has long been controversy concerning the role which Pugin played in its decoration and construction. Ferrey deals in a very balanced and sensible way with Pugin and Barry's roles and also Pugin's involvement with Gillespie Graham's scheme. He rightly stresses that Pugin's great contribution was to the decoration of the interiors (p. 246): 'The designing of the internal fittings, furniture, decoration, encaustic floors, &c., were officially confided to him.' Every aspect of the building has been so thoroughly dealt with elsewhere[21] that Ferrey's remarks should be seen in the context of this new research.

Ecclesiastical Works

These occupy the central role in Pugin's life, due to his fervent devotion to the Roman Catholic faith. To a non-Catholic Pugin's deep devotion to his faith is difficult to understand in that it impinged so dramatically upon his career as an architect and designer. Even a close friend like Ferrey was unable to understand fully Pugin's viewpoint (p. xli) 'feeling that he could not describe Pugin's character from a Roman Catholic point of view, the Author has, at the request of Pugin's widow, admitted an Appendix written by a friend of the family. In some of the sentiments therein expressed he cannot agree.' This appendix by E. S. Purcell in fact gives an interesting and valuable account of Pugin's religious views and their relationship to his architecture and literary work. Since there has been no full modern discussion of Pugin's religious life, the best source is still Michael Trappes-Lomax's book of 1932[22].

Ferrey does not deal at any length with Pugin's churches but other biographers have illustrated and described many of them[23]. The friend and patron who looms largest in the story of Pugin's churches is the Earl of Shrewsbury. From the mid 1830s he paid for the construction of some of Pugin's most important churches, a number on his Staffordshire estates and others on his estates in southern Ireland. Pugin's Irish works both for the Earl of Shrewsbury and other patrons were numerous and noteworthy but have never been carefully studied. The most important was probably Killarney Cathedral, started in 1842 but not completed until after his death. Several major convents and colleges, such as Presentation Convent, Waterford and Maynooth College, still remain in their original use.

Lord Shrewsbury was involved in the important project to build a grand Roman Catholic Cathedral in Birmingham. This was St Chad's, completed in 1841; it and the adjoining Bishop's house originally formed a splendid group almost in the middle of Birmingham. The Cathedral remains, but the Bishop's house has been demolished. Lord Shrewsbury was also the patron of one of Pugin's most splendid and beautifully decorated churches. Pugin frequently suffered in his church building from the lack of money properly to decorate the church internally but Ferrey states (p. 184) 'At Cheadle there certainly could be no excuse from want of funds, his lordship appeared to have given him carte blanche. For richness of colour and general decoration the church has no equal in this country.' The impact of St Giles, Cheadle not only on English but also on continental ecclesiologists and architects was immediate. The consecration in 1846 was attended by August Reichensperger, the editor of the German periodical *Kölner Domblatt*, and Adolphe Napoléon Didron, the editor of the French periodical *Annales Archéologiques*[24]. Pugin knew Didron already and Ferrey published (pp. 235–9) a fascinating letter written to him by Pugin in 1843.

Another of Pugin's major Catholic patrons was Ambrose Phillipps de Lisle for whom he altered two houses, and built several churches and a monastery, all in Leicestershire. The monastery was that of Mount St Bernard which was built in 1839–42 for the Cistercian order on a wild tract of land in the Charnwood forest. Though not finally completed until the twentieth century, it is probably the most successful and impressive of his monastic or conventual works. Pugin formed a close friendship with de Lisle who shared to a remarkable degree his enthusiasm for both the Roman Catholic faith and the art and architecture of the middle ages[25]. Through him Pugin came into further contact with continental scholars and artists; Count Montalembert (p. 138), the great French scholar, came to visit de Lisle's house, Grace Dieu Manor. Work was also carried out at Grace Dieu by German Nazarene artists, some of it in collaboration with Pugin.

Pugin's own church at Ramsgate is certainly the most interesting of all his churches. Ferrey (p. 173) says 'His desire was to build in the most correct and solid manner and in this he was successful'. Eastlake discusses the church at some length and concluded that 'It is evident that Pugin strove to invest the building with local traditions of style. This is shown in its general arrangement, the single transept and other peculiarities being characteristic of Kent . . . in his house and church at Ramsgate one recognizes more thorough and genuine examples of Pugin's genius and strongly marked predilections for mediaeval architecture than elsewhere.'[26]

Secular Buildings

The New Palace of Westminster as we have seen dominates Pugin's career in terms of his secular work. He was however involved in a wide range of country house work especially towards the end of his career. His most important house was Scarisbrick Hall, built for Charles Scarisbrick from 1837 on. It was Pugin's first big country house job and the work went on until 1846, the house being further extended by Edward Welby Pugin after his father's death. Into the splendid interiors which he created Pugin incorporated fragments of ancient wood carving to enrich the modern work. The house still exists and the Pugin designs for it are now in the RIBA Drawings Collection[27].

He also carried out extensive re-modelling and new

works for Lord Shrewsbury at Alton Towers in Staffordshire. A house already existed when Pugin commenced his
work in 1837 and he was involved with work there until his
death. He also built the nearby Alton Castle and St John's
Priory, both at the expense of Lord Shrewsbury. Alton
Towers is now in ruins but the priory and castle exist. As
at Alton most of Pugin's country house work consisted of
alterations and additions to already existing houses. He
worked in this way for de Lisle at Grace Dieu Manor and
Garendon in Leicestershire. In this capacity he also worked
at Chirk Castle in Denbighshire, Oxbrugh Hall in Norfolk,
Eastnor Castle in Herefordshire, Bilton Grange in Warwick-
shire, Leighton Hall in Montgomeryshire, and Lismore
Castle in Ireland. Most of this work was done in the later
1840s and in some cases he probably never visited the house.
But by the later 1840s the craftsmen who executed his
designs understood his ideas so thoroughly that they could
work from drawings only. His growing estrangement from
his patrons within the Catholic Church and from the
hierarchy of the Church itself caused his involvement with
church work to decline sharply in the later 1840s. There
is considerable evidence that he was forced to build up his
work on country houses and his work as a designer of
furniture and metalwork to make up his falling income.
He had a family to support, and he was desperately trying
to complete his church at Ramsgate.

Decorative Design

Pugin was without doubt a major architect, but in sheer
architectural terms his buildings are rarely wholly successful. They cannot compare with the best buildings of architects of the next generation such as Street, Butterfield or
Bodley. These later architects had the tremendous advantage of starting their careers when a proper Gothic Revival
tradition of building existed, which had of course been
largely created by Pugin's efforts between 1835 and 1852.
But even though Pugin was without doubt the greatest
Gothic Revival architect of the first half of the nineteenth

century I am convinced that it was as a designer of interiors and their fittings that he was unequalled. His range and inventiveness as a designer of tiles, carpets, wallpapers, metalwork, stained glass, bookbindings, book illustrations and furniture was immense. In all these fields he made major contributions towards improving the existing standards of design and manufacture.

His great talent for decorative design was the first of his skills to be put to practical use. It must be remembered that he spent the period 1827–35, not as an architect, but as a designer of metalwork, furniture and Gothic carved detailing. In this work he drew upon his wide knowledge of both English and continental mediaeval decorative arts. He constantly travelled, in search of surviving mediaeval artefacts and studying surviving manuscripts and prints[28]. Ferrey (p. 51) tells us how Pugin was discovered in 1827 by a leading goldsmith working in the Print Room of the British Museum. It was immediately obvious that 'His complete knowledge of mediaeval art fitted him admirably for designing plate in the old manner'.

By the late 1830s Pugin had built up a close relationship with John Hardman, the Roman Catholic proprietor of a Birmingham metalworking firm. Together they produced a great deal of very fine church and domestic plate, light fittings, and the whole range of domestic metalwork, including door furniture. Hardman manufactured to Pugin's design hundreds of pieces of metalwork for the New Palace of Westminster, from doorknobs and coatpegs to fire dogs and light fittings[29]. Hardman metalwork rapidly became an essential embellishment to any Pugin building, domestic or ecclesiastical.

Pugin also persuaded Hardman to start to manufacture stained glass and in this field the firm's efforts were also highly successful[30]. They manufactured glass to Pugin's designs for the whole range of his buildings. Hardman also trained craftsmen who were able to carry out schemes of internal painted decoration to Pugin's designs. John Hardman Powell, Hardman's nephew in 1844, became Pugin's only pupil and was later to marry Pugin's daughter. He recorded his reminiscences of Pugin, which start thus 'A youth of 15, with his teeth chattering after an outside coach ride in an east wind from Ashford, knocked at the strong oak door of St Augustines. On giving his name there was much whispering of maids then an interval of a few minutes when a powerful baritone voice called out "is that you Powell?" "Yes Sir" was followed by the shooting back of bolts, taking down of massive bar and candle in hand, was seen the strongly built form of Pugin dressed in pilot cloth his handsome features sparkling with good humour.... "You will find lots of fires, and bread and cheese in the house; compline at 8, supper at 9, bed at 10'[31]. After Pugin's death Powell carried on working as a designer in the Pugin manner.

Another firm with whom Pugin was closely involved in the field of interior decoration was that of Crace. A large number of designs by Pugin for objects and schemes of interior decoration to be executed by this firm survive in both the Victoria and Albert Museum and the RIBA. Several hundred letters covering the period 1844–52 from Pugin to Crace also survive in the RIBA and give a very clear picture of the nature of their business and personal relationship[32]. It seems likely that Pugin's father had first come into contact with the Crace firm when he was painting watercolour views of Brighton Pavilion in 1824 (pp. 8–10). Frederick Crace was responsible for the exotic decoration of the interiors, and his son J. G. Crace worked closely with A. W. N. Pugin on the interior decoration of many buildings both secular and ecclesiastical, the Palace of Westminster being perhaps the most important example. It is obvious from their letters that their relationship became much closer in the late 1840s when Pugin was concentrating for the first time upon domestic work. Crace's firm not only carried out painted decoration on Pugin's instructions but also organized the manufacture of wall-paper, carpets and textiles to his designs. All these elements were used by Crace and Pugin to create unified schemes of Gothic Revival interior decoration of a quality and originality greater than had hitherto been achieved in England. Crace also made or had made a considerable number of pieces of furniture to Pugin's designs, the subject of lengthy discussions in the Crace-Pugin letters. A number of these pieces still survive in the houses for which they were designed; two of the most important are however now in the Victoria and Albert Museum.

Herbert Minton, the proprietor of Minton's the ceramic manufacturers, was a close friend of Pugin's. They both shared a fascination for mediaeval encaustic tiles (pp. 250–5). 'Among the various objects occupying Pugin's attention not one received a greater share than the revival of the manufacture of encaustic tiles. . . . Minton was the great originator of the modern art of making encaustic tiles.' Pugin was certainly a brilliant designer of tiles and Minton was certainly an early manufacturer of them. But Ferrey is incorrect in giving all the credit for pioneering the revival of this important aspect of mediaeval interior decoration to Pugin and Minton alone. Thomas Willement the antiquary and designer (a friend of Pugin's), several of his friends, and a Worcester ceramics firm, were involved in this revival before Pugin and Herbert Minton had discovered the correct manufacturing techniques of producing encaustic tiles. There is however no doubt that by the mid-1840s Minton's firm was the largest manufacturer. With a brilliant designer like Pugin in collaboration with them they naturally secured a large amount of business. Their most important commission was the provision of tiles for the huge areas of floor in the New Palace of Westminster. Pugin secured this contract for them and considered it their greatest work (p. 251) 'I declare your St Stephen's tiles the finest done in the tile way; vastly superior to any ancient work; in fact they are the best tiles in the world, and I think my patterns and your craftsmanship go ahead of anything'. By Pugin's death encaustic tiles both in Gothic and Neo-Classical designs were being very widely used by architects throughout the world.

One friend and associate of Pugin's played a more important part than any other. He was George Myers, Pugin's builder; Ferrey relates (pp. 185–6) how Pugin and Myers met. He also tells us that of Pugin's buildings 'The greatest number were built by Myers ... it is entirely owing to the praiseworthy exertions of Mr Myers that so many competent carvers both in wood and stone are now to be found.' Myers was responsible for the high standard of craftsmanship which is the hallmark of any Pugin building. He also ran a carving works which produced carved wooden Gothic detailing and furniture. The point which Ferrey makes about the numbers of good carvers working in the 1860s is important. Without the inspiration of Pugin the careful and intelligent study of mediaeval models by the carvers themselves would have been far less widespread. At the Palace of Westminster for instance the several thousand examples of mediaeval carvings which Pugin had collected together were used to instruct the carvers themselves (p. 186), 'not with a view to their making servile copies of ancient examples, but that they might imbibe *the feeling and spirit* belonging to mediaeval art and throw like expression into their own productions'.

When Pugin started to design schemes of interior decoration in the late 1820s a very few craftsmen or manufacturers could supply well made Gothic Revival objects or execute the necessary internal carved or painted details. He therefore created almost single-handed over the next two decades a whole industry devoted to the creation of Gothic Revival schemes of interior decoration. Crace, Hardman, Minton and Myers came to so readily understand both the detail and the spirit of Pugin's work that their work required the minimum of supervision and control. By the time Pugin died in 1852 other firms specializing in the production of Gothic Revival objects and the execution of decorative schemes had come into existence. These firms in conjunction with those already mentioned ensured that those of the generation of Gothic Revival architects which followed Pugin were able to carry out

their schemes with an ease and success unknown when
Pugin started his career.

Publications

There exists no full bibliography of Pugin's books and
periodical articles though such a publication would
certainly be of great interest to both scholars and biblio-
philes[33]. Those books produced by his father set a far
higher standard in the delineation of mediaeval buildings
and their ornament than had hitherto been achieved. The
first of his truly architectural publications was *Specimens
of Gothic Architecture*, 1821–23, the text being by the
Lincolnshire antiquary E. J. Willson (p. 17). In 1827 A. C.
Pugin, John Britton, Josiah Taylor and the engravers J.
and H. Le Keux published *Specimens of The Architectural
Antiquities of Normandy* (pp. 17–22). By this date A. W. N.
Pugin was fully involved with his father's work. Also in
1827 was published *Pugin's Gothic Furniture*, consisting
of the plates previously published in the periodical *Ackerman's Repository of the Arts*. These designs seem to have
been the work of both the Pugins[34]. From 1828–31 an
interesting series of lithographic plates were issued entitled
*Gothic Ornaments from Ancient Buildings in England and
France*. In 1831 appeared *A Series of Ornamental Timber
Gables from Existing Examples in England and France of
the Sixteenth Century* which had plates drawn by Ferrey
himself, with text by E. J. Willson (p. 23). The last publication of A. C. Pugin, *Examples of Gothic Architecture*, was
unfinished at his death in 1832 (p. 23). This was Volume I,
published in 1831 with a text by E. J. Willson and plates
superintended by A. C. Pugin himself. Volume II was
supervised by both A. C. and A. W. N. Pugin, had a text by
Willson and was published in 1836. Volume III was not
published until 1837–38 and was by A. W. N. Pugin and
T. L. Walker.

A. W. N. Pugin, after his close involvement in his father's
publications, naturally started to publish in his own right.
In 1835–36 he published four volumes of plates which,

though published separately, often appear bound in one volume entitled *Ornaments of the XV and XVI Centuries*. These four publications were *Gothic Furniture in the Style of the 15th Century* . . . (1835); *Designs for Gold and Silver-smiths* (1836); *Designs for Iron and Brass Work in the Style of the XV and XVI Centuries* (1836) and *Details of Antient Houses of the 15th and 16th Centuries at Rouen, Caen, Beauvais, Gisors, Abbeville and Strasbourg etc.* (1836). In 1836 he also published his most controversial book (pp. 109–16) which was entitled *Contrasts or, A Parallel Between The Noble Edifices of The Fourteenth and Fifteenth Centuries, and Similar Buildings of The Present Day, Shewing The Present Decay of Taste*. This book caused considerable comment and discussion, but his most widely influential book was without doubt *True Principles of Pointed or Christian Architecture, Set Forth in Two Lectures Delivered at St Marie's, Oscott* . . . (1841). In this book he set forth his important theories concerning the proper use of ornament and honest construction, both being principles which were to have far-reaching effects. Two more important theoretical treatises followed in 1843, *The Present State of Ecclesiastical Architecture in England* and *An Apology For The Revival of Christian Architecture in England*.

At this point Pugin moved away from theoretical treatises and became involved in the art and practice of chromolithography. His first colour plate book had immediate and widespread success as a reference book for everyone involved in Gothic Revival design. It was *Glossary of Ecclesiastical Ornament and Costume, Compiled From Antient Authorities and Examples* . . . (1844). It was followed by *Floriated Ornament* . . . (1849) which consisted of coloured plates demonstrating the use of floral motifs for flat pattern design. But Pugin's last major book represented a return to the theoretical and polemical formula of his earlier books: *A Treatise On Chancel Screens And Rood Lofts, Their Antiquity Use And Symbolic Signification* (1851).

These books, which form a very important aspect of

Pugin's career, had world-wide impact, whereas many of his buildings, though illustrated in books and periodicals, were seen by comparatively few people. His books without doubt continued to be read and discussed long after his fame as an architect had waned.

CONCLUSION

Pugin's last great triumph was his role in organizing the Mediaeval Court of the Exhibition of 1851. 'The furniture of the Mediaeval Court forms one of the most striking portions of the Exhibition, and has attracted a large amount of attention. The design and superintendance of these articles are by Mr Pugin, an artist who has studied the leading principles of mediaeval composition and ornamental design until his works are identified wherever they are seen. He has been ably seconded by Mr Crace who has executed his designs . . . Mr Myers of Lambeth who has contributed a large number of the finest articles in wood and stone to the Mediaeval Court . . . Ecclesiastical vessels &c are selected from a large variety of those quaint and beautiful works designed by Mr Pugin and executed by Messrs J. Hardman of Birmingham. They fully realize the style and artistic feeling of the best works of the Middle Ages.'[35] The firm of Minton was also very involved in this enterprise and it is obvious that we again have that team of Minton, Crace, Hardman, Myers and Pugin which could design and execute Gothic Revival schemes of decoration which were of amazing quality and sophistication. Their success in this branch of design was fully recognized by all involved with the Exhibition. Ferrey quotes (pp. 258–9) the verdict of the great German art historian Waagen.

The contents of the Mediaeval Court demonstrated Pugin's genius as a decorative designer to the several million people who came from all over the world to visit the Crystal Palace. Pugin however had little time left to appreciate the praise and to take up the new commissions which would naturally have resulted from his success. Ferrey (pp. 265–73) tells the sad story of his last few tortured months which led up to his death on 13 September 1852. Ferrey must of course be allowed to give a final assessment (pp. 272–3) 'For unrestrained freedom of action he sacrificed the pleasures of society. His genius was great. The part he had to perform in life gave insufficient scope for the energies of his mind, and the incessant exercise of his mental faculties destroyed his physical frame before he had attained the ordinary age of man. He bore little similarity to the other men amongst whom he lived; in many respects superior, he was different and out of his element everywhere except in his own study.'

NOTES

1. *The Builder*, vol. xxxix, 1880, pp. 281–283. *The Trans-actions of The Royal Institute of British Architects*, 1879–80, pp. 219–21.
2. Rev. James Cottle, *Some Account of The Church of St Mary Magdalene Taunton and The Restoration Thereof*, 1845.
3. Michael Trappes-Lomax, *Pugin, a Mediaeval Victorian*, 1932, p. 26.
4. Ibid., p. 334.
5. *The Builder*, loc. cit.
6. *Magazine of The Fine Arts and Journal of Literature and Science*, vol. i, 1833, pp. 322–3. This obituary of A. C. Pugin contains a number of interesting facts concerning his career.
7. Ibid., p. 326. This Diorama was constructed behind the facade of an existing house by John Nash. It still existed in March 1977 but was under threat of demolition. See also 'Daguerre's Pleasure Dome' by David Robinson, *The Times*, 5 February 1977, pp. 8–9.
8. The RIBA Pugin Catalogue deals fully with this matter and includes a list with brief biographies of each.
9. A full discussion of A. C. Pugin's career as a watercolourist can be found in J. L. Roget, *A History of The Old Water-colour Society*, 1891.
10. G. de Bellaigue and P. Kirkham, 'George IV and the Furnishing of Windsor Castle'. *Furniture History*, vol. viii, 1972, pp. 1–35. This scholarly article deals very fully with Pugin's work at Windsor and illustrates some of the surviving furniture.
11. James Macaulay, *The Gothic Revival 1745–1845*, 1975, p. 248.
12. Ibid.
13. Ibid., p. 251.
14. Clive Wainwright, 'A. W. N. Pugin's Early Furniture'. *The Connoisseur*, vol. cxci, no. 767, pp. 3–11.
15. Ibid., pp. 8–10.
16. *Catalogue of Original Drawings, Books of Prints, and An Extensive Architectural Library . . . Unique Collection of Basso Relievo Casts from Rouen Cathedral . . . to be Disposed of by Auction by Mr Wheatley . . . on Tuesday June 4 1833 & Three Following Days . . .*
17. There were three sales of the library and collection. They all took place in 1853 at Sothebys . . *Collection of Mediaeval*

Carvings in Oak . . . 12 February . . . ; followed by . . .
*Framed engravings Drawings . . . Original Drawings and
Sketches . . . 7 April . . .*; and lastly . . . *The Valuable and
Important Historical Topographical, Antiquarian Library
. . . January 27 1853 and Two Following Days.*

18. John Piper, 'St Marie's Grange: The First Home of A. W. N.
    Pugin'. *Architectural Review*, vol. xcviii, 1945, pp. 90–93.

19. A Pugin drawing is illustrated in Phoebe Stanton, *Pugin*,
    1971, p. 15. It shows the house in its original state before
    the alterations.

20. John Summerson, 'Pugin at Ramsgate'. *Architectural
    Review*, vol. ciii, 1948, pp. 163–7.

21. M. H. Port (ed.), *The Houses of Parliament*, 1976. This
    important furniture is also dealt with in *A Report by the
    Victorian & Albert Museum Concerning The Furniture
    In The House of Lords*, 1974.

22. Trappes Lomax, loc. cit.

23. See especially Stanton, Trappes Lomax (cited above), and
    Gwynn (note 25 below). Also of great importance is the
    well-illustrated article by Paul Waterhouse, 'The Life and
    Work of Welby Pugin'. *Architectural Review*, vol. iii,
    1898, pp. 167–75, 211–21, 264–23: vol. iv, 1898, pp.
    23–27, 67–73, 115–18, 159–65.

24. Georg German, *Gothic Revival in Europe and Britain:
    Sources, Influences and Ideas*, 1972, p. 99.

25. For a full coverage of Pugin and de Lisle's friendship, see
    D. Gwynn, *Lord Shrewsbury, Pugin and The Catholic
    Revival*, 1946; and E. S. Purcell, *Life and Letters of Ambrose
    Phillipps de Lisle*, 1900.

26. Charles L. Eastlake, *A History of The Gothic Revival*,
    1872, pp. 163–5. Eastlake devotes a whole chapter to
    Pugin and his work.

27. A number of these will be illustrated in the forthcoming
    RIBA Pugin Catalogue. A view of the Great Hall at
    Scarisbrick was illustrated in Wainwright (note 14 above).

28. S. Ayling, *Photographs of Sketches from the Notebooks of
    Augustus Welby N. Pugin*, 1865, 2 vols. This fascinating
    compilation includes sketches made by Pugin throughout
    the continent. Some are of buildings and others of metal-
    work, woodwork and Gothic ornament.

29. *Houses of Parliament*, loc. cit. Shirley Bury's fascinating
    chapter on 'Metalwork' not only includes information
    concerning the Hardman work in this building but also
    details of Pugin's involvement with Hardman's firm. See
    also two more articles by Shirley Bury: 'In Search of
    Pugin's Church Plate', *The Connoisseur*, vol. clxv, May

1967, and 'Pugin's Marriage Jewellery', *The Victoria And Albert Museum Yearbook*, 1969.

30. *Houses of Parliament*, loc. cit., includes a scholarly chapter on 'Stained Glass' by John Christian which deals with Hardman as a stained glass manufacturer.

31. John Hardman Powell, *A Memory Offering To Lay On The Tomb Of His Master Augustus Welby N. Pugin Whose Example Was Noble and Every Word Instruction By His Faithful Pupil* . . . 1889. A typewritten copy of this manuscript exists in the Victoria and Albert Museum Library. It contains not only a first hand account of life at the Grange but also useful information concerning Pugin's career.

32. RIBA Pugin Catalogue, loc. cit. This includes a précis of the contents of these important letters, arranged year by year.

33. Useful lists of both A. C. and A. W. N. Pugin's major publications are given in Trappes Lomax, loc. cit., Stanton, loc. cit., and the RIBA Pugin Catalogue, loc. cit.

34. For a full discussion of this interesting book, see Wainwright, loc. cit.

35. *The Crystal Palace Exhibition Illustrated Catalogue London 1851* . . ., New York, 1970. This is a reprint of the *Art Journal Catalogue*, pp. 317–19.

PREFACE TO 1861 EDITION

No man of the present generation has distinguished himself more signally in his own peculiar line than Augustus Welby Pugin; anything, therefore, relating to his history and career, may prove interesting to those who take an interest in the revival of Mediæval Architecture.

His original genius and varied acquirements are acknowledged by all who enjoyed the privilege of his acquaintance; while his Publications, by their forcible style and their free utterance of stubborn truths, have made no little stir in the artistic world, and are quoted as affording the best axioms in the branch of Art to which he devoted his pursuits.

Without exaggeration, it may be fairly said that Pugin ranked among the most eminent Architects of the present or former days.

Cut off before he reached his prime, more importance is attached to the early period in which Pugin's talents were developed; and the Writer's intimacy with him commencing from boyhood he had peculiar opportunities of watching his whole career. He has, therefore, been induced to place upon record such leading incidents of his life as, he trusts, will not be found devoid of interest. These have naturally led to some notices of the elder Pugin and others his eminent contemporaries during the rise of a school of art, the progress of which from a very low ebb may be traced, however imperfectly, in the following pages.

The step now taken has been deferred from time to time under the impression that a more competent person might undertake the task; but at the desire of many friends he no longer hesitates, and the moment seems well-timed when a Public Memorial in honour of Pugin is under consideration. Anxious also that this Memoir should be faithful, as well as acceptable to the members of Pugin's family, and feeling that he could not describe Pugin's character from a Roman Catholic point of view,

the Author has, at the request of Pugin's widow, admitted
an Appendix written by a friend of the family. In some
of the sentiments therein expressed he cannot agree; but
their insertion seemed due to the wishes of Pugin's
relatives, who desired that certain opinions attributed to
him on controversial points connected with the Roman
Catholic Church, respecting which he had been misunderstood, might be explained. Beyond these remarks, the
Writer has only to beg the reader's indulgence for defects
in a work compiled during such moments of leisure as his
professional engagements afforded, and to offer his thanks
to the many friends who have so readily placed at his
disposal whatever information respecting Pugin they
possessed.

Benjamin Ferrey

RECOLLECTIONS

A. WELBY PUGIN.

CHAPTER I.

The elder Pugin's arrival in England—Introduction to Mr. Nash—Acquaintance with Sir M. Shee and Hilton—Nash's Town and Country Residences—Marriage of Mr. G. Repton and Lady E. Scott—Intention to publish a work on Gothic Architecture—Introduction to Miss Catherine Welby—Origin of the Society of Painters in Water Colours—Becomes a Member of the Society—Anecdote of George IV. and Nash—His early history.

BEFORE entering upon a narrative of the incidents belonging to the life of Augustus Welby Pugin, it is desirable to give some account of his parents, particularly of his father, whose memory is cherished by many now living, who respected him for his generous nature and amiable disposition. The elder Pugin was born in France, in the year 1762; his birthplace is unknown, but he was descended from a family of distinction, his ancestor being a nobleman who raised a hundred soldiers for the service of Fribourg, the Senators augmenting his arms 'd'un oiseau sable,' for his valour in having defeated a hundred cavalry at Morat,

B

when besieged by Charles Duke of Burgundy, in 1477. Pugin witnessed many of the fearful scenes in the French Revolution, and it is said that he fell fighting for the king, and was thrown with some hundred bodies into a pit near the Place de la Bastille, whence he managed to escape by swimming across the Seine, flying to Rouen, and embarking from that place to England. As a total stranger, almost entirely ignorant of the English language, his position was one of great difficulty. He now eagerly read all the advertising columns of the newspapers, and at last his attention was arrested by an advertisement in which the assistance of a draughtsman was required in the office of Mr. Nash, the celebrated architect, with a further intimation that the services of a foreigner would be preferred. Pugin therefore hastened to Mr. Nash's residence, and when shown into the waiting-room was astonished to find a French nobleman, whom he had known in Paris, a candidate for the same appointment.

Mr. Nash, after considering the respective qualifications of the two candidates, gave the preference to Pugin. Little indeed did he know whether his abilities were equal to the requirements that might be expected, but he resolved to exert himself most strenuously, and endeavour to please Mr. Nash, who was at this time in the full tide of his prosperity, and could find occupation for artists of all kinds. Perceiving that Pugin had taste and skill in the use of colours, he employed him on perspective views of buildings in the Gothic style then erecting under his superintendence in Wales, and also on drawings of the Waterloo Monument, for which Mr. Nash had made a drawing, though it was never carried into effect. These designs Pugin executed on a large scale in body colour, in a bold and effective manner, working with unceasing energy, and availing himself of any leisure time for studying drawing, to render efficient assistance to Mr. Nash. To advance this object he also entered himself as a student at the Royal Academy, and became intimate with the late Sir Martin Archer Shee and Hilton, who were then studying in the same school of Art.

Remembering that a drawing master to his father's family in France was now living somewhere in London, he made a search and discovered him. This person was Merigot, the aqua-tint engraver: under this artist Pugin made great progress in his art. He often related the many difficulties experienced at this early period of his residence in England, owing to his imperfect pronunciation of the few words of English which he had learnt. Pugin, according to the fashion of that day, wore a three-cornered hat, carried his muff and gold-headed cane, and made frequent applications at the post-office for letters. To his repeated inquiries, he constantly received the same petulant answer, ' I tell you there are no letters for Monsieur Augustus Pugin, but plenty for Monsieur Puggen.' The mention of this incident to his friend Mathews in after times, induced that clever comedian to found upon it the well-known character of Monsieur Malet, which he personated with so much feeling. 'Ah!' Pugin would often say, 'people little know that Monsieur Malet should be Monsieur Pugin.'

Perhaps no professional man ever attained greater success in his pursuits than the late John Nash. He was, as is well known, the especial favourite of George the Fourth, being his private architect, and engaged by the King to make the alterations and additions at Buckingham Palace; he also built the Pavilion at Brighton.* Possessed of a large professional income, Nash lived in a style of some splendour at his house in Regent Street, receiving his employers in a spacious and beautiful gallery adorned with the choicest sculpture and pictures; † and possessing East Cowes Castle, in the Isle of Wight, where he was visited by many of the leading families of the aristocracy.

Nash's treatment of his pupils was of the most generous kind, and when staying in the Isle of Wight, he permitted the gentlemen of his office to join the distinguished company who visited him. Amongst them was George Stanley Repton, a son of the famous landscape gardener, and brother of the late respected Canon of Westminster. This gentleman won the heart of no less a person than the daughter of the then

* The Government business, executed under the control of the Board of Works, was then divided between three architects, each of whom received a retaining fee of five hundred pounds per annum, with a commission of three per cent. upon the expenditure. The three architects were Nash, Sir R. Smirke, and Sir J. Soane.

† The apartment referred to as Mr. Nash's reception-room is now completely transformed, and become familiar to the public by the name of the 'Gallery of Illustration.'

Lord Chancellor Eldon, who was a frequent visitor at East Cowes Castle. Mr. Repton was privately married to Lady Elizabeth Scott in March 1817; Lord Eldon was at first much displeased with this marriage, but in course of time he not only became reconciled both to his daughter and son-in-law, but evidenced the sincerity of his regard by appointing the latter one of his executors.

But to return to our subject: About this period there was a mania for building gentlemen's houses in imitation of castellated and monastic structures. Mr. Nash being largely engaged in this way, and feeling the want of practical works upon Gothic architecture (for although beautiful pictorial illustrations of our cathedrals were in course of publication by Britton, no book yet existed in which the details were so drawn as to enable the practical architect to make working drawings from them), suggested to Pugin that by applying himself to this particular purpose he would do the profession a great service and secure a profitable occupation.

Acting upon the advice of Mr. Nash he shortly set to work collecting materials for a publication which would meet the wants of the profession. Pugin was now in a position enabling him to earn a fair income; and while occupied in making sketches for a picturesque work on Islington he became acquainted with Miss Catherine Welby, the daughter of a distinguished barrister, and a relative of Sir William Welby, Bart., of Denton Hall, Lincolnshire. Pugin's position was

hardly such as to make him a desirable candidate for
the hand of this lady, yet, by his gentlemanly demeanour and persevering suit he overcame all the objections of her friends, and they were eventually married
at St. Mary's Church, Islington. Of this lady more
will be said hereafter. She was possessed of no ordinary charms, and known as 'The Belle of Islington.'
Islington, be it remembered, was at that day the head-
quarters of the Royalist Emigration. In proof of her
good looks she was accustomed to relate the circumstance that once at a dinner party, a gentleman sitting
next to her, with whom she had been in close conversation, availing himself of one of those mysterious
pauses which sometimes occur at the table, and
looking her earnestly in the face, suddenly exclaimed,
with animated gesture, ' Madam, how exceedingly like
you are to the devil.' This expression caused no small
surprise amongst the company ; but far from discom-
posing Mrs. Pugin, she gracefully bowed her thanks,
and accepted the remark as a compliment to her
personal appearance. Familiar with the works of
Milton, and especially Paradise Lost, she recognized
in the seemingly rude observation an allusion to the
fascinating form of Satan as there described by the
great poet.

Pugin now came into repute as an architectural
draughtsman, and his drawings were deservedly admired for their truthfulness of form and colour. At
this period there was a marked improvement perceptible in the works of artists who had previously

worked in water-colours. The earlier practice in the
art had been carried out with remarkable simplicity;
broad tints of monotone, possessing something resem-
bling a local tint, formed the groundwork, the objects
being drawn freely with a reed pen, either in dark brown
colour or Indian ink. So far this mode of working in
water-colour had hitherto prevailed, but a change in
the process now took place; the old method of preparing the drawing in uniform tint was given up, and
efforts were made to represent objects with their local
colours and varied effects of light and shade. Many
of the most eminent artists felt that the time had
arrived when a popular annual exhibition of their productions could be successfully established. With this
view, they associated themselves in the foundation of
the Old Water Colour Society. Their first exhibition
took place on the 22nd of April, 1805, at the rooms
built by Vandergucht the engraver, in Lower Brook
Street, Grosvenor Square. Eventually they moved to
Pall Mall East, where the annual exhibition continues
to be held. Of this body Pugin was elected an associate in 1808, in the room of Richard Ramsay Reinagle.
He frequently exhibited in their gallery, and his beautiful drawings of the interior of the Hall of Christchurch, Oxford, of Westminster Abbey, and St.
Paul's, with many views of Lincoln, were well known
as creditable pictures of the earlier exhibitors of this
distinguished society. Pugin always spoke in terms
of the greatest regard for many of his associates in

this body, particularly of Copley, Fielding, and George Robson, men whose friendship he enjoyed.

Although Pugin had for some time ceased to give his exclusive attention to Mr. Nash's works, yet his intimacy with that great architect continued for many years afterwards. Pugin entertained much respect for him, and delighted to relate anecdotes to his pupils characteristic of Nash's generous nature and indomitable spirit. Some of these may fitly be recorded here. It was in the year 1824, while Nash was engaged in building the Pavilion at Brighton, that he received the King's commands to prepare a work illustrating that extraordinary Hindû structure. Mr. Nash naturally requested Pugin to take sketches, make the drawings, and superintend the engravings; and eventually a beautiful work was produced, at great cost, consisting of perspective views etched in outline, printed in colour, and finished by hand. The King's object was to have an elegant book which he might give as a souvenir to those who were honoured by invitations to Brighton. The strictest precautions were therefore taken to prevent the possibility of any impressions of the plates becoming public; but it was hardly to be supposed that in the passage of the copper-plates and proofs through the hands of the engravers, printers, colourists, and others, some stray prints might not be dispersed. This indeed proved to be the case; and in the sale of the effects of one of the engravers who had become bankrupt a few prints of the intended work

were publicly exposed for auction. A most respectable
bookseller, who by chance attended the sale, knowing
Mr. Pugin's anxiety that no impressions of the work
should get into circulation, at once purchased them to
prevent such a result. On this becoming known to
Mr. Nash, he rather hastily, and without waiting to be
made acquainted with the circumstances under which
the prints were obtained, communicated the fact to the
King, and the well-intentioned purchase of the bookseller had nearly made him the victim of a prosecution
as a receiver of stolen goods. Fortunately, however,
a timely explanation saved him from this annoyance.
This fact shows with what vigilance Mr. Nash carried
out the King's command in connection with the preparation of the book, proof impressions of which were
submitted to His Majesty and revised by the King's
own hands. Pugin relates an amusing incident which
occurred while he was making the sketches for this
work. He was engaged in one of the galleries of the
Pavilion colouring a view. Deeply intent upon his
drawing, he did not observe that some one had entered
the apartment, but on looking round, to his surprise,
saw the King, who was then advancing to the spot
where he was sitting. Pugin had scarcely time to rise
when the King, passing by him and not perceiving a
stool on which a colour-box was placed, accidentally
overthrew it. The King stooped, and instantly picking
up the box, gave it to Pugin with an expression of
apology. It may easily be imagined how fully Pugin
appreciated this act of condescension, which he never

failed to mention whenever he had opportunity. The kindly act is quite in keeping with many others which could be related by those whose privilege it was to be brought into frequent intercourse with George IV.; and no one received more proofs of the King's generous nature than Mr. Nash, owing to the confidential relation in which he stood to him as his private architect. Pugin was also engaged in a very costly work by Sir George Nayler, Garter King-at-Arms, upon the ceremonies attending the coronation of George the Fourth, and contributed many illustrations to Ackerman's Microcosm of London; he was also occupied with Turner in the production of a work on Cassiobury for the Earl of Essex.

In order to animate his pupils to perseverance and industry, Pugin frequently set before them the example of Mr. Nash's early career, who when a pupil in Sir Robert Taylor's office, had an early opportunity of bringing himself into notice. Sir Robert, on one occasion, putting before his clerks some plans to which certain alterations were needed in an unusually short space of time, was annoyed at being told that it was impossible to do what he required. This being overheard by young Nash, he ventured to ask if he might undertake the task which had been declined by his superiors. Sir Robert, struck by the earnest manner of the boy, granted his request. Nash immediately went to his room, procured paper and candles, and, sitting up all night, laboured incessantly at the drawings, and by the time appointed appeared before Sir

Robert with the plans completed. This unexpected achievement convinced Sir Robert that Nash would succeed in after life—a prediction which had complete fulfilment. Amongst the pupils in the office with Nash were Cockerell, the father of the present C. R. Cockerell, the accomplished President of the Institute of British Architects, and J. Leach, who, after studying architecture, left the profession for that of the law, which he followed with such success that he rose to the high position of Master of the Rolls, which office he filled for many years. As another illustration of Nash's perseverance in after life, and his determination never to be overcome by seeming difficulties, it is told that on one occasion, having to go to some out-of-the-way place in Wales, he disdained the accustomed road, which was circuitous, and resolved to seek a more direct path to his object. Setting out on foot he encountered many hedges, ditches, and fences, most of which he passed, though not without difficulty. At last, meeting with a locked gate, awkwardly framed and inconvenient to mount, he was seen to retrace his steps several hundred yards, make a sudden run, and attempt to vault over the gate. Failing in this, again and again he put forth his strength, and nearly accomplished his aim; at last, stripping himself of his coat and waistcoat, by a longer run and a desperate spring he succeeded in clearing the barrier. He was then seen to climb deliberately over the gate, retrace his course, put on his clothes and proceed quietly on his way. On being told that this performance had been witnessed at a distance, he observed that it was his rule never to be deterred by seeming difficulties from accomplishing anything which he knew to be practicable.

Those who recollect the accent and impassioned manner of Pugin's recitals, and the amusing way in which he repeated these anecdotes before his pupils to stimulate their industry and perseverance, can fully appreciate the mixture of gravity and drollery exhibited in their repetition.

These traits of Nash's character are mentioned because, whatever may have been the misfortunes which befel him after death had removed his patron George the Fourth, when the ideas of the Court and the public underwent a signal change, there never could be any just reason for denying the great merit due to him for the important metropolitan improvements effected under his directions.   The formation of Regent Street and the skilful arrangement of the terraces and grounds of the Regent's Park are alone sufficient to attest his genius; and although his buildings are deficient in the vigour of outline shown in the best antique examples of architecture, still his combination of plan and fertility of contrivance are deserving of great praise.

As concerns the works at Buckingham House he can scarcely be held responsible for their defects. The original structure was capable of moderate additions, and if only those first contemplated had been carried into effect a consistent design might have been

the result. By the King's command, however, a
mansion suited only for the moderate requirements of
a junior branch or a Queen Dowager had to be meta-
morphosed into a huge metropolitan palace for the
reigning Sovereign; hence all the additions are wanting in congruity of design, and numerous defects in
arrangement perceptible. Besides the difficulties in
the arrangement of the building, which Nash had to
meet in order to please the King, he had also to contend
with the vigilant authorities at the Board of Works,
and was frequently brought into collision with them.
At one time, when he had disputes with the Commissioners, the King requested Sir Jeffrey Wyattville to
examine Buckingham House, which was then nearly
completed by Nash, and report on such works as he
might think would be necessary to render it suitable
for his Majesty's residence. On this Wyattville, to
his great credit, wrote to the Keeper of the Privy
Purse, requesting him to state to the King that,
although he felt flattered by His Majesty's commands,
he hoped to be permitted to decline advising on Buckingham Palace, as long as there remained any possibility of Mr. Nash removing the difficulties between
himself and the Commissioners, which he trusted he
would be able to do.

Here it may not be out of place to correct some
erroneous impressions concerning Nash's origin.

In the autobiography of John Britton, he remarks,
when speaking of J. Nash and Humphrey Repton:
" Both were born in the same year, 1752; the first in

Wales, the second in Suffolk; the one of humble, obscure parentage, the other of a respectable family classing with the gentry of Bury St. Edmunds. Whilst Nash had to contend with difficulties and struggles in early life, Repton was benefited by a good education and exciting associations, and was destined to succeed his father as an English merchant. Our first news of Mr. Nash is of his being a miniature painter; next we find him scene-painter to a company of itinerant players in Wales, where my old friend Mr. Pugin joined him. We afterwards hear of him in London, living with a Mr. Edwards, a relation, in Bloomsbury Square; and of some adventures after his residence there. His daring and important schemes in Regent Street and the Park, in Buckingham Palace and other parts of London are well known to all persons in the metropolis, and have been more censured than praised by the periodical press." He then proceeds to speak in strong condemnation of George the Fourth, and makes severe reflections upon Mr. Nash's proceedings whilst connected with that monarch, which it would have been far wiser to have withheld. His statements regarding Mr. Nash's entrance into public life are entirely wrong. He had patrons in Wales, and acquired property there; and being fond of theatrical representations built a private theatre, in which Mathews, Pugin, and other friends acted for their own amusement, sometimes inviting the surrounding gentry to witness their performances. Mr. Nash was born in London; his parents being

possessed of some private fortune were able to place
their son with Sir Robert Taylor, the leading architect
of that day.   Nor was he an uneducated person, as
implied by the unfavourable manner in which he is
described in contrast to Mr. Repton.

CHAPTER II.

Pugin travels to obtain Sketches for his Works—Goes to Normandy—
Messrs. Langlois and De Caumont—Discountenances the practice of
despoiling Ancient Ruins—Meets distinguished Travellers—Lord
Elgin at Kenilworth Castle—Unsatisfactory character of the per-
vading style of Architecture.

PUGIN now began in good earnest to carry into effect
his promise to Mr. Nash, but it was impossible that
he could collect the materials for so important a work
single-handed.   He therefore sought pupils and readily
obtained them, Mr. Nash and other architects being
glad to recommend his office as the best school for
obtaining a knowledge of Gothic architecture and
other elementary branches of art.   Accompanied by
his pupils he visited different towns for the purpose of
sketching and measuring such details of mediæval
buildings as appeared to him desirable; but the
expense of travelling led him to select those specimens which were most easy of access; and to this
cause may be attributed the want of classification observable in the work, an error he carefully corrected
in his later publications.   But though the examples
chosen by him might not be the best, they were so
carefully drawn and practically studied as to be of

material use to persons engaged in building, and no other publication had ever given details in so desirable a form. In carrying on this work he was assisted by Mr. Willson of Lincoln, who contributed the literary portion; and this gentleman's well-known antiquarian knowledge gave additional interest to the book. The first volume, entitled 'Specimens of Gothic Architecture,' was published in 1821, and dedicated to Mr. Nash as the private architect to the King. The second volume soon followed, and the work met with a most extensive sale, fully justifying the hopes of its promoters.

Encouraged by success, and really animated with a love for mediæval art, Pugin, to whom the magnificent buildings of Normandy were familiar, determined to illustrate some of the French structures with the precision shown in the works he had just published.

Foreseeing the great cost which must attend this new publication, he obtained partners in the undertaking, and Mr. Britton, the Messrs. Le-Keux, and Mr. Josiah Taylor the publisher, were associated with him in the speculation. Although interesting illustrations of Normandy had been previously given by Ducarel, Cotman, and Turner, yet those works were wanting in the qualities which made Pugin's books useful to the practising architect, and his proposed work was still a desideratum.

It was in the month of August, 1825, that, accompanied by some of his pupils, he set out for Normandy, and crossing from Brighton to Dieppe, proceeded to

Rouen, where he commenced the execution of his design. In this ancient and interesting city he found abundant objects for his pencil. The churches of St. Ouen, St. Maclou, the Palais de Justice, the convent of St. Amand, the Hôtel Bourgtheroulde and other buildings furnished excellent details, all of which were measured and rendered in a practical manner. A new and distinctive feature tended to make this work more popular than its predecessor,—the introduction of perspective views, which though not originally contemplated, have certainly imparted an additional interest to the book. In the course of his tour Pugin became acquainted with many of the most distinguished antiquaries and artists of Normandy, to whom he owed much for pointing out to him the buildings most interesting for the purpose of illustration. Two of these friendly assistants deserve a passing notice, being eminent in their peculiar walks.

In M. Langlois, a member of the Society of Antiquaries of France, Pugin met with a remarkable artist. He was the type of a class of men who rank high in French estimation. Well versed in ancient literature, an able professor in science and art, this man of genius occupied with his family a second floor in an obscure street of Rouen. His apartments were meanly furnished, and all his arrangements characterized by economy; but still in everything about him there was an evidence of taste and a cultivated mind. In his person M. Langlois was extremely plain, and his manners were unpretending; but in social position, notwithstanding his humble mode of living, he visited and ranked with people moving in the highest circles.

In this country things are rather different; it must be admitted that, in general, a man of talent unfortunately placed in M. Langlois' circumstances could not mix in society on equal terms. In France a man is estimated by his mind and accomplishments, and treated accordingly, without reference to the size of his dwelling, or the style of his establishment.

The family of M. Langlois was devoted to the arts, and his eldest daughter had become a most accomplished artist. She not only exercised her pencil well, but engraved beautifully, and her etchings may be met with in some of the best illustrated French works upon architecture.

To M. De Caumont, the learned antiquary, Pugin was also much indebted; and a better guide could not have directed him in his researches.

At the period of which we are now speaking the grand monastic ruins and desecrated churches in France were not regarded with much reverence either by their custodians or by tourists; and to such an extent had the sin of sacrilegious pilfering reached, that by bribing those who had the charge of these precious remains, persons were allowed to detach and carry away any ornamental fragment they desired, and thus much of the interest attached to the buildings was lost. Pugin discountenanced this practice most strongly, and admonished his pupils to respect architectural remains,

and to preserve rather than injure them by removing
any of their ornaments.   This injunction was so far
followed that only in one instance was Pugin. unwit-
tingly made privy to a spoliation of this kind ; it
occurred in the following manner.   Within a few
miles of Rouen, upon the banks of the Seine, are
situated the beautiful ruins of the once famous Abbey
of Jumièges.   These Pugin determined to visit,
having been especially invited by the mayor of the
commune.   The passage from Rouen to Jumièges,
by the river Seine, had been made in a market-boat,
which leaving Rouen at an early hour in the morning
returned again late at night.   On the arrival of this
boat with Mr. Pugin, accompanied by four of his pupils,
he was warmly greeted by the mayor, who politely
accompanied him to the abbey, anxious to hear his
remarks upon the peculiarities of its architecture.   In
the course of their examination the pupils found a
beautifully carved capital in a position which offered
such facilities for removal, that they determined, in
spite of previous warnings, to attempt the enterprise ;
but to accomplish the deed it was necessary to divert
Mr. Pugin's attention elsewhere.   This was done by
one of the pupils who, being in the secret, remained at
Pugin's elbow, constantly suggesting fresh points for
discussion between him and the mayor, and adroitly
keeping them away from the spot where a mason was
engaged in breaking away the useless and unnecessary
stone from the capital to be removed.   The noise of
the chipping often roused the suspicions of the mayor,

who was repeatedly on the point of rushing to the spot from whence the sound came, but whose attention was immediately drawn by some remark of the watchful pupil to an opposite portion of the ruins. At length the bulk of the stone being cut away, and the capital made portable, it was concealed under a camlet cloak and stealthily hurried down to the banks of the river just as the Amazonian boatwoman blew a tremendous blast from the cow-horn, to summon the passengers on board, this being the signal for departure.* On Pugin's discovering the manœuvre which had been practised in order to obtain this ornamental fragment, he was exceedingly indignant, and no future attempt of a similar kind was ever ventured upon by his pupils.

A reference to Pugin's work on Normandy will show with what judgment he selected the portions of the most remarkable structures in Rouen for illus-

---

* The despoiled condition of many of the magnificent monuments of our kings and others in Westminster Abbey may be traced to the wicked practices of antiquarian collectors in carrying off any ornament which could be detached from these beautiful tombs. However little the authorities may have valued and appreciated the works of art confided to their care, and been indifferent to their safe custody—yet nothing would justify the wholesale spoliation carried on by educated men under the pretext of forming museums, &c. Since the jealous care of Mr. Scott, who now has the charge of the restorations at the Abbey, much has been done to recover fragments of the royal tombs known to be in private hands; and he has been enabled, in the case of Queen Philippa of Hainault's tomb, to replace an entire canopy, with its tabernacle work on the south side of the tomb, the place from which it must have been torn many years since. The fragment having found its way into the Museum of a well-known collector was purchased at the sale of his effects after his decease, and laudably restored. The iron-work and the gates of Henry V.'s chauntry have also been thus restored.

tration. Having completed his mission in that ancient city he next proceeded to Caen. Here also he found subjects of the highest interest for his work; and after making the necessary sketches and measurements, he extended his journey to Bayeux, the extreme point of his tour. In the course of this excursion many remarkable people were met. In the steam-packet from Harfleur to Havre an acquaintance was formed with Mr. R. Lalor Sheil, the brilliant Irish orator, who was accompanied by several young barristers; and at Bayeux Pugin fell in with Major Todd, who took a deep interest in architecture, that officer himself being then engaged in producing a costly work on the antiquities of India. Nor must we omit the hapless Beau Brummel, whose conversation enlivened the table d'hôte at Calais.

In some of his professional journeys Pugin was accompanied by his wife, and this lady having an only sister, Miss Selina Welby, whom she loved with a degree of affection hardly to be exceeded, it was her practice to correspond regularly with her, giving minute accounts of all she saw, and the various incidents which occurred in the course of their travels. These letters are still preserved, and are in the highest degree interesting. Her descriptions, observations, and reflections are admirably expressed, and show with how much ability she could exercise her pen. There are occasional references in these letters to her boy. Their first visit to France was in 1824; writing to Miss Welby, she says:—

'Sept. 24. My dear boy bears up tolerably; he

dislikes Paris altogether, and rejoices to think we are to set off for Fontainebleau on Saturday next week, to walk in the Forest, take sketches, and eat the finest grapes in the world ; but of the latter *I* must be very cautious. I bless the kind Providence which gave me the means of obtaining them ; and in this manner it seems to me we should think of all our departed joys and pleasures, not so much passing our time in regretting their loss as in gratitude and thanksgiving, that we *have* been indulged in the course of our lives with the possession of them ; for seeing that ourselves, and all things around us, are *intended* to be continually changing, this mode of reasoning can alone produce that sincere resignation which is so much our duty, and is, in fact, that peace surpassing all understanding. It is thus I have reasoned with my sister Lafitte, who, from shutting herself up to uninterrupted sorrow and regret, began to think there were no pleasures left for her ; but I got her, the other day, to go with us to dine in the country, and she seemed really to enjoy it, and the next morning, when I called to see how she was, I found her, both in health and spirits, another creature ! To-morrow, if please God I am well enough, I take her to see my niece and my new little great nephew.'

Of Pugin's other works—the ' Edifices of London,' 2 vols., the ' Examples of Gothic Architecture,' ' Ornamental Timber Gables,' &c.—it is sufficient to say that they are all useful in their degree ; more especially the ' Examples,' as the selection there given is chiefly from

secular buildings. While engaged in collecting ma
terials for these volumes, Kenilworth Castle, amongst
other buildings, was inspected. These far-famed ruins
were visited daily during the summer by large parties
of tourists. Some, as usual, merely gazed at the picturesque features of the buildings and quickly departed; but occasionally persons would be found to
take deeper interest in the architectural details. It
was in the month of September 1830, while Pugin's
pupils were occupied in sketching parts of the Great
Banquetting Hall, that two strangers addressed one of
them and offered assistance in taking dimensions of
the hall. They appeared to be father and son; the
remarks of the elder gentleman were acute and showed
much intelligence. He particularly lamented the rank
growth of the ivy, and pointing to the huge mantel of
the fireplace in the great hall, being a stone of enormous size, 8 ft. 6 in. long by 2 ft. deep, remarked that
it was actually thrown out of its position by a large
stem of ivy which having insinuated itself between the
joints of the masonry, caused great disturbance to the
whole structure of the chimney breast. Conversing
freely upon art with Pugin, among other inquiries he
asked if he had ever seen the original drawings of the
Elgin marbles deposited in the British Museum. On
his replying in the negative—'Then on your next
visit to the Museum,' said he, 'present this card and
request to see them.' Upon looking at it Pugin was not
a little surprised and gratified to find that the inquiring
stranger was no other than the Earl of Elgin himself,

accompanied by his son Lord Bruce, who having succeeded to the earldom has been recently distinguished
by his able diplomacy in China.

The great service which Pugin's labours have rendered to architects is now admitted beyond dispute;
indeed till his time the only practical attempts in
Gothic architecture, though unfortunately made on a
large scale, were imitations of conventual or castellated buildings, exhibiting every kind of incongruity
perpetrated in extensive masses of cement or terra cotta.
Although therefore Augustus Welby Pugin, the son,
by the successful adaptation of Gothic architecture to
modern uses, has shown how applicable the genius of
mediæval architecture is to all ages, and their various
requirements, still, his father merits the tribute of
being considered the great pioneer in this branch of
art; for without the aid afforded by his books it is
doubtful whether this style of architecture would have
ever obtained the hold which it now has upon the
public taste.

The professional career of Augustus Welby Pugin is
so interesting that it may seem unnecessary to dwell
further upon the less striking events of his parents'
life, but to the characteristic talents of both his parents
may be traced some of the peculiarities observable in
the genius of their son.

CHAPTER III.

Early Instruction—Domestic regulations in Pugin's establishment—
Mrs. Pugin's peculiarities—Pugin's intimacy with Mathews, the
Comedian—Studies the theory of Mediæval Architecture—Napoleon
as First Consul—Isabey, David, and Lafitte, the artists—Mr. Pugin's
antecedents.

IMPRESSIONS upon the mind at a tender age through
the fond teaching of a beloved parent are easily
made; but however implicitly this guidance may be
followed in youth, as manhood approaches and the
mind acquires vigour any extreme bias of early teaching is detected, and results too frequently in a revulsion of feeling and causes opposition to opinions formed
in early life. The effects of the system under which
Welby Pugin received his boyish inspirations were so
observable in after life that some more particular account must now be given of his mother and the domestic rule. It has been already stated that the elder
Pugin, when preparing his published works, received
articled pupils for instruction in the elements of their
profession. Some were inmates of his house, and a discipline was enforced in the social system of the establishment which owed its origin to Mrs. Pugin. It was severe
and restrictive in the extreme, unrelieved by any of
those relaxations essential to the healthy education of

Lynch, lith.

Hanhart, Imp!

Augs Pugin

youth, and the smallest want of punctuality or in-
fringement of domestic rules excited the marked displeasure of the lady. Mrs. Pugin usually retired to
rest at nine o'clock, and rose in the morning at four;
she therefore thought it salutary that the pupils
should commence their studies at six o'clock in winter
as well as in summer; indeed, from the moment the
mistress of the house awoke no one was ever permitted
to get any rest. First came the loud ringing of the
bell to rouse the maids, then in quick succession the
bell to summon the pupils from their beds, and the
final peal requiring their presence in the office by six
o'clock. A pitiable sight indeed it was to see the shiver-
ing youths reluctantly creeping down in the midst of
winter to waste their time by a sleepy attempt to work
before breakfast. At half-past eight they were summoned to breakfast, and on entering the room Madame
was seen already seated at the head of the table: on
approaching it each youth made a profound bow, the
neglect of which would quickly have been visited with
reproof. A short prayer was then said, and breakfast
despatched in constrained silence, after which each retired as he entered, making the same obeisance to the
head of the table. During dinner the like silent system
was enforced, similar obsequious respect paid, and then
retiring, the pupils continued to work incessantly at the
desk till eight o'clock. The only leisure afforded them
was from that hour till ten, when they retired to rest.

Nothing could exceed the stern manner in which
this routine was carried out; and excellent as was the

course of studies pursued in the office, the cold, cheerless, and unvarying round of duty, though enlivened by
the cheerful manner and kind attention of the elder
Pugin, was wretched and discouraging.

It was hardly to be expected that amongst a number
of young men of various temperaments there should not
be some who either resented or disregarded these domestic rules, and violent were the disputes which ensued
when the transgressions of some unhappy youth brought
upon him Mrs. Pugin's wrath in no measured terms.
On such occasions the good offices of her husband
were frequently exerted to calm the raging storm and
mediate between the belligerent parties. Nevertheless,
in spite of these drawbacks, Pugin's office was in great
repute and always filled with pupils. It is remarkable,
however, that of the many youths who were articled to
him very few followed the profession of architects in after
life. Some died, others changed their pursuits or succeeded to independent property; but to use one of Pugin's
quaint expressions, none ' *sunk into filth or perished on
the scaffold,*' a prediction which he was wont to make
when much irritated by idleness or want of skill in
any of his pupils.* It may cause some surprise to
know that among Pugin's earliest pupils was Charles
Mathews, the distinguished comedian, who, after com-

---

* Of those still living, who were either articled to the elder Pugin, or
acquired their knowledge of art in his office may be mentioned Lake
Price and Joseph Nash, distinguished members of the old Water Colour
Society; Grantham, the Civil Engineer; G. B. Moore; James Penne-
thorne, the architect to the Board of Works; Talbot Bury, B. Ferrey,
F. T. Dolman, architects; J. D. Egville, J. Amos, F. Whitaker, T.
Cramer, W. Shoubridge, and many others.

pleting his articles with Pugin, proceeded to Italy for the further prosecution of his studies. There he resided for some years, and on his return Mathews succeeded in obtaining from the Middlesex magistrates the appointment to a district surveyorship under the Metropolitan Buildings Act, a post which he filled even after he had made his appearance on the stage. He was soon, however, relieved from the duties of his office, the magistrates declining to recognize the district surveyor and acting comedian in the same person. Mathews's father and Pugin were intimate friends, and the latter was a frequent guest at old Mathews's table when he lived at Highgate, where he surrounded himself by men of eminence in literature and art. Pugin was in the habit of relating many amusing stories of this celebrated comedian, and invariably asserted that it was from himself Mathews acquired the humorous facility of personation and mimicry for which he became so renowned through his performances known as 'Mathews at Home.' Their first acquaintance took place in Wales. Mathews, while returning from a professional engagement in Ireland in 1796, was nearly wrecked on the coast of Wales, and while at Carmarthen fell in with Nash and Pugin, whose love of theatrical representations has been already mentioned. These gentlemen acted in the comedy of 'The School for Scandal,' which was performed at the Carmarthen theatre, and the playbill is now extant in which the part of Sir Peter Teazle is personated by Mr. Nash.

It may be gathered from what has been already stated

that the elder Pugin's labours were devoted more to the theory of architecture than to its practical application. A few country villas and the Diorama in the Regent's Park were the only buildings actually erected under his superintendence, his time being chiefly occupied in the direction of useful publications. Enough has been said to show the character of his office: other incidents relating to him will appear in connection with the account of his son's career. In person he was remarkably good-looking, and in manner displayed overwhelming politeness. His foreign shrug and strong accent often astonished the country people with whom he was brought in contact. Many of his favourite sayings, though quaint, were full of meaning, and the drollest scenes might be described if it were possible to impart to them his humorous accent. When a young man in France he appears to have associated with distinguished artists; he knew David the historical painter intimately, and probably belonged to the same political club. Isabey, the favourite miniature painter to Napoleon the First, was another of his companions. This man boasted of his familiar acquaintance with the Emperor when First Consul. That he was at all events a very presuming person may be inferred from the following practical joke told by Pugin. Napoleon, when First Consul, resided at Malmaison, delighting in the retirement which it afforded him in his moments of leisure from state affairs. There it was his custom to take solitary walks in the avenues, wrapt in contemplation, with his arms folded across his breast.

Isabey one day bragging of his great intimacy with Napoleon, boastingly laid a wager that he would (as boys do in playing at leapfrog) follow the First Consul in his solitary promenade, run behind him and jump over his head. The challenge being accepted, and the opportunity watched, the artist attempted his practical joke, which in fact he accomplished, but at a cost he little expected. Isabey running and planting his hands on the First Consul's shoulder sprung clean over his head, and being recognized, and instantly chased, would have paid dearly for his frolic had Napoleon caught him. Fortunately the artist outran the Consul, who, however, resented the gross liberty by ever afterwards excluding Isabey from his presence.

Another artist from whom the elder Pugin derived much instruction was his brother-in-law, Monsieur Lafitte, a member of the Legion of Honour, and one of the household of the Emperor Napoleon I. This gentleman was most skilful in the composition of historical subjects for sculpture, and designed among other works the panel decorations of the 'Arc de Triomphe' in the Place de Carrousel, representing the victorious career of the Emperor and the various striking incidents in his life.

CHAPTER IV.

Birth of Augustus Welby Northmore Pugin—His education—Amuse-
ments in his father's office—Sketches and measures Rochester Castle
—Searches the Well—Narrow Escapes—Goes to Oxfordshire, Norfolk,
&c.—Travels in France—Attends Irving's Chapel in Cross Street,
Hatton Garden—Mrs. Pugin's Literary Powers—Defence of Lord
Melville—Her Adventures in Lincoln Cathedral.

AUGUSTUS WELBY NORTHMORE PUGIN was born 1st of
March 1812, at Store Street, Bedford Square, where his
father then resided. He was of somewhat delicate
health as an infant, and needed the anxious care
which was bestowed on him by his mother. At an
early age, after receiving from her some preliminary
instruction at home, he was entered as a day boy
at Christ's Hospital, Newgate Street, better known
as the Blue Coat School. The selection of this
place for his education was probably made from
its then being the nearest public school to which he
could easily go and return daily without excessive
fatigue, and thus be kept under parental care. The
Rev. Dr. Trollope was then head master of the school.
Augustus soon began to show that aptitude for acquiring knowledge which was so strikingly displayed
in after life. It was remarked of him by one of the
masters that whether in Greek, Latin, mathematics,

or any other branch of education, he would learn in
twenty-four hours what it took other boys many weeks
to acquire. Thus, as a mere child, he was quick
in all that he attempted, and fluent in speech, expressing his opinions in the most dogmatic manner
with volubility and vehemence. It is not surprising,
therefore, that in after years he should have offended
at times by the roughness of his manner ; indeed such
rudeness would not have been tolerated in a man
of less genius. Rarely is any one endowed by nature
with such abilities, unaccompanied by some drawback ;
and Pugin, who as a child, in addition to his other
nobler qualities, was gentle and refined, gradually
permitted a habit of slovenliness in person to grow
upon him, amounting at last to eccentricity. It was
observed that while at school he mixed very little
with other children of his own age, always preferring
the company of those who were his seniors. After
completing the ordinary course of education at Christ's
Hospital, he did not proceed to either of the Universities, but shortly afterwards entered his father's office.

He had an almost intuitive talent for drawing,
and as soon as he could handle a pencil, commenced
sketching. At first his inclination was towards cari-
cature, and many were the incidents occurring in the
office to give him the opportunity of indulging in this
fancy. Being quick and observant he remarked that
amongst his father's pupils were some who excelled in
their artistic efforts, while others were sluggish and
unsuccessful. The former were always naturally in

D

favour, and his father never failed to express approval or displeasure in a very decided and graphic manner to each youth according to his merits. Augustus (for that was the Christian name by which he preferred to be called) created great amusement by illustrating the ups and downs of the pupils on a wheel of fortune. Every week the rotatory machine was sketched with great spirit, each pupil being represented standing upon a projecting bracket attached to the wheel. The favourite was always at the top, capering and laughing with pencil in hand, while the one least fortunate was seen hurled to the ground by the revolution of the wheel. Others were planted on the ascent or descent, according to the degree of favour in which they stood with their master, their doleful or joyous faces being cleverly expressed by a few spirited touches. Great amusement was produced by this humorous device; and the publication of a new wheel of fortune every week was eagerly looked for by his fellow pupils. Though this was a favourite amusement with him he was not less successful by the droll manner in which he illustrated any passing event wherein he could find subject for fun. Soon, however, his love for architecture showed itself in a decided manner. After passing through the usual elementary courses, and making himself master of perspective, he delighted in taking sketches from Nature, and was scarcely ever seen without a pencil in his hand; more particularly he rejoiced in all opportunities of drawing in Westminster Abbey. Notwithstanding his great power of delinea-

tion he rendered but little assistance to his father in
the prosecution of his architectural works, as the labour
of drawing out the details of building in a strictly geo-
metrical manner from given measurements little suited
his active habits or mental energy. Sedentary occupations were distasteful to him, and his imagination
sought pursuits more congenial to its natural instincts.
As in literature, tales of chivalry and romance delighted him, so in art, the idea of ancient castles and
feudal mansions gave him pleasure, and this led him,
early in the year 1826, to turn his attention very
closely to the study of castellated buildings. Prior
to this, however, it should be stated that he went
with his parents and some of the pupils to Paris, the
elder Pugin being engaged in obtaining sketches for
a work upon that city. He was soon very active
with his pencil, full of fun, and a great favourite with
his father's pupils. Mrs. Pugin, writing from Paris
to her sister, observes :—

'If he understood how to dress himself I should
consider him an universal genius ; and a most orderly
good creature, if he had not had the skin of his nose
twice torn off by a battle of pillows in the suite of
rooms they have above, quite out of my observation ;
however, the second time it happened, I brought him
down to a room near me. He does not dislike a little
play, but he works infinitely more than he plays, while
the rest play infinitely more than they work. His
father calls this work of Paris " Augustus's work," and
well he may, for he has done more than three parts

of it, and made sketches and coloured them for the first time from Nature, and written some very good descriptions. *Nevertheless the fellow cannot dress himself.* When he heard that you left Beverley without seeing the churches, he declared, had he been with you, you would have found him the most restive animal you ever posted with; nor whip, nor spurs, nor anything else would have got him on before seeing those churches.'

The stately Tower of London was very familiar to Welby Pugin, but the other great work of Gundulph, the Castle of Rochester, was little known and had been most inadequately illustrated. He therefore determined that this castle should be the first subject of a strict examination; having, upon application to the Earl of Jersey, the proprietor of the estate on which the Castle stands, obtained full permission to excavate the ground and make all needful investigations.

It was in the month of July, 1826, that he set out for Rochester, accompanied by the writer of these pages, then an articled pupil with his father. On reaching the precincts of the Castle, its commanding situation and grandeur of design at once riveted his attention. He therefore stayed at Rochester some days, taking sketches of every part of the Castle, and measuring carefully its several apartments; he then prepared accurate drawings, showing it in a state of complete restoration.

At that time little was known concerning the foundations of these enormous structures; Pugin there-

fore determined to make excavations, and by forming
huge trenches at the base of the walls, he ascertained
the mode of their construction, which proved to be of a
solidity and depth fully in keeping with the superincum-
bent masonry. There are always amusing traditions
connected with these old buildings, and amongst others
belonging to this Castle it was supposed that treasures
or plate might in emergency have been thrown down
the well constructed in the inner wall of the Keep.
The bare reference to this as a probability only was
sufficient, and Pugin at once resolved to make a careful
search. He immediately obtained the necessary appa-
ratus, and having hired men to descend the well,
fearlessly placed himself in the bucket to be lowered
by the windlass, so that he might direct the operations
at the bottom. It had been previously ascertained
that the well was considerably choked up by quantities
of rubbish; and in the removal of this accumulation
very little was discovered, his zeal being only rewarded
by the acquisition of a few pieces of pottery and glass of
Queen Elizabeth's period. Doubtless if any treasures
were secreted there in troublous times, they had long
since been found and appropriated. It is very likely
that this well might have been the depository of treasures when the Castle was closely besieged, as it communicated with every floor of the building, from the
summit to its base, and the water in it being under
the tidal influence of the river Medway, would conceal
for a considerable time the objects remaining at the
bottom.

It was only through the most providential escapes that Pugin's career was not cut short while he was occupied in these examinations. One day he had descended the deep trench before alluded to as having been sunk to ascertain the materials of which the foundations were composed; remaining there a few minutes, he again ascended the ladder, and had scarcely reached the solid ground when the planks and struts by which the sides of the trench were secured snapped with a sharp crash, and masses of heavy earth filled the trench. Had this happened a few moments sooner Pugin must have been buried alive. At another time, while straining to take a measurement by clinging to a large beam resting on the set-off to a wall, the timber, which was insufficiently fastened, slipped away, throwing him suddenly backwards from some height. Fortunately the beam on striking the ground on its rebound, missed his head, or the result would have been fatal.

Pugin intended that the series of careful drawings which he took of this Castle should form the commencement of a publication to be exclusively devoted to the illustration of castles; but other occupations interfered, and he never realized the scheme. Although his disappointment was considerable at the small extent of discoveries made in the well, yet the vessels and remains of pottery formed the beginning of his collection which gradually increased, and eventually became a museum comprising a considerable number of interesting objects of antiquity. Like other collectors, he was not over-scrupulous as to the means by which he became possessed of these relics, and the opportunities afforded him in the professional excursions which he made were numerous.

During the year 1827 he again accompanied his father on a professional tour in France, and was of great assistance to him, for he sketched well and could speak French fluently. He seems even at this time to have overworked himself, as we find Mrs. Pugin writing to her sister thus : ' My poor Augustus has latterly been very unwell, and on Thursday last alarmed us much ; he went before breakfast to draw in Notre Dame, when suddenly (as he describes his sensation) the whole building on every side seemed breaking and tumbling to pieces, and the pavement so agitated he could not stand ; fortunately Mr. Nash was drawing with him, and got him into a coach and brought him home pale as death.'

Two other passages occur in the same letter which, though referring to family affairs, are remarkable, and ought to be mentioned. Speaking of the customs in France she observes: 'No sooner is a child born here of good family than they immediately are thinking of a proper alliance. Mad^e Lafitte told her brother and me, she had mentioned to her daughter that a marriage between Clara and Augustus would be a very proper union, and hinted she would have a very good fortune ; whether this was said as a matter of politeness, or more seriously, it is impossible to say, for Mad^e Lafitte is very polite. I laughed with my son about it, when

*

he was quite indignant; " *What! marry a Catholic? that surely will never happen.*" But who can read the book of fate, fast closed, except the page that time doth hourly turn?' Who indeed could have foreseen that the boy, so indignantly repudiating the idea of marrying a Catholic, should in after years not only form such an alliance, but become one of the stoutest champions of the Roman Catholic Church.

Alluding elsewhere to the Pugin arms, she remarks : 'You may remember that the family arms which Mr. Pugin's mother burnt in the Revolution, in terror of their being discovered, because of their being of the noblesse of Switzerland, are again restored in the family; they are very handsome in themselves, and very handsomely emblazoned, framed, and glazed. In the account pasted at the back of the frame (which account is given by the Herald's Office), they are said to have been assumed in the fourteenth century. Augustus is delighted with them, but cannot help at the same time observing that Roger de Welby died fighting at the battle of Hastings, which clearly proves the family Saxon, and carries it up at once to William the Conqueror.'

It is not surprising that his quick eye and excellent judgment should lead Welby to admire the wondrous buildings of Normandy; and the surpassing grandeur of many of the continental churches seems to have thrown him quite into raptures. He had then no leaning whatever towards the Roman Catholic creed, and was loud in his denunciations of the men who, wanting in appreciation of the exquisite beauty of mediæval art, could mutilate their buildings by interpolations of incongruous character, fill their churches with altars and decorations of debased Italian design, and permit the very precincts of their sacred buildings to be defiled. Nor was he less severe in his criticisms upon the vestments and all modern ecclesiastical ornaments connected with their ritual.

There were causes, however, in operation even now, at home, which, though long in taking effect, stealthily made their impressions upon his mind, and to which in some degree may be traced his after change in religious faith. His mother, who might be designated a woman of extraordinary intellect, though educated and brought up in warm attachment to the Church of England, was not always satisfied with the abilities of the clergy in the parish where she resided, and frequently wandered to neighbouring churches to hear strange preachers. A moderately eloquent sermon would not satisfy her : she needed strong stimulants. In justice it must be stated that she was possessed of considerable literary accomplishments, and frequently contributed articles to the leading periodicals. She took a lively interest in the political questions of the day, and as a partisan was active and even useful.

During the trial of Lord Viscount Melville—who was impeached by the House of Commons in 1805 for alleged malversation in his office of Treasurer of the Navy, and, after a trial by his peers in Westminster

*

Hall, adjudged not guilty—a pamphlet appeared which, showing no inconsiderable power of advocacy, and written in a very vigorous style, was attributed to Mrs. Pugin. It was entitled 'An Address to the Public, containing a Review of the Charges exhibited against Lord Viscount Melville, which led to the Resolutions of the House of Commons, on the 8th of April, 1805.' The opening paragraph will give some notion of Mrs. Pugin's power of language, and is worthy of insertion here :—

'It is a little singular that in the representations of the drama our sympathy is always called forth in favour of suffering rank, and we feel a desire to soften the misery of afflicted greatness. But in real life we appear to act on the reverse of this policy, and are for the most part inclined to accelerate the fall of human power, and to exult in the condition of a man degraded from high state and put down from the seat of authority. The obscure and feeble prisoner asks our compassion and receives it ; he solicits our aid to testify his innocence, and we lend our prompt exertion to his cause. But when crime is imputed to a man high in power we withdraw ourselves, with something like a feeling of congratulation, to a distance, that we may behold him grappling with the foe ; and however undeserved the attacks, we please ourselves with thinking that at least the pride of his stature will be humbled, and the ermine of his fame be spotted in the wrath and bitterness of the encounter.'

Again, in the middle of her argument, the writer apostrophises Justice in the following strain :—

'Eternal Justice! whose sway is on earth—whose source is in heaven—whose altar asks no sacrifice—whose shrine demands no victim—whose dominion ruled before the world was—whose empire will remain when worlds shall be no more—let not thy sceptre depart from our land ; give us to regard every individual, whether highest in power or lowest in rank, as a member of that commonwealth which links the interests of all; then shall the British Constitution—the reward of the blood of our martyred fathers—be the blessed inheritance of our children. Let not the zeal of party or of prejudice withdraw us from thy worship, but, in the seat of judgment, let us keep our eye on Him who ruleth over all, and who gave thy laws for our guidance, and for our government here and hereafter.'

Just about this period Edward Irving, subsequently the well-known founder of the modern Holy Catholic Apostolic Church, was the popular pulpit orator of the day. People rushed to his meeting-house as to a theatre ; royal dukes, members of both Houses of Parliament thronged the doors of the miserably ugly building in Cross Street, Hatton Garden, where he preached, and hundreds were weekly turned away from want of room. It was to this place Mrs. Pugin resorted, always accompanied by her son, and perhaps by one of the resident pupils. The Sunday morning breakfast was hurriedly despatched that she might be early at the door to gain admission. Wet or dry, no matter what might be the state of the weather, the expedition to Hatton Garden was never abandoned.

Such cold and tedious services as those belonging to the Presbyterian Scotch Church were by no means suited to young Welby's taste, and the long-spun orations of the preacher, though able and eloquent, failed to keep his attention awake. The Sunday, therefore, instead of being a day to which he looked forward with pleasure, became to him a day of ennui, for his mother never went to this place of worship unaccompanied by her son, so that he had no escape from attending a service wholly uncongenial to his feelings. Often on a fine morning, when he would have hastened with delight to Westminster Abbey, his desire was overruled by his mother, who compelled him to accompany her to Hatton Garden. It was rather remarkable that Mrs. Pugin should not have better understood her son's turn of mind and thus spared him this weekly infliction. No one ought to have known him better; she witnessed his habitual enthusiasm in other matters; she even seconded him in the exciting projects in which he embarked, and fed his lively imagination by the relation of marvellous hair-breadth escapes and far-fetched tales. It never could have been expected that such a youth would submit to be pent up for hours together without any relief, in a pew like a cattle-pen when so magnificent a building as Westminster Abbey, with its beautiful and solemn services, was within reach.

However, such was the effect of his mother's want of judgment that it helped forward the change in his religious views which subsequently took place. Pugin always expressed his unmitigated disgust at the cold and sterile forms of the Scotch Church; and the moment he broke loose from the trammels imposed upon him by his mother, he rushed into the arms of a Church which pompous by its ceremonies was attractive to his imaginative mind. Allusion has been made to the exciting stories which Mrs. Pugin was in the habit of relating, and there was one well calculated to create timidity in the minds of her son and the pupils, who were often left by themselves, while sketching and measuring in churches. It was as follows:—When staying with a friend at Lincoln whose house adjoined the cathedral, she frequently visited a prebendary who lived in the Close. The nearest way between their houses was easily effected, when the cathedral was open, by passing through the church and cloisters. The verger also, by way of accommodation, when he knew that it was required, left the cathedral doors unlocked, so that the prebendary and his friends might use this short road of an evening, instead of making a long detour outside the precincts. It happened one summer evening that Mrs. Pugin had been dining at the house of her clerical friend, and on parting at night declined an escort, and took her usual path through the cathedral. Entering the door, she closed it and passed to the opposite portal, which to her surprise was locked. The door by

which she entered being fitted with a spring lock, she
suddenly found herself a prisoner in the cathedral.
She made every effort to arouse attention by shouting
through the keyhole and shaking the door, but without
effect, for at that late hour everybody had gone to
rest. It was a fine moonlight night; thus she was not
left in darkness, and concluding that her absence from
home would soon cause a search to be made and save
her from a cold night's lodging in the cathedral, she
easily composed herself, and seated upon a bench, was
contemplating the beautiful effects of the light and
shade upon the pillars of the nave, when suddenly
there appeared through the silvery light the figure of
a man looking down upon her from one of the openings of the triforium, which as suddenly disappeared.
For the moment she was willing to believe that the
apparition was only a phantom created by her imagination, and having a large amount of courage and
self-possession, thought nothing more of it. A few
minutes afterwards, however, she again saw the appearance of a man looking over the gallery front, nodding
his head and beckoning to her with his hand, who then
again vanished. Her alarm was now really excited,
for it was difficult to suppose that this nocturnal visitor
could be in the cathedral for any good purpose. Impelled by fear, she moved from her position and entered
the choir, seating herself in one of the stalls. Every
minute now seemed hours to her, and, taking a prayer-
book, she sought by the aid of the moonlight to read;
but fancying she heard the unlocking of the outer

door, looked up, when to her horror she saw, staring in the opposite gallery front just above the book-board, a grizzly head, with the face directed towards her nodding and grinning most fearfully. Her courage now forsook her, but happily at this moment the cathedral door was really heard to open, and rushing away she was met by her friend and a servant. Uneasy at her not coming home, they had repaired to the Close, and the clergyman at once concluded that by some accident she might be locked up in the cathedral.

The cause of her alarm was soon explained. A poor idiotic youth who had escaped from the care of his friends, was, like persons thus afflicted, fond of prowling about and prying into odd places. The cathedral was his favourite haunt, and finding the door unlocked he entered and amused himself by running from place to place ; it was his erratic movements and awful grimaces which had well nigh bereft Mrs. Pugin of her senses.

CHAPTER V.

Effect of Calvinistic teaching—Brunel and the first public Cemetery—
Pugin's connection with Public Improvements—Practice of Pugin's
Office—Introduction at the British Museum to Messrs. Rundell and
Bridge—Appointed to design the Furniture for Windsor Castle—
Sir J. Wyattville and the King.

THE elder Pugin had never been very strict in his religious observances; occasionally he attended the services of the English Church, which he preferred to those of any other communion. The son was therefore left to the care of his mother, through whom all his religious impressions were obtained. That the strictness and character of this early training influenced his after life there can be no doubt, for he was often heard to inveigh against the Calvinistic tone of his early religious education.

The period had now arrived when from his acquirements Augustus could become useful to his father in his professional pursuits.

It was in the year 1827 that the scheme for establishing a public cemetery beyond the suburbs of London, in place of the parish churchyards, was first agitated. One of the chief promoters of this project was the late Sir Isambard, then Mr. Brunel. This gentleman united with his friend and fellow-countryman Pugin in preparing plans for laying out the ground, and in designing the several mortuary chapels and gateways for the cemetery; and it was mainly through their joint instrumentality that a company was formed, amongst whom were Lord Ingestre, the late Sir J. Dean Paul, and W. Carden, Esq., for the purpose of applying to Parliament for an Act authorizing the establishment of a public cemetery.

It is somewhat remarkable that we should be indebted to a Frenchman for first calling attention to this subject; and no one but a man of such vigorous mind and strong determination as Brunel would have persevered till he overcame the natural repugnance to separating the burial places of English Churchmen from the sacred precincts in which they and their forefathers had worshipped for many generations.

The public, therefore, were by no means eager to avail themselves of this new scheme, and as a commercial speculation it held out no tempting prospect. The project in consequence languished, and could not then be realized; but a few years later a Company was formed, under the title of the 'General Cemetery Company,' which entirely succeeded, and resulted in the large and well-regulated public cemetery at Kensal Green. From that time, as is well known, numerous other cemeteries have been established in the neighbourhood of London and in the provinces. The subject is here mentioned because it was in the preparation of the preliminary drawings for this cemetery that Augustus began to make himself useful; though it

E

may be added that it would have been well if the
original plan by Brunel and Pugin had been carried
into effect, as it was far more consistent with the ideas
of Christian sepulture than the heterogeneous collection
of monuments, crowded together at Kensal Green.

Another great project, which unfortunately was
never carried into execution, also occupied much of the
senior Pugin's attention. Great efforts were made by
Sir Frederick Trench to effectuate plans for embank-
ing the Middlesex side of the Thames, and form extensive quays with handsome ranges of buildings.
Many designs for this purpose were prepared, under
the suggestion of Sir F. Trench, by Mr. Pugin in 1824.
At a later period he was likewise engaged in the
design for terraces and a bridge of communication
between Carlton Terrace Gardens, so as to admit of a
drive into St. James's Park in a straight line with
Regent Street. This project also fell to the ground.
But a still more important scheme than either of these
was proposed by the late Samuel Rogers, Esq. and
Pugin, having for its object the formation of an additional park on the Bishop of London's estate, to unite
Hyde Park and the Regent's Park, thus to have all
the London parks together. This project was of
course agitated when nothing but green fields were to
be seen west of Tyburn Gate, where now countless
houses are built.

The superior knowledge of Gothic architecture
which the elder Pugin was known to possess, led many
architects whose acquaintance with mediæval art was

superficial, to apply to him for aid. This he was always ready to afford, and through the help of his son and his pupils he assisted others in carrying out their works. Many buildings might in strictness claim him as their author instead of the architect to whom they are publicly ascribed.

It is to be feared that the system of working by other people's hands and wits is not now wholly abandoned; but there is a meanness in the practice which cannot be too much reprobated, and he is unworthy the name of a conscientious architect who condescends to such surreptitious proceedings. This remark does not apply to those who, in the conception and execution of large works, find it necessary to have their ideas carried out by secondary agency, subordinate to their own direction, but to the system of those who are in the habit of throwing upon others the labour and study of design, and then unworthily claim the merit of the performance. His first employment, independent of his father, seems to have been given to young Pugin by the celebrated goldsmiths, Messrs. Rundell and Bridge. One of their firm, while engaged in an examination of some ancient designs for plate in the Print Room of the British Museum, chanced to notice that he was employed in copying the prints of Albert Durer and Israel Silvester. Struck by his skill in drawing the goldsmith accosted him, and soon found that he possessed just the genius his firm was seeking. His complete knowledge of mediæval art fitted him admirably for designing plate in the old manner; his services were immediately secured, and much beautiful plate was executed by them from Pugin's designs. This introduction very soon led to another commission of a still more important character.

The great works which had been for some years in progress at Windsor Castle, under the professional direction of Sir Jeffrey Wyattville, were now drawing to a close, and the important question of fitting the apartments with furniture of suitable design was under consideration. The King took a lively interest in this matter, and resolved that those portions of the interior which retained a mediæval character should be furnished with objects designed in a corresponding style. There was at that time a French upholsterer, Mr. Morel, whom the King had in earlier days patronized by employment at Carlton House; and it was to this gentleman that His Majesty entrusted the great undertaking of suitably furnishing the new apartments, galleries, and corridors of Windsor Castle.

In ancient times this task would have been confided to the architect of the Castle, and it would not have been thought beneath his dignity to design and adapt any detail which might conduce to the artistic effect of the building. This most excellent rule appears to have fallen into desuetude, and was not acted on in the present instance. Sir Jeffrey Wyattville had more than sufficient occupation, and did not desire the additional labour which the management of this branch of business would have entailed upon him. According to the usual routine, the King's orders passed through the Lord Chamberlain's office direct to Messrs. Morel and Seddon. Mr. Morel, feeling the great responsibility of the task thrown upon the firm, applied to the elder Pugin to aid them in the execution of their commission. This was just the opportunity calculated to draw forth the abilities of his son, to whom his father immediately transferred the business. All attempts hitherto made to design furniture in the mediæval style had been feeble and unsuccessful; here was then a good chance for showing what really could be done when the task was confided to proper hands, and where the want of money formed no bar to the production of the best thing which art workmen could produce.

Without asserting that this work, when completed, was wholly successful, it may fairly be said, that the furniture was remarkable for great variety of form and detail, producing an expression of fitness not to be found in any other modern attempts; and it may be reasonably doubted whether any person but Pugin could have designed such a multitude of objects with equally happy results.

Among other schemes suggested for enhancing the grandeur of the Castle, the King at one time proposed that the splendid great roof of the Banqueting Hall, forming part of the remains of Eltham Palace built by Edward the Fourth, should be removed from thence to Windsor Castle; and Sir J. Wyattville made a careful examination of the ancient structure in October, 1827, to ascertain if its condition was sufficiently sound to admit of its being transferred as a roof to St. George's Hall. It was, however, found to be in so decayed a state as to render this proceeding undesirable. Previous to the time of this examination the building, which had been, and still is, used as a barn or lumber-room, had been sadly neglected, but it is now carefully protected from the effects of weather. Upon archæological grounds it may be considered fortunate that circumstances prevented the removal of this beautiful timber roof from its legitimate position.*

It would have been very advantageous if the great works at Windsor Castle had been deferred till the practice of Gothic architecture was better understood. Still it must be conceded, in justice to Sir Jeffrey Wyattville, that, whatever may be the defects in detail, he has succeeded in raising a most effective and picturesque group of buildings; and though we may blush for our other palaces, England can justly boast of Windsor Castle as a residence fit for the sovereign of a mighty empire.

The personal interest which George the Fourth took in the progress of the additions to the Castle is well known, and his constant interference was a matter of much annoyance to the architect. Wyattville was not by habit a courtier, or disposed to give up his own well-grounded opinions to meet at all times the King's

---

* The custom of stripping one palace to furnish and adorn another ought to be especially deprecated, as it deprives places of their well-acquired ancient associations, and produces much confusion in recording their histories. Hampton Court has already suffered much by these means.

fancies; he was plain and honest in his remarks, but the independence with which he insisted upon his own views never offended the King. When Sir Jeffrey was about to begin the erection of the corridor or long gallery on the south and east sides of the court of the upper ward, about 500 feet in length, in order to form a handsome feature in the interior, as well as a commodious access to all the private apartments on the principal story, he proposed that it should be 15 feet wide, but the King would not listen to its being made more than 10 feet for fear of spoiling the effect of the court. As soon as the parapet was finished the King came to see it, and was so surprised at finding that instead of injuring, the corridor actually added greatly to the effect of the court, that he expressed to Wyattville his regret that he did not allow him to make it 15 feet wide instead of 10; on which Wyattville replied that he had presumed to anticipate his Majesty's feeling on the subject, and had actually built it 15 feet wide.

Wyattville did not live to see the termination of the works at the Castle. The stables and riding house built since his death, were designed and carried out under the superintendence of his friend and assistant, Mr. Henry Ashton. This gentleman also prepared the drawings and edited a beautiful work on the Castle, published by Mr. Weale. Probably but one opinion prevails now as to the questionable taste shown by George the Fourth in connection with public works executed by his command, yet the credit of encouraging art according to the best of his knowledge must not be denied him. That his taste was not pure is to be regretted, but he was nevertheless a real patron of art, in spite of the obloquy heaped upon his memory by eminent popular writers of the present day. The erection of the Pavilion in so singular a style, and the placing of artificial ruins about Virginia Waters, do not show sound judgment, yet the King sought to impart artistic effect wherever he thought it possible; he even sent Monsieur Vilmet, his chef de cuisine, to the elder Pugin, that he might instruct him in the art of drawing and design—wishing his table to be decked with taste, and the confectionary, &c., built up in artistic forms.

CHAPTER VI.

Welby Pugin's first connection with Theatres—Employment in the designs of Scenery for the Opera of Kenilworth at Her Majesty's Theatre—Construction of a Model Theatre in his father's house—Bad effects from associating with low society—Establishes an Art Manufactory—Improved condition of Art-Workmen—Failure of the Scheme.

WE now arrive at a period in Welby Pugin's life when, through mere accident, a totally new direction was given to his tastes. During his engagement on the works in connection with Windsor Castle he formed an acquaintance with a person of inferior position, who, amongst other occupations, was employed at night in a subordinate station in the management of the stage scenery at Covent Garden Theatre. This man's description of the scenery, property, and machinery of the stage filled Pugin's youthful imagination with a longing to see the concealed mechanism used for stage effects.* It must be borne in mind that, although entrusted with the important business just mentioned, he was yet but a boy of fifteen years or little more, and never till

* In a diary which Pugin now began to keep is the following entry: 'June 26, 1827. Designed furniture for Windsor Castle. While at Mr. Morel's I became acquainted with a person called George Dayes, son of the celebrated artist of that name, and it was through him that I first imbibed the taste for stage machinery and scenic representations, to which I afterwards applied myself so closely.'

this time had entered a theatre or witnessed any dramatic representations,—the strictness of his mother's principles and domestic regulations being a bar to his attendance at any theatrical performances.

Pugin's first admission behind the stage seems to have filled him with wonder. The complicated and interesting mechanical contrivances were things of which he had not the slightest previous notion ; but his quick perception soon assured him that these admitted of great improvement and might be made to produce far more magical results than had yet been seen. He saw defective design adopted in scene painting, and immediately determined to effect some reform in the scenic department. An introduction being obtained to Messrs. Grieve, the well known scene-painters, he obtained, through them, some knowledge of the art of distemper painting on canvas, and the peculiar colours used; and thus he became enabled to paint scenery, designed by himself in the mediæval style.*

* The author of ' Self-help, with Illustrations of Character and Conduct,' gives an account of Pugin's connection with theatres which is founded upon a mistake. He was attracted to the pursuit of theatrical mechanism by accident ; it occurred at the time that he was engaged in designing the furniture for Windsor Castle. The man who cleaned his drawing-boards, rubbed up Indian ink, and did other duties in the office, happened to be a scene-shifter at Covent Garden Theatre; this fellow was sharp, had a good memory, and could imitate cleverly the voices and mannerism of comic actors. When Pugin required him to do anything, he invariably replied in a droll manner, adding gesture, and imitating the voice of some well-known actor. This amused Pugin amazingly, and he was persuaded to accompany this man one evening behind the scenes; once there, it was not difficult to foresee what would happen, and in order that he might repeat his visits, it is not improbable that he made himself useful; for otherwise he would not

There was certainly a wide opening for any one possessed of talents to improve all the accessories of the stage; for though the Messrs. Grieve and others produced beautiful landscapes, yet whenever architecture was depicted a total absence of knowledge was shown. The most absurd incongruities were called Gothic, and compositions full of the grossest anachronisms presented to the public as genuine forms of architecture. Young Pugin was just the man to correct these errors in judgment, and he no sooner set about it than he achieved great success. Historical operas were then most popular, and they afforded a wide scope for the introduction of beautiful scenery and costume. The manager of the Italian Opera, hearing of Welby Pugin's known skill in mediæval art, sought his assistance, and commissioned him to design all the scenery for the new opera of *Kenilworth* brought out in the season of 1831. A better subject for the exercise of his genius could scarcely have been found; he designed, and had executed under his own control,

---

have been permitted on the stage through the mere introduction of a menial. He soon made acquaintance with Bartley the stage-manager, the Messrs. Grieve, and others, all of whom he aided in some degree by his natural genius. So again his purchase of a sailing ship was not with a view to making a profitable trade—it was a youthful frolic; neither of these pursuits were chosen with the intention of improvement, through ';the discipline of labour.' He was fond of the sea, and it was most natural that he should use his pencil when on landing at any place he saw interesting buildings, which might furnish illustrations for his publications. That he carried on a little commerce while cruising about is quite true, and would often burst into a fit of laughter when accosted as an egg merchant by some of his friends, in allusion to his freight.

all the scenery for this interesting historical opera. Its production created a great sensation, presenting as it did in all its features one of the most gorgeous and correct representations which had hitherto been witnessed. The architectural portion of this spectacle, which was considerable, showed great originality of treatment, being in striking contrast with the old and ill-painted scenes, wings, and sky-pieces which formed the staple for all scenery no matter in what age or country the story of the opera might be laid. The great success which attended the performance of this opera was almost entirely due to the attractiveness of the scenery and costume. So completely did the mania for theatrical representations enthral him that he was for ever making experiments in order to produce startling and novel mechanical changes, and he made himself acquainted with all that had been written and published on the subject; but little was to be obtained either from the designs of Peruzzi or any more modern artist. The only man in comparatively recent times who devoted attention to the subject was Inigo Jones, who displayed great fancy and talent not merely as a scene painter, but in producing pageants and masques, and planning the decorations and machinery for them. Perhaps Pugin might claim to have done as much in his way for producing correct representations of the pageants of the middle ages. With a view to help him in this pursuit his parents allowed him to convert the upper floor of their house in Great Russell Street into a model theatre. This he did at much expense, removing the attic ceiling, cutting away the roof, constructing cisterns, and adapting everything necessary to his object. On this model stage he designed the most exquisite scenery, with fountains, tricks, traps, drop-scenes, wings, soffites, hilly scenes, flats, open flats, and every magic change of which stage mechanism is capable. Large parties were invited to witness his performances, and probably a more skilfully made model theatre had never been seen. It was not a toy in any sense of the word, but a piece of construction sufficiently large to enable Pugin to exhibit experiments and study compositions before they were adopted on the actual stage. The intricacy of the mechanism was surprising, but every part was so admirably adjusted that the changes in the scenes, wings, and sky-pieces were effected with marvellous rapidity, for it was provided with lines, pulleys, grooves, balance weights, machines for ascents and de. scents, &c. His connection with the theatrical world was not of long duration; it served to gratify his taste for a while, but his impulsive mind could not rest satisfied with mere fictitious representations of buildings. His desire was to carry into reality some of the designs which he so skilfully indicated upon a small scale. The gradual steps by which he succeeded in accomplishing his wish will appear in the sequel; but as earlier in life the duties of his father's office became utterly insupportable to the active mind of Welby Pugin, so now his scene-painting and other theatrical engagements had no longer any attractions.

At this time he conceived an ardent desire for a maritime life, and regardless of the eminent position which laid within his reach, he made up his mind to go to sea. First, owner of a small boat which he kept for his own pleasure, he successively commanded a smack, and afterwards a schooner, in which amongst other merchandize he generally managed to bring over many interesting carvings and other antiquities purchased in the old stores of Holland and Flanders. Thus he used these excursions as subservient to the object of forming a museum, which later in life afforded him the greatest pleasure, and became one of the chief attractions in his residence at Ramsgate.

During one of these voyages he was wrecked on the Scotch coast, some distance below Leith, where he and his men all but perished; this event led to his friendship with Mr. Gillespie Graham, the well-known architect, of Edinburgh, which he always prized most highly.

Having lost everything, he arrived in Edinburgh in a destitute condition. Knowing Mr. Graham by fame he applied to him, and was received with the greatest kindness; this gentleman, to use his own expression, completely '*rigged him out*,' provided him with money, and what was more to the point gave him sound advice. Foreseeing the talent of the architect cropping out in every word of his interesting conversation, he conjured him to give up his mode of life, and to pursue the career for which nature had so brilliantly prepared him. Before taking leave Mr. Graham gave him his own pocket compasses as a reminder of his advice, (these were the famed instruments which he used through life, which appear in Herbert's portrait of him. Upon them is engraved James Gillespie Graham, architect, Edinburgh, 1830.)

It may be naturally inferred that from the refined boy and polished gentleman, which were Welby Pugin's characteristics while under his parents' care, his present life had led him to assume the dress and habits of a sailor, with the exception of his innate horror of tobacco and beer.

As before remarked, Welby Pugin was extremely delicate in youth, but his present mode of life had certainly one good effect, by giving him Herculean strength, which doubtlessly enabled him so effectually to carry out the work which he so gloriously accomplished. The life he had hitherto led was, as may be imagined, a source of much pain and anguish to his parents and friends, more especially to the refined tastes of his father, who on meeting a friend, exclaimed with much grief, 'God bless my soul, it was but this morning I met my boy Auguste in the disguise of a common sailor, carrying on his shoulder a tub of water which he had took from the pompe of St. Dunstan.' Few things probably could have so severely shocked the finely poised susceptibilities of the elder Pugin.

Welby Pugin's name had now acquired celebrity in various ways connected with art, in consequence of his well known intimate acquaintance with Gothic architecture.   His power of rapid delineation was likewise appreciated.

The elder Pugin, although well versed in the history of architecture, had devoted himself to its theory rather than to its practice, and, with the assistance of pupils, was largely engaged as an architectural draughtsman. At this time his son was still living with him, and all who were engaged in building in the Gothic style resorted to young Pugin as the great authority in his special department. Many leading architects placed their rough sketches in his hands in order to have the detail drawings accurately prepared.

In those days great difficulty was felt in finding artificers and carvers capable of doing justice to the execution of designs in the mediæval style. The long prevalence of classic architecture had resulted in fostering a school of art-workmen well versed in Grecian and Italian detail, but who were ignorant of the correct forms and expressions of Gothic detail; their notions of ornament being gathered from terra cotta casts and plaster of Paris models, instead of being taken from authentic ancient examples. Very few carvers could execute a foliated string-course or span-dril with correct feeling, and the general notion amongst workmen was that anything grotesque would do for Gothic decorations, as grace and beauty were supposed by them to be alien to the style. As young Pugin now proposed not only to undertake the delineation of working drawings, but also to superintend the execution of the work which he designed, he felt that some step was necessary on his part to educate the workmen, or his acquired reputation would suffer by the bungling way in which objects said to be taken from his drawings would be executed. To obviate this difficulty he determined to have all carved work, whenever it was possible, executed under his own eye. On making known this intention to some leading practical architects they were only too glad to avail themselves of his services in this new capacity, and the promises of business which were quickly given justified him in putting his scheme into action. For this purpose he took the lease of extensive premises in Hart Street, Covent Garden, as he had still a lingering affection for his old haunts; and having secured the assistance of one or two clever carvers whom he had himself already taught, he made it known generally amongst his friends that he would undertake to supply all the ornamental portions of buildings which could by possibility be executed apart from the structure and be fixed afterwards. At first his success was considerable, and he obtained extensive commissions from Scotland and Ireland; for in those countries the want of skilled artificers was even greater than in England, and in the progress of any large and important building the difficulty experienced in securing the proper finish of details was only to be overcome by obtaining carvers from England. In the hands of such a master as Pugin, therefore, a great desideratum was supplied; for by the mere transmission of drawings showing the intended decorations, he at

F

once understood what was required, had all duly executed, and sent off to the buildings under construction. But not being brought up as a man of business he was incapable of estimating the sufficient profit to be attached to labour and materials in order to secure a proper return for his invested capital; nor could he exercise sufficient check over the art-workmen in his employ. This speculation was therefore soon brought to an end, after the sacrifice of a great deal of money which had been sunk in the undertaking; still during the time in which it was in operation a vast amount of excellent detail, both in wood and stone, was prepared under his immediate directions.

CHAPTER VII.

Temporary Embarrassments—Pugin's Marriage, and his Wife's Death —Buries her at Christchurch Priory Church—Intention of building a House at Christchurch—Abandoned through his Father's inter- ference—Seeks another Neighbourhood, and builds St. Marie's Grange, near Salisbury—Intimacy with Mr. Osmond—Indignation at the modern alterations in Salisbury Cathedral—Commences Cor- respondence with Mr. Osmond by a Letter from Wells.

WHILE carrying on the business which terminated in the failure just mentioned he suffered much anxiety, for his pecuniary resources were inadequate to meet many of his engagements; and at one time he was seized for the nonpayment of rent, and placed in a sponging house near Chancery Lane. It was late one summer evening in the year 1831 that his father rushed in an excited state to Mr. Weale and Mr. Hogarth, the well-known architectural publishers, begging that they would go with him to Cursitor Street and become security in a bond for the payment of his son's debts, so that he might be released from confinement. Fortunately their interference was suc- cessful, and young Pugin was spared the misery of a night's lodging in durance vile. This occurrence was particularly distressing to his father, and he always referred to his son's embarrassments with horror; for in all probability he must have become bankrupt but for the final discharge of his liabilities by Miss Welby, his aunt. The failure in this business scheme fully determined Pugin henceforward to stick closely to the exercise of his profession in a regular manner, for he had sense enough to see that he was not fitted for commercial enterprise.

Although his time and attention were necessarily much occupied during this brief but unlucky period, he still found opportunities for occasionally visiting Covent Garden Theatre to see how matters were going on, and to enjoy a little conversation with the Messrs. Grieve, with whom he still kept up an acquaintance. It was about this time that he met Miss Garnet, a grand-niece of Dayes the artist. After a very short court-ship he was married to her in 1831. His choice was not pleasing to his father and mother, but they did not withhold their sanction to the match, fearing to thwart him in a matter of such delicate nature; but it is due to her memory to add that for the short time she was his wife, she showed a most affectionate regard, and exercised a beneficial influence over him.

Augustus was yet a minor, and for a considerable time after their marriage he and his wife resided with his parents in Great Russell Street; and here in May, 1832, she became the mother of her first and only child. Unhappily she died in her confinement, but her infant daughter survived. This melancholy event was a fearful blow to his sensitive mind.* It might have been

---

* In an extract from one of his mother's letters to her sister she says: 'I feel somewhat desolate to-day, for I am without either father

A VIEW OF THE PRIORY CHURCH, AND RUINS OF THE CASTELLAN'S HOUSE, CHRISTCHURCH, TAKEN BY WELBY PUGIN WHEN 13 YEARS OLD.

supposed that as his wife was a native of London he
would have chosen some metropolitan churchyard for
her last resting-place, but, as stated by his mother, he
selected the ancient Priory Church, at Christchurch,
Hants, for her burial-place. A vault was there formed
in the north aisle of the choir, and on the 15th of
June she was buried. The spot is now marked by a
black marble slab, inlaid with a beautiful brass cross,
and bearing an inscription copied in the note to this
page.*

---

or son. My son travelled by the night coach for Christchurch, and
my husband went this morning; the funeral, which will be merely
placing my poor Anne in the vault, will, I suppose, take place on Friday.
It was my intention, as a consolation to Augustus, to have attended
myself, but I feel the journey would be beyond my strength. He is to sleep
in a double-bedded room with his father, so he will not be left alone at
night, that is the dread hour. I have never left his bedside since the death
of his wife, nor known what an unbroken night's rest was before last
night. Wretched he will be, grieved to the soul, but in this world,
where fortitude is so necessary, he must strive to obtain it; and may
Almighty God, of His infinite mercy, sanctify unto him all his sorrows!
I frequently think how often he used (before he was fourteen years of
age) to say, "My own dear mother, how happy I am! nobody can be
happier than I." Alas, alas! look over the six years which have passed
since that period, and we find a whole life of woe, such as is rarely
experienced by the generality of men, huddled into it. From his works
and his woes he has already experienced a long life, and when he dies he
will not die without some dignity, and have his name perpetuated.'
Scratched on his watch is found the following beautiful inscription:
' This day, May 27th, 1832, my dearest Anne died unto this world, but
lived unto God.'
    * This slab was laid down in the year after his conversion to Roman
Catholicism, and the inscription concludes with the pious aspiration
common to such Catholic memorials. It is the only instance in which
he adopted his triple Christian name, Augustus Welby Northmore, and
there may be observed also the French prefix of _de_ to his surname. The
inscription runs thus : ' Here lieth the body of the first and beloved wife

Pugin also presented to the church, at a subsequent time, a finely carved oak altar-table. Of course anything designed by him excited much remark, and this table was the subject of criticism; for, though admirable as a piece of carving, it was wanting in ecclesiastical expression, and too much resembled the richly-carved cabinets of the 16th century. The peculiarity apparent in the selection of so distant and retired a spot for the burial-place of his wife, may probably be best explained when it is stated that a year or two previously to his marriage, he had a severe illness, and upon his recovery a change of air became needful. Accompanied by his mother he went to the south-west coast, and selected the neighbourhood of Christchurch as his temporary residence.

Here he was truly delighted with the magnificent Priory church, the ruins of the castle and castellan's house, as well as the beautiful marine scenery of the town and neighbourhood. The natural quietude was also very congenial to him in his then enfeebled state of health; and the spot struck him as being particularly well calculated for his retreat when desiring to study apart from the turmoil of business in London.

---

of Augustus Welby Northmore de Pugin, Architect, who departed this life at London on the twenty-seventh day of May, one thousand eight hundred and thirty-two. R. I. P. Amen.' The funeral was remarkable. The interment did not take place till the 15th of June at 8 o'clock P.M., the remains being brought to the church on the 8th of June, and deposited during the interval in Prior Draper's Chapel. The service was read in the choir, the coffin being placed in the centre, an unusual practice.

Pugin consequently cherished the idea of obtaining a piece of ground and building a house, in which he might indulge his own taste and show the manner in which a domestic residence should be arranged fitted up in strict accordance with mediæval examples. The hope of accomplishing this was ever foremost in his mind, and the precise part of the country in which it might be realized was immaterial to him, provided there was some great castle or church, of architectural interest, near. Upon hearing that the site for a house in a retired situation near the town of Christchurch, called Holfleet, commanding a view of all the objects he admired, backed by the hills of St. Catherine stretching up the valleys of the Stour and Avon, was to be obtained, a negotiation for its purchase was at once set on foot. Pugin, however, being still a minor, it was necessary for the owner of the land to consult his father upon the propriety of the step his son was meditating, and also on the means for carrying the project into effect. The father, remembering and disapproving his conduct in connexion with the theatrical world, refused to become guarantee, or to give consent. Thus for a while the project fell to the ground, but he never relinquished the hope that at a future day he should carry his favourite scheme into effect; and it was no doubt the operation of this feeling which led him to determine upon burying his wife at Christchurch.

The grief which he suffered through the sad loss of his partner indisposed him from pursuing his favourite idea for some months; but he was too much occupied

in business to suffer any depressing feelings to take
lasting effect upon him, and soon after we find him
again reverting to the project of building. But instead
of renewing his application for the land at Christchurch, he had selected another site for his dwelling,
though still in the valley of the Avon.*

Here he set boldly to work, and designed and built
a house for himself exhibiting all the peculiar arrangements common to domestic dwellings of the 15th

century. The structure was principally of brick. It
was quaint and odd, and much noticed by people of

* It was in 1835 that he purchased half an acre of ground, about a
mile and a half from Salisbury, from Mr. Staples, on the road to
Southampton.

the neighbourhood who took an interest in such matters. It can scarcely be said that he was successful in this work; there was nothing very inviting in the exterior design, and a great absence of modern comfort in the interior arrangement. The building tended rather to show the eccentricity of its owner than his superior skill in design; still it was not without merit, and undoubtedly formed a striking contrast to the class of modern suburban houses generally erected. The place was called St. Marie's Grange. Here he frequently resided, collecting old books, prints, manuscripts, pictures, &c.; and now was first manifested his indignation at the wanton havoc which had been made in Salisbury Cathedral, where, under the plausible guise of improvements or restorations, most reprehensible changes were effected.

Pugin's fiery spirit was strongly roused by the contemplation of these sad doings, now brought so prominently to his notice. Out of the catalogue of spoliation it will be sufficient to enumerate the following:—The destruction of the Hungerford and Beauchamp Chapels, and the removal of the porch of the north transept; the demolition of the screen which separated the Lady Chapel from the choir, and the elevation of the pavement so as to alter all the proportions of the former; the destruction of the Saints' Chapels in the western transept, and of the rood-loft before the choir; the removal of the monuments from their appropriate places transported in order to line the arcades of the Nave; and the destruction of the detached belfry tower. Unhappily, what was done scarcely deserves less censure than what was left undone.

How far the effect of these enormities upon his ardent spirit may have led to the religious change which shortly came over him, it is difficult to say. Judging, however, by his writings it cannot be doubted he was indulging a notion that these acts of spoliation, as well as others of a like nature at Durham, Lichfield, and elsewhere, were due entirely to indifference on the part of the Church of England Chapters; and he believed that these mighty fabrics would, under the care of Roman Catholic authorities, have been spared such disastrous changes. Pugin, however, lived long enough to see the delusion dissipated; but at this moment his feelings of indignation were directed against the Cathedral dignitaries.

It was during his residence at St. Marie's Grange that he made a tour for the purpose of examining several Cathedrals yet unknown to him; and, having formed a close intimacy with Mr. Osmond, senior, of Salisbury, whom he found desirous of acquiring a knowledge of mediæval architecture, he from time to time communicated to him in a series of letters his impressions of the various buildings he saw, illustrating his meaning by the most admirable marginal pen-and-ink sketches. The correspondence abounds in the strongest expressions of disgust at the mutilations which he observed in operation, and he never restrained his pen, but boldly gave vent to his feelings when writing to his friend.

The first letter is dated from Wells in Somersetshire, and is headed by a clever sketch, contrasting a modern marble tablet stuck against a wall with a beautiful canopied tomb and recumbent figure.

He writes as follows:—

' MY DEAR SIR,

' If you want to be delighted, if you want to be astonished, if you want to be half mad, as I at present am, for God's sake come over to Wells. The most magnificent things for detail that can be seen, splendid remains of every style, and every description of Gothic architecture. You have no conception of the magnificence of the cathedral, &c. One day would suffice. I am well acquainted with everything here, and have got introductions to all the most secret corners; and I declare I would not leave you till you had seen every interesting object in the place. Pray come, I entreat of you. I leave here either at the end of the week—that is the beginning of next, about Tuesday or Wednesday. * * I would not think of wishing you so much to come down were I not certain you would be delighted. No *artists* indeed! The figures of the west front are magnificent—splendid specimens of sculpture. Tell that to Mr. Lucas; and tell him that the *antique* fades away before the *ancient*. Gothic for ever! Mr. Caunter, one of the vicars here, is most anxious to see you, so pray come down and don't be ruled by your wife, for without you make a pilgrimage to this shrine you will never obtain absolution for the

number of *blisters* you have been the instrument of
fixing and polluting against ancient arts. Give my
kind remembrances to Mrs. Osmond and all my good
friends at Salisbury, and believe me your most sincere
friend and fellow labourer,

'A. PUGIN,

'Freemason, though not a member
of the man-milliner's lodge.

'Send a line to me by post : direct Mr. Pugin, at Mr.
Hatch's, Vicar's Close, Wells.'

The next letter, written from Ramsgate, is so singularly beautiful in its illustrations that the heading is
here given as a wood cut, being a fac simile of the
original.

'Saint Laurence, Oct. xxvii., Anno Dom. mdcccxxxiii.

'DEAR OSMOND,

'I fear you will by this time have thought me
neglectful in not acknowledging the receipt of a most
acceptable and kind present from you in the shape of
an enormous Cheddar cheese, which although not
strictly Gothic in its present shape may be daily rendered more so by cutting it into 4, which will make it
a quatrefoil. But I fear me much in the course of a
short time its style will be scarcely perceptible, as it
will have gone through such a variety of form, owing
to the extreme partiality of all at home to do full
justice to its merits. It is, in truth, excellent, and the
only drawback on the enjoyment of it is that we have

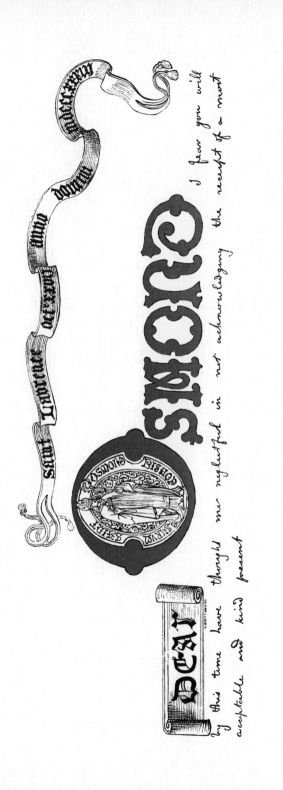

THOMAS

DEAR

by this time have thought me neglectful in not acknowledging the receipt of a most acceptable and kind present

I fear you will

not the kind donor to partake of it with us, which was the case the last time I had the pleasure of tasting such cheese. I should have sent a letter off directly on our receiving your present, had I not been absent on a journey when it came, not in search of the beautiful but the needful, which is not so easily obtained; from which I am only just returned. I have long had it in contemplation to send you an account of my proceedings after I left you at Exeter, and as nothing is like the present time I will proceed, with the help of my memory and memorandum book, to give you a full, particular, and true account of my adventures. After leaving you at Exeter I had a most delightful day's ride to Bristol through Taunton, where I had a *sight* of the magnificent tower whose fame you have no doubt heard of. It is without exception the finest tower of the kind in England, though I must say we are deficient in this country of those magnificent masses which are to be seen in the towns of France, Flanders, and Germany; for beautiful as the Tower of Taunton is it still seems to want something to carry it off at the top. The towers of Boston and St. Nicholas at Newcastle are in this respect far preferable. (See sketch.)

'While at Bristol I paid particular attention to the Cathedral, where I find many things deserving most particular attention. This Cathedral has been generally overlooked as undeserving of notice, but the fact is that there are parts about it equal to anything in the country. The groining of the aisles, the carving in parts of the stalls, the vestry, the tombs in the aisles round the choir, the great west window, the Norman entrance to the Chapter House from the cloisters, all are most interesting, and to real Gothic men, like you and me, it affords a great treat. The east window is so

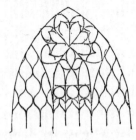 truly beautiful that I have just marked out the tracery of it for you; the original glass is still in it, and the effect is wonderfully rich and varied. I then steamed from Bristol to Chepstow in Monmouthshire; here is, I may say, one of the most perfect castles I have ever seen. The parts about it are magnificent, and the extent of mouldings immense. To give you some idea of its preservation, the wooden gates are all remaining; they are composed of three pieces of oak halved together crossways, then two thicknesses of one and a-half oak plank with a sheeting of iron, and bound with iron bars bolted through all. It is to be remembered that the tide from the Severn rises higher here than at any other part of the world, the rise and fall being at spring tides upwards of seventy feet. Leaving this interesting spot, I walked by the side of the River Wye to Tintern Abbey, distant about eight miles. Although I can manage to give you an idea of

a Gothic building, it is quite impossible to convey by writing any conception of the beautiful scenery of the banks of the River Wye. The richest foliage and loftiest trees arise up amid overhanging masses of rock, and the terrific and beautiful are everywhere blended. I ascended a place called the Wyndcliff, where I had the sight of four cathedrals and fourteen counties. The day was remarkably fine, and those views you and I saw on the Exeter road faded to nothing before it. A heavy thunder-storm coming on, I was glad to push on for the quiet inn at Tintern, where I rested for the night, and next morning proceeded to view the far-famed abbey. The situation is beautiful; as a ruin the building is also; but dare I oppose the torrent of popular opinion and not admire Tintern Abbey as a building? yes I dare, and I say that, as a building, it is anything but admirable. Were I to express this opinion to the tourist and the general observer I should be set down either for an ignorant brute or an opinionated upstart; but I am sure if you and I were to go over it together you would agree with me. The only thing really worthy of admiration is the west window, which is very beautiful, and of which I send you a sketch; but the rest of the building is by no means equal, and the plan, mouldings, windows, &c., are very common-place; I therefore mounted the Here-ford coach with four horses, and a very pleasant ride

brought me to that city,—an old fashioned but not
ancient looking town, common brick houses, dull shops
and empty streets being the features of Hereford.
Maddened by the sight I rushed to the cathedral; but
horror! dismay! the villain Wyatt had been there,
the west front was his. Need I say more? No! All
that is vile, cunning, and rascally is included in the
term Wyatt, and I could hardly summon sufficient
fortitude to enter and examine the interior. In this
church there is much to admire, a good deal to learn,
much to deplore. 1st, Much to admire :—the Saxon
parts of the nave, the stalls, the bishop's throne, the
tombs, the Lady Chapel, the vicar's cloisters, are all
most beautiful and interesting, of which you may be
sure I took complete sketches. 2nd. A great deal to
learn :—there are portions of the Lady Chapel and
the Bishop's throne that are perfectly unique and truly
extraordinary. 3rd. Most to deplore :—what do you
think of a regular Roman altar-screen, a modern
window over it, with the Last Supper from West, like
a great transparency? "What do you think of it?"
said a canon, triumphantly, when he showed it me.
"Think of it!" said I; "why I think it is yet more
execrable than the window of New College Chapel."
The canon was dumb. Then, only conceive the fine
Saxon ornaments imitated in plaster in the most
wretched style; a plain ceiling to the nave; the Lady
Chapel filled with bookcases, and the end towards the
church plastered up; the building ruinous in many
parts, and the cloisters absolutely left to fall. All these

things raise emotions in the breast of the real antiquarian not easily subdued. I next shaped my course to Malvern, to see the abbey there and the celebrated Hills. Here is a church in which the stained glass has not fallen a victim to Protestant zeal. It is truly magnificent, and the drawing of the figures is correct and beautiful, the colouring rich and varied. These windows may be rated among the finest specimens of English glass of the 15th century. The paving-tiles are likewise decidedly the finest in the kingdom; such a variety of patterns and such a quantity of tiles I never saw anywhere. A few years ago a meeting of the fashionables of Malvern was called to subscribe towards the repairs of the dilapidated building, and by the help of raffles, &c., a few pounds were collected. Two hodfulls of mortar were got to repair the church, and the remainder of the money expended in putting in a window of the aisle the arms of the subscribers in stained glass, with their names in full, a monument of their folly and arrogance. The very mullions in which the glass is placed are rotten and falling. The church itself is in dreadful repair; fall it must, and all that is to be hoped is, that in its fall it may annihilate those whose duty it was to have restored it; but of this we may be sure, that if it falls while there is a congregation within its walls, it will clear some away that ought to be got rid of, for such a set of lounging idlers as the fashionables of Malvern are only to be matched at Brighton or Cheltenham. I must now for the present conclude, leaving the rest of my journey, which is too

extensive for one letter ; and if you have the patience
to permit it, I will send you soon the second part of
my travels in search of the beautiful. And now, with
kindest remembrance to your wife and family, believe
me now and ever your most sincere friend and fellow-
mason,

'A. W. PUGIN.'

The graphic description given in this letter of the
various objects he saw is very interesting, and his
independent opinion upon the merits of Tintern Abbey
quite worthy of remark. There can be little doubt
that his criticisms are correct. The public are so accustomed to estimate the architectural character of
buildings, by the description of local guides, without
scanning the details for themselves, and to be fascinated
by the luxuriant masses of ivy and foliage, that it is
quite refreshing to find Pugin assailing so fearlessly
the weak points in the design of this structure. There
certainly is a poverty in the detail which is truthfully
described by him.

But if these criticisms are correct, not less true are
his strictures upon the motives of the so-called church-
restorers at Malvern, whose feeble efforts at restoration
could only be stimulated by the vanity of seeing their
heraldic bearings perpetuated in stained glass. Fortunately there is now a more correct feeling on those
matters than existed thirty years ago.

In January, 1834, Pugin redeemed his promise, and
again wrote to his friend Osmond. Unfortunately he

did not invest this letter with the same interest as his former one; for though written, as it will be seen, with all the piquancy of his style, there is wanting the skilful embellishment which belonged to the first communication. However, the contents are most amusing and instructive.

'Island of Ely!!! January, Thursday, 1834.

' DEAR OSMOND,

'I fear by this time you have thought that I did not mean to fulfil my promise of sending you another long letter, containing the second part of my travels in search of the picturesque and beautiful, but I can assure you I have not forgotten it, as this epistle feebly showeth. I left off my last account at Malvern, from thence I proceeded to Worcester. Here I was much disappointed; with the exception of Prince Arthur's Chantry the church does not contain a monument of any consequence, and the building itself was dreadfully battered about in the Civil Wars, when Worcester was a stronghold of the Cavaliers, and it has been very badly repaired in several places. The cloisters are rather curious, as they contain the ancient lavatories for the monks to wash at. The spirit of the clergy here towards the building is detestable; but in order to give you an idea of it I will recapitulate an anecdote as I had it from the person who is *nominally* clerk of works to the Cathedral. The western gable having become ruinous, the upper part was required to be taken down. The gable terminates in a rich

G 2

cross, part of which remained and was very similar to some at Sarum. Accordingly the mason having received orders to restore the gable, caused a rich cross to be cut, together with a base to it, forming the top stone of the gable. All was complete, the cross was finished, attached to the tackle ready for hoisting. A canon appears, and the following conversation ensues. Persons: Canon, a Mason. The scene the west end of Cathedral.

'*Canon*. Hollo, mason! what is all this? what d'ye call it? what is it for?

'*Mason*. It is the stone cross, sir, to terminate the western gable.

'*Canon*. Who ordered it? who is to pay for it? who gave directions for such a thing?

'*Mason*. The Chapter, sir, directed me to restore the gable, and as the cross was there—

'*Canon*. Don't talk about the cross being there; it is impossible the Chapter intended going to this expense. Why it is perfectly useless; the funds will not permit of such things. (The Dean appears.) Mr. Dean, I was saying it was impossible you could sanction such a useless expenditure as the cross for the west end.

'*Dean*. Cross! what cross? I ordered the gable to be plainly restored; I had no idea of all this.

'*Mason*. The expense of this cross is inconsiderable, and the effect—

'*Dean*. Don't talk to me of effect, sir. I will not suffer the cross to be erected; things must not be done in this manner, or we never shall know where we are.

'The result is plain. The cross I saw lying in his stone-yard, and the gable ends thus, **∧**. As it was the preparation for the music meeting, the church was turned into a carpenter's shop for seven weeks previous and three after. Divine service is suspended during the week. If there were no other, is not this a decided objection to allowing such a performance? You know my opinion well on this subject, and the more I have an opportunity of judging, the more I am strengthened in it. Excepting the Cathedral, Worcester does not contain anything of interest. Disgusted, I was glad to turn my way to Lichfield, where I duly arrived, but late in the evening and dripping with wet.* . . . . . .

'On proceeding to the Cathedral, which from its distant appearance promised great things, what was my horror and astonishment on perceiving the west front to have been restored with brown cement, cracked in every direction, with heads worked with the trowel, devoid of all expression or feeling, crockets as bad, and a mixture of all styles. My surprise, however, ceased on the verger's informing me that the whole church was improved and beautified about thirty years ago by the late Mr. Wyatt. Yes, this monster of architectural depravity—this pest of cathedral architecture—has been here; need I say more? I wound myself up to the pitch to bear the sight of

---

* He here relates an amusing incident somewhat of a Pickwickian character, through a mistake in entering the wrong bed-room, but it is hardly worth recording.

the havoc he had committed. Of course here his
old trick of throwing the Lady Chapel into the
choir by pulling down the altar-screen ; then he has
pewed the choir *and walled up* the arches of the choir,
making the aisles nothing but dark passages. The
man, I am sorry to say, who executes the repairs of
the building was a pupil of the wretch himself, and has
imbibed all the vicious propensities of his accursed
tutor, without one spark of even practical ability to
atone for his misdeeds. The repairs of the Cathedral
are conducted in a most puerile manner. What think
you of replacing finials and crockets upon the pinnacles, &c. ? while flying buttresses themselves threaten
to fall daily. But, notwithstanding all these defects,
there are points in Lichfield Cathedral that render it
extremely interesting. First, the stained glass brought
from a convent in the Netherlands, and which now
fills the east window of the choir, is without exception
the most beautiful I have ever seen for richness of
colours and beauty of design. Then the nave is truly
beautiful, and the chapter house, with library over,
is exceedingly interesting. Lichfield is a dull place,
without anything remarkable ; and I can assure you
in all my travels I have never seen a pleasanter city
than Salisbury. From here I then proceeded to
Oxford, through that most detestable of all detestable places—Birmingham, where Greek buildings and
smoking chimneys, Radicals and Dissenters are blended
together. At Oxford I was much delighted with the
restoration of Magdalen College Chapel by Mr. Cot-

tingham, which I can truly say is one of the most beautiful specimens of modern design that I have ever seen, and executed both in wood and stone in the best manner. It is impossible for me to give you an adequate idea of the interest of the city of Oxford, where at every turning you meet a buttress and face an oriel window. With what pleasure could I walk through the place with you, and point out the various places of interest it contains! Indeed I fondly cherish the hope of some day taking a long journey with you in pursuit of our favourite object; for believe me there is no person existing with whom it would afford me so much pleasure to travel as yourself. I fully hope and expect to join you for a few days in the spring on my way by Havre de Grace for a nine months' journey in Normandy and the Low Countries to collect originals and sketches. What a time to look forward to!—what a treat! I have already completed three new books, and have another in hand to be completed when I return to Ramsgate, as I am at present on another tour, and am now at Ely, where I have arrived to-night. I have as yet seen but little of the Cathedral, but shall be up with the lark to examine it to-morrow.

'I have been at the Cathedral all the morning. How I am delighted! how I am pained! Here is a church, magnificent in every respect, falling into decay through gross neglect. Would you believe it possible? there is no person appointed to attend to the repairs of the building, and the only person who has been employed during the last sixty years is a bricklayer. Not even common precautions are taken to keep the building dry. The lantern never was completed, and I fear never will be ;* but its effect is truly magnificent as it is, and makes one long to see it as originally intended by its great architect.* The fine western tower is falling into great decay, and alarming fissures have taken place and are become menacing to various portions of the western end which receive the pressure of the tower. I truly regret to say that in my travels I am daily witnessing fresh instances of the disgraceful conduct of the greater portion of the established clergy. At a place in Lincolnshire called the ——, the Rev. —— goes to perform the service in *top boots* and *white cord breeches.* Then I have seen the —— of Lincoln Cathedral, the Rev. Mr. ——, son of the late Bishop —— (who refused to subscribe to the erection of his throne in —— Cathedral), *lost £7000 at the last Lincoln races.* I can assure you that, after a most close and impartial investigation, I feel perfectly convinced the Roman Catholic Church is the only true one, and the only one in which the grand and sublime style of church architecture can ever be restored. A very good chapel is now building in the North, and when it is complete I certainly think I shall recant. I know you will blame me, but I am internally con-

---

* Were Pugin now alive what a ' Contrast ' he might draw between the condition of Ely Cathedral in 1834 and its present state !—so beautifully has it been restored by G. Scott (a *Protestant architect*), and even the Lantern is proposed to be constructed according to its ancient form

vinced that it is right. But of this subject I beg you
will make no mention in your letter to me till I see
you, for then I can more fully explain my ideas. I
do most truly long to hear from you. I shall be back
at Ramsgate in less than a couple of weeks, and must
beg you to let me hear from you before long, as it
will be a great pleasure to me. I am very happy to
inform you that the fourth and last number of my
work will be shortly published, and that it is meeting
with the greatest success. I shall have several new
books to show you when I come down, for I work
without ceasing, and trust I continue to improve.
Remember me kindly to all my friends at Sarum, and
last but not least to your wife; tell her I fear my wife
will imitate her example, for a few weeks will, I expect,
bring a little Gothic boy or girl, I don't know which
yet. God bless you. I trust to find you and yours
well in the summer, till then I am, believe me, your
most sincere friend and fellow craft,

'A. W. PUGIN.'

This letter contains some very severe strictures, but
probably not more than the facts warranted; however, it is to be hoped that the sad state of things
here described has now passed away. Had Pugin
lived to this day he would have seen reason to speak in
terms of approbation of the works now carrying on at
Lichfield, which are conceived and executed in a
manner worthy of ancient times, and in a way far

superior to the works at Magdalen College, of which he speaks so favourably. But at the period these letters were written the spirit of correct restoration had hardly been awakened, and a really good work of renovation had seldom been accomplished.

During the tour he took for the examination of ancient buildings he seems to have been somewhat shocked by the apathy, not to say misconduct, of a few of the clergy with whom he came in contact, and he here gives the first intimation of his intention to leave the Anglican Church. But there is no sufficient reason assigned for the change; and though he reflects with severity upon the failings which he had observed in some of the clergy, this could not, to a man of Pugin's discrimination, have been a sufficient ground for his abandoning the faith in which he had been educated. Other causes must have operated, and it is not difficult to suppose that his enthusiastic love of ancient art, of which he had seen so much in his recent tour through France and Belgium, mainly influenced his desire to be reconciled to a Church which gave in former days such encouragement to his darling taste.

Nothing could exceed his enthusiasm when prosecuting antiquarian projects. In another letter, without date, to his friend at Salisbury, he says: 'I expect to sail next Thursday for France, and if the wind proves fair I shall soon be up to my ears in dilapidated chateaux, ruined abbeys, ancient libraries, venerable cathedrals, ancient towers, and splendid remains of every description of the middle ages. Leave your *blisters,** leave your Doric porticoes, leave all and follow me. When I return I will unfold such a tale as will eventually seduce you from home and lethargy to continental beauties and glory ; but I must tear myself from all sublime ideas, and return to common-place matters of fact.'

To this letter there is the following P.S.

' Please to relate the following fact to Mr. Fisher.

' Not long since during divine service at a small church that has been lately disguised by some modern repairs, a person was struck blind by a flash of lightning, which was attracted by an *iron head of tracery* placed in a wood panel immediately behind him. The electric fluid then descended on the top of the seat, where it left the following extraordinary marks ! ᑕᐱᖇᐱᐁ During the same storm the house and shops of the founder himself were struck, and 200 tons of one sort of tracery shivered to atoms.

' Yours most truly,

' A. W. PUGIN.'

About this time Pugin's mind appears to have been much impressed by the doctrines of the Roman Catholic faith, but we do not hear of any actual change in his religion taking place until after the death of his

---

* This term, frequently employed by Pugin, referred to the numerous tablets which Mr. Osmond was in the habit of affixing to the walls of churches as memorials.

mother. She was in many ways a remarkable woman, shrewd and caustic in her observations, and with an eye which in a rapid glance summoned up all that came under her notice.

She impressed the casual stranger by the readiness of her wit and knowledge of the world. Her letters are full of interest: minute, and graphic in detail: spirited in their tone: and, when alluding to her son and his occupations, most tender. Her influence on his mind was visible, and to her suggestive imagination may be traced the plan which was afterwards so ably developed by her son in the ' Contrasts.'

CHAPTER VIII.

His Second Marriage—Industry in copying Illustrations in the Cathedral Library—Success in his Profession—Proposes to sell St. Marie's Grange — Designs for altering Longford Castle—Eccentric Habits — Amusing Anecdote — Improves the Vestments at the Roman Catholic Chapel — Readiness to give Professional Advice—Death of his Father and Mother.

IN 1833 Pugin married Miss Louisa Burton, and went to reside at Salisbury, a city he greatly admired, having visited it with his mother, and stayed some days there, on his way to Christchurch in 1828. Mrs. Pugin being a friend of the Reverend Mr. Greenly, the librarian of the Cathedral, this gentleman gave Pugin free access to the valuable volumes under his charge, a privilege of which he was not slow to avail himself. For many hours together he was in the habit of shutting himself up copying the beautiful illuminations of the ancient missals and service books. There was not a page of any interest from which he failed to glean something; and he made a surprising number of drawings in an incredibly short space of time. His sketches also of the Cathedral fill a quarto volume, illustrating in practice the precepts which he afterwards laid down in his famous 'Apology for the Revival of Christian Architecture in England,' 'whose glorious cathedrals are volumes of ancient art which lie open for all inquirers.'

While residing at Salisbury he became intimate with the Reverend Mr. Greenly, Lord Radnor, and Messrs Lambert, Reed, and Fisher ; and although his secession from the Church of England grieved some of his friends, the circumstance occasioned no interruption in their friendship. On his first visit finding the house in an unfinished state, excepting the room which Pugin used as his study ; Lord R——r, omitting to remove his hat at once entered into conversation, the only reply he met with was a look of astonishment. Pugin rang the bell and ordered his hat ; placing it on his head, he said, 'Now, my lord, I am ready.' In this well-merited rebuke Pugin resembled his father, who was very susceptible of affront, and sometimes even threatened to show people the door if proper courtesy was not shown him in conversation.

The erection of his house on so novel a plan, and the publication of the ' Contrasts,' were the main causes of his success. His business soon greatly increased, and led him in so many various directions, that he found Salisbury hardly central enough for a fixed residence ;—and his wife not liking the place, he determined if possible to let the house and grounds. In his letters to Mr. Fisher at this time, he refers to the overwhelming amount of business pressing upon him, and indicates the class of buildings on which he was engaged. Writing from Alton Towers in June 1839, he says : ' I am full of business, and long to talk over my operations with you. My church at Birmingham will be a truly grand affair, filled with rich carving and decoration. I have several large churches to do in Ireland, and five near Birmingham, so that I am almost worked to death, and all my business, excepting Downside Priory, lies quite wide of Salisbury. I do not see the probability of my being able to reside there for years. I must do something regarding my house; it cannot go on in this manner, and I am most anxious to have your advice about it. My whole prospects are entirely changed since I built it. I was then almost without architectural business, and I have now more than I can well do; indeed every moment of my time is occupied. I wish to let my house at a moderate rent. I do not like the idea of selling it, because I have no occasion for so doing, but I do not like so much money sunk without any return whatever.'

In another letter he says: 'I have now an immense deal of business, and if I live on two or three years shall have done something worth looking at. Some of my buildings in Derby, Wexford, &c., will be completed early this summer. I have got the great church at Liverpool, with a crypt 150 feet long by 60 wide, well vaulted.' Again in the next communication he says: 'I have twice as much as I can do, though I work early and late. Were I not driven at this moment beyond my strength, you should not wait a moment.' After a lapse of some time, he writes once more: 'I shall come down to Salisbury, when I

shall want the deeds of my house, as it is most improbable I shall ever be able to live there, and I have
quite determined on disposing of it.' This he eventually did in 1841, the property being put up to
public auction and purchased for £500 by Mr. Staples,
the gentleman from whom he had originally bought
the ground.

This was a great sacrifice of money, for Pugin had
expended upwards of £2000 on the building alone,
and never thought, when erecting it according to his
own fancy, (the rooms communicating without any common passage,) that the house would be unsuited to
other people's requirements in the event of his wishing
to sell it. To build a house according to Pugin's early
notions was no easy matter, so many modern usages
had to be given up ; and several humorous disputes
arose with the builder during its progress. He would
have enormously thick walls and deep splays to the
windows, strong oak bars for fastenings, and not a
scrap of plaster or battening where such materials were
usually put. There was attached to the house a small
oratory, with a window opening to his bed-room, so
that in case of illness he might participate in the
service going on at the altar ; he also spoke of providing an endowment for a Priest to celebrate the
services, but he never carried his intention into effect,
probably seeing the impossibility of retaining St.
Marie's Grange as his fixed residence. It does not
appear that Pugin obtained much business in the
south-western counties. Additions and alterations at

Longford Castle were under consideration, but nothing was carried into effect. There are, however, in the possession of the Reverend Mr. Greenly, of Salisbury, some beautiful drawings which he made for improving the façades of that curious structure, and also for the building of a bridge of suitable character over the river near the castle. These designs are very masterly, and showed the perfect knowledge he possessed of the peculiar combination and details of the Jacobean period. He had studied buildings of this date very closely, having in 1829 made the most elaborate drawings of Hatfield House.* Unfortunately the fashion of the day was favourable to the erection of buildings in that debased style, so that Pugin's attention was rather too much devoted to its details, when he would have preferred adopting the architecture of a purer type. The design for the bridge just mentioned is extremely graceful: it consists of three elliptical arches, the central arch being much the widest; the piers are surmounted by pedestals, bearing the arms and insignia of the Radnor family, the ends and sides of the bridge flanked with massive pillars, and the pierced parapets are also ornamented with excellent devices.

The only works which Pugin really executed at or near Salisbury, were the Roman Catholic church, a pleasing building in the town, and a lodge for Sir

---

* In his diary are these entries : ' September 21. Went to Hatfield House with my friend Ferrey to make sketches.' ' October 1st. Started with Ferrey for Hurstmonceaux Castle, to make sketches for Gothic examples.'

Frederick Bathurst at Clarendon Park. He was now, as will be seen by extracts from his letters, chiefly engaged on Roman Catholic buildings. His slovenliness in dress at this time amounted to eccentricity. He was in the habit of wearing a sailor's jacket, loose pilot trousers, jack-boots, and a wide-awake hat. In such a costume landing on one occasion from the Calais boat, he entered, as was his custom, a first-class railway carriage, and was accosted with a 'Halloa, my man, you have mistaken, I think, your carriage.' 'By Jove,' was his reply, 'I think you are right; I thought I was in the company of gentlemen.' This cutting repartee at once called forth an apology. The remainder of the journey was most agreeably passed in examining his portfolio filled with sketches just taken in Normandy.

His oddities clung to him through life, but they were of a harmless character, and could easily be overlooked and laughed at by those who knew what a generous nature he possessed, and how straightforward he was in all business transactions, scorning any petty or mean action in his dealings with every one. His utter contempt for dandyism and effeminacy in dress was founded upon acute observation, for he had noticed that those who indulged in such frivolities were generally men of no attainments, and wasted their time in trifling pursuits. In this way he was much tormented by the frequent visits of a relative, a young man, affected in his manners, and showy in dress. Pugin abhorred him, but he was at times forced to endure his society. To the ladies of his acquaintance Pugin's carelessness in appearance was very distasteful: but when remonstrated with on the subject, he never condescended to give a patient hearing, but cut the matter short by saying: 'It's all very well, my dress will do perfectly.' A friend with whom he was at one time staying, after thus expostulating, retorted, with some amount of warmth, 'It is not all very well,' and thought that her remarks had made some impression; and true it was, for on the following morning he presented himself in a smart blue coat with gilt buttons, and a buff waistcoat, exclaiming, 'Well, are you satisfied now?' His mother observes, in one of her letters, that 'if he only knew how to dress, she would consider him an universal genius,' thus showing that this habit began early in life.

Pugin's professional pursuits did not admit of his making many social visits, but he occasionally accepted an invitation. Lord R——r once calling at St. Marie's Grange during its erection, and desiring to make his acquaintance, asked if he would dine with him, to which Pugin assented. 'Very well then,' said his Lordship, 'I'll expect you to-morrow at six o'clock.' Thither at the time Pugin repaired, and as he was admiring the stately rooms and objects of art and vertû with which they were enriched, his Lordship, who was well known for his simple habits and encouragement of agricultural pursuits, observed, with perhaps generous feeling, that he would as soon live in one of the smallest cottages on his estate as in his large and magnificent mansion. Upon this, Pugin, jumping up and pacing the room in apparent excitement, exclaimed, ' The d—l you would—the d—l you would, my Lord; then what is to become of me and all other artists?'

Whenever any work of improvement in the city of Salisbury, or suggested restorations of the churches were under consideration, Pugin was always ready to give his gratuitous advice or assistance. When the interesting ancient hall, since converted into the show-rooms of Mr. Payn, the china manufacturer ('Hall of John Hall') was in course of restoration, Pugin with his own hands executed in colour the coat-of-arms supported by an angel in the end wall of the apartment, and decorated the chimney-piece and other parts of the hall. When the re-seating of the church of St. Thomas was under consideration, he offered some excellent suggestions. Unfortunately they were not adopted, and thus an opportunity for doing the right thing was missed: the present wretched arrangement of pews being substituted for open seats of appropriate character.

In reference to the Cathedral he never ceased to deplore the mutilations to which the magnificent building had been subjected; but knowing how little chance there was of any restoration being effected, he studiously kept aloof from the dignitaries of the church, knowing that his disturbed spirit would be roused by discussions which might arise, and that he might be tempted to launch out in unmeasured terms of invective.

His finest work at this time consisted in the rebuilding of Scarisbrook Hall, Lancashire, for the late Charles Scarisbrook, Esq., one of the richest commoners in England. Here Pugin had money at his command, but unfortunately (as in almost every one of his later buildings) he was hampered in his ideas by the determination of Mr. Scarisbrook to build upon the foundations of the old house. Notwithstanding this the architecture is of the highest merit, and the great hall is quite unsurpassed by any modern buildings of the kind. It is very much in the style of the present Houses of Parliament, and the clock tower bears undeniable resemblance to the present graceful structure at Westminster. The plans fill six large folios, one of which contains exquisitely finished perspective sketches of various parts of the building.

Pugin was now deprived of his father and mother; the former died in December 1832, after a long illness, at the age of sixty-three, and Mrs. Pugin survived her husband but a short time, her decease taking place in 1833. Both were buried in the churchyard of St. Mary's, Islington, the parish where Mrs. Pugin's sister, Miss Selina Welby, had lived for many years. By the death of this lady Pugin became possessed of some property, being her nephew.

CHAPTER IX.

Article in the 'Times'—Publishes his work entitled 'Contrasts,' &c.—
Remarks on the character of the Book—Strictures upon the practices
of the Roman Catholic Church—Anecdote referring to Vestments
—Erroneous Notions, limiting Art to those in connection with the
Roman Catholic Church—Public Opinion upon the 'Contrasts'—
Humorous Songs in reference to the work.

DURING the early part of his residence at Salisbury, and
before he inhabited St. Marie's Grange at Laverstoke,
Pugin was still in communion with the English Church,
and regularly attended divine service in the Cathedral.
But after his secession, he frequented the Roman
Catholic chapel of the town,—an ill-shaped room,
having no pretensions whatever to an ecclesiastical
character. This change in his attendance, from the
glorious cathedral to the miserable chapel, was a sacrifice of no small kind for a man of Pugin's taste to
make. It was out of the question to alter the building, but he did his utmost to impart dignity to the
externals of public worship, which were at that time
sunk to the lowest level of bad taste.

Many, both in and out of the pale of the Roman
Catholic Church, did not scruple to attribute Pugin's
conversion *solely* to the love he had for the outward
splendour of the middle ages.

This was far from being the fact. His faith in the Catholic Church rested probably on far higher grounds than on his admiration for external magnificence. In reply to a charge of this character made in a public journal, he stated that he did not for a moment deny that the study of ancient ecclesiastical architecture was the primary cause of the change in his sentiments, by inducing him to pursue a course of study terminating in his complete conversion.

'My education,' he goes on to say, 'certainly was not of a description to bias me towards Catholicism; I had been taught to view it through the same distorted medium as the generality of persons in this country; and by the time I was at all capable of thinking on the subject, I was thoroughly imbued with all the popular notions of racks, faggots, and fires, idolatry, sin-purchase, &c., with all the usual tissue of false-hoods so industriously propagated throughout the land, that by such means men may be led to detest and fear what they would receive with joy and reverence, could they but behold it in simple truth.

'It was, I say, with such perverted feelings I first became a student in ancient art. Soon, however, I found it necessary to begin a new and different course of study to what I had hitherto pursued. The origin, intention, and use of all I beheld around was then perfectly unintelligible to me; but, applying myself to liturgical knowledge, what a new field was open to me! with what delight did I trace the fitness of each portion of those glorious edifices to the rites for whose celebration they had been erected! Then did I discover that the service I had been accustomed to attend and admire was but a cold and heartless remnant of past glories, and that those prayers which in my ignorance I had ascribed to reforming piety, were in reality only scraps plucked from the solemn and perfect offices of the ancient Church. Pursuing my researches among the faithful pages of the old chronicles, I discovered the tyranny, apostasy, and bloodshed by which the new religion had been established, the endless strifes, dissensions, and discord that existed among its propagators, and the devastation and ruin that attended its progress: opposed to all this, I considered the Catholic Church; existing with uninterrupted apostolical succession, handing down the same faith, sacraments, and ceremonies unchanged, unaltered through every clime, language, and nation.

'For upwards of three years did I earnestly pursue the study of this all-important subject; and the irresistible force of truth penetrating my heart, I gladly surrendered my own fallible judgment to the unerring decisions of the Church, and embracing with heart and soul its faith and discipline, became an humble, but I trust faithful member.

'I therefore hope that in Christian charity my conversion will not any longer be attributed solely to my admiration of architectural excellence: for although I have freely acknowledged that my attention was first directed through it to the subject, yet I must distinctly state, that so important a change was not effected in me, but by the most powerful reasons, and that after a long and earnest examination.'

In this outspoken and characteristic letter Pugin completely vindicates the change of his religious opinions, from the light and frivolous motives so freely imputed to him at the time. Had he, however, remained in the Church of his birth, what a noble field would have been open to him in the restoration of those ancient churches and cathedrals with whose beauty he was so familiar!

The following letter bearing upon this subject is interesting, coming from a member of his own communion. The hopes so clearly expressed do not appear to have been ever realized. Greatly as the Roman Catholics ought to feel indebted to him for all he did, they have never shown by any united public recognition their sense of his invaluable services. It has been left to the members of the English Church to initiate a lasting memorial to his honour.

' MY DEAR SIR,

'It is likely that many of your subscribers are not habitual readers of the " Times " newspaper: will you therefore allow me, for their benefit, to insert in your columns two quotations from recent numbers of that periodical, touching our late friend Mr. Pugin? The first paragraph is from a " Leader " on the subject of domestic and street architecture, wherein the writer closes some severe remarks on the prevalent taste in these matters, with the following words:

' " Whether successful in treatment or not, what we regard with so much satisfaction in this and some other late specimens of architecture is the honesty of the work; and for this we have to thank, in the first instance, the late Mr. Pugin. With all his crotchets, and with an absurd attachment, not merely to the spirit, but to the letter of mediævalism, he has perhaps done more for architecture than any of those who run him down. He it was who first exposed the shams and concealments of modern architecture, and contrasted it with the heartiness and sincerity of mediæval work. He showed the fair outside of a modern building, having no relation to its construction, except that of a screen to hide its clumsy makeshifts. He then showed how the first principle of mediæval work was to expose construction, and not to hide it, but to adorn it. A modern building, for example, conceals its flying buttresses with a dead wall; an ancient one exposes them and derives a principal charm from these contrivances being seen. It is the law of all the old architecture,—there is nothing which it fears to show; it rather invites inspection within and without; whereas concealment was for long the rule of modern British architecture—concealment of the real material—concealment of the manner of construction. Pugin is dead—died, we believe, in distress. Let us remember to his honour that, if now there seems to be the dawn of a better architecture, if our edifices seem to be more correct in taste, more genuine in material, more honest in construction, and more sure to last, it was he who first showed us that our architecture offended not only against the laws of beauty, but also against the laws of morality."

'The "crotchets," the "absurd attachment," &c., the truth of which under other circumstances might be called in question, may be allowed to pass in the face of such a compliment. On the day after the publication of the above, a letter appeared in the same journal signed A. R., which echoed the sentiments of the "Leader" on our friend's merits, and concluded with these words, "I further thank you for your generous testimony to the late Mr. Pugin. No man has done a tithe of what he has done in a given time for the reformation of our national architecture, yet no one has been more reviled. It is true that a man who comes forward as a reformer and an exposer of the vices of his age, must expect his share of vituperation in return; but he has met with injustice from those who advocated the same principles with himself, as well as those whose fallacies he has exposed."

'My object in submitting these extracts to your readers is twofold; 1st, to invite them to join with me in a legitimate triumph in favour of our deceased friend; and 2ndly, to use them as a text for something further.

'1st. There are surely few Catholics who will not rejoice at witnessing so unmistakeable a homage paid, however tardily, to one to whom our Church in this country is so deeply indebted. Had Mr. Pugin *not* been a Catholic, his services to architecture and fine arts

would have been acknowledged long ago ; and therefore when they are at length recognized, and by the
"leading journal" of these kingdoms in this honourable way, we must feel doubly proud of having had
in our ranks the man, who, despite of his religion, and
of the intrepidity with which he invariably defended
it, is now declared on such competent authority, and
in the face of such persevering efforts to decry him, to
have been the *one* successful individual to whom " if
now there seems to be the dawn of a better architecture, if our edifices seem to be more correct in taste,
more genuine in materials, more honest in construction,
and more sure to last," the chief if not the whole
credit is due.   " Let us," says the writer, "remember
this to his honour."

' 2ndly. The moral which I am desirous of extracting
from the above text is this: that if those who are not
of the fold, begin at last to appreciate the immense
benefits conferred by the subject of this memoir on
architecture and the fine arts, we to whom he especially belonged, and of whose faith he was ever the
unflinching champion, ought certainly to aim at something more.   The article which I have quoted states
that Mr. Pugin " died in distress."   This is perhaps
hardly correct ; but though the pecuniary inheritance
which he bequeathed to his children was certainly not
ample, he has, nevertheless, if we may judge of all
by one specimen, transmitted to them sparks of genius,
and that spirit of persevering industry which must, in
course of years, be a fortune to any one.   But if the

great man whose loss we deplore did not leave large
revenues behind him, to what cause must we attribute
the circumstance? To no other than his intense devotion to the Church of God. The beauty of God's
House was his dream by night and by day, and the
Royal Prophet could not say with more *literal* truth
than he: *Zelus domûs tuæ comedit me.* His substance was
eaten into, or, according to the writer in the "Times,"
well nigh consumed, by his insatiate zeal for the glory
of the House of God. This, I presume, will not be
considered by us a blot on his fair fame, but rather
an honourable feature in it, and certainly his family
are far from reproaching him with the result. It is
not therefore to relieve any real or supposed necessities of his family that I am now going to propose
some suitable testimonial. Time was, when a subscription was projected, the proceeds of which were to
be given to himself, and well do I remember the
honest indignation with which he met and rejected the
proposal. The same, I feel, would be the case with
his family now.' . . . .

The immediate fruit of Pugin's secession from the
English Church was shown in the work entitled ' *Contrasts; or, a Parallel between the Architecture of the
15th and 19th Centuries, by A. Welby Pugin,*' published at St. Marie's Grange, near Salisbury, 1836.
The book was well calculated to create a sensation,
its tone being severe and personal. Had he never
published any other architectural work than this, his
literary power would have been established, the style

of writing being clear and forcible, injured only by a violence in some expressions arising from his great zeal for the cause of the religion he had so recently embraced.

The illustrations, drawn and etched by his own hand, are very spirited and clever, yet certainly not all selected with fairness. His desire to put everything connected with Protestantism in a bad light, led him to select objects for contrast, which, being erected under totally different circumstances, ought not to have been placed in comparison with buildings raised during the palmiest period of mediæval times. Architectural art was certainly in a miserable state when this work was penned; but the modern buildings erected for Roman Catholic purposes by professors of that creed were equally obnoxious to criticism, and selections might have been made from them for comparison, to show the difference in treatment between ancient and modern ecclesiastical structures, without taking every example of failure from buildings erected by members of the Anglican Church. Nor, again, was it fair to pick out, what are confessedly the worst buildings of the 19th century, to compare with those which on all hands are acknowledged as gems of art of the 15th century. Still, admitting this defect in the plan of the book, it must be conceded that many glaring abuses are here brought to light, and the mutilations of our cathedral buildings well exposed. Yet no impartial reader can fail to see that Pugin's judgment was manifestly warped; he treated many things with scornful and unmitigated censure where, if he had been so disposed, he might have found ample grounds for palliation. Moderation in most matters was unknown to him, and it was not likely that he would practise that virtue when dealing with the system of the Church, from which he had just seceded. Observe, for instance, the exaggerated character of the following passage in the 'Contrasts:'—

' When we reflect on the horrible repairs, alterations, and demolitions that have taken place in our venerable edifices, ever directed by a tepid and parsimonious clergy, brutal and jobbing parochial authorities, and ignorant and tasteless operatives, I do not hesitate to say that the lover of ancient art has more to regret during the period the present Establishment has had the churches in possession, than ever during the fatal period that drove the ancient churchmen from them.'

The circulation of this work, however, did much good. It set people to look into matters hitherto neglected, and the beginning of several improvements in our cathedrals and large churches may be attributed to the effect of the exposures it made. But if Pugin here commented severely upon the architectural deformities perpetrated by Protestants, his later publications will show that he was not more sparing in the exposure of blemishes in the Roman Catholic system. His attacks upon the meretricious style of music employed in the service of that Church, to the exclusion of the early Gregorian chaunts, and his vehement reprobation of the depraved and paltry character of some of

the sacerdotal vestments, made him many enemies in
his own communion; for he spared no one, and feared
not to speak evil of dignities, nor to engage in literary
conflict with the most distinguished theologians.   On
one occasion, when enjoying himself among a few congenial spirits in a college at Oxford, the conversation
turned on the original character of the chasuble and
other vestments which he was then trying to revive.
After dwelling with great delight on the beauty of
Gothic forms, and the dignity gained by the ample
folds of a soft material, instead of the stiff tabards of
the French and Italian school, he broke out with an
even more than wrathful malediction:—' But after all,
my dear sir, what's the use of decent vestments with
such priests as we have got? a lot of blessed fellows!
Why, sir, when they wear my chasubles, they don't
look like priests, and what's worse, the chasubles
don't look like chasubles.'   One great fallacy in the
remarks made in his ' Contrasts ' must not be passed
over: he labours hard to prove that no work of high
art can be produced by any one not within the pale
of the Roman Catholic Church.   In his view, it is
only with the feeling inspired by that communion that
anything excellent in religious art can be inspired.
Thus, he says:—'The mechanical part of Gothic
architecture is pretty well understood, but it is the
principles which influenced ancient compositions, and
the soul which appears in all the former works, which
is so lamentably deficient; nor, as I have before stated,
can anything be regained, but by a restoration of the

ancient feeling and sentiments; 'tis they alone can restore Gothic architecture.'

This is the whole gist of Pugin's arguments. He appears wholly insensible of the merit which belongs to works of the classic period, and we find not a word even in toleration of that great school of art. Conceding very readily the unsuitableness of the severe Greek and Roman styles of architecture for giving the most impressive character to religious edifices, still the assertion that it is impossible to effect great and masterly productions unless inspired by the genius of the Roman Catholic Church is untenable. No one denies that the ceremonial character of the ritual of that Church, and the intensity of feeling generated by its doctrines and traditions, afforded a wide scope for the exercise of those branches of art, such as architecture and painting, which have flourished chiefly in connexion with it; nor that a revulsion of feeling, not yet wholly extinct, which took place at the Reformation, chiefly through the fanaticism of the Puritans, affected most seriously the cultivation of fine arts. Still, to conclude that none but Roman Catholic artists can produce works of merit and feeling, even in a religious sense, is a lamentable mistake, of which Pugin himself must have been convinced before his death. Beyond all doubt a debt of gratitude is due to him for the remarks in his 'Contrasts,' calling attention to the degraded state of modern architecture; but the public fail to recognize that identity of cause and effect, which, in Pugin's view, would give the monopoly of art to

I

the Church of Rome. The many structures erected by Pugin himself, though superior to the generality of modern buildings, and exhibiting much of the architectural truthfulness for which he contended, are yet far from being perfect; on the other hand, several churches and schools in connexion with the Anglican communion have been built since he commenced practice, which beyond all question, both in design and feeling, will bear comparison with anything executed by him. Nay more, they may be considered superior, since they manifest an amount of study and care in design, which are sometimes found wanting in Pugin's best works. The very soul and expression which he claims as exclusive prerogatives of his own Church are present in the carefully considered details of some of our own recently built churches. But in justice to Pugin it should be added that this excellence has been really attained through the impetus which his writings gave to the study of ' the true principles of Gothic architecture.'

In the remarks which will be found in succeeding Chapters upon his executed works, notice will be taken of the infraction of some of the fundamental rules laid down by Pugin himself, with great emphasis, in his published works, from which it will appear, that although he could point out defects in the performances of others with unsparing severity, making no allowance for the difficulties under which they laboured, yet his own productions are justly censurable when tested by the same severe rules.

Still the general current of public opinion was certainly very favourable to the ' Contrasts,' and on the whole the book was well spoken of by the Press. It gave, as might be expected, some offence, but at the same time it caused much amusement by the pungent character of its remarks. The following lines, droll and clever, written by Mr. M'Cann, an Irishman, were first circulated privately, but at length got into 'Notes and Queries,' and were subsequently copied into the ' Builder :'

SONG ON PUGIN'S ' CONTRASTS.'

Oh ! have you seen the work just out
    By Pugin, the great builder?
' Architect'ral Contrasts ' he's made out
    Poor Protestants to bewilder.
The Catholic Church, she never knew—
    Till Mr. Pugin taught her,
That orthodoxy had to do
    At all with bricks and mortar.

But now it's clear to one and all,
    Since he's published his lecture,
No church is Catholic at all
    Without Gothic architecture.
In fact, he quite turns up his nose
    At any style that's racent,
The Gracian, too, he plainly shows
    Is wicked and ondacent.

There's not a bit of pious taste
    Iver since the Reformation ;
'Twas Harry the Eighth, the nasty baste,
    That introduced the Gracian.
When they denied the truth outright
    Of Transubstantiation,
They built them in the Composite—
    That great abomination.

Next thing their frien's to build dozing pews
   In the most systematic way go;
They'd be kilt, they say, the other way,
   With rheumatics and lumbago.

Some raise a front up to the street,
   Like ould Westminster Abbey ;
And then they think the Lord to cheat,
   And build the back part shabby.
For stuccoed bricks, and sich like tricks,
   At present all the rage is,
They took no one in ! those fine ould min !
   In the ' pious Middle Ages ! ! !'

CHAPTER X.

Pugin's introduction to the Earl of Shrewsbury—Letters addressed to his Lordship on various occasions—Letter from the Rev. Dr. Rock —Memorials to Pugin from Maynooth and other places—Letter from Count de Montalembert—Letter to the Lords of the Committee of Trade.

IT was in the summer of 1832, when calling at the well-known furniture-dealers, Messrs. Hull, in Wardour-street, that the Earl of Shrewsbury first became acquainted with Pugin's great talent for design. Observing some drawings upon a table executed in a beautiful manner, he inquired the name of the artist, and on learning that it was Pugin, he desired to be introduced to him, a request which was immediately complied with. The introduction had no sooner taken place, than this illustrious and wealthy nobleman, the premier Peer of England, and most devoted son of the Roman Catholic Church, immediately availed himself of Pugin's professional skill to aid him in the alterations and additions to his princely residence, Alton Towers; but perceiving, also, Pugin's zeal for the Catholic Church, and fully appreciating his eminent qualities, both as a man and an artist, he at once extended to him a friendly confidence, seldom found to exist between men in such different positions of life. His lordship, though warmly attached to the Catholic Church, knew that much was defective in her external rites and ceremonies, and was conscious of many abuses needing remedy. In Pugin he found a man fully alive to these blemishes: eager and panting to correct them, at any risk, and who needed but the moral support of so powerful a patron as the Earl of Shrewsbury to make his efforts completely successful. Having then the same objects in view, Pugin, without reserve, communicated to his lordship every fact which came to his knowledge showing neglect of ritualistic ceremony, or flagrant abuse of architectural propriety. In a series of letters, addressed to his noble friend, commencing in 1841, and extending over several years, there is much interesting matter on different subjects, and not one letter which does not contain some observations worthy to be recorded. Many of them relate, necessarily, to details of the architectural work he was carrying on at Alton Towers, and might not be generally interesting; still, a few extracts are given, to show the independent manner in which he insisted upon carrying out his own views. One cannot but admire the manliness with which he intimates his determination to resign the superintendence of works he had in hand rather than be made the instrument for effecting alterations which his superior knowledge convinced him would be wrong. He had fondly hoped that, in designing buildings for his lordship, he would have been spared the mortifying interference so often encountered with public committees, and been permitted to erect structures in every respect suitable to the dignity of his employer; but in this he was in some degree disappointed, as the following letter shows :—

'Hornby Castle.

'MY DEAR LORD SHREWSBURY,

' I cannot admit that I am to blame respecting the design of the dining-room. Of course I intended to make a fine thing, suitable to the purpose for which it is destined, and not a common room, fit only for a hotel. This is the very first room at the Towers that I was called upon to design, and it was quite natural that I should wish to produce something that would have a striking effect, especially when so many persons were loud in condemning the alterations, and declaring that the present room was far better than anything that could be done : yes, indeed, on the plan proposed by your lordship, at present, I do think the present room *far better* as regards design ; for the new room would be the most common-place apartment that can well be imagined. If I am not enabled to exercise any judgment, and make use of my knowledge and experience, I am reduced to the condition of a mere drawing clerk to work out what I am ordered, and this I cannot bear ; and, so far from knocking under, I really must decline undertaking the alteration, unless your lordship will consent to its being made worthy of your dignity and residence. It shall never be said that I have spoilt the dining-room at Alton : I would not do it for a thousand pounds. I always opposed the win-

dow, and at one time your lordship suggested it would
do for the east window of a church, to which I quite
agreed, for it is a church window in design. From the
first moment I spoke of a screen, and it is indispensable
to break the current of air into the room. I never
proposed anything for *mere effect*. I know my design
was quite right, and again I entreat of your lordship
to carry it out, or to leave the present building unaltered. . . . Nothing can be more dangerous than
looking at prints of buildings, or trying to imitate bits
of them : these architectural books are as bad as the
Scriptures in the hands of the Protestants. I am very
unhappy about it ; and as regards the hall, I have
nailed my colours to the mast,—a bay window, high
open roof, lantern, two good fire-places, a great side-
board, screen, minstrel-gallery—*all or none*. I will
not sell myself to do a wretched thing. Lady Shrewsbury told me, when I was last at Alton, that she
would rather see the present room left, unless the new
one was a truly fine work : and I am sure her ladyship
is right.

' Ever, dear Lord Shrewsbury, &c.,

' A. Welby Pugin.'

The readiness with which Pugin exposed any abuse,
in one instance made him the subject of a hoax. On
receiving the annexed letter, he promptly wrote to
Lord Shrewsbury, and did not discover, till some days
afterwards, the trick which had been played.

'Dear Sir,

'It is with deep sorrow that I venture to inform you of a circumstance which has just come to my knowledge'; and, though an entire stranger, I take the liberty of addressing you, being aware of your zeal for the *honour* and welfare of the Catholic Church. What, then, will be your grief and indignation (if you have not already heard it) at being told that—fearing the bazaar* in behalf of the Monastery of St. Bernard may prove unsuccessful—it has been thought that more people will be drawn to it were the *monks to hold the stalls!* Was there ever such a scandal given to our most holy religion? It may have been done ignorantly or innocently: but it is enough to make a Catholic of feeling shudder! *I* am not in a situation to have the slightest influence in putting an end to this most dreadful proceeding: but knowing you to be well acquainted with the head of the English Catholics— the good Earl of Shrewsbury—would you not write to him, and request him to use his influence (which must be great) in stopping the *sacrilege*—for such it really is? Think of your holy Church, thus *degraded*, and made a bye-word in the mouths of Protestants! I know how you love and venerate her. Aid her then now: and attempt to rescue her from this calamity! Pray excuse the freedom with which I have written, and, believe me, dear Sir,

'A Sincere Lover of my Church, but an
Enemy to the Protestant Principle
of Bazaars.'

* See woodcut from Pugin's sketch, page 189.

In reference to this trick, when writing to Lord Shrewsbury, he says :—

'I have found out at last that the alarm about the monks at the bazaar was all a hoax ; and rumour mentions some ladies not far distant from the Towers as the authors. I must own it was capitally done, and put me into a perfect fever for some days. I only read the letter late in the day, and sent a person all the way to the General Post Office to save the post. I never gave the day of the month a moment's consideration. I shall be better prepared for the next first of April.'

Pugin, at this time, was much gratified by receiving the following complimentary letter from the Rev. Dr. Rock : they had both common objects in view, as the letter indicates ; but there evidently grew up a little rivalry between them ; for, in a later communication with Lord Shrewsbury, Pugin complains that a charge of piracy had been made against him by the learned Doctor. It was extremely likely that men interested in the same cause might, in their researches, quote the same authors : they had too much respect however for each other to let a slight mistake interfere with their friendship, and a little explanation soon healed the breach.

'   'Alton Towers, Ashbourne, Derby,
'DEAR SIR,   August 19, 1836.

'Though, as yet, I have not had the good fortune of making your personal acquaintance, but know

you only by your admirable and very valuable works
on the architecture of our country, still I cannot resist
the pleasure of addressing a line to you, to offer you
my most cordial congratulations and sincere thanks for
the manner in which you have contributed to honour
our holy religion, by the way in which you have executed the screen part more particularly, of your Book
of Designs for silversmiths. The work is a most elegant
and correct one : the designs are really beautiful.   In
the second part I was quite at home, amid chalices,
monstrances, cruets, &c. : and I cannot tell you how
much I feel indebted to you, not only for the delight
you afforded me as an individual who is enthusiasti-
cally attached to the study of the architecture and
church antiquities of Catholic England, but for the
assurance which I felt that your designs of Catholic
church-plate would, on many occasions, propitiate the
good-will of the man of taste towards the olden faith,
and, perhaps, induce some to inquire into, and adopt
its tenets.   The first moving cause of several of our
countrymen returning to the faith of their forefathers
has, more than once, originated in similar trivial incidents.   Truth is, very often, at first, like the grain of
mustard-seed.

' Having written a work, entitled " Hierurgia," in
which I attempted to trace the origin, and note
the accidental changes in the vestments of the priests
and his attendant ministers at mass, and to explain
to our Protestant fellow-countrymen the meaning
of our church ceremonies, I feel very interested in

everything which can illustrate the subject. May I, therefore, request of you to inform me where you found the originals or models of the second part of your Designs? I have an ancient chalice and a very old bronze processional cross, much in the style of the one you gave, but without the figures of the blessed Virgin and St. John. I should be most happy to show them to you. I should very much like to know if there be still existing, in England, any Catholic church-plate, and the places where they may be seen. I know that much may be detected figured in illuminated MSS., in painted glass, in the sculptures of our beautiful old churches, and in collegiate and monastic seals. When you favour me with a line, direct "The Rev. Dr. Rock," and send your letter under cover to Lord Shrewsbury. Thus you will be conferring a kindness on one of the numerous admirers of that correct and refined taste and accurate knowledge which you have displayed in the illustration of our splendid and venerable national ecclesiastical antiquities. While I take this opportunity to offer you my many thanks for the instruction and delight which I have derived from the sight of your works, allow me to congratulate with you on having discovered the pearl of great price—the knowledge of the true faith—while exploring those monuments of ancient piety which were erected by the generous zeal and religious feelings of our ancient Catholic predecessors. Believe me, dear sir, with sincere esteem and regard, yours most truly,

'DANIEL ROCK.'

He was extremely angry in finding that his buildings were no sooner completed than they were subject to mutilations through the indifference of those intrusted with their care, and expresses himself with much indignation :

'I regret to say that there seems little or no appreciation of ecclesiastical architecture among the clergy. The cathedral I built, at Enniscorthy, has been completely ruined. The new bishop has blocked up the choir, stuck the altars under the tower ! ! and the whole building is in a most painful state of filth : the sacrarium is full of rubbish, and it could hardly have been worse treated if it had fallen into the hands of the Hottentots. I see no progress of ecclesiastical ideas in Ireland. I think if possible they get worse. It is quite useless to attempt to build true churches, for the clergy have not the least idea of using them properly.'

In one of his communications Lord Shrewsbury had referred to the illegible character of some of Pugin's letters, which is not to be wondered at.

It is indeed surprising to think that he could design all his buildings, make every working drawing, and carry on a voluminous correspondence, single handed. He might well, therefore, be excused for occasional careless writing. Thus he says in one of his letters : ' I am very sorry for my bad writing, but really I have so many letters to write, so much work to do, and get so driven up for time, that my ideas go so much faster than the pen, I fear I cut the syllables short, but I will be more careful in future.'

Amongst several letters written by him to Lord Shrewsbury while he was travelling on the Continent, the following are very amusing.

'Florence, Ascension of our Lord,
May, 1847.

' MY DEAR LORD SHREWSBURY,

'Ever since I left Rome I have been delighted with Italy. By good luck, instead of coming here by sea, I took a veturrino from Rome, and saw Assisi, Perugia, Arezzo, Cortona, &c. I am certain that your lordship never could have seen those places, for they contain the most magnificent things in the world. I have seen three of the finest Gothic altars in Christendom, and one of silver about 12 feet long. As for the stained glass there is nothing so good on our side of the Alps ; and the sacristies are full of Gothic shrines, reliquaries, chalices, &c. I am in a perfect mine of mediæval art. I used to imagine that there was nothing of the kind in this country, and I find more than in any other part of the world. Florence is enchanting. The glass at Santa Croce is perfectly beautiful, and the frescoes of Angelica di Fiesoli enchanting. Rome is certainly a miserable place, quite disgusting and depressing ; but Italy is yet the richest country for true Christian art, and I do not despair of St. Peter's being re-built in a better style. I saw two prelates at Rome in immediate attendance on the Pope, who quite agreed with me. What absurdities people have talked and written about the pointed style not being adapted for Italy ! Why, it is full of it ; there is not a little town that does not contain some fine specimens, to my astonishment. When I was at Pistoia one of the Canons, seeing I was an Englishman, asked me if I knew a Mr. Pugin, a Catholic architect, and when I told him I was the man, he embraced me, &c.'

The horror which Pugin felt at the depraved taste, shown by some portion of the Roman Catholic priest-hood, and so forcibly dwelt upon in the modern Ambonoclast, is more particularly described in the following extract.

After remarking upon the mischief done to the Catholic cause by the articles in the ' Tablet,' he adds :

' Has your lordship heard that the Oratorians have opened the Lowther Rooms as a chapel ! !—a place for the vilest debauchery, masquerades, &c.—one night a MASQUED BALL, next BENEDICTUS. This appears to me perfectly monstrous, and I give the whole order up for ever. What a degradation for religion ! Why, it is worse than the Socialists. What a place to celebrate the mysteries of religion in ! I cannot conceive how it is allowed. It cannot even be licensed or protected by law, since they only have it for a time. It is the greatest blow we have had for a long time; no men have been so disappointing as these. Conceive the poet Faber come down to the Lowther Rooms ! The man who wrote " Thoughts and Sights in Foreign Churches ! ! ! " hiring the Lowther Rooms ! Well may they cry out against screens or anything else. I always said they wanted rooms, not churches, and now they have got them. Sad times! I cannot imagine what the world will come to, if it goes on much longer.

'Ever, my dear Lord Shrewsbury,

'A. W. PUGIN.'

'London, Tuesday in the Octave of the Assumption.

'MY DEAR LORD SHREWSBURY,

'I arrived home quite safe last week after experiencing most miserable weather. I encountered one gale of wind between Rotterdam and Antwerp which was awful, and to make the matters worse I was in a wretched steam-boat that I found after I was on board had been condemned, and after the week was to be replaced by a fine new vessel. We had both pumps going, and the vessel strained as if she would go to pieces. I was very thankful to get safe ashore. Immediately on leaving your lordship, I was the victim of the grossest piece of villany that I think was ever perpetrated in broad daylight in a Christian country. I sat in the coupé, and immediately before me was a black, ferocious-looking rascal in a conical hat, moustaches and beard, a compound of both Infidel and Republican. He brought an enormous pipe, at least three feet long; this he laid on the seat unperceived by me. After a short drive the postillion said everybody must dismount, as there was a dangerous bridge to pass. It was impossible to get out of the coupé without pushing up the seat. The fellow had left his pipe behind the cushion, and of course down it went and broke the bowl. On this he attacked me most furiously, and declared I should pay 25 francs!! for his pipe not worth 30 sous. And if it had been worth 500 francs, *he* placed it in a position where it was impossible even to perceive it. I refused, and remonstrated, and this went on till we got to the place where we join the high road to Liege; he was going to Aix. As soon as I got out of the coach he rushed on me and declared he would have the satisfaction of a man of honour, or 25 francs. He drew a knife and desired me to defend myself; this of course I refused to do, for I had no idea of fighting. He then swore that if I did not instantly pay 25 francs, I should not leave the place alive. Not a soul came to help. The other passengers, who saw the whole injustice of the business, left me to this horrid ruffian; I had no alternative but to pay. What could I do? My diligence was waiting; he was going to Aix, I to Liege; I had not even time to seek redress. The furious ruffian would have stuck me at any rate; but I never paid 25 francs with such bad grace; and yet what other chance had I to free myself from this beast? Whenever I see a man with a conical hat, a beard, and a pipe, I shall avoid him most carefully. . . . .

'With kindest respects to her ladyship, believe me, my dear Lord Shrewsbury, with great respect,

'Your most devoted and faithful servant,

'A. W. Pugin.'

'Ramsgate, July, 1840.

MY DEAR LORD,

'I intend proceeding to London on Monday,
and shall not fail to call at Mivart's, where I shall have
the greatest delight in going over that glorious church
of St. Peter's, Westminster, with your Lordship. I have
just returned from St. Omer's, where the glories of
Catholic antiquity and modern trash are surprisingly
contrasted. I witnessed a procession of the Fête Dieu,
in which ecclesiastical ornament and vestments were
burlesqued in the most outrageous manner. I reserve
particulars till I have the pleasure of seeing your
Lordship; but such a collection of paper wings, sashed
and pinked acolytes, petticoat albs, board-like chasubles and dalmatics I never before witnessed, and the
ressosoirs were worthy of Bartholomew Fair.'

'Hotel des Trois Rois, Basle;
October 2nd.

'MY DEAR LORD SHREWSBURY,

'I have arrived safe at Basle, and never was
better repaid by a journey. I think this is one of the
most interesting places I have seen next to Nurem-
burg. I wonder your lordship did not recommend me
to come here before. There are several exquisite
things, especially in lead work, and everything is so
picturesque. I feel a great deal better than I have
done for some time; the journey has done me good in
every way. I shall return laden with treasures of
detail. It is wonderful to find so much that is new

even to me, and I have had dreadful weather all the time, but I have managed, by working in doors during the worst rain, to get on. I arrived here in a dreadful thunderstorm, and we have another to-night. I never saw heavier rain, and those who had any luggage got it soaked; thanks to my large pockets and mackintosh I escaped dry. It is quite delightful to travel without incumbrances. I care nothing for custom houses and baggage offices. *I have everything about me, and cannot leave anything, it is the only way to travel with comfort.* I met two Oscott students with six large packages, out for three weeks' tour!!! It is quite a duty to sketch all the fine old places, for they are modernizing in every direction, and in a few years we shall have nothing left. Mayence is utterly ruined, nothing but modern streets and great square houses. I begin to return on Monday, and purpose coming down to Alton soon after my arrival in England. As soon as I get back I will write again to your lordship, but I thought you would be glad to hear that I was well, and had accomplished the object of my journey.

'Ever, dear Lord Shrewsbury,
'With great respect,
'Your most devoted and faithful servant,
'A. W. Pugin.'

'I have just returned from Ireland, and to all appearances, everything is arranged about Maynooth, but, after the great experience I have had of the uncertainty of human affairs, I shall not calculate on it till we have actually begun.   I was very kindly received both by the authorities of the colleges and the Lord Lieutenant, *who invited me to a grand state dinner on Tuesday.*'

' I was horrified, on arriving at Manchester to-day, to find that some pious persons had bought those horrid figures that came out of your lordship's chapel, cast iron brackets and all, and given them to be fixed in the church I have built at Manchester, St. Wilfrid's, with that French image of the blessed Virgin for the lady chapel : it is dreadful.   I will never advise sending anything to bazaars again.   Good gracious ! the horrid things to come back again : they pursue me like the Flying Dutchman.   I thought I had seen the last of them, and they actually go into a church that should be perfect in its way.   What to do, I know not.'

' I am now on my way to Gloucester, to build a small chapel, and alter a house for Mr. Leigh, who became a Catholic some time ago.   I am doing a great deal in various ways, but nothing now of any great importance ; the new Houses of Parliament occupy a great deal of my time, and I work incessantly.   There are great difficulties about Maynooth ; the grant is quite insufficient for the building, and it appears that the Government will neither give any more, nor consent to Dr. Crolley's proposition to take a sum from the yearly grant for its completion, so I am quite at a stand and have no idea how it will end.'

'I have latterly nothing but Protestant business, but that pays, and by erecting my church I turn it to Catholic purposes. There are so many Catholic architects now, that there is not a chance of any new buildings. I believe I design for all of them, for I see actually my own casts and figures used, and then they abuse me afterwards. These men can afford to sell cheap, for they *steal* their *brooms ready made;* however, the movement progresses, and the right sort of thing becomes general, and that is the great point.'

The perplexing suggestions interfering with his own better knowledge, which he had to resist with his friend Lord Shrewsbury, were trifling as compared to the difficulties he met with in dealing with committees. He had been appointed by the Government to prepare plans for the additions to Maynooth College in Ireland. After producing a satisfactory design, from some causes beyond his control, the proposed expenditure was reduced from £30,000 to £18,000. This unexpected reduction put it out of Pugin's power to do anything which he felt could be creditable to him; he, in consequence, tendered his resignation as architect. This step on his part caused the greatest disappointment to the local authorities. They were so fully impressed with his superior abilities, that they addressed a memorial to the Executive Board as follows:—

'We the undersigned have learned with deep regret that Mr. Pugin has ceased to be the architect to the

College. We are fully convinced that his long experience in ecclesiastical architecture, and his thorough acquaintance with the noble churches and colleges of former times, eminently qualify him for the task of building the new church and making other improvements which have been already intrusted to him by the Board. We are strongly of opinion that there is no other person likely to be appointed who is in any degree equally qualified with Mr. Pugin for executing buildings of this kind. In confirmation of this conviction, we appeal to the beautiful plan which he submitted to the trustees last summer, and of which they unanimously approved. May we be allowed to suggest to your lordship, and to the other members of the board, that the circumstances which have induced Mr. Pugin to resign are not of an insuperable nature, but that, on the contrary, they may be overcome by hearty co-operation, and we fully calculate on the kind and powerful support of our illustrious hierarchy in making our College worthy of Maynooth and of Ireland.

'P.S. We have taken the liberty of forwarding a copy of this note to each of the members of the Board.'

N.B. This document was signed by the several professors.

Mr. Gaffney.	P. A. Murray.	J. Behan.
Mr. Lee.	G. Crolly.	D. McCarthy.
J. Gunn.	T. Furlong.	D. Gargan.
T. Fanelly.	C. Russell.	M. Kelly.
T. Dixon.	N. Callan.	J. Tully.
E. O'Reilly.		

Mr. Gaffney, also a leading member of the College, addressed this letter to him:—

'Maynooth, 6th of April, 1846.

'MY DEAR MR. PUGIN,

'I would in vain endeavour to convey to you, by letter, our anxiety here on this important question, which every one puts to himself and to his confrères, "Who will build our new church and college?" Some months ago we hailed, with delight, the appointment of a man, whose genius, whose talents, whose truly Catholic spirit were sure to leave a solemn impress of Catholicity, within and without the walls of this national establishment, which for fifty years has presented no emblem, to the eye, as of a Catholic seminary, save the sacred tabernacle which decorates the altar. You were the man, in whom our fond hopes were centred, through whom we expected the realisation of them. Conceive then, if you can, what our feelings were, when we heard that you had ceased to be the architect to our College. This news was bad news indeed; it was a severe blow, it was deeply felt. We were disheartened, but we did not despair. One of us waited on His Grace Dr. Murray, who feels as intensely as we do regarding your resignation. By the Archbishop's advice, we sent a document to each of the members of the Board of Trustees. I send you a copy of this paper, which was signed by all the members of our body except three. These gentlemen are, however, anxious that you should be the architect to the College. We have received many answers to our circular, all of which agree with us in opinion. Doctors McHale, Brown, McNicholson, and Lord French, declare, in their answers, that they will use all their influence as trustees, to secure to the College the services of Mr. Pugin. There will be a meeting of the trustees in Dublin on the 22nd day of the present month, for the sole purpose of coming to a decision on the buildings. Mr. Owens will submit his plan (without a new church) on that day, but I am almost certain that the great majority of the trustees will not have any other plan than the one proposed by you last summer and approved of by all. We have £30,000 ; let us begin with that sum, and when exhausted, Providence will not be wanting. The new church and buildings will not remain unfinished. This is the idea of some of our most distinguished prelates. We agree most heartily with them. We all here are full of hope that two months will not pass away until you are again the architect to St. Patrick's College. We all desire it, we all pray for it, and no one more ardently than he who has the pleasure of subscribing himself,

'Most sincerely yours,

'M. GAFFNEY.'

Though Pugin was greatly annoyed either by the opposition or indifference to his views, showed by many leading men in the Roman Catholic Church, yet he had reason to be pleased with such spontaneous communications as the following.

To A. Welby Pugin.

'St. Edmund's College, near Ware, Herts.

' DEAR AND RESPECTED SIR,

'Feeling ourselves highly honoured by your presence amongst us, long anxiously expected, we hasten to present you with a testimonial of our sentiments. While others more favoured have lived in the very circle of your actions, we, in our retirement, have communed with you solely in your writings. But think not that, therefore, our esteem has been less enthusiastic. We have watched your constant exertions in the revival of the real glory of art, we have witnessed your successful labours for the beautifying of the House of God, and great has been our respect, heartfelt our gratitude. A time has at length arrived when these feelings, so long secret, may be made manifest, and we rejoice in the hope that this small manifestation will give some passing satisfaction to you as highly deserving. The approving voice of many truly learned has already gone forth to cheer you in your career of utility and fame. And amongst these may we not number several of our own body, several amongst the anointed of God? They have been happy in their appointment to raise the broken altars of Israel—they have been further happy in having one who might render the beauty of these altars a fitting throne for the Eternal. In this twofold honour may a share be reserved for us. May we be one day their successors, and may we too have the advantage of

your co-operation. That for many years your mind
may be guided by the Framer of all beauty, that you
may long continue the worthy embellisher of His
temples is the united earnest prayer of

'THE STUDENTS OF ST. EDMUND'S.'

The only drawback to this token of approval must
have been the form in which it was sent, for the
letter paper was headed with the view of a most detestable and commonplace building in the Grecian
style which can possibly be conceived ; but still these
approving communications were very grateful to
Pugin, as showing that there were certainly some
amongst his own communion who appreciated his zeal
and devotion to their Church, and he might well
excuse the somewhat forced and far-fetched language
in which the testimonial was couched.

It may easily be supposed that Pugin, filling so
distinguished a position as an architect, would be in
communication with the leading men of all countries ;
and so he was ; but the letters mostly relate to professional business, and are therefore scarcely suited
or interesting to the public. One, however, from the
Count de Montalembert, commending an artist of eminence to Pugin's notice, is worthy of insertion.

'Paris, in Festo S. Marci Evangel, 1848.

'MY DEAR MR. PUGIN,
          'Allow me to introduce to your kind notice and
protection M. Emile Lusson, one of our best Catholic

artists. As a painter, in the modern Christian style, I sincerely think he has no superior in France; and I should be very much astonished if he had any in England. The sad and discouraging state of every concern depending on art and intellect, owing to the late catastrophe in France, induces him to try his fortune in England; and, if I am not greatly mistaken, he would do honour to any of the churches and chapels with which your genius has adorned your native land.

'I abstain from all reflections on the astounding events which we are now going through. The French clergy has taken a part which has astonished and grieved some of its best friends; but, whatever happens, the Almighty will know how to save His Church from the frenzy of its enemies and its false friends.

'Believe me ever cordially and faithfully yours,

'W. C. de Montalembert.'

In 1851 Pugin was appointed one of the Commissioners of Fine Arts in connexion with the Great Exhibition. During his absence from one of their meetings, a recommendation was made for the purchase of a shield ornamented in a style he did not approve. This caused him some annoyance, and, feeling strongly upon the subject, he addressed a letter of remonstrance to the Lords of the Committee of Trade, exonerating himself from any implication in this act of his colleagues. The letter, couched in strong terms, affords another illustration of the manly outspoken manner in which he always expressed his opinions.

'St. Augustine's, Ramsgate,
' My Lords,   December 10th, 1851.

' I hasten to acknowledge with most earnest thanks the communication which I have just received respecting the purchase of the shield of Vechte, No. 25. It enables me to present myself as the *uncompromising opponent of that purchase*, to which I *have never, by word or deed, consented*. The purchase appears to have been decided by the three other commissioners on a day when I was unavoidably absent on Government business at Westminster; and, when I was informed of what had been decided, I exclaimed that they would never obtain my consent. I repudiated the very idea of purchasing the shield, as, although it was, in the abstract, an exceedingly clever piece of chasing, yet it was diametrically opposite to the style and principles which I considered we ought to put before the students, and the object of the collection we were entrusted to form. I trust, therefore, that your Lordships will exonerate me from all participation in this shield purchase, the cost of which is out of all character for such an object, useless and obsolete, excepting as a space to exhibit metal chasing ; and I do not hesitate to say that, clever as this chasing may be, it does not in any way illustrate the English character of the POET to which it pretends to refer, but is a positive revival of Pagan art, and unfit for our National school of design, and as such, as well as from the great cost, I consider it a most objectionable object to select, and out of all character with the purpose for which we have had the honour of being appointed. I am very happy to add that we have, on the whole, worked most cordially, and I may truly say that our purchases, as a collection, will be of infinite service, especially in the Oriental productions and works designed on natural principles. Cannot this matter be reconsidered by your Lordships, and the money, which is a considerable sum, far better applied? I imagine the East Indian importations of costly articles might be revisited with great benefit. I have been preparing a short account of our reasons (barring the shield), which has unfortunately been retarded by my late severe attack of nervous fever, from which dangerous malady I am only very lately delivered, and the state to which it has reduced me prevents my returning too quickly to anything that requires much mental exertion ; but if, by the blessing of God, my faculties are again restored to their former strength, I will send a fair copy to Mr. Cole (from whom I have received the kindest attentions), or, in his absence, to Mr. Dodd. I feel confident that my friend Mr. Herbert will only echo the sentiments I have expressed, if his opinion be taken.

' I remain, my Lords, with all respect, your most devoted and humble servant,

'AUGUSTUS WELBY PUGIN.

' To the Lords of the Committee for Trade, Whitehall.'

---

*Note.*These letters have been brought together into one chapter without reference to their dates : they form no portion of connected correspondence bearing on one particular subject, but are inserted here as illustrating the force of character so observable in all Pugin's affairs, and as showing the high esteem in which his talents were held.

CHAPTER XI.

Publishes 'True Principles of Gothic Architecture'—Cruises at Sea—
Facility of Drawing and Etching while in the Boat—Sound Principles of Design—Tact requisite to carry them into execution—Exposure of unrealities, and censure of wrong Roman practices—Publishes his great work, 'A Glossary of Ecclesiastical Ornament and
Costume'—Its effect.

THE success attending on the publication of the 'Contrasts' induced Pugin very soon afterwards, in 1841,
to prepare another work, entitled 'True Principles of
Gothic Architecture.' This volume was published by
Mr. Weale, the architectural bookseller. It has been
already noticed that Pugin's former work, 'The Contrasts,' was published by himself at St. Marie's
Grange. He was compelled to take this course in
consequence of his failing to find a publisher who
would incur the responsibility of giving to the world a
work so strongly seasoned with personal abuse.

His present aim was to further the correct revival
of ancient architecture, by exposing the miserable
way in which all branches of trade connected with
mediæval art were carried on, and the unsatisfactory
result arising through the artifices and deceptions practised in the production of fabrics of every kind used in
buildings of this description. Such true and incon-

trovertible principles are contained in this book, that it may be safely affirmed we owe more to its influence in correcting public taste than to all other causes combined. The simple and masterly manner in which first principles are insisted upon constitute the key to the extensive usefulness of the volume, which is illustrated in the most happy manner by diagrams and sketches, all drawn and etched by himself.

While occupied in the preparation of this work Pugin was pursuing a rather eccentric mode of life; it has been previously remarked that he was fond of the sea : he now frequently made cruises along the coast, sometimes extending them to the opposite shores of France, and in fair weather reaching the coast of Holland. In this way he was frequently afloat for many days together; yet, amidst this seeming neglect of his legitimate demands on his time, he contrived to give sufficient attention to what was in progress at home. The following incident is somewhat characteristic. After an absence of some weeks Pugin unexpectedly called at his publisher's, who observed that his dress, which usually was untidy, appeared more strange than ever. He was enveloped in a huge pilot-coat, large enough for a man twice his size. On this strange exhibition Mr. Weale, his publisher, remarked :

' Why, you appear to have made a mistake, and have got a coat belonging to somebody else.'

' Oh,' observed Pugin, ' it is of no consequence—I caught up the first garment that came in my way, getting into harbour after a stiff gale off Calais; but here are the plates for my book:'—at the same time pulling out a heap of copper-plates from under the ample folds of his coat. 'They are all ready for proving.'

'But how and where did you finish the etchings?'

'Oh,' said Pugin, 'I finished them in the boat.'

'Impossible,' replied Mr. Weale.

'Not a bit of it,' retorted Pugin; 'the motion of the sea makes no difference to me;' and, truly, many of the outlines illustrating the 'Apology' were etched by him under these apparently impossible circumstances.

There is a tendency, whenever any measure sound in principle is made strongly manifest, to carry it to extremes in practice. Nothing, for instance, can be more true than Pugin's theories, laid down in the 'Apology,' and, among other axioms, that the plan of a building should combine all the convenience required for its intended purpose, and when once the plan is settled, then the elevations may be considered. In all the buildings erected by Pugin this rule has been acted upon; and they are very happy illustrations of his theory. There is an obvious character and fitness about them, no stiffness or studied uniformity, but graceful adaptations of plan and elevation. As in the plans, doors and windows are placed where convenience needed them, so in the elevations, their heights and positions are regulated by the natural requirements of construction. Still the application of this same rule can scarcely be successful unless the artist, while planning his building, can see by anticipation the general outline of the superstructure to be raised from his ground plan. The system of drawing a plan and disposing of windows and doors without reference to the gracefulness of exterior design must end in a composition remarkable for eccentricity and awkwardness, rather than for pleasing appearance. A great disposition is shown among the young architects of the present day to fall into this error : and indeed, amateur architects who, charmed with the truthfulness of Pugin's views, have boldly acted upon his rule without suspecting any difficulty, have found themselves cruelly disappointed in the result. At the time when the 'True Principles' were written, few beyond strictly professional men ventured to carry into practice the axioms so plainly laid down by Pugin. There were then, however, as there are now, some men whose natural taste for drawing and application to the study of mediæval art rendered them almost as competent as professional men. A few such the writer of these pages has had the pleasure of knowing. The attempt of one of these gentlemen to work out Pugin's theory will afford a good illustration of the difficulty in design just referred to. The late Lord T—— was an ardent admirer of Pugin's writings, and, being really a scientific and accomplished man, he determined, unaided by any professional advice, to build a parsonage in the mediæval style, and strictly upon the 'true principles' embodied in the work he so much admired. Selecting, then, his site with much judgment, in the village of A——, in S——, my Lord arranged the ground plan to his own mind perfectly, and in so convenient a manner that a triumphant result seemed certain; and in due course, though unexpected difficulties continually presented themselves, the parsonage was finished. The embarrassments, however, attendant on the building of this house were almost endless, and the various shifts by which false bearings were overcome, small gutters carried from the roofs over ceilings, and other expensive contrivances made to meet new and unforeseen checks, were many. 'Well,' said a friend one day to his lordship, while inspecting the parsonage, 'and now what has been the cost of this example of truthful construction?' To which he received the short but expressive answer, 'For heaven's sake don't ask me.' No doubt all this disappointment might have been avoided if his lordship had called to his aid competent professional assistance, and the mention of the failure is only made to show that a sound principle in theory is not sufficient; but to be useful must be worked out with professional practical knowledge.

Perhaps the greatest service has been done, through the agency of this work, by Pugin's unsparing exposure of the system of SHAMS in architectural design. Every kind of unreality is pointed out and denounced. The good effect of his decrying this most vicious practice may certainly be witnessed in many works

executed since his day; for whatever may be their
other faults, there is a much greater degree of honesty
and sterling character in them than is to be found in
modern buildings erected previously to Pugin's publication. The circulation of this work established his
reputation, and he rapidly obtained extensive business, reaping the pecuniary advantages accruing
from large commissions. Had he now reserved but a
moderate share of his annual income, he would have
left a handsome fortune behind him; but Pugin's
love for all that was interesting and useful in connection with his art was so strong, that he never
could resist the temptations of purchasing ancient
works of art and literature. Whenever opportunities
offered of obtaining choice pictures, books, and prints
by early German masters and divines, the cost of
such objects was readily incurred, so that in a short
time he possessed a very valuable library of the most
choice books, and a large collection of rare articles of
vertû.

Pugin seems about this time to have been more
than ordinarily annoyed by observing that in all the
accessories connected with the Catholic worship where
art should be apparent, there had been a sad declen-
sion since the period of the Reformation; and having
exposed in no sparing manner all the abominations,
as he was accustomed to call them, of the Reformed
Church, he now sought, by the influence which his
genius gave him, to effect an improvement in ecclesiastical vestments, furniture, holy vessels, and other

objects connected with the ritualism of the Roman
Catholic Church. His intimacy with many learned
ecclesiastics enabled him to obtain such an amount of
historical information in reference to these matters,
that, aided by them, he produced the most elaborate
and beautiful work which had been hitherto attempted,
under the title of ' A Glossary of Ecclesiastical Ornament and Costume ; with Extracts from the Works of
Durandus and others, faithfully translated by Bernard
Smith of St. Michael's College, Oscott.' The book
is illustrated with the most exquisite chromolithic
examples of ancient design, besides many beautiful
woodcuts, and many ingenious devices of his own.
The subject was one so entirely congenial to his taste
that he seems to have exhausted all the resources of
art bearing upon the sacred furniture and decoration
of the Church. The influence of this work upon poly-
chromatic decoration has been immense. No well-
directed attempts in recent times had been made to introduce coloured embellishments into churches ; but a
stimulus was now given to such efforts, and although
Protestant prejudices were opposed to coloured decorations, yet they were depicted with such fascinating
effect in the pages of the Glossary that many of his
symbols, suited only for the walls of a Roman Catholic
edifice, were innocently repeated in our English
churches. Although not immediately, yet in great
measure, we owe the successful application of poly-
chromatic decoration in the Chapter-houses at Salisbury, Chester, Wells, Ely, and elsewhere to the well-

directed efforts of Pugin to revive this art. None who studied his books could fail to see the truth of his reasoning on art, and the diffusion of his writings among the public tended much to abate the blind prejudice against colour, so that the cathedral authorities could in some degree count upon support where hitherto they had met opposition. Whenever coloured wall spaces were advocated the prejudice was strange which led the same people who approved filling windows with painted glass to raise objections when painting was sought to be applied to stone surfaces.

CHAPTER XII.

Publishes 'A Treatise on Chancel Screens'—Severity of his Remarks
upon a section of the Roman Catholic Church, when disregarding
proper Church Arrangements—Precedents taken from Lombardic
Churches — 'Modern Ambonoclast ' — 'Calvinist Ambonoclast '—
Anecdotes.

AFTER labouring hard both by pen and pencil for
many years to bring about a revival of purer art,
chiefly in connection with the Catholic Church, Pugin
published his last book in 1851, entitled ' A Treatise
on Chancel Screens and Rood Lofts; their Antiquity,
Use, and Symbolic Signification. Illustrated with
Figures copied on Stone, from Drawings by the
Author;' with the motto, ' Ne transgredearis terminos
quos posuerunt patres tui.'

In this publication he traces with remarkable clearness the uses of screens of every description, from the
earliest period of the Christian Church to the present
time. It was not in his nature to express himself
feebly on any matter, and his lively imagination finds
ample scope in fervid description while engaged on
this topic. But the most remarkable feature of the
work consists in its extreme severity upon the modern
usages of the Roman Catholic Church. Whereas in
his earlier writings no terms of condemnation were
sufficiently strong to express his dislike of the prac-

tices of the Reformed Church, we now find him exhausting his vocabulary of censure upon the learned ecclesiastics of his own creed. Speaking of screens, he says : ' Screens are, in truth, the very least part of the cause of their animosity to the churches of their fathers, for if any man says he loves Pointed Architecture and hates screens, I do not hesitate to denounce him as a liar ; for one is inseparable from the other, and more inseparable from Catholic arrangement in any style, Byzantine, Norman, Pointed, or Debased.'

The numerous illustrations of this work, consisting in delineations of ancient screens of every kind, are admirably drawn. The author does not confine himself to examples in the pointed style only, but gives several specimens of early Italian designs in support of his theories. He appears to have studied the arrangement of the ancient Basilicæ with much care, and derived several of his best screens from the noble mediæval churches of Lombardy. His precedents are wholly taken from buildings of well-known early date and authority, during this period. Pugin's tour in Italy did not in any degree alter his opinion of classic architecture. When at Rome a story was current of his going round St. Peter's in a state of rage, exclaiming, ' Why they can't even carry out decently their own miserable style ;' and on his return to England he told his friends he got out of Rome as soon as he possibly could, ' for every hour he was there he felt endangered his faith ; that the metropolis of Christendom should delight in such monstrosities of architecture was,' he observed, 'almost enough to make a man an infidel.'*

He sums up his treatise by four sketches of great interest, entitled 'The Calvinistic Ambonoclast,' 'The Pagan Ambonoclast,' 'The Revolutionary Ambono-clast,' and 'The Modern Ambonoclast,' each showing the retribution which attends those who despise, and destroy holy things. The work concludes with a severe philippic against a certain section of the Roman Catholic clergy, who, ignoring the usages of antiquity, directed all their efforts to the establishment of places of worship wherein a total disregard might be shown of the many objects which Pugin so much venerated. Those who remember the fittings up of the oratory in King William Street, Strand, with all its tawdry and unartistic embellishments, will see how well-merited was his denunciation, conveyed in the unflinching terms of the chapter of his book describing the 'Modern Ambonoclast.'

'The Modern Ambonoclast.

'This character is of comparatively recent creation, some of the species having been seen in this country previously to the consecration of St. George's Church. About that time two or three made their appearance, and though not by any means in a flourishing condi-tion, they have somewhat increased. It has been asserted that their first dislike of screens arose from

* In a letter to a friend, speaking of Rome, he says: 'The bad archi-tecture there belongs to a *period*, not to a *nation* ; for Italy is full of Gothic work, and within a short distance of the Eternal City.'

a desire of literary notoriety; and that, finding several old women of both sexes had taken a most unaccountable and implacable offence at the ancient division of the chancel and the restoration of the Crucifix, which had been so wisely destroyed in the good old days of Queen Bess, they profited by the occasion to increase the sale of a periodical. But this may be mere calumny; and, indeed, it is very probable that it is a case of pure development, as at first they did not exhibit any repugnance to Pointed churches, which they rather lauded, and only took objection to certain upright mullions and fanciful images. But they speedily developed other propensities and ideas, and latterly have exhibited symptoms almost similar to hydrophobia at the sight—at mere mention—of Pointed arches or pillars. The principal characteristics of modern ambonoclasts may be summed up as follows: —Great irritability at vertical lines, muntans of screens, or transverse beams and crosses; a perpetual habit of abusing the finest works of Catholic antiquity and art, and exulting in their admiration of everything debased, and modern, and trumpery; the inordinate propensity for candles and candlesticks, which they arrange in every possible variety. They require great excitement in the way of lively, jocular, and amatory tunes at Divine service, and exhibit painful distress at the sound of solemn chanting or plain song; at Divine worship they require to sit facing the altar and near the pulpit, and then if the edifice be somewhat like a fish-market, with a hot-water pipe at their feet, a gas-pipe in the vicinity, and a stove in the rear, they can realize a somewhat Italian atmosphere in cold and cheerless England, and recover some sparks of that devotion of which the gloomy vaulting of Westminster and the odious pillars of a new rood-screen had well-nigh deprived them of. It must be however stated to their credit, that the modern ambonoclasts, unlike their predecessors, confine their attacks to strokes of the pen; and we do not believe that they have hitherto succeeded in causing the demolition of a single screen. Indeed it is probable that if the development of their real character had not proceeded so rapidly they might have caused some serious mischief to Catholic restorations; but the cloven foot is now so visible that men are looking out in expectation of the tail, and are already on their guard.'

The interesting description which he gives of the city of London with all its ancient churches in Catholic times, and his graphic account of the destruction of the roods and fittings, are so powerfully written under the title of the 'Calvinist Ambonoclast,' that the temptation to insert it in these pages cannot be resisted.

'THE CALVINIST AMBONOCLAST.

'When we now behold the city of London, with its narrow lanes lined with lofty warehouses, and gloomy stores leading down to the banks of the muddy Thames, whose waters are blackened with foul discharges from gas-works and soap-boilers, while the air is darkened with the dense smoke of chimneys rising high above the parish steeples, which mark the site of some ancient church destroyed in the great conflagration, it is difficult to realize the existence of those venerable and beautiful fabrics where the citizens of London assembled in daily worship, and whose rood-lofts shone so gloriously on Easter and Christmas feasts. But this great and ancient city was inferior to none in noble religious buildings; and in the 16th century the traveller who approached London from the west, by the way called Oldbourne, on arriving at the brow of the steep hill must have had a most splendid prospect before him : to the right the parish church of St. Andrew's rising most picturesquely from the steep declivity, and surrounded by elms, with its massive tower, decorated nave, and still later chancel; on the left the extensive buildings of Ely House, its great gateway, embattled walls, lofty chapel and refectory, and numerous other lodgings and offices surrounded by pleasant gardens, as then unalienated from the ancient see after which it is called, presented a most venerable and ecclesiastical appearance. Further in the same direction might be perceived the gilded spire of St. John's church of Jerusalem and the Norman towers of St. Bartholomew's priory. Immediately below was the Fleet river with its bridge and the masts of the various craft moored along the quays. At the summit of the opposite hill the lofty tower of St. Sepulchre's which, though greatly deteriorated in beauty, still remains. In the same line and over

the embattled parapets of Newgate, the noble church
of the Grey Friars, inferior in extent only to the
cathedral of St. Paul, whose gigantic spire, the highest
in the world, rose majestically from the centre of a cruci-
form church nearly 700 feet in length, and whose
grand line of high roofs and pinnacled buttresses stood
high above the group of gabled houses, and even the
towers of the neighbouring churches.   If we terminate
the panorama with the arched lantern of St. Mary-le-
Bow, the old tower of St. Michael Cornhill, and a
great number of lesser steeples, we shall have a faint
idea of the ecclesiastical beauty of Catholic London.

‘ But to return to our more immediate subject : each
of these fine churches was provided with its screen and
rood.   Numerous are the entries in the old church-
warden's accounts yet remaining of pious offerings
made by the citizens to beautify the devotional sculptures which decorated them, and to provide tapers and
branches to deck them for the returning festivals.
There were veils for Lent, when the glory of our Lord
was partially obscured by his approaching Passion ;
and there were garlands for Easter, and paschal lights,
and crowns, and diadems.   The old parish church of
St. Mary-at-Hill was inferior to none in the beautiful
partition of its chancel.   It was principally the work
of a pious citizen, who on the decay of the older work
renewed the same ; or, as the old chronicle expresses
it, “ For the love he bore to Jesu and his holy Modir
did sett up at his own proper costes and charges, and
most artificially dispensit the image of Christ, Mary

and John and many saynts and aungels, with the loft whereon they stood ; and for the due maintainyng of a perpetual light to hang burnyng before the same, and for a priest to synge at his anniversary he also left 2 tenements in the paryshe of Barkynge ; and when he died he was buried under a grey stone over and against the holy doors of the chancel, and till the sad time of the civil wars was his portraiture in brass and that of his wife and 3 sons and 5 daughters at their feet, and his shield of mark, and the arms of the honorable Company of the Fishmongers, and round the bordure, with an Evangelist at every corner, with this inscription : ✠ 'Good Christen people, of y^r charitie pray for the soulys of John Layton, citizen and fyshemonger of London, who deceded on the feast of St. Stephen, in the yeare of our Lord 1456, and of Margaret his wyffe, on whose sowlys and the sowlys of Christen men may Jesu have mercy. Pater ave, Amen.' And on the brestsumer of the rood loft were carved divers devices, such as St. Peter's keys for his Patron, and the dolphins and sea-luces salterwise for the company, and scrolls with lays coming out of tuns for the founder, and above all was a most artificial bratistring, with large bowls of brass, with prickets for tapers on great feasts, and there was a staircase of freestone, closed by an oak door, set up on the south side of the aisle, for the convenience of ascending to the same ; and on each of the lower panels of the holy doors, and of the bays of the screen were pictures of saints and martyrs, on grounds of gold diaper, each with their legend. For nearly a century this goodly work had stood the pride and delight of the parishioners, who bestowed much cost on sustaining its lights and ornaments, as the church books yet testify. But a sad and fearful change was approaching—new and heretical doctrines were circulated, and even heard at Paul's Cross; men became divided in heart and mind; the returning festivals exhibited no unity of joy and devotion, many gloomily stayed away, and it was currently reported that nocturnal meetings were privately held at some citizens' houses, where preachers from beyond sea taught novel opinions, and inveighed against altars and priests, and sacred images and ancient rites; and soon there was a quest to examine into the ornaments of the churches, and many a goodly pyx, and chalice, and chrismatory were seized by the sacrilegious spoilers for the state; and shortly after the ancient service was interrupted by the scoffers and infidels, and they who adhered to the old faith of England's Church were filled with sorrow and dismay, and they worshipped in fear and sadness, and every day brought new troubles and greater sacrilege.

'It was late in the evening, or rather the early part of the night, that a number of persons, evidently of very varied ranks and conditions, were crowded into a back-chamber in the habitation of a citizen notoriously disaffected to the ancient religion. They were listening with considerable earnestness of attention, to the exhortations, or rather ravings, of a man of sour aspect, whose dress and gestures announced him as

belonging to the class of unordained preachers called
the New Gospellers. The subject of his discourse
was the extirpation of idolatry. The triumphs of the
Jewish people over the unbelieving nations was the
principal source from whence he drew his denunciations.
The texts relating to the destruction of the heathen
idols he transferred to the ancient images of the
Church, and he succeeded in rousing the passions of
his hearers to the utmost frenzy. " But why," he exclaimed, "do we waste time? Let us lay the axe to
the root of the tree; the famous rood of St. Mary-at-
Hill standeth hard by, to the shame and reproach of
Christian men. Let us pluck it down and utterly
deface it, so let it perish and be seen no more."

'Some of the most zealous of the fanatics instantly
acted on this suggestion. Descending to the street,
they soon surrounded the residence of the aged sacrist
(who still retained his office, though the duties were
sadly curtailed), and rousing him from his rest, de-
manded the keys of the church. Alarmed by the
uproar, many casements were opened ; but the numbers
of the clamouring party appeared so considerable, and
the prospect of any assistance from the watch, which
was then only perambulatory, so remote, that none
ventured down to the assistance of the old clerk, who,
terrified by the menaces of his assailants, and without
any companion, except a lad who acted as his servant,
at length surrendered the keys. A few links had by
this time been procured, and by their smoky and
lurid light the southern door was opened, and the

whole party tumultuously crowded into the venerable edifice.

'The lamp so liberally provided by John Layton had ceased to burn for some time; its revenue had been sequestered as superstitious, and the chancel was shrouded in unpenetrable darkness. Against this gloomy background the rood and its attendant images stood out in red reflected lights, but the Jews themselves who scoffed on Calvary's Mount were not more bitter in their scorn than the New Gospellers, who uttered loud shouts and cries as they beheld the object of their sacrilegious vengeance. The sound of hollow blows echoes through the church, the lower door is forced, ascending footsteps are heard on the staircase; then the rebounding tread of heavy feet on the loft itself, torches appear—axes gleam—heavy blows fall thick; some cleave, some pierce, some shout, and with one great crash it totters and falls—images— cross—all lie a ruin on the ancient pavement. The work of destruction now proceeds: some wrench the extended limbs from the sculptured cross; broken and dismembered, the sacred image of the Redeemer is dragged down the nave, while others deface and cleave the evangelistic symbols, tossing the fragments in wild derision; some curse, some spit, some foam, others exclaim "Into the fire with it!" and a glare of light striking through the western window, showed that the suggestion had been followed. It crackled in the garth, and now the mangled images are piled on the roaring mass, while furious cries, " Away with it!"

"Destroy it utterly!" break through the stillness of the night, and scare the affrighted parishioners, who behold this horrible spectacle from their gabled residences. Nearly three hundred years have elapsed and the rood was again raised in glory in this very city, and the cry "Away with it" was again heard. Came it from the blaspheming Jews? No. Came it from the bitter Calvinists? No. Came it from the incarnate fiends? No. It proceeded from a modern Catholic ambono-clast!!!'

When Pugin was in Dorsetshire, engaged in re-building a chancel and parsonage, a friend started him upon a subject on which he knew that Pugin felt very uneasy just then, viz. The Italian taste that was rife amongst the Roman Catholics in England. To the utter bewilderment of those present he began vehemently to denounce the Romanizers; and, a well-known name in the Anglo-Roman hierarchy being mentioned as one of them, he exclaimed, 'Miserable! my dear sir, miserable!' The clergyman for whom he was building, who at that time was more than half inclined to think everything Roman must be right, was utterly astonished to hear so distinguished a convert giving vent to such heresies; and his friend had to explain that the heresy was on the other side, but that it was only architectural.

M

CHAPTER XIII.

Ruskin's severe Criticism upon Pugin's Buildings—Inconsistencies pointed out—Strong religious Bias—Troublesome Interference of Committees—Incidents relating to the Foundation of St. George's Church and Conventual Establishment, Lambeth—Remonstrates against unusual Expectations, and exposes their Fallacies—Defects in the Design from want of due study.

PUGIN, who had hitherto stood almost unrivalled as the great champion of mediæval art, soon encountered a powerful rival in a person whose learning and literary genius were of the highest order. The name of Ruskin had long been associated with art and archæology. His work, 'The Seven Lamps of Architecture,' was read with eagerness, and gave rise to new and more exalted views of art than had yet prevailed. Devoted to art and the means for its promotion, he looked at the subject from a different point of view from Pugin. Familiar with Italy, and well versed in the peculiarities of the foreign schools, abhorring the Romish religion with an intensity as strong as Pugin's affection for it, he could not endure the fulsome language in which Pugin indulged when writing of anything belonging to the Catholic Church ; and in his publication entitled the 'Stones of Venice,' when speaking of modern Romanist ar , he expresses himself in these words on Pugin and his works.

Extract from Ruskin's ' Stones of Venice.'
Appendix 12.

'I had hardly believed that it was a thing possible, though vague stories had been told me of the effect, on some minds, of mere scarlet and candles, until I came on this passage in Pugin's " Remarks on articles in the Rambler :"—

' " Those who have lived in want and privation are the best qualified to appreciate the blessings of plenty ; thus, to those who have been devout and sincere members of the separated portion of the English Church ; who have prayed, and hoped, and loved, through all the poverty of the maimed rites which it has retained to them, does the realization of all their longing desires appear truly ravishing. . . . . Oh ! then, what delight ! what joy unspeakable ! when one of the solemn piles is presented to them, in all its pristine life and glory ! the stoups are filled to the brim ; the rood is raised on high ; the screen glows with sacred imagery and rich device ; the niches are filled ; the altar is replaced sustained by sculptured shafts, the relics of the saints repose beneath, the body of our Lord is enshrined on its consecrated stone ; the lamps of the sanctuary burn bright ; the saintly portraitures in the glass windows shine all gloriously ; and the albs hang in the oaken ambries, and the cope chests are filled with osphreyed baudekins ; and pix, and pax, and chrismatory are there, and thurible and cross."

'One might have put this man under a pix, and left him, one should have thought; but he has been brought forward, and partly received, as an example of the effect of ceremonial splendour on the mind of a great architect. It is very necessary, therefore, that all those who have felt sorrow at this, should know at once that he is not a great architect, but one of the smallest possible or conceivable architects; and that by his own account and setting forth of himself. Hear him :—

' " I believe, as regards architecture, few men have been so unfortunate as myself. I have passed my life in thinking of fine things, studying fine things, designing fine things, and realizing very poor ones. I have never had the chance of producing a single fine ecclesiastical building, except my own church, where I am both paymaster and architect; but everything else, either for want of adequate funds, from injudicious interference and control, or some other contingency, is more or less a failure. . . .

' " St. George's was spoilt by the very instructions laid down by the Committee, that it was to hold 3000 people on the floor at a limited price; in consequence height, proportion, everything was sacrificed to meet these conditions. Nottingham was spoilt by the style being restricted to lancet—a period well suited to a Cistercian abbey in a secluded vale, but very unsuitable for the centre of a crowded town. . . .

' " Kirkham was spoilt through several hundred pounds being reduced on the original estimate. To effect this, which was a great sum in proportion to the entire cost, the area of the church was contracted, the walls lowered, tower and spire reduced, the thickness of walls diminished, and stone arches omitted."—(*Remarks, &c., by A. W. Pugin:* Dolman, 1850.)

' Is that so? Phidias can niche himself in the corner of a pediment, Rafaelle expatiate within the circumference of a clay platter; but Pugin is inexpressible in less than a cathedral! Let his ineffableness be assured of this, once for all, that no difficulty or restraint ever happened to a man of real power, but his power was the more manifested in the contending with, or conquering it; and that there is no field so small, no cranny so contracted, but that a great spirit can house and manifest itself therein. The thunder that smites the Alp into dust can gather itself into the width of a golden wire. Whatever greatness there was in you, had it been Buonaroti's own, you had room enough for it in a single niche; you might have put the whole power of it into two feet cube of Caen stone. St. George's was not high enough for want of money? But was it want of money that made you put that blunt, overloaded, laborious ogee door into the side of it? Was it for lack of funds that you sunk the tracery of the parapet in its clumsy zigzags? Was it in parsimony that you buried its paltry pinnacles in that eruption of diseased crockets? Or in pecuniary embarrassment that you set up the belfry fools'-

caps, with the mimicry of dormer windows, which nobody can ever reach nor look out of? Not so, but in mere incapability of better things.

' I am sorry to have to speak thus of any living architect; and there is much in this man, if he were rightly estimated, which we might both regard and profit by. He has a most sincere love for his profession, a hearty honest enthusiasm for pixes and piscinas ; and though he will never design so much as a pix or a piscina thoroughly well, yet better than most of the experimental architects of the day. Employ him by all means, but on small work. Expect no cathedrals of him ; but no one, at present, can design a better finial. That is an exceedingly beautiful one over the western door of St. George's ; and there is some spirited impishness and switching of tails in the supporting figures at the imposts. Only do not allow his good designing of finials to be employed as an evidence in matters of divinity, nor thence deduce the incompatibility of Protestantism and art.'

The withering sarcasm of these remarks can scarcely be said to be warranted under any circumstances. It so far exceeds the bounds of fairness, that thoughtful people feel shocked at finding a man of Ruskin's ability descending to such gross personalities, in order to embody in them the expression of his bitter aversion to Romanism.

Nothing but the most bigotted feeling could have prompted the writer to abuse Pugin for studying with minuteness the details of art so inseparably connected with the ornament and costume of the Roman Catholic Church. If there is one thing more than another upon which Mr. Ruskin insists in all his lectures and papers on art, it is on the necessity of artists attending with unremitting care to all the minutiæ, and accessories of architecture. In the ' Stones of Venice,' whole chapters are written and spun out in eulogy of the beauty and meaning of small and unimportant details; while in his lectures he almost invariably brings forward, as one of the most distinctive contrasts between genuine ancient and modern art, the extraordinary care bestowed in the former, even in the design of the smallest objects. Nor are his remarks upon Pugin's executed works animated by a spirit of fairness. Looking at his buildings as the first evidences of a better knowledge of pointed architecture, they deserved to be judged by a different standard, and nobody can doubt that if adequate funds had been forthcoming he would have erected edifices free from the defects of which he was fully sensible, and so feelingly deplores in the passages which Ruskin quotes against him.

Where was the man at the time of Pugin's early career who could design and execute works at all approaching the excellence of his productions? Indeed, it is admitted on all hands that Pugin was immeasurably in advance of his day. That his works are perfect no one asserts; but his indulgence in some small enriched details upon a building otherwise plain and poor in general character, ought not to expose him to the anathema launched against him. The

small saving which might have been obtained by the
omission of the questionable enrichments, could never
have supplied means for giving St. George's the
solidity and gracefulness which would have satisfied
his own desires; and, as to the strictures upon the
design of the finials, parapets, &c., they are not
founded upon sound judgment, but are the arbitrary
opinions of a critic who is determined that nothing
shall be right if it emanates from a Roman Catholic.

None but those who have been obliged to submit to
the dicta of Committees can form any adequate idea of
their interference with the functions of professional
men when engaged in the exercise of their art.   Pugin
had suffered much annoyance in this way, and was
often heard to complain of the mutilations made in his
designs by pretending and meddling ecclesiastics.
His impatient disposition sometimes led him to rebel,
and even to set at defiance the ordinary rules of courtesy
when acting with ill-informed employers.   It is related
of him that when, owing to the increasing number of
Roman Catholics in London, the prelates and influential laymen formed a Committee to take steps for
providing a cathedral with a convent and schools,
Pugin was applied to for plans.   He at once prepared
with his usual skill very beautiful designs, and the
Committee were duly summoned to receive him, and
hear his plans explained.   They were of an elaborate
kind, and provided for a cathedral with chapter-house,
cloisters, conventual buildings, and every usual adjunct.
The drawings excited great admiration, and many

questions were asked to which Pugin gave most satisfactory replies. Indeed, all promised well, and nothing seemed likely to prevent the realization of this magnificent project, when a member present very naturally asked the amount at which he estimated the cost of the entire work; others put the like question, and inquired also the time which it would take to carry his scheme into execution. These requests met with no direct reply; entering upon that part of the subject, was, for the present, evaded, and the conversation turned to another point. Meanwhile Pugin, in a manner not to excite observation, swept up the several drawings which were on the table, politely asking those who were admiring the details to be good enough to hand them to him for a few minutes.

Having thus collected his plans, Pugin deliberately rolled them up, took his hat, wished the gentlemen good day, and walked out of the house, leaving the Committee in perfect astonishment at his inexplicable conduct.

The next day some members of the Committee calling on him for an explanation, met with a rough reception. 'You asked me,' said he, 'to furnish designs for a cathedral, chapter-house, cloisters, and conventual buildings, upon a grand scale. I complied with the request, and supposed that I was dealing with people who knew what they wanted. The absurd questions, however, put to me soon showed my mistake. Who ever heard of a complete cathedral being built in the life of one man? Those structures have been the gradual work of centuries, begun by one founder, and carried to completion by his successors. How could

I possibly frame an estimate for a building, a small portion of which might possibly only be raised during my lifetime ?   That which would cost little one year, might, by the increased price of materials, be doubly expensive in future years.   Everybody acquainted with building operations knows the fluctuating nature of these things.   Common sense should have taught the Committee not to put such absurd questions to me. If you approve my design, adopt it, and carry out all or part, in its integrity, as the means may be forthcoming.'   However just these views might be, it certainly did not warrant such abrupt conduct on Pugin's part.

The Committee had mistaken their power of raising funds for the great purpose on which Pugin was to be employed, and we may wonder that after this outbreak of his sentiments he should have agreed to further a scheme, which resulted in so meagre a fulfilment of the original intention.   It appears, however, that after this, the building was put up to competition, and at the earnest solicitations of a friend, he consented (quite contrary to his usual custom) to send in a new design.*   As a proof that a building worthy of Pugin's skill was at first contemplated, two views are annexed showing the size and grandeur of the church which was to have been erected on a scale worthy of

* While these pages are in the press Mr. A. J. Beresford Hope has published a very interesting book under the title of 'The Cathedral of the 19th Century.' He refers in this work to St. George's Cathedral, and points out very fairly its defects. Pugin was fully sensible of the mistakes he had made in this building, and always deplored the necessity which led to the rejection of his first design.

INTERIOR OF ST. GEORGE'S ROMAN CATHOLIC CATHEDRAL, AS ORIGINALLY PROPOSED BY PUGIN.

O. JEWITT. SC.

Pugin
1841

NORTH-WEST VIEW OF ST. GEORGE'S ROMAN CATHOLIC CATHEDRAL, AS ORIGINALLY DESIGNED BY PUGIN.

ancient times. There are in the church, as now built, amidst many beauties, defects which may be found in his other productions, arising from the rapidity with which he sketched his designs, and his never deigning to revise or modify them. Hence many crude notions were adopted, which would undoubtedly have undergone change had he exercised the patience required for revision. In this particular he might have learned much from the great artists of the middle ages, the very best of whom, however happy in their first sketches, did not rest satisfied till, by successive modification and grouping, they were convinced that no further improvements could be made. How fully do the sketches of Raphael illustrate this fact! what intense pains-taking they exhibit! And hence the excellence of the final result.

The annoyance to which Pugin was subjected by applications for designs to be executed from ridiculously insufficient funds, made him at times very irritable. A story is told of his once receiving a letter from a Roman Catholic prelate, requesting designs for a new church of the following description. It was to be ' *very* large,—the neighbourhood being *very* populous ; it must be *very* handsome,—a fine new church had been built close by ; it must be *very cheap*,—they were very poor, in fact had only £ — ; when could they expect the design ?' Pugin wrote in reply :—

' MY DEAR LORD—Say *thirty shillings* more, and have *a tower and spire* at once. A. W. P.'

Pugin's patience was often tried by the irresolute conduct of those who sought his professional services ; thus on being sent for by a noble lord, whose seat in Lincolnshire had been greatly injured, and partly destroyed by fire through the overheating of a stove, to advise him on the work of restoration, and suggest such improvements as might occur to him ; he at once pointed out what ought to be done, re-marking upon the bad taste yet remaining in the details of the portion of the house not destroyed, plainly intimating that the whole building should be re-constructed. Being interrupted occasionally by the noble proprietor asking, 'Well, what shall I do? what shall I do?' 'Do,' exclaimed Pugin, 'why put a barrel of gunpowder and blow up what remains, and when it is demolished then I'll tell you what to do;' a piece of advice not acted upon, and the house was restored in the same debased style, but not, as may be imagined, under the professional guidance of Pugin.

CHAPTER XIV.

Quits Salisbury and comes to London—At the same time commences
building a House and Church at his own expense at West Cliff,
Ramsgate—Description of the Church of St. Augustine—Loses his
second Wife—His presentiment of her approaching Death—Buries
her at St. Chad's Cathedral, Birmingham—His great Patron and
Employer, the Earl of Shrewsbury—His Lordship's remarks upon
Pugin's Works—Much assisted in his Buildings by Mr. Myers—His
first Meeting with Myers—Designs Alterations for Balliol College.

UPON quitting Salisbury in 1841, Pugin came to London, and took up his residence at Cheyne Walk, Chelsea. Here he resided some time, but he had previously purchased ground at the West Cliff, Ramsgate, and commenced building a house upon a much larger scale than the one he sold near Salisbury. He also began to build there a church at his own expense. This building, which occupied some years in construction, was advanced from time to time as he could spare the means from his yearly income. His desire was to build it in the most correct and solid manner, and in this he was successful. The church, as it now stands, consists of a nave, chancel, centre tower, south aisles, and transept. Everything about it is truthful. The exterior is faced with flint banded with courses of stone; the oak roofs are covered with ornamental Staffordshire tiles, the walls with ashlar; the chancel and Lady Chapel ceilings are panelled and emblazoned; the

floors laid with beautiful encaustic tiles; the altars
and tabernacle are elegantly designed and executed
in costly materials, the latter being entirely lined
with plates of silver gilt, and the rood screen and
stalls richly carved in oak. The font and cover are
of unusual beauty. The painted glass by Hardman
is excellent. Many of the fittings are yet wanting,
the church not having been completed before his
death, and for the present there are only temporary
seats and screens, without pretensions; but his family
and friends purpose to complete these accessories in a
manner worthy of the rest of the work.* While he
was at Chelsea he found opportunities of running
down to Ramsgate to advance these private works
of his own. It is to this building Pugin refers in the
passage which Ruskin so severely censures. He
never could have seen the church, or he would have
moderated his language. He had now another trial soon
to undergo; his wife, to whom he had been married
ten years, was attacked by a severe illness, and died
in August, 1844. Thus in the short space of about
twelve years he had become twice a widower.
Being now a member of the Roman Catholic Church, it
was unlikely that he should remove her remains for
interment to Christchurch. The place chosen for her
burial was the church of St. Chads, Birmingham, a
building which he had himself designed. Here the

* The cost of the church, land, and fittings, has been upwards of
£15,000. One gentleman, a great admirer of Pugin, has offered money
without limits for the completion of all that remains unfinished in the
Pugin Chauntrey.

THE CHURCH OF ST. AUGUSTINE, WEST CLIFF, RAMSGATE, FOUNDED BY PUGIN, TOGETHER WITH PUGIN'S RESIDENCE—THE GRANGE.

funeral took place, conducted with as much pomp and
ceremonial as he could command.

The Earl of Shrewsbury signified his intention of
being present by the following letter :—

'MY DEAR PUGIN,

'I am coming to St. Chads to pay my tribute
of affection and respect to you by attending the solemn
service, and in which we all feel so deep an interest.
Douglas comes with me, and young Bodenham returns.

'I hope you will allow me to see you after the sad
ceremony.   'Yours, &c.,

'SHREWSBURY.'

Nothing was wanting to give solemnity to the obsequies. Some bishops took part in the ceremony, and
by their presence showed the high respect in which
Pugin was held. When travelling from Derby a
short time before his wife's death, the author of
these pages met him at the railway station in a
state of the greatest agitation. He accounted for
it by mentioning, that he had been staying a few
days at Alton Towers, and on the last night had
twice dreamt that his wife was taken alarmingly
ill, and her life despaired of. Oppressed by these
omens he resolved at once to go to town, and leaving Alton Towers for this purpose was met by a
special messenger, urging him to come home instantly
if he wished to see his wife again alive. He was now
on his journey back, and in this instance his presentiment was indeed realized; for though on reaching

home his wife still lived, she was in a state of insensibility, unable to recognize him, and died within a short time after his return. In conversation during the journey he constantly expressed his belief that he should find his wife dead, though when he parted from her a few days previously, she was in tolerable health.

Although suffering greatly from his severe loss he is said to have found consolation in the solemn rites of the Catholic church and the prayers offered up for the repose of her soul.

About this time Pugin may be said to have reached the height of his professional career. His house at Chelsea became a place of great resort, especially by a certain section of his artistic friends, and in their society many a delightful evening was passed, enlivened by his wit and brilliant conversation.

It was not only on matters of art that he was consulted, for the great revivalist was at this time in constant communication with the leaders of the high church movement, and doubtless the recognition of his principles in art was, to many, the bridge which first led them to join the Church of Rome; but, strange as it may appear, these afterwards became the very men who formed the vanguard of his antagonists, and who seem to have taken the greatest delight in destroying that work which they, in common with Pugin, at one time considered of so much importance. Not to break the thread of these memoirs, it will be necessary that this delicate question should be treated by one better versed in the matter than the writer of these pages;

he has therefore accepted the assistance of a Roman Catholic gentleman, who, in contributed chapters, will set forth the results of this fierce and important controversy which marked an era in Pugin's life, and will give an insight into his great theological knowledge, his character and religious principles, too important to be passed over by a biographer who is not indifferent to the main springs of action.

Although much courted in the highest intellectual circles, Pugin's dislike to this kind of life was rooted too deeply to be easily overcome; he therefore determined to return at the earliest possible period to St. Lawrence, the spot where he passed his early life, previous to the death of his aunt, Miss Welby. Visiting the Isle of Thanet for this purpose, he happened to find land for sale on the West Cliff at Ramsgate, a portion of which he immediately purchased, which is the site now known as 'The Grange, St. Augustine's,' intending to build a house of the simplest possible character: this idea, however, was much modified at the request of his wife, who induced him to erect a building in some way commensurate with his present position. Here he appears to have led the life of almost monastic regularity. His constant practice was to be in his private chapel at six o'clock; and as sure as the church bell tolled the Angelus, so sure might be heard the withdrawal of the four heavy external bolts which fastened the door of the chapel. Here it was his custom to say a few private prayers and make an offering of his forthcoming work to God.

N

After this he worked in his library until half-past seven, at which time the bell tolled for morning prayers, which he always said habited in a cassock and surplice; this was followed by breakfast, which seldom lasted more than seven minutes. At eight o'clock on feast days he always heard mass in the adjoining church. · He then worked until one o'clock, when, punctual to a moment, he dined. His fare was of the simplest description, neither taking wine nor malt liquor. This meal lasted but a quarter of an hour.

After dinner he generally inspected his buildings, and visited his only pupil and afterwards son-in-law, Mr. John H. Powell.

In the afternoon he resumed his work, which was often enlivened by the visits of a few of his confidential friends and admirers.

He was generally occupied with his post letters until nine o'clock, after which Pugin amused himself preparing designs for his own buildings until ten, when Compline was sung in his own private chapel.

The last hour of this busy day was devoted to the study of historical and theological works; Collier, Lingard, Dugdale, Stow, and Du Caunge being amongst his most favourite authors.

It may be here remarked that on his return from town he invariably had answered the whole of his letters, having written them in the railway carriage.

He had an intense and holy horror of all charity

balls, dinners, ecclesiastical and pious entertainments, bazaars, lotteries, &c., so much so that he never contributed to anything of the kind. Yet Pugin's fundamental charity was unbounded; it may be said that he was literally the father of the poor and shipwrecked sailor, as well as of the indigent of the towns in which he happened to live.

In his generosity he spared neither money nor personal exertion, and relieved all, without distinction of country or religion. For this end he had in his hall a chest filled with entire suits of clothes, and one of his greatest pleasures in life was to send away clothed and fed those who came to him ragged and hungry. His active benevolence originated the Sailors' Infirmary at Ramsgate, the embryo of which was to be found in two small houses he hired in King-street, where he engaged nurses to attend the fever-stricken sailors who were left destitute in port.

This effort attracted the attention of his fellow-townsmen, who generously raised the present infirmary, to which Pugin handsomely subscribed.

He was idolized by the workmen, and in fact by all those who were in his service, notwithstanding the severe discipline he so rigorously enforced, for in spite of his kindness of heart he was not what may be termed an indulgent man.

The following incident is characteristic. Visiting one Sunday afternoon the captain of his lugger, who had sprained his leg, and finding him destitute of what he considered necessary for his comfort, he at once returned home, and finding no man about the place he sallied forth, to the astonishment of all who met him, with a mattress, blankets, &c., on his shoulder, and a bag of provisions in his hand, for the use and comfort of the damaged sailor.

On another occasion when two hundred German emigrants were detained in port by stress of weather this thoughtful and kind-hearted friend of the friendless not only attended to their corporeal wants, but at his own expense invited the priest from the German chapel in London to come down and look after their spiritual necessities. On the morning of their departure, a deputation of thirty of their principal men waited upon him, and being unable to make themselves understood, their chief and would-be spokesman, threw himself on the ground and placed his head under Pugin's foot in token of gratitude, and as an expression of homage towards their kind-hearted benefactor.

While living at Ramsgate his love for cruising in the Channel was easily gratified; yet he did not sail for pleasure only, but was always ready in the roughest weather to put out to sea and aid in the rescue of crews whose vessels were cast upon the Goodwin Sands. The only social entertainments he gave were at Christmas and on twelfth nights, when he would collect a few friends and invest them in ancient costumes, personating the different characters they assumed : the king and queen were splendidly got up, and some acting indulged in ; after which there was a handsome repast.

He was sometimes very amusing by the way in which he issued his invitations, as the following letters illustrate. Desiring to collect some friends at his house he adopted this form :—

'The humble petition of the inhabitants and so-journers of St. Augustine's, Ramsgate.

'Whereas on the Feast of the Epiphany forth-coming, commonly called Twelfth Day, divers revels are to be held at St. Augustine's ; and whereas much of contentment and joy of the said revels would be lost if Mr. J. Thornton of Sturmy be not present to assist thereat ; the petitioners therefore most humbly pray that he will not fail to come, together with all belonging to him. God save the Queen !

'Signed, A. WELBY PUGIN, JANE PUGIN, E. B. DANIEL, KEZIA HERBERT, ANNE PUGIN, J. R. HERBERT, J. H. POWELL, A. HERBERT, CUTHBERT W. PUGIN, CATHARINE PUGIN, MARY PUGIN, EDWARD W. PUGIN, A. HERBERT.'

Fearing lest his friend should disappoint him or leave some members of his family at home, he writes—

' MY DEAR THORNTON,

  ' From what Edward says I have every reason
to hope and expect that you will act honestly, and
come on Saturday. We shall expect you by the train
which gets in at ten minutes past six. Tea ready—
good fires. Why is one of your little girls left
behind? Pray bring her. It will make me unhappy
if you don't; for it will be a great grief for her to be
left behind, and we have plenty of room for her; so
now do bring her with you, and let her enjoy herself at Xtmas. The more the merrier. I am your
sincere friend,

        ' A. WELBY PUGIN.'

  These letters show great good nature, and were quite
in keeping with his generous disposition. He invariably illustrated his letters with some marginal
sketches, admirably expressed by a few spirited
touches. The following note is an instance of the
kind :—

' MY DEAR THORNTON,

  ' I find Christmas Day comes on Monday, so
of course you must all come here on Saturday, by
which means we shall have the benefit of another day
out of you (Capital!). I could not in conscience allow
you to travel on Sunday; so Saturday afternoon, by
the six o'clock train, we shall expect you.

on arrival.

'Remember us kindly to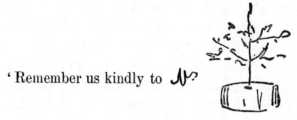

'Yours very truly,
'A. W. Pugin.'

Pugin suffered some annoyance at the period of the celebrated Durham letter, when Lord J. Russell protested against the sub-division of the country into more Papal ecclesiastical divisions. The boys greatly enraged him by chalking 'No Popery' on his walls and doors, and some unhappy lads were severely cuffed and kicked when unluckily caught in the act.

His professional practice now still increased, especially amongst the Roman Catholics. Among his greatest patrons was the late Earl of Shrewsbury, who employed him extensively at Alton Towers and Cheadle. The several letters given in the former pages, show the friendly intercourse which subsisted

between them. He was wont to cite the church of
Cheadle and its accompanying buildings as amongst
the most successful of his undertakings. A friend having asked him, on one occasion, whether there was any
building executed under his superintendence which he
considered free from defects, he replied, ' Yes, St. Giles
Cheadle ; I don't think there is any fault there.' This
remark being repeated a few years afterwards to Lord
Shrewsbury, he smiled and said, ' He won't say that
now though ; he abuses it as much as everything else
that he has done.' At Cheadle there certainly could
be no excuse from want of funds, his lordship appear-
ing to have given him carte blanche. For richness
of colour and general decoration the church has no
equal in this country, if perhaps we except the new
church of All Saints, Margaret Street, London. But
what Pugin had a right to complain of was, that when
he first had to execute the design he was ignorant
of the sum which was to be placed at his disposal ;
the building being commenced as a parish church
only, with a suggested outlay of £5000, whereas afterwards the expenditure was increased, and the character of the building entirely changed, and made to
assume a degree of dignity and richness never previously thought of. Undoubtedly these buildings
attest the consummate skill of the artist. In design,
choice of material, and execution, the master mind is
visible.

Perhaps it is hardly fair, in awarding the well-earned
commendation these works deserve, to omit the mention

of the art-workmen to whom Pugin was indebted for the successful way in which his designs were executed ; and foremost must in justice be mentioned the name of Mr. Myers, the eminent builder, to whom Pugin in all cases entrusted the execution of his works when he was not overruled by his employers.

The way in which Pugin first fell in with him was singular. Pugin became acquainted with Myers at Beverley. He was then a working man in that town, and while Pugin was sketching at the Minster, rendered him some assistance in procuring ladders and scaffolding to enable him to reach the lofty portions of the building, manifesting much interest in Pugin's proceedings ; but here their acquaintance for a time ended.

It happened, however, that Myers, and other builders, were invited a few years afterwards to tender for the erection of a Roman Catholic church at Derby. On going to the town to see the plans, he found, (as is frequently the case,) that in all probability a local builder would be selected, there being a strong feeling in favour of employing a native tradesman.

Determined, however, to obtain fair play, he desired an interview with the architect, and to his surprise found it was Pugin whom he had previously known. Pugin quickly recognized in Myers the enthusiastic mason who had taken such interest in what he was doing at Beverley, and had there rendered his help. Rushing to him he clasped him in his arms, exclaiming, 'My good fellow, you are the very man I

want, you shall execute all my buildings;' a promise
which he nearly kept to the letter : for of the numerous
edifices executed from his designs, of which forty-two
were churches, the greater number were built by
Myers. Pugin knowing how imperfectly builders were
acquainted with the true spirit of mediæval work, was
glad to meet a man of energy like Myers; who with
admirable tact gathered about him a body of young
workmen, and they being impressed with the true principles, soon became efficient auxiliaries. It is entirely
owing to the praiseworthy exertions of Mr. Myers that
so many competent carvers, both of wood and stone,
are now to be found. He spared no pains in obtaining
casts and directing them to proper models for studies,
not with a view to their making servile copies of ancient examples, but that they might imbibe *the feeling
and spirit* belonging to mediæval art, and throw like
expression into their own productions. We must also
here mention that Mr. Hardman devoted himself to
Pugin from the commencement of his career, and
brought both men and money to aid him in his work.

Being now looked upon as the highest authority in
all matters relating to mediæval art, his professional
assistance was much sought by those who were engaged
in any private or public works executed in the style of
the middle ages.

The fellows of Balliol College, Oxford, contemplating
some extensive additions to their College, applied to
him for designs, and he submitted a very beautiful set
of drawings, which met their entire approval. But

they were not adopted, owing to the refusal of the then master, Dr. Jenkyns, to permit the employment of a Roman Catholic architect. His plans were therefore discarded, and a great opportunity lost of achieving a really magnificent work. Two clergymen calling one morning at his house at Chelsea asked to see these plans. He had been at work on them for a fortnight only, but they found not merely the usual architectural drawings for a new chapel, master's house, gateway and rooms, but large perspective drawings of all these in water colours —interiors as well as exteriors—lining the entire walls of his room. Not content with these, he was then amusing himself with filling a book with the most beautiful finished outlines of all these drawings. This book he designed for a present to Mr. George Ward, the fellow of the College to whom he owed his appointment as architect to the new buildings.

He was at work standing, stooping to the table. When asked why he didn't give the mere mechanical part of his working drawings to a clerk to do, ' Clerk, my dear sir, clerk, I never employ one ; I should kill him in a week.' And true it was that he had gone down to Oxford, stayed a few days, formed his plan in his own mind, and then returned to London to get out the whole of these elaborate and detailed drawings in a fortnight with his own hands. The new buildings were ultimately erected upon a more limited plan by Mr. Salvin, and the chapel, a still more recent structure, by Mr. Butterfield.

Though Pugin was not much professionally em-

ployed at Oxford, yet he frequently visited friends at
the colleges; and his opinions on architecture were
held in great estimation by a large body of the members of the University. On one of his journeys to
Oxford he became acquainted with Bartley the comedian in the following curious manner. Bartley having
buried a son at Oxford, was anxious to place an
obituary window in St. Mary's Church as a memorial.
The incumbent having made an appointment to meet
him in the church, Bartley left London early in the
morning and found himself in the railway carriage opposite a very roughly-dressed young man, with a two-foot
rule sticking out of his pocket, and other indications
that he was in some way connected with building.
They entered into conversation, and Bartley soon
found that his odd companion was a person of no
ordinary character. On reaching Oxford, Bartley went
to the church, where the incumbent was waiting his
arrival, expecting momentarily the artist whom he
wished to design the window for Bartley's approval.
It was then within a few minutes of the time for
morning service, the clergyman being robed and waiting the verger's summons, when in rushed Pugin,
whom the comedian immediately recognized as his odd
travelling companion.

'It is too late now,' observed the clergyman; 'we
must defer the consideration of this matter till after
the service.'

'Why not now?' exclaimed Pugin, looking at his
watch. 'There is plenty of time—ten minutes or

more to spare.' Then, pulling out his sketch-book, began, addressing Bartley, ' Now what is your son's name ? Thomas ? Ah, Thomas : subject, incredulity of St. Thomas, &c. ;' asking, with his usual rapidity, a number of other questions, sketching all the time. In less than a quarter of an hour he had made two or three masterly sketches for the subject of the window, to the astonishment of all present.

The only building erected by Pugin in Oxford is the new entrance gateway to Magdalen College. But few works were in contemplation about this period at the University, otherwise, in all probability, Pugin would have been consulted; for it would be a slur upon the heads of houses to suppose that they would have rejected the services of an architect, confessedly then the most competent in the practice of the mediæval styles, simply on account of his being a Roman Catholic. For the credit of the University it is hoped that the decision of the late Master of Balliol College may be viewed as an exceptional case.

CHAPTER XV.

Consulted by the late Lord Stuart de Rothesay at High Cliff—Leaves
the place hastily—Contemplates a third Marriage, but meets with a
disappointment—Publishes a Pamphlet in vindication of his conduct
entitled, 'Statement of Facts '—Extracts from Pamphlet.

CURIOUS stories are told of Pugin in reference to
his independent spirit while corresponding with employers or directing their works. The following specimen is an instance of this. The late Lord Stuart de
Rothesay, having found some beautiful remains of
a conventual building in the south of France, and
being about to build a residence on the south-east
coast near Christchurch, determined to purchase the
materials, have them removed to England, and use
them as far as they could be made applicable to the
design of a new and large mansion.

The site chosen by his Lordship was a part of the
high cliff facing the Isle of Wight. Near this spot
there had formerly been a house belonging to the Earl
of Bute, the celebrated minister, which, owing to the
encroachment of the sea on that part of the coast, was
literally by degrees washed into it. Still Lord Stuart
thought that by draining the land springs and taking
other precautions he could prevent the spread of

further mischief. Acting on this belief, he began the erection of a stately pile at such a distance from the edge of the cliff as was thought sufficient to leave a good margin to the buildings for ages to come. But notwithstanding all precautions the drainage has not been so effectual as to save the cliff from disruption. By the expansion of frozen land springs after severe frosts, and the encroachment of the sea, land-slips still occasionally take place.

Lord Stuart not being perfectly satisfied with the design of the building, which was being conducted under the superintendence of the late Mr. Donthorn, and desiring to obtain the mature judgment of Pugin, invited him to High Cliff to act as his consulting archi-tect. He at once assented, and repaired to High Cliff to inspect the works.

Arriving in the afternoon, he engaged himself busily in examining all that was going on ; soon made him-self master of his subject, and with his usual rapidity, before the close of the day had prepared sketches for Lord Stuart's approval.

After dinner he exhibited his plans, entering into explanations, and pointing out all the alterations which he considered indispensable. His suggestions, unfor-tunately, did not fall on such willing ears as he ex-pected. Lord S. had spent large sums in the work already done, and was not disposed to pull down heavy stonework just finished ; and some amount of demoli-tion was quite necessary to meet Pugin's views. After much discussion, therefore, they separated. Lord

Stuart intending to resume the subject on the next morning, but in this he was disappointed. To meet Pugin's convenience, an early breakfast hour was appointed for the next day, and at the time fixed some surprise was expressed that he did not appear. Inquiry being made, it was discovered that Pugin had risen at six o'clock, taken his carpet bag in hand, walked some distance to a little wayside inn, and thence taken his departure by coach to London, without previously giving the slightest intimation of his intention to any one in the house. Thus terminated his connexion with Lord Stuart de Rothesay. All this abruptness arose from the simple circumstance that his employer did not at once adopt his recommendations. Probably this discourtesy would not have been shown at an earlier period of his career, but he had now obtained such a professional standing that he could afford to disregard giving offence.

Pugin was now looking forward to enter the marriage state a third time. It was at Alton Towers that he first met Miss Amherst, niece of Lord Shrewsbury, and was soon captivated by her fascinating manners and her evident admiration of his talents and conversation. A proposal of marriage followed, but many obstacles were interposed to prevent the union. The disappointment was a heavy blow to him. On the advice of the parents, Miss Amherst broke off the engagement, and afterwards retired to a convent. This, however, was not so severe a trial to him as a later event of a somewhat similar kind, which, having already been made public, can hardly be passed over without some notice in these pages. Pugin had been a second time widower for some years, when certain circumstances led to his again forming an ardent attachment to a lady of position, of considerable accomplishments, and of views on most important subjects which were congenial with his own. The attachment becoming mutual, marriage engagements were solemnly exchanged between the parties. On Pugin's side, various characteristic and costly preparations had been made for the solemnization of the nuptials, when the connection was abruptly broken off, to the great distress of both, by the interposition of the lady's family. The circumstances attending this affair forms a curious episode in the story of Pugin's life, to which it is impossible to do justice, without laying before the reader a ' STATEMENT OF FACTS ' relating to it, printed by Pugin for his own justification. This paper is here given *in extenso,* with the omission, only, of some passages at the close of the pamphlet in which Pugin reflected in strong terms of vituperation on the conduct of the lady's father and friends. Allowance may be made for the use of even intemperate language by a man of Pugin's stamp, when smarting under a keen sense of the injury inflicted : but it would be unpardonable to give them further circulation.

A Statement of Facts, &c.

' It is with feelings of the deepest pain that I put forth the statement contained in the following pages ;

and nothing but imperative necessity would compel me to adopt such a course. I must beg to state most emphatically, that, in so doing, I am not actuated by any vindictive feeling towards the unhappy person who has caused me such bitter distress; but the very extraordinary circumstances connected with this case having already given rise to reports prejudicial to my reputation, and as it is probable that, in the absence of any authentic account, the real circumstances will be still further misrepresented, I have, after full deliberation, considered it most advisable to adopt this course, as the only means by which I could make a public justification of my conduct.

'I purpose to confine myself, as nearly as possible, to a mere statement of facts; as, in the present state of my feelings, were I to indulge in making comments, I might be betrayed into some expressions which would not accord with that spirit of charity which we are bound to maintain even towards those from whom we receive the deepest injuries; and which it has been my most fervent prayer and endeavour to preserve all through this most trying business.

'I became acquainted with Miss L— nearly three years since, when she came with her parents on a visit to Ramsgate; but our intimacy did not commence till the winter of 1846: at that time I was suffering from a most severe illness, produced by anxiety of mind; and Miss L—, who was staying in the neighbourhood, came frequently to pass a great part of the day at my residence, and her extreme kindness and attention

contributed, in no small degree, to my ultimate recovery. It was then I had an opportunity of appreciating the many admirable qualities she possessed; and,
notwithstanding all that has subsequently happened,
I feel bound to say that my opinion, as regards her
talents and accomplishments, remains unchanged.
When I discovered, in addition to her just appreciation
of art, that her mind was strongly imbued with Catholic principles, I considered her one of the most admirable persons I had ever seen; and I speedily became
strongly attached to one who held such a communion
of ideas with myself on so many important subjects.

'As she was exceedingly anxious to obtain information on various points of Catholic doctrine and discipline, I not only explained them to her verbally, but I
supplied her with various Catholic works explanatory
of the faith, both while at Ramsgate, and also after her
return to H—.

'Early in the spring I left England on a continental
journey; and while abroad Miss L— frequently corresponded with me, principally on matters connected
with religion. In a letter dated May 20, she writes
thus: "I do love every thing Catholic; and nothing
gives me more pain than the things I hear against it:
so much bitterness, and so many things which I know
to be utterly false. At the same time this very thing
makes me dread to look forward; for if people are so
inveterate against Catholics in general, what would be
the consequence if they were to discover that I am
leaning that way?" &c.

' *Extract.*

' " How magnificent the service at Amiens must have been! What would I not have given to have the same privilege! I never wished to be a Catholic more than on Easter Sunday : how much we lose in the Protestant Church! I really hardly know what I wish or feel. I am convinced you are right; and my convictions are supported by what I read at night : pray for me that I may have perseverance and courage," &c.

' *Extract.*

' " Your welcome letter from Avignon was forwarded to me here. I prize your letters above *all* others; you cannot think how I long for them; your description of the churches, and other antiquities you have seen are most interesting. I wish you were not so kind to me, for I never can be grateful enough to you ; you are my best friend, and I would confide anything to you. I have just finished Vicentius de Lirens against heresy, which I like very much : it seems to me the Church of England is so inconsistent ; it receives some things and rejects others which have equal authority. We had the curate of Broadstairs' letter sent us the other day ; and I really felt more convinced of the view which the Catholic Church takes of the subject after I had read it than before." '

' *Extract.*

' " I long to have a talk with you : there is no one to whom I can open my mind ; and I hear so much against the Catholic Church, that it often distresses me exceedingly. I shall be obliged to attend a Bible meeting this evening at Dover, where I am now staying for a few days. I was at one at C— Castle the other day. I never liked the Society, and of course I dislike it more. I wish you could have heard the poor arguments against Popery that one of the speakers brought forward the other night. I declare, even with the *little* that *I* know on the subject, I could see how very absurd they were."

'There were many letters of the same tendency; but these were destroyed at Miss L—'s request, in a letter she sent July 21, which will be referred to hereafter.

'Immediately after my return from the continent, Miss L— came to Ramsgate, and she then told me that she was quite convinced of the truth of the Catholic religion, and that she could not bear to continue in her present position. I represented to her the vast importance of the step she was about to take; and although, on one hand, she was bound in conscience to confess the truth openly, yet there was a fear that a premature declaration, which she might not have the courage to act up to, would be productive of more evil than good. However, her resolution remained unchanged; and in a letter dated July 19, she writes:

' " I thought, on the whole, the best thing I could do was to let the change that had taken place in my sentiments be known at once. Oh, the courage it required to do so! My eldest brother was furious, and declared he would quarrel with me if I did not give up reading those accursed books; but papa was so grieved, and yet so mild, that my heart bled for the pain I have given him and darling mamma. If I did not feel firmly convinced I had learnt the truth, I would ease their minds at once, by declaring I would give up what they call errors; but I could not do this conscientiously."

' *Postscript in Pencil.*

"Matters are worse than ever: believe nothing you hear except from me. I may not be able for some time to *keep* to my opinions *openly,* but I do not think I shall ever inwardly lose them. I suffer such grief, I hardly know how to bear it. I know where I should find peace ; that is, in the communion of *the* Church, and *this shall be the end.*"

' Two days after this, I received a letter written in pencil, and under the greatest distress of mind, as the following extract will show : " However painful it may be, I must NEVER write to you or any body belonging to you again. My opinions regarding the Church are the same, and it seems very improbable they should ever be altered; but as to any further communication, it must cease, cost what it may. I beg and entreat of you *never* to write to me, or any body connected with me; or, if you do, you will ensure me the greatest misery ; and please to destroy any letters you have of mine," &c.

' Up to this period, I had never mentioned my affection for Miss L— to herself or anybody else, although I had loved her in secret for a considerable time ; and it is worthy of remark, that her religious change was accomplished without any knowledge of my sentiments towards her, by which she might have been biassed.

' The receipt of this letter distressed me exceedingly, but I determined to comply with the desire expressed in it ; and *I did not write, or take any means of further communication with Miss L—, till she recommenced the correspondence of her own accord some months later.* And I can most solemnly affirm that, had it not been renewed by her, I should never have written, and all the misery which her subsequent conduct has inflicted on me would have been avoided.

' In the latter part of October, the evening post delivery brought a letter from S— in Miss L—'s handwriting. I was so astonished and delighted, that I hardly dared to break the seal, for fear of a disappointment ; but the contents were most satisfactory. She began by stating that she feared I should despise her for her weak conduct, but that she could no longer refrain from writing ; that her opinions were unchanged in every respect, although her friends had succeeded in making her, for the time, *a hypocrite in religion.* She concluded by naming a day on which she could receive a reply, and that she should count the hours till it came. In a postscript, she strictly charged me to burn the letter, which I did ; but the following extract from my own reply will fully prove the arrival of the letter, and the nature of its contents.

'*Extract from my Letter in reply.*

' " My dear Miss L—,

' " I can hardly express the delight I felt at again beholding your handwriting; it seemed almost too good to be true, and I hardly dared to break the seal, for fear of a disappointment. After that dreadful letter you sent me from H—, I lost all hope. I read it over and over again, but you did not leave me a chance of replying; and, fearing I should only make matters worse, I was reluctantly compelled to remain silent. But I was terribly cut up; I could do nothing for some time ; and, excepting that unhappy matter which I explained to you, I never felt anything so much. When you abandoned me, I felt more lonely than ever; and, a few days after, your books and seal were left by a servant without message. I knew not what to think, and I was racked by perplexing ideas. However, I never ceased to pray night and morning for you, even under all these discouragements; and I am now indeed rewarded by seeing your handwriting and hearing from you. I felt sure you could not be a consenting party to such unkindness, and I resolved to bear patiently any insult or reproach for your sake, and to remain perfectly quiet. Do not for an instant suppose that I despise you for the unhappy part you have been compelled to take ; it is *impossible* for me to despise you, or even think unworthily of you; but I am indeed grieved at what you have suffered, and I cannot sufficiently deplore such premature resolution which you were so ill able to sustain. I do indeed feel and sympathise with you in all the difficulties of your position, for they are many, and hard to contend with. I well know all you suffer, having gone through the same ordeal, though under less trying circumstances; but I dare not conceal from you that your present position is one of extreme danger. You have made a profession of your faith, and you are now practically denying God before men. It is far safer to remain in ignorance of the truth, than, having known it, to fall back on error, even in appearance. I know you will forgive me speaking so strongly; but I have seen such terrible examples of persons falling from the verge of truth into a state of indifference, that I feel it a sort of sacred duty, to warn you of your danger; and surely the letter you sent to your aunt (Mrs. B——) was a positive denial of the Catholic faith. I am willing to believe that this was extorted from you by terror and distress of mind; and certainly the trial was a severe one—most severe; and even the strongest might have fallen under such circumstances. But after this, you must forgive me for urging on you greater resolution for the future, &c.

'"I have burnt your letter, according to your wish, and will only write when you direct; but do not desert me again. I have *really suffered* in mind and body from that dreadful letter you sent me from H——; it seemed so unkind, so unlike yourself, that it com-

pletely upset me.   However, I can freely forgive all
the pain you have caused me, if it was only for the
pleasure of receiving your letter from S——.

 ‘ “ Ever yours most devotedly,

        ‘ “ A. W. Pugin.”

 ‘ To this I received a reply, in which Miss L—
stated, that my letter, not having arrived the day she
expected, she was in great distress, fearing I should not
reply to her.   She also excused herself as to denying
God before men, on the ground that the true God was
worshipped in the Protestant Church, &c.

      ‘ *My reply to the above.*

 ‘ “ My dear Miss L—,

   ‘ “ I cannot conceive how my last letter was
behind time ; but how could you for one instant imagine I should not write ? You would have had a letter
by return, only I was obliged to act by your instructions. You quite mistake what I meant by your denying God before men.   I did not mean God (*per se*) ;
for the Jews acknowledge the true God, but they deny
Him in the Second Person of the Holy Trinity, One
Lord.   Persons may deny God in His Church and in
His ordinances ; this is what I mean.   The Church
being founded by Him, and supported by His Divine
power, is to be obeyed as the *vox Dei* ; if persons
therefore, either through fear of human considerations,
or for the sake of temporal advantages, neglect the
observances of the Church, and to profess the faith,

they certainly deny God before men, however they may think and feel internally; and those who persevere in such a course must undoubtedly meet with dreadful punishment in the world to come; for our Lord says, 'He who denieth Me before men, I will deny him before the Father.' And, after all, what need we really fear but the *anger of God?* If the primitive martyrs could bear all the dreadful tortures inflicted on them for the sake of the faith, should we not go through the comparatively easy trial of the displeasure of relatives and contempt of the world? Do not imagine that I am underrating all you have suffered in this matter; but everything is comparative, and, by the side of the trials of all the early Christians, all that we have to undergo is light," &c.

'It should be remembered that I addressed these exhortations to Miss L—, as I believed, from her own statements, that she was inwardly fully convinced of every Catholic doctrine, but hesitated to profess her faith openly, for fear of the displeasure of her relatives; under these circumstances I was not only justified in the course I pursued, but positively bound in conscience so to act. I explained to her the vast distinction between a person in her position and a conscientious Protestant, who worshipped God with sincerity of heart, to the best of his knowledge. In a subsequent letter I wrote as follows:

' " *I do not seek to precipitate you;* but remember I have already told you that those who know the truth, and do not openly confess it, are in a most dangerous position. I have explained to you the doctrine of the Church relative to the salvation of Protestants; but this cannot apply to you. God hath visited you with His Divine grace; He has singled you out; He has enlightened you; He has called you to become a member of His holy Church on earth, and to enjoy eternal life in heaven; He has offered Himself to you in the Holy Eucharist; He has promised you His Holy Spirit in confirmation; He will enroll you in the communion of His Saints and faithful servants who have confessed Him from the beginning; He invites you to celebrate the mysteries of the Redemption, as they occur in the succeeding festivals of the year, and to partake of every privilege and blessing;— and yet you turn away, and allow yourself to be driven, Sunday after Sunday, to a miserable mockery of a service, established by that Church-destroying Knox and his associates; and you have no other, or better, reason to give for this inconsistency, than the fear of displeasing your relatives. But will they save you? Were they the most powerful nobles of the land, could they weigh one grain in the balance of Divine justice? Remember, when great graces are vouchsafed, much is expected, and most certainly much will be required from you."

' This correspondence continued for some time; Miss L— always writing in the kindest and most confidential manner, until feeling that it was neither sincere nor honourable to go on without fully declaring my sentiments to her, and being about to undertake a journey to Hornby Castle, I wrote to her to propose an interview at E—, to which she consented in a letter, from which the following is an extract:

' " I have just received your most welcome letter. How delightful it would be to see you in Edinburgh next week! The only way that I think it would be possible to see you, would be at Aitcheson's the confectioner's, a shop at the west-end of Queen Street, at half-past one o'clock, on Tuesday next, the 30th. But you see I could not positively say that I could be there, as, although no other engagement of *any sort* would keep me away, yet supposing it should be a very bad day, although *I* should not mind the weather, my brother and sister would not let me go out," &c.

' In the same letter, in reply to a complaint of mine about being frequently called away from my art to attend to domestic matters, she writes: " I wish I were so situated that *I* could prevent your having a *moment's* anxiety on such subjects; then my happiness would indeed be *perfect*."

' On receiving this letter, I immediately wrote the following reply, containing my proposal of marriage:

' *Reply and Proposal of Marriage, written Nov.* 26.
' " MY DEAREST MISS L—,
' " Do you think I would hesitate going three

times the distance on such a chance? I will not fail
to be at the place you mention on Tuesday; and
should you be prevented, I will remain about Edinburgh till I have the great delight of meeting you. I
would not miss you on any account, for there is no
one left whom I am so anxious to meet. From the
first moment I had the happiness of seeing you, I
found the greatest consolation and comfort in your
society; and I cannot describe the delight I felt when
you unfolded your sentiments to me on religion.
From that moment I really ventured to hope that you
were raised up by God to support me in my great
undertakings, and to become my guardian angel. I
must rely on your kind heart to forgive me, if I am
too presumptuous; but I cannot refrain from opening
my heart to you. I love you with all the intensity of
affection that a Christian man can love one who has a
perfect communion of soul and feeling with himself;
I know you possess every quality that could make a
home happy; and I do believe I could accomplish
double what I do at present, if I had the support of
your society, and the infinite consolation and comfort
of knowing that I possessed a being in whose affection
I could rely, and to whom I could communicate all
my ideas. At present I am desolate and miserable;
and when your sad letter came from H—, I felt as
if everything was cut from me. Your dear letter
from I— revived all my hopes; and I cannot
remain any longer, without laying before you the true
state of my heart. You know I am a sincere man,

and you will pardon the abruptness of this communication. I am well aware that I am soliciting you to make a great sacrifice in many respects; but I rely on the noble qualities of your mind; and I will not insult you by imagining that you would prefer the luxuries of fashionable society to the consolations of religion, and the comforts of domestic life. I will not attempt to disguise from you that objections will be raised against our union on different grounds; first, on religion; second, on my position; third, from my having already a family of children. Now, to reply to these: on the first, religion. With your opinions, you are bound in conscience not to allow any objections or opposition, even of parents, to prevent you occupying a position in which you can have the free exercise of the Catholic faith; and I need scarcely remind you that, as my wife, you would have comforts on this score which few can possess.

' " Secondly, although I am a professional man, yet it is a most glorious profession that I follow, and a far more honourable state than that of independent idleness. Moreover, unoccupied persons are apt to fall into a state of *ennui*, and to seek amusement in society instead of their home; and rely on it, if husband and wife are not all in all to each other, happiness is at an end. I mentioned to you once that my income averaged about —— a year; of this, I have made a rule to lay by —— for investments, and with the remainder to live and carry on my ecclesiastical buildings, &c.; while I can work—and by the blessing

of God I hope to do so for many years—I have, as
you see, a fine income; but if I were deprived of my
powers by illness, my fortune would be very small,
about —— in money, bringing me in —— a year.

‘ “ I have my freehold residence, and other property,
worth about —— more, but which does not bring in
any interest; however, I do not owe *one shilling*, and
I pay every week; and I would of course take means
to secure you a good independence. I lay all this
before you as I am in duty bound; for, of course, as
regards attendance and style of living, I fear you
would find a considerable change from your present
habits; and I must tell you sincerely and candidly,
no increase of fortune, consequent on my extending
business, would induce me to keep up a costly establishment, or indulge in luxurious living. According
to Catholic principles, every man is only a steward of
his wealth, for the expenditure of which he is answerable to God; and while so many souls require instruction, and so many bodies food and clothes, I dare not
waste my means on superfluities; and I hope you
have the same views on these points.

‘ “ Thirdly, as regards my family. I am willing to
grant that there are some evils to be feared; but, on
the other hand, as I once remarked to you, that the
experience which the father of a family has gained is
calculated to contribute, in no small degree, to the
comfort of a wife. Inexperienced persons are apt to
imagine that marriage is a mere love-romance; hence
they are disappointed with the realities of the state of

which they had no idea. Now, in my case, having already gone through all sorts of troubles and difficulties, I am better prepared to meet them; and I do believe, by the blessing of God, I could make you very happy. And now, my dearest Miss L—, I have stated my case, and considered all the difficulties, which I hope I have solved. I need not say with what anxiety I await a few lines from you; pray give me some comfort; at least let me know I have not incurred your displeasure, &c.,

'" Ever, dearest Miss L—,

'" Your devoted,

'" Augustus W. Pugin.

'"P. S.—What a horrible place you have named for our meeting—a confectioner's shop!! cheesecake and mock-turtle! The ruined abbey of Holy Rood would have been a far more appropriate spot."

'I proceeded, as arranged, to Edinburgh, where I met Miss L— according to her appointment; the interview was most satisfactory. And on my return I received a letter, in which she stated that she felt she must overcome any difficulties to become mine, and consented to be united to me.

'The matter of our union being thus agreed, the next point to arrange was the manner in which it could be best and most prudently accomplished. Although at that time I had not been unfortunate enough to come into contact with Mr. L—, yet, from

P

some circumstances that had occurred, I judged him to
be a man so deeply prejudiced against the Catholic
faith, that it was next to impossible that he should
consent to my union with his daughter.   Taking into
consideration that Miss L— was four-and-twenty years
of age, and foreseeing the danger of all that has since
happened, I was strongly in favour of a private
marriage.   I frequently wrote to Miss L— on this
point, warning her that in *marrying me she would have
to give up her family*, and that her father never would
consent, except by miracle.   She cannot possibly
plead want of consideration on this point, for half my
letters were on this subject.

' *Extract.*

' " *If you expect to obtain any sanction to our union
from your parents beforehand, you will be miserably
mistaken, and it will only be exposing me to a repetition
of all I have suffered before*, and if you abandon me, I
shall give up in despair.   I cannot tell you how I
suffered from that letter you sent me from H—,
although our relative position was so different from
what it is at present.   But *I could not bear it now*;
anything of the kind is too horrible; indeed, I will
not imagine you capable of forsaking me, or I should
work myself up to distraction."

' I also warned her of the loss she would sustain in
temporal matters by her marriage, not knowing that
she was entitled to one shilling in her own right.

' *Extract.*

' "Of course, in marrying me, *you will have to forego any expectation of temporal benefit, either from your parents or family*—that you must expect. But I trust to make ample amends on that score; and in itself it is not a question that can be balanced for one moment, either with your duty to God, on the score of religion, or even with respect to the acquisition of temporal happiness in the married state."

' *Extract from another Letter on the same subject, written in February.*

' "If you regard our troubles in a true light, you will see that they have been the means of testing the sincerity of our affection. Suppose, on the one hand, that, instead of making some sacrifice to become mine, I was a man of high worldly position,—what people would call a very advantageous match for you,—could I feel that *gratitude,* that *absolute obligation* of doing everything in my power to make you happy, which our present circumstances enjoin on me? Again, supposing that, in marrying you, I was to receive an accession of temporal goods, instead of incurring the sacred duty of making a suitable provision for your support, under any circumstances that may happen, could you feel so satisfied of the sincerity of my attachment as you must do at present?"

' It was at first arranged that our union should be private; but I was induced to concede this point contrary to my better judgment, in consequence of Miss L—'s assurances that she had the necessary fortitude to face her father, and, in case of his refusal, to act on her own responsibility.

' *Extract.*

' " I have been thinking that the best plan would be for me to be reconciled to the Catholic Church before I leave Edinburgh; and then, after I get home, I would tell papa and mamma that I was *engaged* to be married to you; they could not reproach me with having taken such a step without their knowledge, and they could never wish me to break my solemn promise to you; besides, as I should then be a Catholic, a great part of their objections would be removed. It strikes me that, although my plan requires an immense deal of courage on my part, yet it is the right one to pursue; however, I shall be guided by you, &c. But you may rest assured that, should anything occur to divulge our secret, *I shall stand firm as a rock;* nothing shall *move me or tempt me* to forsake one whom I *love* and *adore.* You are my all in all,—my only support and consolation."

' Trusting to these assurances, in an evil hour I gave my consent to the course that has been adopted, partly from the considerations advanced in her letter and partly from feeling that a private marriage could not be celebrated with the solemnity becoming a person of her position.

'On the 25th of January Miss L— sent me a formal written promise of marriage, the counterpart of one she received from me. The following is a true copy:

"I—, M—, Jan. 25, 1843.

'"In the name of the Father, and of the Son, and of the Holy Ghost. Amen. I, the undersigned, most solemnly promise to take Augustus Welby North-more Pugin, of S. Augustins, in the county of Kent, to be my wedded husband, according to the laws of Holy Church and of this realm, as soon as conveniently may be after the feast of Easter next forthcoming.

"Witness
    my hand
    and seal.   "S— H— S— L—"

'As soon as my union with Miss L— had been de-finitely arranged, I immediately proceeded to make the necessary arrangements, by altering and com-pleting my residence, making new furniture, plate, &c., and providing dresses, jewellery, &c., with the full knowledge and approbation of Miss L—.

'*Extract from a Letter, Feb. 7.*

'"I am full of work at the house, improving every-thing before you come, so that we shall have nothing to do but enjoy the place afterwards. I am panelling the best rooms, putting new stained glass into the windows, redecorating the ceilings, and the three cros-letts will not be forgotten. I am fitting out in every department, and I do trust everything will please you. You have no idea of the work we have to get done by Easter. I have between thirty and forty people working different ways. There are five at your jewellery at Birmingham; of course I cannot pretend to vie in intrinsic value with thousands of people; but no woman, not excepting the Queen, will have better ornaments, as regards taste, than you will."

'*Extracts from Miss L—'s Letters relative to her Dresses, &c.*

' "I will send you the pattern of the dress directly it comes home, and also the size of the bracelets,— how beautiful they will be! I see you are determined to lavish all your care and attention on me; and if it *were possible*, my love would be increased by your never ceasing kindness; but this is impossible, for I could not love you more ardently than I do," &c.

' *Extract* (*in an envelope containing a ring and piece of tape.*)

' " The ring is rather a tight fit for my third finger; a size larger would fit my second; the tape is the size of my head."

' " My dearest Augustus,

' "I send you the pattern of a dress; the piece of tape is the length of the skirt, the back, and where the pin is put, the length of the front; the slip of paper is the proper length of a bracelet. My own dearest, how much trouble you are taking on my account; I can never do enough to testify the love I have for you," &c.

'All the things made for her being of a most costly description and in the first style of ancient art, amounted to large sums of money—including the alterations, and various matters connected with this unhappy business, altogether more than two thousand pounds.

'And in the mean time Mr. J—, solicitor of Ramsgate, had prepared a deed of settlement, by my instructions, by which I made £5000 over to her absolutely, and my residence, with all its contents, worth at least, £8000 more, for her life, besides a life interest in other property; and thinking it might be a satisfaction to her family, I appointed her brother, Mr. E— L— one of the trustees. In all these arrangements, I was actuated by the one idea of providing, to the best of my ability, for an affectionate woman, whom I imagined to be giving up temporal advantages to unite herself with me.

'Every particular relative to these matters was communicated to Miss L—, who expressed herself more than delighted with all I was doing for her. She frequently expressed her anxiety to be received into the Catholic Church at Edinburgh during Lent, instead of waiting till after Easter, as I had proposed. From one of her letters, it would appear that her relatives had strong suspicions of her religious feelings, and were endeavouring to counteract them, for she writes as follows:

' " Papa sent us the other day a heap of sermons, &c. against Popery, one of them by my uncle in London, which my brother read to us on Sunday. It just contains the old abuse which has been answered so often, &c.

' " If Protestants would only allow themselves to investigate the Catholic religion as it really is, and leave their prejudices behind them, they could not fail in being convinced of its truth."

' On March 1, owing to her being likely to leave Edinburgh, she wrote to say it would not be right to defer her profession of the Catholic faith later than the week after next.

' My reply to this did not reach her so soon as I expected; and I received a second letter from her to the following effect:

" Why on earth do you not write to me? I have been in the greatest anxiety in consequence. Pray write by return of post; and direct to me at M— S—'s. Next Tuesday is the day I should like to be reconciled to the Church. I do not think it would be safe to defer longer. You must arrange everything, and let me know. I shall be wretched till I hear from you."

' I accordingly went down to Edinburgh on the

12th, found a letter at the hotel, appointing an interview in the country, near R—, for the 14th, where I met Miss L—, and settled all for her reception at St. Margaret's on Wednesday the 15th, which took place accordingly, in a most solemn and edifying manner.

'Immediately after the ceremony, she despatched a letter to her father, informing him of what had taken place, and likewise of her engagement to me; and in this letter she enclosed another, addressed to Mr. L— from myself, entreating his consent to our union.

'On Friday, by particular desire of Miss L—, I went to see her at Mr. I—'s, at I—, and met, on the part of her relatives, with the most inhospitable reception I ever experienced north of the Tweed, which was, however, more than compensated for by the affectionate kindness of my affianced wife.

'On Sunday, the 19th, she was actually prevented by Mr. I— from attending the Catholic service, as she states in the following letter, sent to me at Birmingham:

' " MY DEAREST AUGUSTUS,

' " I am sure no one can regret more than I do being prevented from going to church to-morrow. It is indeed dreadful to absent myself the first Sunday after my reconciliation to the Church. Were I at home I should *insist* on going, and must certainly next Sunday; no power on earth shall prevent my doing so, wherever I may be."

'In the same letter she returned her wedding-ring to be finished off, as it had been sent to her to try if it fitted exactly; and she informed me that she was going up to London by the express on Monday, and would write as soon as she arrived. I accordingly joined the train at Rugby, and came up to town at the same time.

'On Wednesday I received a letter from her, dated from I—; and its contents are remarkable, as they prove that she received very different treatment and language on her arrival to that she afterwards experienced:

' " They (my parents) will not *forbid* our union; but I think it probable they would wish it delayed for a little while. You cannot think how kindly and gently they treat me here. Write to me directly you get this; and do send me a rosary and the book you lent me; also tell me which days I am to fast, now I am in the London district. Will you also send me my little Missal papa took away, and my book of instructions? Oh, my dearest Augustus, what a comfort it is to have you to apply to!"

' In accordance with the wish expressed in this letter, I wrote to C— Park without obtaining an answer, and addressed four other letters without any result, as they were all intercepted. The utter uncertainty in which I was thus kept, as to what had befallen Miss L—, occasioned me the most intense anxiety; and on Fri-

day, not being able to endure the suspense any longer,
I went to I—, when I was informed that Miss L—
had gone down to H—, at least two days previous. I
immediately quitted London for Ramsgate, despatch-
ing a letter that evening to H—, stating the extreme
agony of mind I felt at the absence of all intelligence
from her, and entreating for some information.

'Late on the evening of Saturday, Mr. B— came to
my residence with a communication from Miss L—,
and my astonishment and anguish may be readily conceived on my perusing a document, in which she *declared, in the name of the holy and ever-blessed Trinity,
the blessed Virgin, and all the Saints, that she would
never, under any circumstances, unite herself in marriage
with me, or see me, or receive any letter or communication from me.* Such a document, coming suddenly
from a woman who was my affianced wife, whose previous letters and conduct breathed nothing but the
most devoted affection and fidelity, completely over-
powered me. I fell to the ground, and was for a time
deprived of my senses. Mr. B— was exceedingly
shocked and alarmed at the effect which his mission
had produced; and although at that time he was rather
prejudiced against me from the false and garbled
account he had heard of the affair at H—, yet he determined on making further investigation into the
facts; and I feel it a sacred duty to state that, from
the moment he was satisfied of the real truth, and of
my honourable conduct, he acted in the most firm, impartial, and kind manner possible; and indeed I may

say, that had it not been for his friendship and support, I should probably have sunk under these most trying circumstances.

'The next morning he came to my chamber, as I was confined to my bed, and having perused some of the most important documents relative to the affair, he was literally astounded by the facts, and horrified with the gross injury that would be inflicted on me by any violation of the marriage engagement; and he proceeded at once to H— to lay the facts of the case before the family.

'It will scarcely be credited that, on his return, this poor woman, who, only the evening previous, had sent a paper, as above, discarding me for ever, told her uncle that she would *crawl on her knees to Ramsgate; and sent me a message by him, that if I did not marry her, it would be her death.* Can it be considered surprising that, under these circumstances, I should resort to every expedient to see and communicate with her?

'The result of Mr. B—'s statement was the deputation by Mr. L—, of Mr. B—, the Rev. J. S—, and Mr. I—, of I—, to come over to Ramsgate and examine the documents mentioned by Mr. B—. They accordingly arrived at S. Augustine's on Monday afternoon; and on the supposition that I was dealing with honourable men, and that if I was able to make good my case, as stated by Mr. B—, the union would be permitted, I opened the whole matter, even to my own private resources and pecuniary affairs, without reserve; and even forwarded through Mr. S—, the most important letters of my own and Miss L— for her father's inspection. Certainly both Mr. S— and Mr. I— expressed themselves, while at my house, and afterwards at Mr. B—'s, as very favourably impressed with the result of the investigation, and when they left, there seemed every hope of a speedy adjustment of the difficulties. It is impossible to say how far they acted in accordance with their professions, but the result would lead me to infer a great deficiency in this respect. No letter arriving from H— in the course of two days, Mr. B— went over, and was received in a manner that would not induce him to repeat his visit; and the next day the letters sent from his home were returned unread, with a desire that no further communication might be sent from him. A most unaccountable proceeding, and strangely inconsistent with his appointment as one of the arbitrators of the case, made by Mr. L— himself.

'After a fortnight of most cruel anxiety and suspense, after all this investigation into my most private affairs, and after full proof of his daughter's being morally and legally affianced to me, I received a note of *literally three lines* from Mr. L—, merely stating he should oppose the marriage to the utmost; and, on my replying, my letter was returned unopened! All direct communication being thus cut off from H—, a most unsatisfactory correspondence was carried on by the medium of Mr. J. S—. In the commencement of the business I was disposed to give that gentleman credit for some sincerity and good feeling; but I soon discovered that he was as determined, and perhaps a more dangerous opponent, than his violent brother. It appeared to me that he wrote against time. Half his letters were written to say that he could not find leisure to write, such was the pressure of his parochial duties. A confirmation and a religious tea-party served him as an excuse for three weeks; and between apologising for omissions, and proposing vexatious objections, he managed to eke out the time, which I conceive was employed by those at home to harden Miss L— for the very unfeeling and disgraceful part she was to act towards me.

' At length, in a very off-hand note, in which he rather impudently told me that the immediate resignation of my pretensions was only a due and proper reparation for the pain *I* had caused the family, was enclosed a note in Miss L—'s hand-writing, addressed to her uncle, but intended to be forwarded to me. It was to the following effect :

' " That she was deeply grateful to him for all the kind interest he took in her welfare; and as she was resolved not to fulfil her engagement, she begged him to let me know that any further *intrusion* (sic) on my part, or on that of my friends, would be exceedingly offensive to her," &c.'

*　　*　　*　　*　　*

Many of Pugin's friends will be of opinion that this paper does credit both to his head and his heart.

It was printed only for private circulation, and a man of even less ardent temperament than Pugin might perhaps be excused for taking such a step to set himself right in the estimation of his friends under circumstances so painful. But the ' Statement of Facts ' must speak for itself, and the general reader will form his own judgment upon it. At the same time, it must be remembered that we have no counter-statement, nothing in writing from Miss L—'s friends, which discloses their reasons for the strong aversion entertained to the match. It may, however, be gathered from the ' Statement ' that their objections were mainly based on religious grounds.

CHAPTER XVI.

Remarks on Jewels prepared for the intended Wedding—Pugin makes a
Tour in Italy—Reception by the Pope—Expresses his annoyance that
many of the Priesthood disregarded his theories upon Christian Art
—Contrasts their apathy with the earnestness of many in the Anglican Church, who readily adopt his "True Principles."

In anticipation of his intended marriage with Miss L—
Pugin designed most beautiful bridal jewels, and had
them made under his personal directions.   These, it will
be remembered, were exhibited amongst the productions
of mediæval jewellery in the Great Exhibition of
1851.

They were deservedly admired, and on Her Majesty's
visit to the Exhibition, she specially requested to see
them, before inspecting the other objects in the collection.

The expense incurred in these ornaments must have
been considerable, and he evidently intended that his
marriage ceremony should be of no common kind.

Pugin in the year 1847 for the first time extended
his travels beyond Germany, and after visiting all the
leading cities in the north of Italy, proceeded to Rome.
His studies hitherto had been exclusively confined to
the mediæval architectures of England, France, Bel-

gium and Germany. With all his appreciation of the beauties of foreign art, he never hesitated to claim for the English churches and cathedrals a degree of excellence not to be surpassed by anything on the Continent; but admitted that in domestic and municipal architecture, foreign countries supplied a multitude of beautiful examples not to be found at home. He was especially delighted with Nuremberg, and the picturesque features of this ancient city afforded him most interesting studies. Although fully alive to the merits of real art in whatever style it was found, still his deep-rooted antipathy to classic forms unfitted him for receiving those strong impressions of satisfaction which people generally receive, from the contemplation of the magnificent buildings of Rome and the south of Italy. Nor does he appear to have modified his opinions in any material degree after examining them. For on his arrival at Rome he writes to a friend near Durham, in unmistakable terms, expressing his disappointment at the buildings in the Eternal City. He says:

'Rome, May 1st, (1847).

'I have now seen Rome and what Italian architecture can do, and I do not hesitate to say that it is an imperative duty on every Catholic to defend true and Christian architecture with his whole energy. The modern churches here are frightful; St. Peter's is far more ugly than I expected, and vilely constructed—a mass of imposition—bad taste of every kind seems to have run riot in this place; one good effect however results from these abortions: I feel doubly grateful for living in a country where the real glories of Catholic art are being revived and appreciated. In Rome it is hopeless, unless by miracle. I assure you I have felt quite depressed and miserable here; I shall be quite glad to get away. Were it not for the old Basilicas and the associations connected with the early Christian antiquities, it would be unbearable— the Sistine Chapel is a melancholy room, the Last Judgment is a painfully muscular delineation of a glorious subject, the Scala Regia a humbug, the Vatican a hideous mass, and St. Peter's is the greatest failure of all. It is quite painful to walk about; Italian architecture is a mere system of veneering marble slabs; it is enough to make one frantic to think, that these churches with their *plaster pilasters* and bad windows, have not only been the model for all larger churches erected during the last two centuries, but have been the means of spoiling half the fine old buildings through the efforts that have been made to assimilate them to this wretched model. They must have had some fine things at one time, for there are several tombs and incised stones of the right character, and the subterranean church of St. Peter's contains several bishops and popes in fine chasubles, &c. I hope you will tell everybody that this is the place to confirm people in the true style, and I can now speak of all their matters from personal observation. I leave here on Tuesday (the 1st of May) ; as soon as, D. V., I return to England I will come down to Ushaw.

'My legs are still very weak, but otherwise I am stronger, and I shall feel better when I can get sight of a mullioned window again. The old Basilicas are very interesting, and if they had not given such a miserable modern dress to all the holy places, one might realize all the wonderful events connected with the early ages of Christianity within the city ; but how is it possible to realize an idea of the residence of St. Peter, when we see a thing like a side chapel of Versailles ? or the relics of a saint in a flower-pot ? we must nail our colours to the cross, not to the mast. I never surrender ; if my health will permit me, I shall publish this journey and my impressions of Rome ; it will have novelty, at any rate, to recommend it.

'I remain yours respectfully,

'A. WELBY PUGIN.'

Unfavourable as were his impressions of Rome, yet he was not insensible to the beauties of mediæval art to be found in the great cities of Northern Italy, and expresses himself warmly concerning them in his letters to Lord Shrewsbury.

In the libraries and galleries, rich with ancient manuscripts and the works of the early Italian artists of the thirteenth century there was much to interest him ; and he did not fail to draw largely from these valuable stores. As may readily be supposed, he was

received with marked attention by all the leading
dignitaries of the Church. The fame of his great
exertions in the revival of church architecture, and
the successful results of his co-operation through the
medium of the arts in fostering a taste for external
and ceremonial display, were duly appreciated at
Rome. The Pope, to mark the sense His Holiness
entertained of services he had rendered, presented him
with a splendid gold medal. This token of approbation
from the Pontiff gratified Pugin more than any other
event in his life. For it should be mentioned that,
although his merit as an architect was acknowledged by
a large section of the Church Catholic, and his talents
used wherever possible : there were yet many ecclesiastics, who, if they did not altogether dislike mediæval
art, showed a great indifference to Pugin's efforts.
These persons, obstinately persisting in setting at defiance his notions of true art, continued to erect their
buildings in late Italian architecture, and to fit up
their churches with all sorts of cheap and tawdry
ornaments, artificial flowers, candles, plaster figures,
coarse paintings, and (as he termed them) other
"abominations," these being the external objects
through which they sought to make the forms of devotion attractive. This course of procedure greatly annoyed Pugin, and he often found himself at issue with
dignified ecclesiastics, who instead of advancing his
objects, countenanced some of the clergy in their per-
verse doings. He frequently expressed a more favourable opinion of the Anglican clergy, than of those

belonging to his own Church, for however abhorrent his religious opinions might be to the former, the clergy of the Church of England as a body were entirely favourable to the revival of architecture of which Pugin was so masterly an exponent.

CHAPTER XVII.

Pugin's third marriage—Lord Shrewsbury's congratulation—Account of
Roman Catholic Buildings in course of erection—Assumed completion of Structures partially built—Strictures upon Pugin's Buildings
in the 'Ecclesiologist'—Insufficient record of his negotiations with
employers and others to make a full Biography—Addresses a Letter
to M. Didron, giving an account of all that he is doing in England
in the revival of Ancient Art.

AFTER remaining a widower five years Pugin again
entered the marriage state. This his last marriage
was a most happy union. Miss Knill, the lady whom
he now espoused, was the youngest daughter of Thomas
Knill, Esq. of Typtree Hall, Herefordshire, a descen-
dant of the ancient family of that name in the same
county. She was married from the house of her uncle,
the late John Knill, Esq. of Blackheath, and the ceremony was performed at St. George's Roman Catholic
Cathedral on the 10th of August, 1848. By this marriage there are two children. Mrs. Pugin was enthusiastic in her love of ancient art, and appreciating her
husband's genius, entered into all his projects: and when
his health gave way, watched over him with the most
affectionate care. He often refers in his letters to the
soothing manner in which she nursed him when he
was suffering intense pain. How agonized her feelings
must have been to witness the derangement of that
great mind which she had known in its fullest power!

Pugin's wedding card. In the 1861 Edition
this illustration appeared in colour.

On the occasion of his marriage, Pugin announced the fact to his friends by sending a very pretty card,[*] expressing by heraldic devices the happy union which had taken place. Foremost amongst those to congratulate him was the Earl of Shrewsbury, who wrote—

'Mivart's.

'MY DEAR PUGIN,

'I can assure you that nothing has given me more pleasure for a long time past than the announcement of your sudden and happy marriage. Providence I am sure has now rewarded you for all your past sufferings, and given you a happy home for the rest of your days. Lady Shrewsbury desires me to say everything that is kind upon this occasion; we are here till Thursday, and hope to be back at Alton on Saturday. Your card is beautiful, and I am sure you may well be satisfied with your new armorial bearings.

'Believe me, my dear Pugin,

'Most truly and faithfully yours,

'SHREWSBURY.'

The Duke of Norfolk and other distinguished people also wrote to him, expressing their pleasure at his marriage.

The readiness with which the Anglican clergy adopted Pugin's principles of art, was forcibly alluded to in a long and interesting article, published in the Dublin Review of February 1842, entitled 'The Present State of Ecclesiastical Architecture in England.' In this

* Chromolithograph of the wedding-card is annexed.

paper a very full description is given of all the Roman Catholic churches and religious houses building in England, and great praise incidentally bestowed upon the Protestant clergy for their judgment in acting upon correct architectural principles, while the most bitter invectives are launched against the doctrines of the Reformation. Although the writer of that article, (which is accompanied by numerous plans and elevations,) has not appended his name, there can be little doubt that Pugin was the author. It is written in a vigorous tone, but loses much of its point by the inflated descriptions of Catholic ceremonies. The prints are entirely illustrative of churches, &c., built from Pugin's designs, etched by him, comprising the principal Catholic structures then in course of erection. Judging by some of these representations it would be thought that the Roman Catholic churches and monastic institutions were of gigantic dimensions. Few, however, if any of the projects are completed. They show certainly what Pugin intended, but if any person curious to see the effect of one of these groups of buildings were to visit the establishment, great would be his disappointment at finding but an inconsiderable part of the scheme really executed. No blame attaches to Pugin on this account. It cannot be doubted that the founders of these ecclesiastical institutions intended to complete them, and they naturally desired to exhibit them pictorially in their completeness.* It also

* A friend always asks the question, "Do the Romanists in England or Ireland ever finish the pretentious buildings they design?"

answered another purpose as tending to show how rapid was the alleged extension of Romanism in England, which could demand such extensive churches and monastic buildings.

The 'Ecclesiologist' of January 1846, contains an article upon 'the artistic merit of Mr. Pugin,' in which some very severe observations are made upon the several designs published in the 'Dublin Review.' The writer remarks that 'these buildings with one exception are the work of Mr. Pugin himself; and they are, to speak generally, all represented, whether yet commenced or not, as in a state of ideal perfection; to which humanly speaking there is very little probability of their attaining, excepting in a few cases, for an indefinite period. And yet from the whole tenour of the letter-press, one might suppose that they all were already far advanced towards such a consummation. This,' it is observed, 'is scarcely dealing as he should with his readers; for not only does he represent the buildings as in a state of perfection, but he gives the impression of their being larger and more stately than they turn out on examination to be.

'Of such pictorial architecture, perhaps the most striking example is the Benedictine Priory of Saint Gregory's at Downside, near Bath. Here we are presented with a bird's-eye view of an immense monastery with four quadrangles and a huge church, crowned by three lofty spires; stately indeed to look upon, but when will it be finished? how far is this priory an example of the present state of architecture of England in 1842, any more than the gorgeous palaces which form the backgrounds of Mr. Martin's pictures? The safe generalities of the letter-press leave this question very doubtful. Such a proceeding on Mr. Pugin's part is calculated to throw an unreal halo, not only around his own reputation, but (are we uncharitable in the sentiment?) round that of the communion to whose services he has devoted himself. We know its numbers; and assuming his prints as the outward index of its religious liberality, its earnestness, its increase, we should not fail to form a very exaggerated opinion of its present condition in England; more especially when we consider that, but for the pious munificence of one excellent nobleman of that communion, these performances would in all probability have been far less than they are.'

Having traced Pugin's career up to this period, and noticed his principal professional works, some idea may be gathered of the character and ability of the man. But in order to appreciate the peculiarities of his mind, there needs a faithful record of his sayings and doings in connexion with the many distinguished employers, and other persons of eminence amongst whom he moved. The materials for such a biography are wanting, as Pugin unfortunately destroyed all letters received during the early years of his practice. And although it is not unlikely that he himself would at a future day have brought together his memoranda (such having been his expressed intention), yet the suddenness of his removal terminated this expectation.

Observing that a laudable spirit of ecclesiastical restoration had commenced in France, and taking a deep interest in the movement, he addressed a long letter to Monsieur Didron, explaining all that he was himself doing in England. This communication is printed in the '*Bulletin Archéologique, publié par Le Comité Historique des Arts et Monumens*, 1843;' and shows clearly the importance Pugin attached to a careful study of ancient art. Nobody could design new forms with greater ease than himself, yet so fully did he appreciate the value of ancient examples, that we find him scrupulously adopting the forms and manners of constructing old objects in preference to modern modes of workmanship. By adhering to this principle he succeeded in producing the most beautiful revivals of ancient metal-work, tiles, glass, enamel, &c.

This letter is so valuable that it is subjoined *in extenso*.

'M. Pugin, architecte Catholique Anglais correspondant, a écrit la lettre suivante à M. Didron, qui en donne lecture; cette lettre témoigne du mouvement archéologique et religieux, tout à la fois, que l'Angleterre favorise en ce moment.

'" Monsieur,

' "Je suis fort content d'apprendre que le désir de restaurer le véritable art chrétien, si longtemps négligé, se représent avec force en France. On doit encourager de pareilles tentatives, et je vous donnerai sur mes travaux, avec le plus grand plaisir, tous les renseignemens que pourraient vous être utiles. Mes travaux ne se bornent pas aux monumens religieux ; je m'attache encore à la restauration des moindres accessoires, et je m'occupe même des étoffes pour les chapes et les chasubles. Je n'ai pas besoin de vous dire en effet que rien n'est plus choquant à l'esprit d'un véritable connaisseur de l'art chrétien que de voir une église magnifique avec des autels, des chandeliers et des ornemens dans le style moderne ou *rococo*, comme ceux qu'on trouve dans les plus belles cathédrales de la France et de la Belgique. J'ai donc établi, il y a quatre ans à peu près, des fabriques de tous les objets qui peuvent contribuer à la décoration et à la richesse des monumens ecclésiastiques.

' " Dans ces fabriques, on confectionne des objets en or, en argent et en cuivre, tels que burettes, calices, ciboires, ostensoirs, chandeliers, lampes, couronnes ardentes, tabernacles en forme de tour, croix processionales, reliquaries, châsses, et enfin tous ce qui appartient au culte catholique. J'ai fait copier ces objets d'après modèles anciens avec la plus grande exactitude, et je suis parvenu à former des ouvriers qui travaillent tout-à-fait dans l'ancien style. Les calices, larges à la coupe, sont posés sur des pieds émaillés, même enrichis de pierreries et dessinés dans des formes géométriques. Les chandeliers sont de toute grandeur, mais moins élevés qui ceux qui s'exécutent à présent. Je n'ai pas trouvé dans les autorités anciennes que les chandeliers fussent très-élevés autrefois. Je dois vous dire que ces objets sont exécutés dans l'ancienne manière. Ils sont ciselés, gravés, émaillés, battus, et non pas coulés en fonte comme à l'habitude de faire aujourd'hui. Le procédé de la fonte rend tous ces ouvrages lourds, tandis que les anciens ornemens en métal sont legers et travaillés avec art et sentiment. Pour les ostensoirs et les reliquaires, j'ai imité les plus beaux qu'on trouve en Belgique.

' "J'ai fait faire pour les cierges une couronne ardente qui a trente-six pieds de circonférence. Elle est chargée en écussons couverts d'inscriptions et suspendue avec des chaînes ornées. Lorsqu'elle est allumée pour les grandes fêtes, cela produit un effet magnifique.

' " J'espère que le temps n'est pas éloigné où tous les mauvais lustres, qui préviennent des salles de bal et qu'on voit aujourd'hui dans les églises, seront remplacés par des couronnes de cuivre doré qui sont d'un caractère tout-à-fait ecclésiastique. J'ai déjà envoyé en Amérique plusieurs ornemens de ce genre, et toutes les églises que j'ai bâties sont décorées d'objets qui portent le même caractère et sont dans le style de l'époque reproduite par le monument. L'autel de la chapelle de la Sainte Vierge, dans l'église de Birmingham, est extrêmement riche, et dans le style Gothique du temps de Saint Louis. Il porte un tabernacle précieux en forme de tour, orné de pierreries et des quatre évangélistes en émail. Cet autel est tout couvert de bas-reliefs dorés et peints dans le style chrétien ; de chaque côté sont suspendus des rideaux richement brodés. Tous nos autels ont des rideaux, comme on

en voit dans les tableaux anciens et dans les miniatures.
Nous avons plusieurs triptyques avec des portes cou-
vertes de peintures ; nous les plaçons au-dessus des
autels dans les chapelles.   J'ai parfaitement réussi à
faire des pavés incrustes ; l'église de Nottingham sera
pavée de ces briques émaillées de différentes couleurs,
chargées d'inscriptions et de divers ornemens colorés
en bleu, rouge, jaune et vert.   Ces pavés produisent
un effet magnifique, et rappellent la richesse des vitraux
peints.   Les vitraux de couleur, si essentiels aux
églises, sont bien faits chez nous.   Un morceau de
verre épais, attaché par la plomb, ne porte qu'un
seule couleur.   Je ne cherche pas à faire des tableaux
sur verre, mais à suivre la sévérités des anciens verriers
qui accordaient leur style avec l'architecture des fenê-
tres.   Vous seriez forte content, j'en suis bien sûr, des
vitraux que j'ai placés dans les églises que j'ai fait
construire.   Tout ce que je cherche c'est de restaurer
ce qu'on faisait anciennement, et non pas d'inventer
de nouveaux procédés qui ne réussissent jamais.
Quant aux draps d'or et de soie, quant aux galons, je
les ai copiés sur des tombeaux anciens d'évêques et
d'autres ecclésiastiques, et j'en ai fait faire une assez
grande quantité.   J'aurai très-grand plaisir de vous
envoyer des échantillons de ces galons qui sont fort
légers. Avec cette lettre, je vous adresse la gravure
de quelques-unes des briques incrustées dont je surveille
l'exécution.   La liste suivante des travaux que je
dirige pourra vous être utiles." '

[*Here he gives a list of his finest churches, &c.*]

' " Je compte commencer quatre églises nouvelles dans le courant de l'année 1843.

' " Tous ces bâtimens sont construits dans le véritable style chrétien. Ils sont plus ou moins riches dans les détails ; plusieurs ont des murailles et des plafonds chargés de peintures et de dorures. Les autels, les fonts baptismaux, et surtout les jubés qui séparent les chœurs et qui portent le grand crucifix, les images de la Sainte Vierge et de Saint Jean, sont tous dans le même style. J'espère que vous viendrez un jour ici pour voir ce que nous avons fait. L'église de Saint Georges à Londres vous fera plaisir ; elle a 246 pieds de long.* Le clocher aura 317 pieds de hauteur jusqu'à la croix de la flèche. Je vous adresse un paquet de gravures pour vous donner une idée de ces constructions.

' " J'aurais grand plaisir à vous envoyer des renseignemens plus précis sur tout ce que vous voulez savoir, et je reste, Monsieur, votre serviteur bien devoué,

' " A. WELBY PUGIN." '

---

* The base of this tower is only yet built, and according to present appearances there seems little hope of the structure being ever completed according to Pugin's design.

CHAPTER XVIII.

Destruction of the old Houses of Parliament—Pugin assists in preparing
Designs for the new Palace—His subsequent employment, under Sir
C. Barry to superintend certain details—Sir C. Barry's Testimony to
Pugin's Genius—Pugin's readiness to accord merit wherever due.

An opportunity soon presented itself of showing the capabilities of mediæval architecture which had hitherto never occurred in this or any other country in modern times. The destruction by fire of the Royal Palace of Westminster, containing the two Houses of Parliament, although in itself a great calamity, has been the means of giving to the metropolis a new building which in splendour and extent is equal if not superior to any other building in the world. When the commission appointed by Parliament in 1836 made their report, preferring the mediæval styles to those of Greece and Rome, no one doubted that Pugin would in any competition be at the head of the list. It was therefore generally expected that he would furnish a design immeasurably superior to those of his professional brethren. But, strange to say, amongst the names of eighty-four competitors, who submitted designs, his did not appear. This may be considered the great mistake in his professional life. Had he but applied himself to the consideration of this national work with his full power and energy, and entered the competition ; who can doubt but that he would have gained one of the premiums (which were large) even if he failed to obtain the execution of the design. Still, although he declined joining openly in the contest, there was a design offered by a Scotch architect, Mr. Gillespie Graham, in which the hand of Pugin was so evident that its real authorship could not be doubted. In fact he never denied that the drawings were his, and the composition to some extent his own.* This design did not find favour with the commissioners to whom was entrusted the power of selecting five designs to be classed for the premiums according to their respective merits. The commissioners selected designs in which symmetry of plan and elevation were conspicuous, rather than pictorial outline combining bold and striking contrast.

Pugin's design was perhaps wanting in dignity, but it was marked by the most successful treatment in the disposition and grouping of its parts. No attempt was made to produce an extended river façade of uniform character. The Houses of Peers and Commons, the Speaker's residence, St.Stephen's Chapel, committee rooms and officers' residences were severally treated in subordination to each other, either detached or united as the plan might require, but presenting a sky-line

---

* The Commissioners appointed by the Crown to make a selection were, Hanbury Tracy, Esq. (now Lord Sudeley), Lieut.-General Sir Edward Cust, Thomas Liddell, Esq., George Vivian, Esq. These gentlemen made their report to the King (William IV.) on the 29th of February, 1836.

R

of singular and picturesque beauty. There was undoubted merit of the highest order in this design, for
it was strikingly mediæval in treatment, and the very
irregularities of the plan gave point and expression to
the composition. However, there was so strong a
feeling in the minds of the umpires for breadth of
effect and simplicity in plan, that they refused to
recognize the great qualities which were certainly embodied in Pugin's design.*

The appreciation in which Pugin's knowledge of
Gothic art was held, secured for him at a later period,
when Mr. Barry's design was adopted, a large share
in the actual execution of the work : but even of the
original design some portion of its merit must be
assigned to Pugin. Frequent reference is made to
the great demand on his time, caused by his occupation on the drawings for the new Houses of Parliament ;
and the following extracts from his small diary of
1837 may not be without some interest; unfortunately
a great portion of his memoranda prior to *that date*
has been lost.

 Feb. 4*th*.—Finished work on timber-houses. Ditto
Holyrood chapel drawings.

 6*th*.—Came up to London. At Hull's.

---

 * In the 'Morning Post' the following critique upon this design
appeared : 'Gillespie Graham has given a plan, in the genuine spirit of
Gothic architecture, defying symmetry and order, but presenting combinations of convenience and picturesque grouping in perfect keeping
with the character of the style, and most delightful to contemplate.
The designs evince the author's intimate acquaintance with the style.
The drawings by the same hand which appears to have assisted No. 64,
are masterly, and *entirely* peculiar.'

7th.—Ackerman started on work of houses, which I trust will do something towards reviving a love for the ancient thing—but it is not calculated to do much.

9th.—On composition of new river front.

10th.—Begun lodges. Wind N. N.W.

11th.—On composition of centre and wings, drawing centre tower; also

16th.—Upper part of same. Taken ill.

17th.—Ill all day. Wind N. NE.

18th.—Better. W. N. NE.; stormy. Ackerman's bill. Finished timber-houses. Dined at Mr. Stodeim's.

19th.—Much better. Returned Barry 10*d.*

31st.—Finished all Barry's drawings.

Feb. 5th.—Left London for Sarum. The more I think, the more I deplore the degraded state of the public taste.

10th.—Finished chapel for Mr. Barry. Ditto for Wolfe.

11th.—Began Mr. Scarisbrick's hall.

15th.—Left Oscott college at night for Walby. From Walby to Manchester.

16th.—Back to Oscott. Here all day. Earl Spencer came. Left with Bishop for London. All day in London. Called on Bury, Webb, and Hull. Left Sarum at night.

21st.—Sent drawings to Dr. Weedall, Messrs. Moore and Hull.

Worked hard all day. Sent off drawings of great room to M. G. G. Commenced sketches for a work to be
entitled ' Contrasts.'

Aug. 15*th.*—At Moorfields; afterwards to St. John's
Wood. Saw Etty. Dined with Nash.
Left for Birmingham.

20*th.*—Left Oscott for Priory, Stafford. At
Caverswell Castle and Aston Hall.

21*st.*—Stafford Castle. From Stafford to Liverpool. From Liverpool to Scarisbrick.

24*th.*—Writington Hall. Left Scarisbrick· for
Manchester.

25*th.*—Lichfield, at Sir Charles Worsley's, to
Alton.

Sept. 15*th.*—Took lodgings at Chelsea. A poor boy
lost on the Goodwin Sands.

16*th.*—Began Dr. Rock's work.

17*th.*—Read lecture at Oscott, etc.

From this, some little notion may be formed of his
immense energy, as well as of his iron frame, which
allowed him absolutely to annihilate space even before
the introduction of steam.

But to return to the particular object of this chapter : Sir Charles was always ready to admit the great
assistance he derived from Pugin, although much has
been said to the contrary. Strange to say, the following letter from Sir Charles is the only one now to be
obtained, most of the others being destroyed prior to
Pugin's death, and what remain have been unfor-

tunately mislaid. This however testifies how highly
Barry prized all that Pugin touched.

'Foley Place, 22nd October, 1836.

'DEAR SIR,

'Being from home yesterday I could not acknowledge by return of post the receipt of the drawings of the House of Lords, King's Stairs, &c., which
came safely to hand last night, and afforded me a rich
treat. They will in all respects answer the purpose
most admirably. I can easily imagine the great labour
they must have cost you, and knowing all the difficulties, I cannot but wonder that you have been able
to accomplish so much in the time. I am not much
surprised to hear that your health suffers from excess
of application. Do not, however, I beseech you, carry
too great a press of sail, but take in a reef or two if
you find it necessary in due time. I send by this
morning's mail a packet containing tracings of the
Grand Public Entrance, and approach to the Houses
and Committee Rooms. They are most wretchedly
made by a youngster, who is as dull and destitute of
feeling as the board upon which he draws: they will
nevertheless, I doubt not, afford you all the data you
require. The groining and interior generally of the
King's or Record Tower entrance you may make of any
design you think proper: you need not be shackled as
to height, but the groin should, I think, be concentric
with the arch of the opening to the vestibule at the
foot of the King's Stairs, which you already have.

The design of this part of the building should, I think, be of a simple and massive character, and a pillar in the centre of the tower must be avoided. I am much flattered by your hearty commendation of the plan, and shall know where to look for a champion if I should hereafter require one. Truly it has cost me many an anxious thought, and an extraordinary degree of perseverance. With many thanks for your glorious efforts in the great cause, and best wishes for Mrs. Pugin's early recovery, believe me, dear sir,

'Yours most truly,

'CHARLES BARRY.'

In a building of such vast magnitude the architect was naturally glad to secure the best assistance possible for directing and attending to the multifarious details belonging to such a structure. Pugin therefore, by direct wish of the Commissioners, and with the approbation of Mr. Barry, was afterwards appointed to aid in the great national undertaking. The designing of the internal fittings, furniture, decoration, encaustic floors, &c., were officially confided to him, and to his unremitting energy and attention in the formation and selection of carvers, glass-stainers, metal-workers, &c. &c., may be attributed the great excellence and beauty here attained, as well as the masterly skill shown by him in their conception. Barry was accustomed to spend a considerable time every year with his friend Pugin; this practice commenced at Salisbury, and only terminated with death. Here the greatest good feeling existed, and many and most interesting topics (mostly of scientific interest) were discussed, whilst Pugin drew and Barry suggested, and digested, the several parts in which the skill of Pugin was required.

When asked how it was he had not himself endeavoured to obtain the great prize, for which he appeared so eminently fitted—he frankly said: ' Barry's grand plan was immeasurably superior to any that I could at the time have produced, and had it been otherwise, the commissioners would have killed me *in a twelve-month*. No, sir, Barry after all is "the right man in the right place ;" what more could we wish ?' In fact, he lost no opportunity of expressing his admiration of Barry's genius, and took pains that no misapprehension should exist in the public mind, whereby Barry should be deprived of the merit due to his skill. To many of his most intimate friends he was accustomed to speak in the highest terms of him, desiring that whenever any undue share of credit was assigned to himself in the great national undertaking the statement might at once be contradicted. Notwithstanding this honourable avowal, there are still many who adhere to their conviction that the great merit of the entire Palace of Westminster belongs to him, and since the lamented decease of Sir Charles Barry this statement has been revived. Much as Pugin admired Barry's work, he still entertained his own private view of the treatment of the general design. A friend of his recollects that on one occasion, when accompanying him in a steam-boat from Chelsea, on passing the new Houses of Parliament, at that time without their corona of towers, he waved his hand over them, exclaiming : ' All Grecian, Sir ; Tudor details on a classic body.' Although unquestionably Pugin's knowledge of mediæval detail was superior to that of any other person of his day, and was absolutely necessary for the conception of much as well as the effective execution of the actual work—still those who were familiar with Sir C. Barry's facility of drawing and design, cannot doubt that he possessed skill of the very highest order, and that Pugin's assistance was based on the general plan provided by Barry.

Those who knew Sir C. Barry could also testify to the affectionate regard which he entertained for Pugin, and his grief at the distressing malady by which he was afflicted. Indeed the first open manifestation of his derangement occurred in the presence of Sir Charles and his family, and he with the greatest promptitude called in a most eminent physician before even the sad fact was communicated to Pugin's own family.

Unflinching as he was in holding up to ridicule, in his ' Contrasts,' the works of modern artists, comparing them with ancient productions, yet he was most honest and generous when noticing the works of others who had benefitted by his labours and erected successful buildings. Speaking to a friend he observed ' that the only merit he claimed was giving to other architects the *key* to the use of knowledge which in theory they already possessed ; that since he opened the door other men had surpassed him in the goodness of their work.'

This was indeed true, for Pugin really never fairly had a chance of showing the wonderful resources and capabilities of his fertile brain, and shows how justly he appreciated himself and others, and how generously he gave credit where credit was due. In short he was a *great* man ; his chief object was the advancement of his favourite art, and faith, for which he sacrificed both *mind* and *means*, and in his pursuit of *this* he was wholly unselfish, quite as ready to rejoice in the excellence of another man's work as in his own, provided only it tended to the advancing of true principles and the glory of God.

CHAPTER XIX.

AMONG the various objects occupying Pugin's attention, not one received a greater share than the revival of the manufacture of encaustic tiles. In the gradual formation of his antiquarian museum, while he lived in Great Russell Street, he had collected many beautiful ancient specimens, and well knew what an effective means of ornamentation they formed in both ecclesiastical and secular buildings. The old builders neglected no part of their structures, the floor was rendered pleasing though trodden under foot, as well as the coloured and emblazoned roofs and stone groinings; and even the constructive parts concealed from public view were finished with the same care and attention as those details more prominently in view. In Mr. Minton, of Stoke-upon-Trent, Pugin found a man of most enlarged views, who ably seconded him in his endeavours to re-establish the ancient method of making these tiles; no pains nor expense were spared

to obtain the proper clay, and impress them with
ornaments of different colours.   Many fruitless efforts
were however made before such an amount of pressure
could be obtained, and a process of kiln-burning discovered so as to render the tiles hard and true on
their surface; but at last success was achieved, and
we owe entirely to Mr. Minton the beautiful means
of enrichment supplied through the multiplied form
and colour which his tiles afford.   Other manufac-
tories have, indeed, since sprung up where tiles of
almost equal quality can be procured: but Minton
was the great originator of the modern art of making
encaustic tiles.   A warm intimacy existed between
him and Pugin; they had been associated many
years in their endeavours to recover the lost art, and
Pugin had excellent opportunities of using encaustic
tiles in the many Roman Catholic churches he was
building, besides the one great work of the new
Houses of Parliament.   No pains were spared by
Pugin in his efforts to produce beautiful and effective
tile floors.   He was ever suggesting some new method
by which brilliant colouring might be secured, and in
his correspondence with Mr. Minton extending over
several years, there are amusing passages in which he
enforces his views in his own racy and emphatic
manner, accompanied by numerous illustrative sketches.
Pugin was evidently much delighted with the result
of Minton's manufacture of tiles, for when writing to
him in January 1852, he says: 'I declare your St.
Stephen's tiles the finest done in the tile way; vastly

superior to any ancient work; in fact they are the best
tiles in the world, and I think my patterns and your
workmanship go ahead of anything.'

It was in the commencement of the year 1852, that
the first indications were seen of his failing health,
arising from over exertion of body and mind. He
observes in one of his letters: 'I have been dreadfully
ill, so ill that it was at one time doubtful if I could
ever recover; but by the blessing of God I am
certainly gaining strength very fast, and I have
lost nothing of mental power, as I think you will find
by the work I send to you. There is no probability of
my being in London for the next month or two, and the
medical men recommend perfect rest till the advanced
time of spring, and then to travel in an easy and gentle
way.' Unhappily the improvement of his health was
but of short duration, for he was soon again afflicted
more than ever.

It was now that his intimacy with Mr. Minton,
which had existed in an unbroken degree for some
years, was interrupted by a misconception on Pugin's
part of some remarks made by Mr. Minton on his
professional charges. Nothing could be further from
that gentleman's intention than to say or do anything
which could give offence to his friend, but he was then
in such a state of nervous debility as to be scarcely
responsible for his actions. In letters at this time
he repeatedly alludes to his shattered health. Thus
in January 1852, he says: 'I believe I have been too
hurried so soon after such an illness. I cannot get my

bodily strength up at all, and I perspire intensely, to that degree as to be obliged to put on five or six shirts a day, &c.' In another letter to Mr. Minton of a later date, he writes: 'I am in such a deplorably nervous state that I am at times scarcely answerable for what I write; I am so dreadfully afflicted in the head. You seemed to think I had cheated and sent you a false account (though now I don't believe you did), and I cried like a child, and trembled all over in dreadful perspiration, and I thought my fever had returned. Pray, my dear Minton, don't agitate me, the doctors say I am not to be agitated. If you saw your poor old friend so reduced as I am—thin, trembling, hollow-eyed, changed, and yet working tremendously at times—you would be very careful not to distress me.'

His condition was now truly distressing, and each succeeding letter showed fresh symptoms of suffering. His sight, which had hitherto been good, now failed him. He writes: 'You have no conception of the dreadful agony which I still suffer, the least thing agitates me; I feel trembling and my eyesight is dimmed. I am obliged to bathe my eyes with sea water, and to drink the coldest water to bring my sight again.' Even still worse sufferings are described in other communications; it can therefore scarcely excite surprise that he should misinterpret some of the letters addressed to him, and in a moment of irritation, he wrote a letter reproaching Mr. Minton in severe language, withdrawing from him his confidence, and threatening to transfer all business commissions to other manufacturers. Mr. Minton was much distressed by this proceeding, well knowing that he had done nothing to merit such displeasure. To remonstrate however he knew would be vain, for Pugin refused either to see or receive any communication whatever from him. He therefore addressed a very feeling letter to Mrs. Pugin, protesting his ignorance of the cause which could have given such dire offence, at the same time offering to retract any expression he had used, and offer any apology rather than lose the friendship of one he so highly valued. This letter had its desired effect, and Minton was overjoyed at receiving one of the most touching communications ever penned. During the infliction of the severest visitation to which he was subjected by the inscrutable will of the Almighty there were occasional lucid intervals when gushes of warm-hearted feeling evidenced the tenderness of his nature. It seemed indeed as though affliction brought out the best dispositions of his heart. Notwithstanding the harsh manner in which he had expressed himself, when Mr. Minton's appeal was made to him through his wife he replies, February 14, 1852:

'MY DEAR, EVER DEAR MINTON,

' Your capital letter to my wife has just arrived, thus leaving nothing, my dear friend, but a perfect reconciliation between us. You must attribute a great deal to the dreadful irritation of nerves left by this terrible fever under which I suffered; but nothing would contribute so much to the final re-establishment of my improved health, as a real and hearty reconciliation with you. It is ridiculous, and a delight to the many, to see two such men as you and I quarrelling. We cannot afford it long, let us cut the row and embrace. I will endeavour when sufficiently restored to settle it over a leg of mutton at Huntfield; and if you will come and see me I will give you a better reception at St. Augustine than the Emperor; for all my things are in the true style, which is more than you can say for the fancy patterns. I have written to Mr. Barry by this post that we are quite reconciled: it would be too affecting to see us really embracing over a happy combination of four tiles, so it must pass in imagination, though not less real.

'Your devoted old friend,

'A. W. PUGIN.'

There is a rough sketch appended to this letter exhibiting Pugin and Minton embracing each other over an altar inscribed: 'Pax Pugin et Minton,' and on each side a crowd of people shouting 'Pax Minton et Pugin.' At the foot there is placed in old characters as a border tile, 'Pax in eternam.' The last pattern. 'A. W. Pugin, Fecit.'

On the 16th of February, he again writes:—

'Many thanks for your kind letter, my dear friend. I don't think I have been myself. This nervous fever is a dreadful delusion: since I wrote I am no longer an *architect*, that is in a general way. After I wrote to you I was taken with a terrible relapse and a *stagnation of blood*. I soon became cold in all the vital parts, and I felt that without instant relief I must die. I ordered three strong glasses of brandy:—my doctor came in:—and by the mercy of God, and by about half a pint of sal volatile which I drank off, and by my dear wife putting on hot flannels all over me, with rubbing, in which others assisted, at last the circulation returned. My medical man said this could not go on any longer, and he had a consultation of all the first medical men, who declared that I could not live a week if I did not give up my profession. There was no hesitation on my part: I immediately relinquished all my buildings except Lord Shrewsbury's and Sir C. Barry's, and of course yours, which will not kill me; but I am a private gentleman, a grand fellow. The relief of mind, as the doctors predicted, was instantaneous, and succeeded perfectly, and I am, thank God, out of danger. I shall enshrine your kind letter among my most esteemed epistles. My mind has been deranged through over exertion. The medical men said I had worked one hundred years in forty. I have not time to say: more I am ordered to Italy as soon as possible.

'A. W. Pugin.'

This was the last communication between them, the state of his health did not improve, and the distressing malady soon returned with increased force.

CHAPTER XX.

Pugin's opinion of the Great Exhibition Building in Hyde Park, 1851—
Exhibits largely in the Mediæval Court—Praise given him by Professor Waagen—Consulted, in 1852, upon the formation of the
Architectural Museum—His opinion upon Art-Workmen—Power of
persuasion in Argument—A work on Sculptured Ornament contemplated but never carried into execution—Desire to see a Mediæval
Club established.

ON the occasion of the Great Exhibition in 1851,
Pugin became much interested in the project, so far
as to evince a great desire that there should be a
department for the display of successful modern works
executed in the true spirit of mediæval art. However, he took no active part in suggesting or designing
the character of the building ultimately adopted and
known as the CRYSTAL PALACE. In truth he was rather
disgusted at the notion of enclosing everything under
the shelter of a huge GREEN-HOUSE, and considered the
construction of the building rather an instance of
retrogression than of advancement. Cast-iron pillars
were odious things in his sight, and notwithstanding
the astonishing mechanical skill shown in the conception of the building, Pugin viewed the whole scheme
with feelings of aversion. He could see no evidence
whatever of artistic treatment.in its composition, and

s

railed vehemently against the style of ornament employed.

One day, on visiting the building when it was nearly completed, he met Mr. P— the originator of the design, who naturally asked him what he thought of it. —'Think,' said he ; 'why, that you had better keep to building green-houses, and I will keep to my churches and cathedrals.'

Powerful as were his objections to the structure, he nevertheless took great pains that the objects exhibited in his own department of art should be fairly represented. No one who remembers the picturesque arrangement of the Mediæval Court can doubt that he had a great share in its success—the various and beautiful objects it contained were entirely executed from his designs, by Mr. Myers, and amongst other things, were exhibited the wrought gold and silver ornaments made for the intended marriage with his third wife.

Great praise was awarded to him by the jury who reported on the mediæval department; and Professor Waagen, in his notice on the various sectional divisions of the Great Exhibition, says, when speaking of this particular court: 'To conclude this notice, I must also mention the Mediæval Court fitted up by Professor A. Welby Pugin, one of the most distinguished amongst English architects, as a designer of Gothic buildings and ornaments. In this court he has endeavoured with great success to present to the spectator a general idea of ecclesiastical art, by exhibiting an assemblage of altars, shrines, tapestries, painted windows, chalices, and patens, vestments and other ecclesiastical furniture and objects. Most of these articles are executed from his own drawings. The merit of the collection has been duly acknowledged by the jury.' His name is also mentioned honourably, in connection with the metal productions of Messrs. Hardman of Birmingham, whose articles are chiefly executed from his designs.

When, in March, 1852, several architects and others interested in the promotion of art sought to establish a school for ' art-workmen, and a museum of architectural casts,' they naturally desired to enlist Pugin in favour of their undertaking; and with a view to elicit his opinions, Mr. Bruce Allen, one of the originators of the scheme, addressed the following letter to him.

'Cannon Row, Westminster;
March, 1852.

'Sir,

'We are trying to establish a museum of architecture, and a school of art for artist workmen, *i. e.* a school for all the workmen in any way employed in carrying out architectural works;—to do, indeed, for the men just what the Royal Academy does for students and painters. I enclose you a prospectus I have drawn up, which, as you will see, has been approved by many architects and others, and thought capable of realization. If you will kindly read it and tell me what your opinion of it is, I shall feel greatly obliged, and I feel sure that your opinion when repeated to others will greatly help me (if you approve of it), in the very difficult task of inducing people to assist such an undertaking. It is, as you will at once see, capable of almost indefinite expansion. We intend to include all styles, but have commenced our collection with the Gothic as the one of churches and ecclesiastical structures. As I am quite a novice at this work, I trust, Sir, you will pardon my writing without introduction.

'I am,

'Faithfully yours,

'C. BRUCE ALLEN.'

To this communication he sent the following short but characteristic reply; it has neither date or address.

'SIR,

'I have just returned home and received your prospectus and letter. I wish you every success, but it appears to me you are going to work on too extensive a scale in bringing up men to work in all styles. Practically, I expect you will find no end of difficulties. Workmen are a singular class, and from my experience of them, which is rather extensive, are generally incapable of taking a high view on these subjects,—and ready at a moment to leave their instructors and benefactors for an extra sixpence a day for the first bidder that turns up. I have been all my life instructing men, while others profited by the result of my labours. In the present state of society, and the total absence of anything like the faith and religious feeling that actuated men in past ages, I believe it is impossible to do much good; however, I have no doubt your inclinations are excellent, and time will show if they are attended with practical benefit.

'I am yours most sincerely,
'A. W. PUGIN.'

There is observable in the tone of this letter the same leading delusion which enthralled him continually. Pugin could see nothing likely to be successful which was attempted by those separated from the Roman Catholic Church. Still much good sense is displayed in the remarks on the slight hold which employers have on their skilled workmen; unfortunately there is too much truth in them. Great, however, as would have been the difficulties attending the working of the projected school, it must be admitted that the establishment of the Architectural Museum has been productive of real benefit to art-workmen. Some advantage has been gained by bringing together into a central situation, casts taken from all the most beautiful fragments of sculpture known, and art-workmen have not been slow to avail themselves of the opportunities for consulting these valuable authorities. As a further inducement, prizes are annually offered to those who produce the best designs for different subjects submitted for competition. The designs and objects of sculpture submitted at various times in answer to these invitations,

afford convincing proofs that the establishment of this
Museum has realized some of the objects contemplated
by its founders.

In describing Pugin's personal character, it should
be noticed that though his general manner was brusque
and vehement, and his mode of asserting facts somewhat overbearing, yet he had great powers of persuasion when he tried gentler means than were his wont.
No subjects excited him so much as discussions on religious matters. He could scarcely ever converse
calmly and quietly with those who differed from him ;
but occasionally he did so, and his power of persuasion was very considerable when he chose to adopt
that mode in the interchange of ideas. He used to
relate that when travelling from Derby in a railway
carriage, alone with an elderly lady, she on seeing
him cross himself as he was reciting an office, exclaimed
with horror, ' You are a Catholic, sir ;—Guard, Guard,
let me out—I must get into another carriage ;' but as
that could not be accomplished at the moment, Pugin
reasoned gently and quietly with her, so that on arriving
at the next station the lady had no desire to get out,
and before the journey's end, she was shedding tears
of sorrow and regret for her past hatred of such good
Christians. Those who knew him well, can readily
understand how soon he could disarm a weak opponent,
and the fascinating manner in which he would present
his arguments when he chose to adopt a persuasive
tone.

Much as he had done for the promotion of genuine

ancient art by his publications and executed works,
yet had he lived longer, there can be no doubt that
he would have realized other useful schemes in connection with his art. He had it in contemplation to
publish a great work upon Architectural Ornament
and Foliated Sculpture, and frequently spoke of the
benefit which he anticipated would result from his ex-
positions on the subject. That he would have dis-
coursed successfully on this branch of art no one can
doubt; and there would then have been added to his
natural powers the benefit of many years' experience
in practical work.

Although Pugin at no period of his life sought to
associate himself with any institution or chartered
body, having for its object the promotion of the arts,
yet he never withdrew himself from the society of his
professional brethren, and was always ready to give
assistance or advice when asked by any of them to
do so. It should however be mentioned that (without
his consent) Pugin was nominated to fill a vacancy
amongst the members of the Royal Academy; unfortunately he was not elected, a circumstance much
to be regretted, as so eminent a man ought to have
been associated with a body of artists pre-eminently
distinguished by royal favour, his genius being confessedly of the highest order: his friends Herbert, Etty,
and Stanfield much lamented this untoward event.

The very strong views he entertained regarding
the fitness of mediæval architecture for all purposes,
was probably one of the reasons which led him to

hesitate in associating himself with societies in which classic architecture is held in equal honour with the mediæval styles; on the other hand, so strongly was he impressed with the desirableness of furthering pursuits connected with Gothic architecture, that he took great interest in a proposition made to him by an earnest clergyman for the establishment of a Gothic club in London, to be called the 'Old English.' It was to have been for all the purposes of an ordinary club, only the building was to be English Gothic, to show, among other things, how applicable the style is to the wants of the present day, and how much more beautiful it is, as street architecture, than any other.*

Pugin's mind was never at rest, and notwithstanding the great labour thrown upon him by his professional practice, carried on it must be understood mainly by his own hands, as he scarcely ever deigned to seek assistance—except occasionally from an old friend, a pupil of his father, Mr. T. Talbot Bury, he could yet find time to engage in religious controversy.

---

* Since Pugin's death this project has been again revived, and the establishment of a club house, with the distinctive character he proposed to give it, would be most acceptable to a large body of active men both in literature and art. It is indeed strange that a want so long felt has not yet been supplied. All other professions have their distinctive institutions for social intercourse: why then should not men devoted to mediæval art make a united effort to realize this scheme? Amongst the nobility and wealthy commoners of England there would be many willing to become its patrons. The only existing club in which professional men and others attached to art and archæology can find a place is the Athenæum, but, amongst its members, they form only a small minority.

CHAPTER XXI.

Pugin writes to Mr. Minton that he is engaged on a work to produce Mutual Charity amongst Members of different religious Communions —The Work never published—Premonitory symptoms of disturbed intellect—Public sympathy and intended Subscription for his support—Letter of Lord John Russell—Mr. E. Welby Pugin, his son, discountenances the proposed public Appeal as unnecessary—Rumoured change in his Religious Views—No sufficient foundation for the report.

EARLY in the year 1851 he observed, in a letter to Mr. Minton: 'I am almost distracted, for in addition to all other labours, I have a most important work on the real cause of the change of religion in the 16th century, which will place matters in a totally new light, overthrow the present opinions on both sides, and may be the means of tending to much mutual charity on both sides, and a better understanding. The present state of things in a Christian country is afflicting, and it all proceeds from men not being able to separate the temporal tyranny of Catholic States from the religion itself, which suffers all the odium of the system to which one was bound up and tied.'

The work here alluded to was never published. Pugin's opinions respecting the Roman Catholic Church had latterly undergone some change, and he was now wont to speak of her system with greater freedom and independence than he had ever hitherto done.   During the dreadful malady which afflicted him, one of his hallucinations was, that there had been a perfect reconciliation between the separated Churches, and in the course of one night he wrote upwards of sixty pages to his cousin Sibthorp, respecting the union of the Churches, stating that he could now again embrace his previously unfortunate brother—that there was now but one Church—no distinct Roman Catholic, Anglican, nonconformist, or other denomination, and he drew imaginary cheques to be given to clergymen and others for distribution to the poor of their neighbourhood.

Whether the book on which he was occupied contained any actual renunciation of his previous opinions does not appear; but that some great change in his mind was then in progress, rightly or wrongly, was generally believed.   The language in which he announces his intended publication to his intimate friend, Mr. Minton, can only be understood on the supposition that a reaction of some kind had taken place.*

The premonitory symptoms which had shown themselves during the last few years, and had been noticed

---

* A prospectus of this work, entitled 'An Apology for the Church of England' was printed, but never circulated; the contents of the book were classified in chapters with their headings, from which it might be gathered that his opinions had undergone considerable change, and more charitable interpretations were now placed upon historical events which had formerly extorted from him expressions of strong condemnation.

by his friends, were now unhappily to be succeeded by that mental darkness than which nothing more dreadful afflicts the human race.

The first undoubted proof of his insanity was discovered by his friend and medical attendant at Ramsgate, when meeting him one evening returning to Saint Augustine's. Pugin, impetuous as usual, began by asking him if he had heard of the dreadful calamity outside the harbour,—five merchant ships having sunk while striving to reach the entrance. He described the catastrophe in such apparently clear and truthful terms, entering minutely into every particular, that his medical man left him impressed with the full belief of the reality of the event, and proceeding to meet some friends at a dinner party soon after related the account he had just heard. The astonishment was great, for none of them knew the occurrence; and upon an inquiry being made it was found that there was not a particle of truth in the story. His extraordinary conduct was also afterwards noticed by his acquaintances in London, whither he had hurried from Ramsgate. He greatly alarmed Sir Charles Barry, as already mentioned, and that gentleman immediately called in Dr. Tweedie. Pugin was then removed to the Golden Cross in Wellington Street, Strand, and put under proper restraint; but his violence became so great that all moderate attempts to tranquillize him were useless. The fact of his deplorable condition soon became well known, and the deepest sympathy for him was felt amongst all classes of society. In a publication devoted to the interest of the arts and sciences, letters were written, under the most erroneous impressions, suggesting subscriptions. It was said he was reduced to beggary by his religious zeal, that there were no funds to support him, and that he had actually been removed to a public asylum. Invectives of shame and reproach were hurled against his fellow Roman Catholic friends for permitting this degradation to overtake a man so distinguished, and who had rendered such important services to their Church. The Editor of the 'Builder,' participating in the writer's remarks on the melancholy subject, recommended that some endeavours should be made by subscriptions to place him in a private asylum, instead of his remaining in a public hospital for the insane.

The effect of this appeal was instantaneous, and the first response was from a no less distinguished person than Lord John Russell, who in a letter dated Pembroke Lodge, July 10th, 1852, says—

' SIR,

'I do not know whether there is any truth in the assertion of a correspondent of your paper, that Mr. Pugin has been reduced to beggary. I hope not. But if there is any truth in the statement, and a subscription is opened for Mr. Pugin's relief, I beg that my name may be put down for ten pounds.

' I am, Sir, your obedient Servant,

' J. RUSSELL.'

It would be too painful an investigation to re-open the circumstances under which Pugin's temporary removal to Bethlehem Hospital took place. By many persons the fact is even now contested, and the idea of his having been conveyed to a public receptacle for insane patients entirely rejected. There is something abhorrent in the very name of ' Bedlam,' but perhaps it may not be generally known that this noble institution is the refuge of many educated persons and professional men, who unhappily have become proper subjects for the shelter and treatment it affords. There can be no doubt, however, that for a short time Pugin was under the mild restraint practised in this hospital, where he was visited by some of his most intimate acquaintances; but no improvement in his condition taking place, Mrs. Pugin, aided by his old and true friend, the Rev. Mr. Glennie, transferred him to a house in the Grove, Hammersmith, where he resided some time in the midst of his family, under the care of Dr. Dickson (the author of the ' Fallacies of the Faculty '). While there, great hopes were entertained of his recovery; so much so, that he was removed thence to his own residence, the Grange, Ramsgate; where he appeared to enter into the delights of his old home, visiting with great delight all portions of his buildings. On entering the library, the first thing he noticed was the absence of his original sketches, then in the possession of his son Edward, at Birmingham. At first he was extremely annoyed; but afterwards became calm, and hearing they were safe, expressed a hope that they would be serviceable to him in the course of his professional career. The circulation of a statement that Mr. Pugin had been removed to a public hospital 'for want of funds for his support,' met with a prompt denial from his son, Mr. Edward Pugin, who protested that the idea of making a public subscription ought not to have been put forth without at least some authority. 'For the rest,' he said, 'I trust I may be able to carry out my father's professional engagements; and with the continued assistance and encouragement of his friends, to maintain the family till such time as it may please God to restore him to us.'

Had Pugin not been taken to an eleemosynary asylum, the idea that he was in a state of pecuniary destitution never could have gained currency. Every one must have known the large professional practice Pugin possessed, his buildings are found broadcast throughout the land, and instead of being in a state of poverty, it might reasonably have been inferred that he had realized a comfortable fortune. Such indeed ought to have been the case, yet although he spent large sums in the purchase of rare and costly books, &c., and in the erection of the beautiful church of St. Augustine, there was sufficient property realized to afford the means of supporting him without recourse to a public subscription.

Reference has already been made to a reported change in Pugin's religious views previous to his insanity, but no positive evidence can be adduced to support this notion. It is very likely that, in a moment of exasperation at the perverseness of a section of the Roman Catholic Church in resisting his architectural recommendations, and with the recollection of the bitter terms in which he had in earlier days vilified the Anglican Church, he may have said, 'the rest of my life must be one of penitence to seek forgiveness for the wrongs I have done to the Anglican Church,' words ascribed to him in a notice elsewhere of his last illness.

During the short time he was under the care of his friends at the Golden Cross, an incident occurred which showed that, even while under the torments of frenzy, his innate love for his profession was not extinguished. One night he became much excited and attacked Mr. Myers, but was ultimately calmed; and the latter, in order to turn his attention to a subject of interest, reproached him for keeping the scaffolding up at Beverley, as they were waiting for drawings.* 'Give me a pencil,' said Pugin, and on the back of a large envelope he designed an elegant vane, clear and precise, which has since been placed on the corner pinnacle of St. Mary's at Beverley.

The hope which had been raised by the improvement in his health on his return to his residence, was soon to be dispelled; for his physical frame was so shaken by the severe attacks he had undergone,

---

* See the 'Builder' of Sept. 25, 1852, containing a brief but well-written notice of some leading facts connected with Pugin's career, from the pen of Mr. Talbot Bury.

that he could not rally : and on the night of September 13th, 1852, his medical attendant was hastily summoned to his bed-side, where he found him agitated by strong convulsions, which defied all attempted remedies, and continued till the morning of the 14th, when he sank from exhaustion. Thus terminated the life of a great and remarkable man at the early age of forty. By singular coincidence, on the same day, in the same county, and within a few miles from Ramsgate, died also the greatest man this country has produced, the Duke of Wellington.

Although Pugin when he attained manhood was strong and hearty, yet his labours aged him prematurely. Continued anxiety, feverish exertions, and sleepless nights had done much to undermine a naturally strong constitution ; and towards the close of his life, his personal appearance underwent great change. He had a quick and piercing eye ; his nose and lips exhibited a Grecian outline, on which usually played a humorous expression ; his forehead was broad, and indicated his mental power. In him there was nothing studied. Whenever, and however he was found, he was always the man, a true child of nature. In his character the fervid Celtic spirit often appeared through the nature of the Saxon. For unrestrained freedom of action he sacrificed the pleasures of society. His genius was great. The part he had to perform in life gave insufficient scope for the energies of his mind, and the incessant exercise of his mental faculties destroyed his physical frame before he had attained the ordinary age of man. He bore little similarity to the other men amongst whom he lived ; in many respects superior, he was different and out of his element everywhere except in his own study. Such was Welby Pugin before his last malady.

By his three marriages Pugin has left eight children. The eldest son, Edward Welby Pugin, succeeds to his father's practice, and as an architect displays considerable talent. Those who remember the elder and the late Welby Pugin cannot fail to observe that Edward inherits much of the refinement of his grandfather with the genius of his father, though he does not possess the literary power of the latter.

On the 21st of September the funeral obsequies of Augustus Welby Northmore de Pugin took place in St. Augustine's, the church which he had himself founded. Part of the service was performed on Monday evening with all the ceremonials of the Roman Catholic Church, and in the morning his remains were placed in a vault beneath the south transept. Besides the members of his family and the priesthood, Sir C. Barry, Mr. Herbert, Mr. T. T. Bury, Mr. Hardman, Mr. Crace, Mr. Myers, Mr. Scott Murray, Mr. Daniel, Mr. Knill the father of Mrs. Pugin, and some other friends took part in the ceremony. The crowd of strangers in the church was great.

The funeral oration, eulogizing the talents of the deceased, was delivered by Bishop Grant.

The appreciation of the service which Pugin had rendered to art was shown by an act of great kindness

T

of Her Majesty, who, immediately upon hearing of his affliction, directed a pension to be granted to Mrs. Pugin from the Civil List, this resolution being communicated to Mrs. Pugin, in the most complimentary manner, by the Earl of Derby.

In addition to the publications noticed in former Chapters, which by the enunciation of great principles have become extensively useful, many others were produced by Pugin which deserve commendation. Among these are works on *Gothic Furniture*, published in 1835 ; on *Ironwork,* in the same year ; and on *Ancient Timber Houses,* in 1836. These works were admirably illustrated with spirited etchings by his own hand, fully worthy of their author.

To give an enumeration of the various buildings which Pugin executed would be difficult, but the following list is a selection somewhat in the order of their erection. His first church was that of St. Mary at Derby, where he renewed his acquaintance with Mr. Myers in the manner already described. The little Norman Chapel at Reading soon followed; it is built of flint. He was next occupied with St. Chad's at Birmingham, and the schools, nunnery, and bishop's house attached. Then followed St. Edward's, St. Mary's, and two other churches at Liverpool; a chapel and convent at Edge Hill ; St. Wilifred's, Manchester ; churches at Kenilworth, Cambridge, Stockton-on-Tees, Newcastle-on-Tyne, Preston, Ushaw, Keightly in Yorkshire, Sheepsteen, Warwick, Rugby, Northampton, Stoke-upon-Trent, Breeswood, Wool-

wich, Hammersmith, Pontefract, and Fulham; St.
John's, Walham Green; St. Edward's near Ware; St.
Martin's, Buckingham; St. Wilifred near Alton; St.
Barnabas Nottingham, with a convent and chapel in
the same town; St. Bernard's church and monastery,
Leicester; the convents of the Sisters of Mercy at
Birmingham, Liverpool, and London; St. Gregory's
Priory, Downside near Bath; colleges at Radcliffe,
Rugby, and Maynooth, Ireland; being engaged on
the latter by the Government of the time. The
Roman Catholic cathedrals of Killarney, Enniscorthy,
and St. George's, Southwark, with the schools, priests'
houses, and other offices connected therewith; also
Sibthorpe's almshouses, Lincoln; schools at Stone;
chancel, Winick (one of his finest works); restoration
of Tofts, near Brandon; his magnificent plans, which
were never executed, for the entire restoration of
Hornby Castle, for the Duke of Leeds; the partial
rebuilding of Alton Towers, for the late Earl of Shrewsbury; the entire rebuilding of the castle on Alton
Rock; the church, hospital, and schools of St. John's,
Alton; the Jesus Chapel near Pomfret, for the late
Miss Tempest; the cathedral church at Uttoxeter;
the restoration of Jesus College, Cambridge; the
chantry of the late Lady Sutton; the chapel at Danes-
field, for Scott Murray, Esq.; the Catholic church at
Lynn; the completion of St. Mary's College, Oscott;
St. Wilfrid's, Manchester; the design he prepared for
the cathedral of St. John's, Salford, which building
was afterwards erected by Mr. Hadfield, as Pugin

could not be induced to give way on some point of
principle; the chapel in Douay College; the restoration of the parish church at Winswold; the Catholic
church at Salisbury; St. John's, Kirkham; the church
of St. Mary's, Southport; the church of St. Oswald's,
Old Swan, near Liverpool; the church of our Lady of
the Annunciation, Bishop Eton; the convent at Ber-
mondsey; the completion of St. David's, Barnstaple;
the convent and school at Nottingham; the church,
and restoration of Grace dieu Manor, for Ambrose Lisle
Phillipps, Esq.; the chapel for Sir William Stuart, in
Scotland; the magnificent designs prepared for St.
Margaret's cathedral, Edinburgh; the church at Whit-
wick; the church of St. Augustine, Solihull; the
church of our Blessed Lady, Dudley; the church of
St. Peter's, Great Marlow; the tower and spire of St.
Mary's, Edinburgh; St. Stephen's, Blargowrie; Scarisbrick Hall, near Ormskirk; the Catholic churches of
Tagote and Gorey, and several other churches in Wexford; the convent and church at Parson's Town; the
convent and church at Waterford; the convent at
Gorey; the Catholic church at Guernsey; the Catholic
church, Macclesfield. He also designed many churches
for Australia, and the other colonies.

It was not likely that Pugin would be extensively
engaged by the clergy and friends of the Anglican
Church; in some few instances only was he consulted
by these authorities on the restoration of their churches.
His time and energies were so devoted to Catholic
buildings that few private gentlemen applied to him

for domestic mansions. Still mention must not be forgotten of Scarisbrick Hall, Bilton Grange, Warwick; Lord Dunraven's seat at Adare in Ireland; Mr. Drummond's house; restorations to Chirk Castle, Denbighshire, for Colonel Biddulph; gateway and chancel of the church at Pepper Harrow, for Lord Middleton; and his magnificent designs for Hornby Castle, for the Duke of Leeds.

CHAPTER XXII.

General Retrospect of the Progress of Modern Architecture—Peculiarities of Lombardo-Gothic—Pugin's treatment of Mediæval Architecture—Recognition of the labours of Architectural Authors preceding Pugin's time.

DWELLING upon what Pugin accomplished, especial reference must be made to the period and the state of architecture at the time when he commenced his studies. Without entering into the interminable question as to the merits and fitness of either the classic or mediæval styles (for the battle of the styles is now being fought with greater violence than in Pugin's days), it must be borne in mind that the then prevailing taste was in favour of Greek architecture. The learned and beautiful publications of the Dilettante Society, the acknowledged ability and skill of those architects who had devoted themselves to the investigation of classic remains, were the plausible means of introducing the claims of a style of art, practised by the polished people of Greece; little effort however was made to modify the antique types, and make them applicable to modern wants, or to meet the requirements of our more northern climate; but a system sprung up of minutely copying both the general designs as well as details of temples and monuments of heathen character, applying them indiscriminately to churches, theatres, asylums, and institutions of every kind. Well-proportioned porticoes without any reference to their positions; pediments where roofs could never exist, and multitudes of like inconsistencies, were continually erected. It seemed a sufficient warrant for expecting public approval that an undoubted antique example was followed, without any regard to its fitness or congruity.

Added to these misapplications, a further evil prevailed of executing buildings with an extent of unreality which had never hitherto been known in this country. The earlier period of the Georgian Era, if not remarkable for the pure taste to be found in the public structures then built, at least exhibited some admirable examples of sound brickwork and durable stone; roofs substantially constructed with oak and fir, either covered with lead or Westmoreland slate; elaborately wrought iron-work, as well as bold and effective carving. But in the early part of the 19th century, cements of all kinds for facing and ornamentation took the place of real good brick or stone. Walls were built of mere rubbish coated with cement jointed and coloured to look like stone, and numberless other cheap and tricky artifices resorted to for outward appearance, showing a total disregard to constructive honesty.

Amidst the prevalence of such glaring mistakes, Pugin, possessing a large amount of daring, came out with his brusque and powerful pen, to what purpose the present practice of mediæval architecture will best answer ; but wherever improvement is visible in recent works, it may be unmistakably traced to the architectural reformation set on foot by Pugin thirty years ago. The value of his exertions must not be measured by the merits of his own executed buildings, they are justly open to the criticism of matured knowledge now gained from his own published books, but by the present state of architecture throughout Europe, which certainly evidences an advance to be attributed only to the effect of ' True Principles.'

It is now much the fashion to decry Pugin ; another development of mediæval art has obtained popularity ; and the study of the peculiar character of Italian Gothic now cultivated, has brought into favour a different type of pointed architecture little known in Pugin's days, and not introduced till some time after his death. Of the great merit to be found in the architecture of the middle ages of Lombardy, there can be no question: the adventitious aid of beautiful local marbles, the skill of great Italian artists, the effect of climate, and the chisel of the Lombard sculptors combine to produce monuments of art singularly grand and imposing, and a debt of gratitude is justly due to those great architects, by whose skill such excellent illustrations are handed down to us. But it is still questionable whether the merit of this class of Gothic buildings equals the beauty and fitness always found in the magnificent buildings on this side the Alps. The great facilities for obtaining local marbles and other materials since the introduction of railways, have probably led to the recent use of the transalpine forms of Gothic abounding largely, with coloured wall-decorations, introduced by the easy use of local marbles. The architect should be ever ready to avail himself of each and every succeeding new substance, applying it in the manner which its natural properties justify, either in construction or decoration. There are now brought into notice Devonshire, Cornish, Derbyshire marbles, and other coloured limestones which, till within the last few years, if known, were not available, excepting within the confines of their immediate localities; now, however, through the facilities of steam conveyance, they can be carried easily to any distance at a moderate cost, and are thus at once applicable for building purposes. Already the effects of these changes may be observed in many recently-erected buildings, more particularly in the Museum at Oxford, where our native marbles are introduced with the happiest results; and there is no reason why all newly-discovered products may not be used in the development of architectural forms, provided they are introduced with skill and judgment. Viewing the forms of Lombardo-Gothic buildings apart from the advantages of the beautiful material with which they are erected, it may still fairly be questioned whether they are equal to either the French or English examples. There is a want of purity in their compositions, and some strange admixture of classical details which destroys the harmony so remarkable in the best buildings of France and Germany. While borrowing therefore those features of interest belonging to the Italian type, such as the spiral marble columns, the inlaid door and window panels, friezes, circular sunk niche, and boldly-carved bust projecting before the face of the wall, the open niche and canopy, the balconets and other distinctive parts of Italian character, care should be taken not to import the less happy peculiarities of general design, in which there is a marked inferiority when compared with our northern architecture.

The façades of the most celebrated mediæval palaces in Italy are confessedly inferior to the palatial buildings of France and Belgium, and the monotony of the Venetian elevations is only redeemed by portions of beautiful sculpture and coloured marbles. To abandon therefore the principles of our northern composition, and exchange them for the faulty mannerism of the Italian school is indeed a mistake. Let advantage be taken of those features in detail which are wanting in our own climate, infusing them harmoniously into our designs; but never let us give up those leading characteristics of pure Gothic composition so conspicuous in the palatial and domestic architecture of Normandy and the south of France. True that in the hands of a great artist, any style may be so treated as to produce a successful result, yet it must be remembered that the licence permissible to such a man cannot be exercised by the less accomplished architect, or tyro: who imitating the quaint treatment of his subject by a man of genius, adopts the peculiarities and deviations from ordinary rules in a capricious manner, and produces a building remarkable rather for oddity than the discriminating exercise of the latitude which in more able hands results in success. Many of the strange buildings now erected with the most exaggerated details, utterly wanting in grace and proportion, rendered mainly attractive by the introduction of striped brickwork in imitation of coloured marbles, are the fruits of a fashion which appears to set aside all the sound canons of architecture, and gives reins to every kind of eccentric treatment which the young architect may choose to adopt.

This country abounds with admirable examples showing the skilful manner in which our ancestors availed themselves of stone, brick, and flint, in the character of their designs. The most elegant and elaborate details in carved and cast bricks, are to be found in the baronial mansions of Norfolk; and the aptitude with which cut flints are used in combination with stone, may be seen in all the churches of Suffolk and Norfolk. The moment seemed to have arrived when through the exertions of Carter, Britton, Pugin, Parker, Rickman, Brandon, and others, by their published works, a knowledge of the grammar of Gothic architecture was at length attained; and buildings were daily showing evidences of the study and thought which had been heretofore sadly wanting in Gothic structures. At this juncture, the principles of the style being nearly mastered, and ample scope given for realizing them, the continental type is suddenly thrust on the public notice, diverts attention from the beautiful forms of northern Gothic, and claims consideration for the Lombardic peculiarities. This is to be regretted, because it has diminished the opportunities of showing the full capability of our national architecture. The laborious studies of past years, the painstaking researches of the author of ' The Glossary of Architecture,' and numerous others who have laboured successfully in collecting and publishing the most beautiful details, showing the marvellous fitness of our ingenious architecture when thoroughly understood, are set aside for this foreign school. Since the rebuilding of the Houses of Parliament, no building of any magnitude has been erected in our vernacular mediæval style; every competition for a public structure has called forth designs almost exclusively cast in the new mould. One might imagine that many of them were drawn on gutta-percha, capable of expansion or contraction according to the required size, so similar are they in their servile imitation of some favourite idea. Thus the extended façade of an hôtel de ville is not unfrequently taken as a model for a railway station, union workhouse, literary institution, or some much smaller establishment. And it would be difficult to say how many designs have been founded upon the outline of the Oxford Museum, fitness and propriety being quite set aside in order that the popular mannerism should be followed. Now this is manifestly wrong, and results entirely from the love of seeking to give novelty instead of aiming to produce convenience in plan, and elevation, suitable to the purposes of the intended structure.

Upon this topic nobody has ever spoken more truly than Welby Pugin, who has laid down rules of universal application. And though unhappily they are now too frequently disregarded, yet some happy illustrations of his principles may be found in recently-erected buildings, where judicious freedom of design is exemplified without forced treatment.

So admirable are his remarks, that though they have been already quoted by Mr. Scott in his able work on 'Gothic Architecture, Secular and Domestic,' they may rightly claim to be inserted here.

* * * * *

'In the second place, when modern architects void this defect of regularity, they frequently fall into one equally great with regard to irregularity; I mean, when a building is designed *to be picturesque*, by sticking as many ins and outs, ups and downs, about it as possible. *The picturesque effect of the ancient buildings, results from ingenious methods by which the old builders overcame local and constructive difficulties.* An edifice which is arranged with the principal view of looking picturesque, is sure to resemble an artificial waterfall, or a made-up rock, which are generally so *unnaturally natural* as to appear ridiculous.

'An architect should exhibit his skill by turning the difficulties which occur in raising an elevation from a *convenient plan* into so many *picturesque beauties;* and this constitutes the great difference between the principles of classic and domestic architecture. In the former *he would be compelled to devise expedients to cover these irregularities;* in the latter *he has only to beautify them.* But I am quite assured that all the irregularities that are so beautiful in ancient architecture, are the result of certain necessary difficulties, and were never purposely designed; for to make a building inconvenient for the sake of obtaining irregularity, would be scarcely less ridiculous than preparing working drawings for a new ruin. But all these inconsistencies have arisen from this great error—*the plans of buildings are designed to suit the elevation, instead of the elevation being made subservient to the plan.*

'They were substantial, appropriate edifices, suited by their scale and arrangement for the purposes of habitation. Each part of these buildings indicated its particular distinction: the furreted gatehouse and porter's lodging, the entrance-porch, the high-crested roof, and louvred hall, with its capacious chimney, the great chambers, the vast kitchens and offices, all forming distinct and beautiful features, not *masked or concealed under one monotonous front*, but by their variety in form and outline increasing the effect of the building.

*   *   *   *   *

'I must mention here two great defects, very common in modern pointed buildings, both of which arise from the great fundamental principle of decorating utility not being understood. In the first place, many architects apply the details and minor features of the pointed style to classic *masses* and arrangements; they adhere scrupulously to the regularity and symmetry of the latter, while they attempt to disguise it by the mouldings and accessories of the former. They must have two of everything, one on each side : no matter if all the required accommodation is contained in one half of the design, a shell of another half must be built to keep up uniformity. What can be more absurd ? Because a man has a real door to enter his house on one side, he must have a mock one through which he cannot get in on the other. How inconsistent it is to make and glaze a window which is to be *walled up* ab initio !'

No better proof can be given of the value of Pugin's teaching than that it should have led to the further development of his principles by the publication of Mr. Scott's work. If Pugin laid down general rules, Mr. Scott has shown the manner in which they should be applied, pointing out in the most discriminating manner the caution to be observed in following his maxims and suggesting thoughts for new combinations of a most interesting kind in connection with the introduction of Italian details into our own Gothic styles. What Pugin's notions might have been upon this subject it would be presumptuous to say. Although acquainted with the mediæval architecture of North

Italy he had not given special attention to its claims; but that in the gradually improved practice of his favourite styles he would have availed himself of the continental details which might consistently be infused into English Gothic can hardly be doubted; but how far he would have recognized the propriety of mingling the characteristic details of different countries may be questioned. Whatever defects exist, in the works executed by him there is always a great unity of effect visible in their composition; proportion and harmony of parts are never neglected, and in matter of minute detail there is nothing wanting. Fertility of design and delicacy in execution are specially remarkable. Nobody was so thoroughly master of detail; his memory could recall to him the beauty and fitness of any ornament which he had ever seen, and he would apply it whenever a fitting opportunity offered for its introduction. Added to his intuitive taste for architectural form he possessed an excellent eye for colour. This gift is not necessarily associated with the love of picturesque outline. Some men are utterly incapable of distinguishing with nicety the various tints and gradations required for harmonious effects, or the just proportion between positive and complemental colour, but Pugin was a master of this art, and many excellent decorations were carried into effect by the Messrs. Crace under his immediate guidance. The same capacity for colour made him a good landscape artist. Some of his sketches of coast scenery are most truthful—executed on rough paper with few touches they are crisp and spirited. He had not patience to finish drawings; thus all his efforts were slight but masterly. Much as he loved colour, yet he never at any time tinted his architectural designs; his established habit was to draw them firmly in Indian or common ink, not relying upon the aid of either colour or shadows, giving them force by a few light lines or spirited touches thrown in when necessary. Whenever he moved about the country it was his custom to travel in a gig, if he could possibly do so, in preference to any other mode of conveyance, in order that he might stop and examine every old church that he passed in his way; and although his memory was most retentive, yet, in order to assign dates quickly, he carried about with him a tabular compendium, written and drawn upon vellum, in the most minute and beautiful manner, containing a chronological list of the kings of England and France, the anniversaries of the saints in the English Calendar, the dates of great national events, a chart of the British Channel (indicating the shoals), tide tables, sectional outlines of the mouldings and forms belonging to different dates, and many other aids to memory connected with religion and architecture. He could draw and talk upon any subject at the same time, and has been known to originate and complete the design for a monastic institution, sitting at the edge of a table with his drawing board, while tea was going forward, carrying on a running conversation, and in the course of the evening showing the successful result of his occupation. No adequate idea

of the rapidity with which he sketched can be formed
by anybody who has not seen him draw. The several
volumes of beautiful outlines in the possession of his
family, afford the most convincing proof of his wonderful power. Great as this gift was, it would never
have secured for him the lasting honour attached to
his name : the great ' Fundamental Principles ' which
Pugin revived and laid down could alone do this.

Scarcely reaching the middle age of man, Welby
Pugin lived to see the whole state of architecture
revolutionized by the standard which he himself had
raised. A long war had utterly erased the last germs of
truth, principle, and beauty in architecture. Gothic was
no longer thought of, except for the purposes of an artificial ruin, or an absurd castellated mansion ; for ecclesiastical purposes it was alone known. The schools
of Wren and Jones had passed their day, and were
dead,—even the red brick buildings of the early Georgian era, with their protruding stone quoins, and heavy
pediments, and truthful panellings, had been forgotten
in the universal decay. Europe had suffered too long
from an utter absence of art, not to have been eager
and hungry for a change. Public taste looked, but
hoped in vain, for a movement to emanate from the
ranks of the profession. All felt the existence of the
void ; many sought for an external expression of their
times, and some called for a renewal of the glories of
the past. These were answered by the efforts of
Rickman, the researches of Carter, the theories of
Milner, and the examples of the elder Pugin and others.

These accomplished nothing but the galvanism of the ancient body.   Gothic buildings Rickman produced it is true.   The tree bore a strong resemblance to the old one ; it had stem, branches, and even leaves, but one thing was still wanting—it had no root.   The spikey pinnacles, cast-iron tracery, consumptive and attenuated columns, showed at a glance that the sap was wanting, and where it had begun it must end, and would germinate nothing.   One man only could be found sufficiently bold, and sufficiently devoted, to realize the colossal works which all felt were wanting. The wit, humour, and exaggerated views adopted by Welby Pugin for the accomplishment of the revolution, were often personally abusive, always painful, and sometimes dangerous.   But they were weapons to achieve victory, and instruments for effecting great results.   Others tried different roads and failed, whilst the mass of men wallowed in the vulgar utilitarian style of the nineteenth century ; a few carried away by the enthusiasm, but without a knowledge of the grammar, followed only in a servile manner, the glory of extant examples.   All were found wanting.   Some men must be judged, not by their accomplished works, but by their conceptions ; the buildings Pugin has left behind him are nothing in comparison to his splendid theories.   England called for a renovation, Welby Pugin answered the summons.   The country looked for the spirit of reformation, Welby Pugin imposed upon her the despotism of the ancient art, whilst giving her the alphabet by which to form her own expression.

To the hopes of the Anglicans he replied by submission to the Roman Catholic Church. Few men were ever destined to accomplish more, yet his greatest works were to be realized only in theory.

CHAPTER XXIII.

Further Illustrations of Pugin's Character—Appeal to his Co-religionists on the subject of the Papal Hierarchy in England—Neglect in the recognition of his great services by the leading Roman Catholics— A Memorial in honour of his memory, founded by the Protestants, to perpetuate the great service he rendered to Architecture.

THE following eminent qualities are observable in Pugin's eventful life. First, his untiring industry : from the time he began his professional career to the moment of his fatal malady, no day was ever wasted by him. His vigorous mind was always at work ; a simple change in the object of his pursuits afforded him the only kind of recreation he desired. He entirely abstained from light and frivolous amusements. From the moment he embraced the tenets of the Roman Catholic Church, to the close of his life, he laboured incessantly in promoting true art in connection with the structures and ceremonies of that Communion. His devotion was intense, and has never been duly appreciated nor acknowledged by the most eminent members of that Church.

His independent spirit was not less remarkable. He would rather forego great pecuniary advantage than lend himself to carry into execution any building which he knew to be inconsistent with the principles of design he had promulgated. This exercise of consistency is deserving of great praise. Whatever he laid down in theory he carried into practice, setting a noble example, unhappily not always followed by present fortunate professors, who seem to possess less power of abnegation than belonged to the great revivalist.

His impartiality was also conspicuous towards his professional contemporaries. He rarely engaged in public competitions, though often invited to do so, and therefore was not brought into collision with them. Yet on many occasions, when his opinions were sought (towards the end of his career), he eulogized the talents of the rising young men whose works deserved praise. No mean or petty jealousy ever actuated him. He desired to see the glories of ancient art revived, and whoever furthered that object received from him due share of commendation.

Various as have been the reports regarding the motives and tendency of his religious life, in consequence of his having separated himself from the Church in which he was baptized, yet it is impossible to doubt this momentous step was taken under a deep conviction that his soul's welfare was in peril. This overwhelming consideration eventually impelled him to enter the fold of the Roman Catholic Church, though by his own admission he was at first drawn towards her through the fascinating influence of art. His earnestness in the cause of Catholic art was immense, and his sincerity patent to the world by the costly sacrifices he made. What a noble pattern of self-devotion he exhibited, and that without the least ostentation, annually putting aside a good part of his income to build and endow a church. When Pope Pius IX. in the year 1851 determined on subdividing England into papal dioceses, Pugin hailed the intention with joy, and on that occasion addressed an appeal to the Roman Catholics of Southwark, showing the difficulties which must arise in obtaining sufficient funds to support the newly consecrated bishops, unless the Romanists made sacrifices according to their respective incomes to meet the new order of things. His appeal was as follows:—

'CATHOLICS OF THIS DIOCESE.

'We beg to draw your attention to a system which, we believe, under the blessing of God, may be the means of restoring religion in this land, and supporting that hierarchy which has just been established to our great consolation.

'We hope and trust that all good Catholics are thoroughly agreed in recognising the hand of God in this great act, which has imparted full episcopal powers to our bishops, and constituted us, who were before a scattered remnant, into a regular church. As a body, indeed, we have addressed the Holy Father with grateful thanks for the blessing he has conferred on us—we have addressed the bishops themselves in language of congratulation and affection. But the time has arrived when we must do more; we must

prove the sincerity of these preliminary acts by coming
forward and affording a practical support to religion
and its ministers.   The duties which are inseparably
connected with the offices of the new bishops entail
great additional expenses on their position; the very
publication of the necessary pastorals and official
documents for the government of their dioceses—the
visitations they must make for the preservation of
discipline and administration of their sacred duties,
however economically conducted, are necessarily attended with much cost.   Moreover, if our bishops are
really to become that benefit to religion which their
sacred office, when efficiently carried out, may legiti-
mately lead us to hope and expect, they must be placed
on such a footing and supported with such means as
will enable them to fulfil their high office and duties,
and make them practically what they were intended
by Providence to be—the channel through which aid,
both spiritual and temporal, has to be conveyed to the
very extremity of their dioceses.   How is this to be
accomplished? To raise such a sum as, when invested,
would enable them to do anything with the interest is
out of the question.   Moreover, large sums of money
lying by as investments are practical evils, and sources
of dissension and scandal of which we have already
had too many sad examples.   Again, the very idea of
locking up money in imaginary securities is in itself
an evidence of some want of confidence in Almighty
God and His promises to the church.   But what we
have to propose on the present occasion is this—that

we, the faithful of the English Catholic body, should become *a living investment* for our bishops, and through them to the church. Let every man, independent of local obligations, see what amount of capital he can afford to represent by an annual or biennial offering. For instance, one man is wealthy, he represents 1,000*l*., and sends 50*l*. a year; another 400*l*., and he sends 20*l*. a year; another 100*l*., and he sends 5*l*.; another 20*l*., and he sends 1*l*., and so on, more or less. There is no responsibility binding to sin in making this resolution before God, and no legal responsibility incurred to man, but a great revenue would be at once obtained for church purposes out of a true and apostolic investment in the *hearts, souls, and devotion of baptized men,* an investment with which no parliamentary decrees could interfere, no state laws confiscate, no rapacious tyranny could grasp, by legal fiction; and an investment which would be a reciprocal tie between the church and the people. Moreover, in its collection there are no expenses incurred, no odious list of comparative contributors published, no committees, no waste of time or money. Each man has only to go into the nearest church or chapel, examine truly what amount of capital he can represent for the church, make his solemn resolution, go home, and send his cheque or Post-office order, as the case may be, direct to his bishop, and repeat it at the appointed times unless hindered by circumstances he cannot control; and he may rely that God, who sees this in secret, will reward him openly in the development of his holy religion, in the efficacy of the episcopal rule, in the increased aid afforded to the various parochial churches of the diocese, in the greater solemnity of the services of religion, in the multiplication of priests and religions, the erection of schools, and all those glorious works connected with the revival of Catholic faith and practice. By this endowment all legal difficulties of trusts, mortmain, and lapsed legacies will be avoided, for this should supplant the old rotten system made only to fatten lawyers and create hatred among men : no stamps required except the penny one on the envelope that conveys the money ; no deed except the good deeds of those who contribute without expense or difficulty twice every year, and thus would the ample means of supporting religion be placed in the hands of our apostolic rulers. The church was intended to be a *self-supporting institution* by its apostolic constitution, *creating its own supplies through the continual sacrifice of its faithful children, always succeeding, and always contributing.* Such a perpetual endowment as this is exempt from all dangers, and, as we have already said, will place our spiritual rulers completely beyond the reach of state enactments in temporal matters.

' We intreat every zealous Catholic in the land, whatever be his position and means, to contribute accordingly, to the temporal support of that church which the Holy Father has established amongst us, and which we do not hesitate to say, without some great exertion on our part, will become our shame and re-

proach instead of our glory. We cannot allow the
episcopal power to become, in a manner, paralyzed
for want of that temporal support for which it has an
apostolic claim on the faithful children of the church.
Unless we are prepared to show what Catholic faith
and Catholic zeal can do in the free support of a free
hierarchy, our thanks to the Holy Father are a mockery
and our addresses a sham. But we will hope for better
things. We trust that this event has been ordained
of God to raise our hearts and instil into us some
of that true zeal, devotion, and spirit of offering which
was inseparable from the profession of Catholic truth in
early ages. We have now laid before you the means by
which a considerable revenue can be raised to relieve
the necessities of religion; and we may truly say they
have never been greater than at the present time.
Let, then, any man who has Catholic interests at heart
look to his means and conscientiously think what
amount he can represent as an investment, of which
he contributes the interest. We have already paid
our instalments into the treasury, and others have
done the same; and we have made a solemn resolution,
whilst we have a hand or an eye left to work with, we
will repeat it twice every year; and, by God's help,
we will bring up our children to the same principles;
and we exhort all to do the same, that the succession
of contributions may be kept up with that of the
bishops. We intreat all on this important occasion to
sink private feelings and all paltry considerations in
the respect due to the office of their bishops, appointed

by apostolical authority, apart from any temporal or state intrigue whatever, and in a hierarchy perfectly *free in principle;* we say, if these men are not worthy objects of our entire confidence and our most strenuous aid, if these be not men in whose endeavours for the advancement of religion we can fully believe, there is an end of all belief in apostolic succession and church government. Had a concordat existed between our government and the Holy See; had these names ever passed through an ambassador's portfolio, there might be room for suspicion and doubt; but under present circumstances *there is none.* They come to us from the highest ecclesiastical authority on earth, as from the *Vox Dei* itself; and while they keep their free and honourable position inviolate, we are bound to them as children to their spiritual fathers; and the man who, possessing temporal means, holds back on this most important event, must be dead to every sense of duty and unworthy to rank among the faithful.'

This scheme was worthy of all praise as a means to an end, but how feebly was it responded to by those to whom it was addressed! Pugin had personally set an excellent example, acting up most fully to the precepts he taught, but through the degeneracy of the Roman Catholic laity his recommendation was followed by no satisfactory result. No greater blot rests upon the Romanist community of this age than the disregard shown by them for Pugin's great exertions in strengthening their cause by advocating a restoration of neglected Catholic usages, and the correction of modern abuses. What a stigma upon the Roman Catholic body, of which he was so bright an ornament! and to the edification of whose temples he devoted his life, believing the most successful efforts in art to be compatible only with the highest inspirations of her creed! that her dignified ecclesiastics and wealthy noblemen should allow many years to roll by without making the slightest effort to honour his memory for the invaluable services he rendered to art —leaving this act of simple justice to be accomplished by members of the Reformed Church of England. It might reasonably have been supposed that the dignitaries of his own Church would have been first to contribute liberally to a fund raised in honour of their great church architect; but to their shame it must be recorded, that out of their whole hierarchy only two or three names appear on the list of contributions to ' the Pugin Travelling Fund,' while other men, of all shades of opinion, and in various grades of society, not members of the Roman Catholic Church, came forward spontaneously to do honour to the memory of one who did so much, and so well, for Christian Art; thus confirming the solemn truth, 'a prophet is not without honour save in his own country, and in his own house.'

In all that has been said relating to Pugin, every endeavour has been made to represent him in his professional character, to do justice to him in the great occupation of his life, and not to dwell more than necessary on his religious opinions. His reputation as

an architect has been gained by the excellence of his
writings on art, and if they were divested of every
sentence bearing a religious impress, there would still
remain the residuum which must ever be received as
offering an invaluable 'vade mecum' for the professional architect; yet, it must be observed, that he
never wrote on any subject but from a Roman Catholic
point of view, and loved to trace all excellence in
architecture and art through that channel, maintaining
stoutly that the only really great works could be executed by Roman Catholics. His family, sharing in these
impressions, have felt that, however desirous Pugin's
biographer might be to do him justice, yet that the
author of these pages, being a member of the Anglican
branch of the Church Catholic, and not a son of the
Roman Catholic Church, it was impossible he could
appreciate the motives which actuated Pugin in all he
did, and hence might unintentionally deprive him of
the halo inseparable from his labours. The author of
this book has therefore, in deference to these opinions,
readily admitted the contribution of the succeeding
chapters, relating, amongst other matters, to a great
dispute on the hierarchy question of 1851. He feels
it incumbent on him to add that he cannot agree in
some of the conclusions drawn by the writer in his
notices of Pugin's published works. The chief object
of the author of this memoir has been to give in some
popular form a connected sketch of Pugin's career as
a professional man, avoiding, wherever possible, topics
which might lead to controversy ; and with this leading

purpose he has not dealt, as he might otherwise have done, upon many questionable passages in his writings, leaving the enlightened readers of Pugin's works to form their own judgment thereon. In reference, however, to the dispute on the Roman Catholic hierarchy question of 1851—a subject not treated of in any of his architectural publications—the author of these pages has felt that this matter could only be handled by a Roman Catholic familiar with the points of controversy, whose acquaintance with the persons engaged, and knowledge of the facts involved, could qualify him to write authoritatively on transactions connected with which Pugin played so prominent a part.

AN APPENDIX:

IN WHICH

THE WRITINGS AND CHARACTER

OF

Augustus Welby Northmore Pugin

ARE CONSIDERED

IN THEIR CATHOLIC ASPECT.

BY

EDMUND SHERIDAN PURCELL.

"The greatest privilege possessed by man is to be allowed, while on earth, to contribute to the glory of God."—*True Principles.*

INTRODUCTION.

THE name of Pugin is familiar to the world. His dramatic and eventful life, from the brilliant development of its early dawn down to the darkness of its untimely and tragic close, has not escaped the notice of the moralist or the preacher;* but the character of his mind, the views which he has unfolded in his writings, and the genuineness of his religious belief have been ill-understood by too many, and misinterpreted by not a few. To remove the accidental misconception, to rebut the false charge, and, by a fair and dispassionate examination of his artistic and religious principles, to throw light upon the character of his mind, and the peculiar nature of his genius, is the purport of these pages. It would best please him, whose habits of thought and character of life we are about more closely to consider, and whose image and likeness we are endeavouring to set up before the eyes of those who had not the good fortune of knowing him, that in his biography there should be no concealment and no re-

* *Vide* Dr. Weedall's Funeral Oration on the death of the Earl of Shrewsbury.

serve.   Were, indeed, the secret motives of his heart, and the character of his mind as well known as his name, it would but enhance his reputation, and add still more to our admiration and love.

The first aspect, however, in which Pugin presents himself to the mind of all, is as the prime mover in the revival of Christian art, as the great mediæval architect who considered the highest honour that could fall to the lot of man was to raise a church to the glory of God.   To his patient and often unrecognized labours, —to his studious researches and striking comparisons between modern and mediæval productions,—is mainly owing, not only the revival of a higher standard of excellence and a purer taste in our national architecture, but the more general recognition of those true principles of Christian art which are now, indeed, accepted by all who have a right to pronounce an opinion, as normal rules and fundamental axioms.   In his writings, so rich in illustration, so full of antiquarian knowledge, and so powerful by their earnest eloquence, Pugin has done more than any man in the present age to promote the study of mediæval art, and to revive again the glories of our national architecture. In the 'Contrasts,' a work which first fixed public attention on the rising artist and man of letters, the Author unfolded as they gradually became familiar to his mind the principles of his art, which, in his latest works, found their fullest development.   Pugin was not an artist merely, his genius had a larger range and his mind a greater grasp than to be satisfied

with the technicalities of any school or the limits of a
single pursuit. The investigation of the great principles which underlie all knowledge, and of which art
is only a partial expression, had an attraction for his
mind, and was the source of his originality as well as
the cause of the errors into which through inadvertence
or immaturity of judgment he sometimes fell. This
investigating spirit he carried into historical subjects ;
and on matters of church-government and history he
had often bold and original, and sometimes, what many
termed, hazardous, views to propound, and in fine, no
small portion of his laborious life was devoted to
theological studies. To him religion was no idle
form, and the Catholic faith no mere æsthetic fancy,
as many have supposed, which gratified, by its grand
ritual and sublime symbolism, his sense of the beautiful and his love of the ancient. It was rather the
informing spirit of his mind, on which his principles
rested, and the guide of his heart in the battle of
life.

Religion, there is no question, is the stamp and seal
set upon the character of a man's life ; it is the finger-
mark of God upon the soul. To have broken this seal,
to have obliterated the tracings of the Divine Hand, to
have been a renegade at heart to the faith of his
Church, and to the principles which were the very
foundations of his character, was a charge that was
never deliberately and distinctly brought against the
great Christian artist. But the doubt as to the completeness of his attachment to Rome has been more

than insinuated ; therefore on the very threshold of this closer inquiry into his life, I have thought it right to be explicit and outspoken on the genuineness of his faith ; and if, in the course of these pages, I shall be enabled to remove the imputation of incipient heresy—for to such a length did the prejudice or misconception extend—good service will have been done to the cause of truth in thus preserving from tarnish the fair fame of a great and extraordinary man.

CHAPTER I.

Pugin's principles as manifested in his writings—The 'Times' on the 'truthfulness' of Pugin's principles—His chief works considered—'Contrasts; or, a Parallel between the noble Edifices of the fourteenth and fifteenth centuries and corresponding Buildings of the present day'—Causes of the decline of Gothic architecture—The revival of letters in the sixteenth century—Paganism in art and literature—The neglect and decay of the English Cathedrals a quarter of a century ago—Pugin's hatred of shams and unrealities—His severe criticisms on modern church builders—'The True Principles of Pointed or Christian Architecture considered'—Pugin's principles generally adopted as fundamental axioms in Mediæval architecture—His criticisms on the Grecian style—Pointed Architecture best suited for Christian purposes—Its symbolism, strength, and beauty—Appropriateness the principle of ornamentation—'An Apology for the Revival of Christian Architecture'—A defence of his own principles—Their antiquity—The Gothic revival and its results.

PUGIN was the Gibbon of architecture. In the 'Contrasts,' he wrote the history of its decline and fall, not in the mocking spirit of the great disciple of Voltaire, but with the earnest and vehement eloquence of Savonarola. Like the Italian Dominican, the English architect was a reformer and denouncer of Pagan abuses; as orthodox as Savonarola, he was more fortunate in having lived in happier times, when to denounce abuses is not to be a candidate for martyrdom.

His life marks an era in the history of the architecture of his country, and the name of Welby Pugin will be for ever identified with the revival of a purer taste in art, and of a severer and more critical judgment, which now promises to remove the reproach that has so long rested upon the artistic fame of England. The almost universal recognition of those fundamental axioms for which he so long and so ably contended, is a proud tribute to his memory, and one which the author of the ' True Principles of Christian or Pointed Architecture ' well deserved at the hands of his countrymen.

Wren's epitaph, mutatis mutandis, might be justly applied to Pugin—'SI MONUMENTUM REQUIRIS, CIRCUMSPICE.' Look around on the churches and public edifices which are now being raised in England, and whatsoever is grand and solid in construction, or Christian in principle, and whatsoever is in keeping with the traditions of the ancient architectural glory of England, is a proud and eloquent monument to him, who was the first to raise his voice against the abominations of an adopted paganism, against the base imitation of a corrupt style, foreign to our soil, to our climate, and to our national character. When Welby Pugin began his labours, there was not a single building of modern date, either public or private, which was not a reproach and a disgrace to the country. The finest site in Europe, as the late Sir Robert Peel himself declared, was spoiled by the ugliest building the imagination of man could conceive. And no less an

authority on all matters which concern public convenience than the 'Times' newspaper, declared in an
article on street architecture, that to no man do we
owe more than to Pugin, for the improvements which
have already taken place and for those which may
yet be effected in our public and private buildings.

Leading article in the TIMES *on Pugin and the revival
of architecture in England.*

'Of all those arts which combine the useful with the
beautiful there is not one that has descended in this
country to such degradation as architecture, and there
is not one which now gives greater hope for the future.
That very little of the architecture of the last century
and the present is beautiful is not the heaviest charge
that we have to bring against it, the heaviest charge is
that it is utterly false, utterly inappropriate, and not
durable. Domestic, palatial, or ecclesiastical, no matter
what the style of building, there is not much of the
masonry of the last hundred years which the educated
eye can contemplate with pleasure. Which of us in
his heart admires Oxford-street or Regent-street?
Forget for a moment the immense wealth in the warehouses that line those busy thoroughfares, forget that
the streets are paved with gold, and look up calmly
at those plastered walls and wooden pillars and fixtures
of stucco flowers, and say whether the nature of the
materials, or even the forms into which these materials
are wrought, can be more false, inappropriate, clumsy,
futile, transitory.'

After some further remarks on the recent manifest improvement in street architecture and in church building, the 'Times' concludes its article with the following laudatory but well applied observations on Pugin's earnest endeavours to promote a purer taste in architecture.

'Whether successful in treatment or not, what we regard with so much satisfaction in this and some other late specimens of architecture is the honesty of the work; and for this we have to thank, in the first instance, the late Mr. Pugin. With all his crotchets, and with an absurd attachment, not merely to the spirit but to the letter of mediævalism, he has perhaps done more for architecture than any of those who run him down. He it was who first exposed the shams and concealments of modern architecture, and contrasted it with the heartiness and sincerity of mediæval work. He showed the fair outside of a modern building having no relation to its construction except that of a screen to hide its clumsy makeshifts. He then showed how the first principle of mediæval work, was to expose construction and not to hide it, but to adorn it; a modern building for example conceals its flying buttresses with ·a dead wall; an ancient one exposes them and derives a principal charm from these contrivances being seen. It is the law of all the old architecture; there is nothing which it fears to show, it rather invites inspection within and without; whereas concealment was for long the rule of modern British architecture, concealment of the real materials, concealment of the manner of construction. Pugin is dead. Let us remember to his honour that if now there seems to be the dawn of a better architecture, if our edifices seem to be more correct in taste, more genuine in material, more honest in construction, and more sure to last, it was he who first showed us that our architecture offended not only against the law of beauty but also against the laws of morality.'

Far from being ornamental, our public buildings are not even convenient. To a practical people, like our-, selves, this failing in their chief purpose ought to be their final condemnation; but our national character inclines us to avoid rash reforms, even when most required, and makes us conservative even of abuses. Yet, when we reflect, that in no age have buildings so public and so important—constructions so vast and so novel—been undertaken as in the present, and that in no age or country has so little been shown for the vast outlay of public money, this consideration alone ought to induce the public to listen to the counsels of a writer, who in his various works has not only laid down the true principles of architecture, but has shown in how ready a manner they may be put in practice. In considering Pugin's writings, however, it is necessary to remember, lest his criticisms should appear severe and overstrained, that his labours at reform commenced about a quarter of a century ago, when apathy and irreligion combined, had allowed the great

ecclesiastical buildings of the country to fall into a
state of neglect and degradation, ill-suited to the holy
purposes for which they were built. If a purer taste
in art and a higher sense of duty have now removed
this national scandal, it ought not to be forgotten how
much of this revival was due to the bold and unsparing criticisms of the writer of ' Contrasts.' This
awakened regard to propriety in art, and reverence in
public worship, is a triumph of the principles for which
Pugin life-long contended,—a triumph of reverence
over irreligion, of the Christian over the Pagan principle.

In the ' Contrasts ' the author institutes a parallel
between the noble edifices of the fourteenth and fifteenth centuries and corresponding buildings of the
present day, and shows in a striking manner, and with
unconcealed delight, the wonderful superiority of the
architectural works of the middle ages over those of
the present century. In a philosophical spirit, and
with the logical acumen, which were distinguishing
qualities of his mind, the great defender of Gothic architecture next proceeds to inquire into the causes
which led to the decay of taste, and assigns as the chief
reason for the present degraded state of architecture,
the substitution in the sixteenth century of Pagan for
Christian ideas. The first axiom which Pugin lays
down, as the great foundation on which to build his
argument, is that the great test of architectural beauty
consists in the fitness of the design to the purpose for
which it is intended, and in the correspondence of the

style of a building with its use. He then shows that the
ideas and ceremonies of different people, as well as the
nature of the climate, have given rise to various styles
of architecture. Every ornament, too, every detail, in
the temples of Pagan nations had a mystical import.
'The pyramid and obelisk of Egyptian architecture,
its lotus capitals, its gigantic sphynxes and multiplied
hieroglyphics, were not mere fanciful architectural
combinations and ornaments, but emblems of the philosophy and mythology of that nation.' In classic
architecture, likewise, not only the forms of the temples, but the very ornaments, down to the minutest detail, were symbolic. In all the works of Pagan antiquity, from the caverns of Elora to the Druidical
remains of Stonehenge, the writer shows how the connexion between architecture and religious belief is
invariably found in the mystical plan or emblematic
decoration. With its stupendous mysteries Christianity
introduced an architecture of its own, symbolical of
the sublime doctrines of the Christian religion. It
is not the mere beauty of Pointed or Christian architecture which renders it so immeasurably superior to
all the productions of ancient Paganism, but the wonderful power it exhibits, in embodying and illustrating
the faith and practices of Christianity. The three
great doctrines of the redemption of man by the sacrifice on the Cross, the Trinity, and the resurrection of
the dead, are, the author of 'Contrasts' maintains, the
very foundation of Christian architecture. The Cross,
he says, is not only the very plan and form of a Catholic

church but it terminates each spire, and gable, and is imprinted as a seal of faith on the very furniture of the altar. The second doctrine is fully developed in the triangular form and arrangement of arches, tracery, and even subdivision of the buildings themselves; and the third doctrine is beautifully illustrated by great height, the vertical principle having been from the earliest period acknowledged as the emblem of the resurrection, and on this principle we may readily account for the adoption of the pointed arch by the Christians.

And do not all the churches erected during the middle ages, continues the author, set forth their origin as well as exhibit the triumphs of Christian truth? Like the religion itself, their foundations are in the Cross, and they rise from it in majesty and glory. The emblem of the Christian's brightest hope, the shame of the Pagan, placed between the anger of God and the sins of the city, crowns, in token of mercy and forgiveness, the sacred edifice. Not the external magnificence alone is to be contemplated with feelings of awe by the Christian, ' for if the exterior of the temple,' to quote the eloquent words of the author, ' be so soul-stirring, what a burst of glory meets the eye on entering a long majestic line of pillars rising into lofty and fretted vaulting! The eye is lost in the intricacies of the aisles and lateral chapels; each window beams with sacred instructions, and sparkles with glowing and sacred tints; the pavement is a rich enamel.'

Not pecuniary reward, not even the applause and

admiration of mankind, but devotion for, and faith in,
the religion for whose worship they were erected, can
enable the mind to conceive and compose buildings
which shall produce such imposing effects. Unless the
mind of the builder feel, is the writer's argument, that
to raise a temple to the worship of the true and living
God is the most glorious occupation that can fall to
the lot of man—unless he be imbued with the faith, the
zeal, and the unity of spirit which prevailed when the
term Christian had but one signification throughout
the world, and when the glory of the house of God
formed an important consideration with mankind,—
he will be utterly unable to conceive and raise wonderful fabrics, like those of our ancestors, which still
remain to excite our wonder and admiration. In the
second chapter of 'Contrasts' the author treats on the
revived Pagan principle, and shows that as prior to
Christianity 'all art was devoted to the service of
error and impurity, so that Christian art itself was the
natural result of the progress of Catholic feeling and
devotion, and its decay consequent on the decline of
faith itself; while all revived classic buildings, whether erected in Catholic or Protestant countries, are
evidences of a lamentable departure from the true
Catholic feelings and principles.'

He agrees with the opinion of M. le Comte de
Montalembert, that the ancient Pagans at least were
consistent, since in their architecture, symbols, and
sculpture, they faithfully embodied the errors of their
mythology; whilst modern Catholics have revived

these profanities in opposition to reason, and formed
the types of their churches, their paintings, their
images, from the detestable models of pagan error
which had been overthrown by the triumph of Christian truth. Not feelings of devotion, but a desire to display their art, or to increase their fame, have during the
last three centuries, Pugin contends, inspired the works
even of the most celebrated artists in every country.
This mania for Paganism has not only infected every
church which has been erected in modern times, from
St. Peter's at Rome downwards, but what is still far
worse to such a lover of antiquity as Pugin, it has
scarcely left, unencumbered by its unsightly and incongruous additions, one of the glorious fabrics of the
olden days. What does the Christian artist find in the
most celebrated palaces of Europe, but the veriest
heathen buildings? Not a Christian emblem nor ornament is to be seen. In the halls and galleries, on the
ceiling, window, and wall, we are indulged with a
more than Pagan luxury of gods and goddesses,
demons and nymphs, tritons and cupids. Holy subjects are exchanged for the fables of Ovid, classic
heroes take the place of the saints, and Paganism in
literature and art supersedes the principles of Christianity.

So fatal indeed has this rage for Pagan novelties
proved to Christian art on the Continent, that after all
the demolitions and destruction they have escaped, the
old English churches have retained more of their original features than most of those in foreign countries.

They enjoyed all the advantages of neglect. To Protestant apathy, continues the author, we are not a little indebted, since neglect is a greater preservation of antiquity than either modern innovation or restoration. When Protestantism originated anything *of itself*, its work was ten times worse than the extravagances perpetrated by its Catholic contemporaries, since it embodied the same wretched Pagan ideas, without either the scale or richness of the foreign architecture of the same period. It is most fortunate for English architecture that during the greatest rage for classic art, in consequence of Protestant ascendancy and indifference, the desire for church building was nearly extinct. Protestantism and the revived Pagan principle both date from the same epoch, both spring from the same causes; and neither could possibly have been introduced, is the argument of the author, had not corruption and internal decay prevailed to so fearful an extent, as to undermine the very principles and faith of Catholicism.

'I was perfectly right in the abstract fact,' Pugin contends, against a charge of misstatement which had been brought against him, ' that the excellence of art was only to be found in the Catholic Church, but I did not draw a sufficient distinction between the Catholic Church in its venerable garb, or as disguised in the modern externals of Pagan corruption.'

The third and fourth chapters treat of the pillage and destruction which the churches and great abbeys suffered under Henry the Eighth, Edward the Sixth, and during the Puritan ascendancy. The latter is a

Y

period in English history, too well known and too
generally regretted, to need much comment. The destruction, by the hand of fanaticism, of altar and
shrine, of chapel and abbey, which in perfect beauty
adorned every hamlet in England, roused, as may well
be imagined, in the mind of the great Christian artist,
an indignation that knew no bounds. It is not necessary to do more than merely indicate the train of his
argument, because the sacrilegious and impious destruction of these glorious works of our forefathers is
now to every cultivated and Christian mind a subject
of painful and humiliating regret. None will deny,
unless perhaps the most recent historian and eulogist
of Henry the Eighth, the rapacity which neither respected art nor sanctity, and which, by the help of the
axe and the halter, replenished the royal coffers from
the rich spoils of the monastic institutions. The
arrogant and impious step of proclaiming himself supreme head of a Christian Church, roused against the
King the noble resistance of those who preferred the
interests of religion to the will of a despot. Amongst
the numerous victims who suffered under the bitter
persecution which followed, the author cites the glorious
names of Bishop Fisher, Thomas More, and Abbot
Whiting, to show the injustice and cruelty of this
merciless tyrant, under whose reign the work of sacrilege was inaugurated. The suppression of the religious
houses proved, as the writer shows, the occasion of the
total overthrow of art, and paved the way for all those
disastrous events that so rapidly succeeded each other.

In a treatise like the 'Contrasts' the author could do no more, although he could hardly do less, than indicate some of the advantages accruing from these splendid institutions. He points out how the poor were entirely maintained by their boundless charity and hospitality, and how well the monastery was adapted alike as the training place of youth, and as the quiet retreat of mature age. The vast results in all classes of art and science, in the preservation and advancement of literature, show the excellent use the monastic bodies made of that time which was not consecrated to devotion, and the immediate duties of their orders. How sublime and admirable the splendour of their churches, how precious the material, how exquisite the form of their sacred vessels and sumptuous vestments the author delights in showing, and then the shelves of their libraries, who shall describe the host of ponderous and valuable volumes under which they groaned? I can well enter into the feelings, and understand the indignation which filled Pugin's mind, on the contemplation of the entire overthrow of the religious houses, the dispersion of so many treasures of ecclesiastical art, and the destruction of so many glorious monuments of ancient piety. To satisfy the wasteful extravagance of a profligate court the very lead was torn from the roofs and spires of venerable churches, and the shrines of the saints were rifled for their precious ornaments, and the vessels which had served for centuries in the most solemn rites of the Church were melted in the fire of the sacrilegious crucible.

The suppression of the monasteries Pugin considers to have been a fatal blow to the progress of architecture, and from that period he traces only a melancholy series of destructions and mutilations, by which the most glorious edifices of the middle ages have either been entirely destroyed, or so shorn of their original beauty, that what remains only serves to awaken our regret at what is for ever lost.   The author of 'Contrasts' enters into details, and verifies the facts he adduces by the weighty authority of Dugdale and Peter Heylin, and by the testimony of Stowe and other writers.   Numerous references and quotations are given in a valuable Appendix attached to his volume.

The hand of the church-builder was indeed paralysed, for who would build new churches when they saw the old buildings ransacked or allowed to fall into decay ? The parochial churches, when they were used for the new service, were cut to pieces, as the author feelingly laments, 'by galleries of all sizes and heights, the nave blocked up with pews, wooden panelling of execrable design, smeared over with paint, set up with the Creed and Commandments, entirely covering some fine tabernacle work, the projecting parts of which have been cut away to receive it.'

'Large portions of the church,' continues the writer, ' for which there is no use, were walled off to render the preaching more snug and comfortable, porches enclosed and turned into engine-houses; and when all has been done, what are they but inconvenient, inappropriate buildings, for the purpose they are used for ?'

Nor were these enormities confined to obscure villages only, but abominations equally vile, he alleges, and far more reprehensible, were to be found in collegiate and cathedral churches.

In fine, the author contends that the fall of architectural art in this country is intimately connected with the rise of the established religion, not only on account of the check it received from the destructive rapacity of Henry the Eighth, and from the avarice and fanaticism engendered by the growth of the new opinions, which had plundered and destroyed all those splendid works of art that, under the fostering care of the ancient faith, had flourished for so many centuries, but chiefly because to the new system the ancient architectural symbolism was both unsightly and inappropriate, and because oneness in faith and form of worship, and that inward unity of mind, which had hitherto bound men together, were utterly fled.

'In fact,' continues the remorseless author of 'Contrasts,' 'from the moment the new religion was established, all the great architectural edifices ceased to be of any real utility; the new rites could have been equally well performed in a capacious barn.' Were not the spontaneous offerings, the heartfelt tribute, the liberal endowments by which the ancient churches had been raised in splendour, exchanged for rates wrung from an unwilling people? The destructive principle triumphed. 'No longer were village priests looked on as pastors of the people, or those high in ecclesiastical authority with veneration and respect.'

In the ruins of the old religion its venerable architecture perished.

The two concluding chapters treat on the degraded state of ecclesiastical buildings at the period when Pugin lent his powerful aid to the Gothic revival movement, and contain some reflections on the probable state of the English churches, had this country remained in communion with the Catholic Church.

The author states, in the first place, that none, who were acquainted with ecclesiastical antiquities, but must have felt the emotions of astonishment and admiration, which the examination of the glorious cathedrals and churches of England had raised in their minds, rapidly give place to regret and disgust at the barren, meagre, and inappropriate use to which these edifices have been reduced, and at the miserable unfitness of the present tenants for the vast and noble buildings they occupy. He laments that the gates of these once ever open churches were fast closed, excepting for the brief space of time set apart twice a day to keep up the form of worship, and regrets still more the necessity of fastening up the churches lest, as was alleged, they should be exposed to destruction and desecration by the people in whom the ancient devotion and piety had become extinct.

'Few there are,' he continues, 'who amid the general change and destruction the ancient churches have undergone, can conjure up in their minds the glories of their departed greatness, and who, while they bitterly despise the heartless throng that gaze about the sacred aisles, mourn at the recollection of those ages of faith now passed and gone, which produced minds to conceive and zeal to execute such mighty, glorious works.' The author here points out the state of neglect and decay in which so many of these wonderful churches were allowed to remain, mouldering away from the want of the commonest care; and under the name of restoration, he exclaims, what mutilations have not been committed, what abominations perpetrated! 'There is no sympathy,' he continues, 'between these vast edifices and the Protestant worship. So conscious of it were the first propagators of the new doctrines that they aimed all their malice and invective against them. The new religion may suit the conventicle and the meeting-house, but it has no part in the glories of the ancient days; the modern Anglican establishment is the only one among the many systems that sprung up, which retained the principle of cathedral establishments and episcopal jurisdiction; and so badly put together were these remains of ancient church government with modern opinions and temporal jurisdiction, that they have ever proved the subject of popular clamour, and might be suppressed at any time by a legislative act. Then what a prospect to look to! What new ordeal, what new destruction would these ill-fated fabrics undergo? The mind shudders at the thought. Would they be walled up as in Scotland, and divided into preaching-houses for the Dissenters, the Unitarians, and the Free-thinkers? Would they be made into factories or store-houses, like the churches in France during the fatal Revolution of 1790? or—ruined, roofless, neglected—be left to decay like the many glorious fabrics that perished at the change of religion, of which only a few mouldering arches remain to indicate the site? One of these results would in all probability be produced if the present Establishment ceased to exist. One ray of hope alone darts through the dismal prospect; that, ere the fatal hour arrives, so many devout and thinking men may have returned to Catholic unity, that hearts and hands may be found willing and able to protect these glorious piles from further profanation, and in the real spirit of former years restore them to their original glory and worship.'

Pugin argues, in conclusion, that had even this country remained Catholic, it is not to be supposed that it would have been able to resist the inroads of those Pagan principles, which, since the revival of letters in the sixteenth century, had invaded and overrun most of the countries on the Continent, until scarcely a vestige of Christian art escaped the hostile hand of a revived and dominant intellectual Paganism. The animadversions of the author of 'Contrasts' were as severe on the corruptions of art in Catholic countries, as on Puritan abuses and Protestant apathy. He was too honest a man, and too candid a writer, not to stigmatize Rome, the seat of Catholicism, as the headquarters of the Pagan revival, and even to attack St. Peter's, raised at such unparalleled cost, for exhibiting in its decoration the symbolism rather of a heathen temple than of a Christian Church. That pointed architecture is not repugnant to the genius of Italy, nor unsuited, as often alleged, to papal ceremonial, the author has no difficulty in proving from its prevalence in the Peninsula during the middle ages. In the prolonged absence of the Popes from Rome during the purest period of Christian art, he discovers the cause of the comparative barrenness of the Eternal City in monuments of Christian art. He advises those students, who go to Italy to study art, to follow in the footsteps of the great Overbeck,—to avoid alike the contagion of its ancient and modern Paganism, and to confine their researches to its Christian antiquities. ' They would then indeed,' he says, ' derive inestimable benefit, for Italian art of the 13th, 14th, and 15th centuries is the beau idéal of Christian faith and purity, and its imitation cannot be too strongly inculcated ;' but when it forsook its pure, mystical, and ancient types to follow those of sensual Paganism it sunk to a fearful state of degradation, and for the last three centuries its productions of every class should only be looked upon for the purpose of being avoided. Now is the time, he urges, to break the chains of Paganism, which have enslaved the Christians for the last three centuries. Why should we any longer be content with mere natural and sensual productions in art, in place of the mystical and divine ? ' When I see a man,' he says, ' professedly a Christian who, neglecting the mysteries of the faith, the saints of the Church, and the glories of religion, surrounds himself with the obscene and impious fancies of mythology, I may presume, without violation of charity, that although he is nominally a son of Christian Rome, his heart and affections are devoted to that city in the days of its Paganism.'

In illustration of his text the author appends at the end of his volume a splendid collection of drawings, in which he shows the striking contrasts between modern and mediæval architecture. But how can these productions of Pugin's pencil be described,—how is it possible to convey to them who have not seen these now celebrated 'Contrasts' an idea of their beauty and power? They tell their own tale at a glance. They speak volumes. What amazing cleverness is not exhibited in their selection and juxtaposition! What humour and ridicule do they not throw on the grand and pretentious efforts of modern art! What quiet fun lurks in the brilliant pages of the great mediæval artist! But his sarcastic pencil reserves its strength to expose and attack the hollow shams and ostentatious vulgarity in which the architects of the day revelled, in glorious ignorance of the first principles of correct taste and true harmony. The angry manner in which his work was received, showed how true was its mark, and how it hit home into the very heart of the evil which it sought to destroy. Not an architect of the unreal and pretentious style, but recognised the truth of the contrast and felt its application. The self-love of many was wounded, and the vanity of all disturbed.

The rough hand of the great mediævalist had torn the veil from vulgar pretence, and exposed to contempt the hollow claims of modern art to original power, beauty, or genius.

In reply to the accusation of being either ignorant or disingenuous in not having noticed the charge preferred, amongst others, by Mr. Hope, the eminent architectural writer, against the Catholic Church, of having engrafted many heathen rites on Christianity, Pugin, in a letter addressed to the editor of Fraser's Magazine, contended that it would not be difficult to show, that ample authority was found in holy writ for the use of emblems, without referring their adoption to an imitation of Pagan usages ; and as for the assertion, that Christians borrowed their idea of consecrating their churches and protecting them from profane uses, from similar practices among the idolatrous Romans in regard to their temples, Pugin remarks : ' I think we may attribute the zeal of the early Christians on this score to far nobler motives and ideas than the bare imitating of idolatrous customs. As touching the use of lustral water, incense, and lights, all of these can be traced to an infinitely higher origin than either Greek or Roman Paganism. We find it employed in the worship of the true God, and *that* by his own command, centuries previous. The adoption of these practices by the heathen did not certainly render them evil ; it is the object to which external acts are addressed by which their propriety is to be tried, and not by the mere acts themselves, otherwise prayer itself might be proved to

have existed among Pagan nations, and consequently
to be objectionable and unfit to be exercised among
Christians.'

The author of 'Contrasts' then notices another
charge or taunt brought against that work. 'With
regard,' he says, 'to the omission of my own house
among the "Contrasts," which my reviewer says
cannot be attributed to excess of modesty, I beg to
say, I am by no means possessed of so large a stock
of impudence as he supposes; at any rate I have too
much common sense and feeling of propriety to exhibit
as an example, a small dwelling, erected with very
limited means, and simply calculated for a retired
residence. I really fear, that the earnestness with
which I have set forth the glorious works of past
days, and my forcible reprobation of modern abominations, has caused a mistaken notion that I have no
low idea of my own judgment and excellence. Such,
however, I beg to say, is far from the case. I am in
too continual contact with the noblest achievements
of ancient art to lose sight of my own extreme inferiority, and my vain endeavours even to follow
those, whom my wishes would be to rival, are quite
sufficient to repress any feelings of self-satisfaction.
But in giving vent to my admiration of works which
have ever been my study and admiration, and exhibiting, by their scale, the inferiority of our own times,
I will contend I have by no means laid myself open
to a charge of either arrogance or presumption.'

In the 'Contrasts,' as in his other works, and in his

life itself, the energy of Pugin's mind and the labour
of his hand were ever devoted to the broad principle
of erecting the most glorious temples to the worship
of God, and consecrating the highest efforts of art to
his honour.

' The True Principles of Pointed or Christian Architecture.'

In two lectures delivered at St. Marie's Oscott,
in which college he was professor of ecclesiastical
antiquities, Pugin, at a time when they were but
little understood, undertook to explain the 'True
Principles of Pointed or Christian Architecture,' and
to lay down rules by which architectural excellence
might be judged and tested. His treatise is the
grammar of architecture. Its laws are no more to be
violated than the ordinary rules of language. That
architectural principles are set at nought with im-
punity is only the result of the profound ignorance
which prevails on the subject, not only in the public
at large, but among those who are not ashamed to
style themselves professors and teachers of the art.
The two great rules for design which the lecturer lays
down are these : ' 1st, That there should be no features
about a building which are not necessary for conveni
ence, construction, or propriety ; 2nd, That all ornament should consist of enrichment of the essential
construction of the building.' In pure architecture,

the writer maintains on principle that the smallest detail
should have a meaning or serve a purpose, and that
construction itself should vary to accord with the properties of the materials employed. In pointed architecture alone, he contends, are these principles carried out.
He then proceeds to examine more fully ancient examples of stone, timber, and metal construction, and to show
that no features were introduced in the ancient pointed
edifices, which were not essential, either for convenience or propriety. The pillars, the arches, the vaults,
the ramified tracery of a stone building are all peculiar,
as the author well points out, to stone, and could not
consistently be executed in any other material. The
great altitude obtained by the ancient masons, and
the wonderful strength and solidity of their buildings,
are shown to be the result, not of the quantity or size
of the stones employed, but of the art of their disposition. A comparison is then instituted between the
pointed architecture of the middle ages and the classic
buildings of Greece, and the text is illustrated by
various wood-cuts which are of material assistance to
the reader. Grecian architecture, according to the
author of 'True Principles,' originated in wooden buildings, and its professors never possessed either sufficient
imagination or skill to conceive any departure from
the original type. Their buildings, in the earliest
period, exhibit the most ancient and the most barba-
rous mode of construction that can be imagined. But
what the learned professor of ecclesiastical antiquities
evidently considered most extraordinary, was, that

when the Greeks commenced building in stone 'the *properties of this material did not suggest to them some different and improved mode of construction.*' The author loudly and justly declaims against the monstrous absurdity, which has originated in the blind admiration of modern times for everything Pagan, of holding up their buildings as the standard of architectural excellence, and as the types on which the modern edifice and the Christian temple are to be formed. The writer then enters into details, for the consideration of which I must refer the reader to the work itself. He proves, however, that buttresses, the distinguishing feature of pointed architecture, are essential both for strength and beauty, and examines in which style, Christian or Pagan, these breaks and projections, so necessary in architecture, have been most successfully carried out. He maintains that it is the great principle of pointed architecture not to conceal, but to beautify its construction, while classic architecture seeks to conceal, instead of decorating, its supports. The writer next proceeds to criticise 'St. Paul's,' London, and ridicules the miserable expedients adopted to disguise those essential supports of the building, which in Gothic constructions are made the means of light and elegant decoration. In St. Paul's, one half of the edifice is built to conceal the other. This system of shams and unrealities is Pugin's abhorrence. He does not fail to point out its fictitious dome as one of the greatest defects in the metropolitan cathedral. The author takes high ground in his argument, and indeed maintains that 'if we view pointed architecture in its true light as Christian art, as the faith itself is perfect, so are the principles on which its architecture is founded.' 'It is as easy,' he says, 'to improve in mechanical contrivances as it is difficult successfully to deviate one tittle from the spirit and principles of the pointed style. After having proved that the ornamental parts of pointed stone buildings are merely the decorations of their essential construction, the author proceeds to treat on metal-work, and shows that the same principles of suiting the design to the materials, and decorating construction, were strictly adhered to by the artists of the middle ages in all their productions in metal, whether precious or common. He then briefly notices the exquisite productions of the ancient gold- and silver-smiths, and laments that the Reformers and Puritans have left us nothing but the mere name of the glorious shrines and ornaments, which formerly enriched our cathedral and other churches, and states, that were it not for a few places on the Continent, which have preserved their ancient treasures from heretical and revolutionary violence, we should be unable to conceive half the art, half the talent, half the exquisite beauties of this class of ecclesiastical ornaments.

Pugin is severe on the ignorance and incapacity of the modern artisan. Silver- and iron-smiths were in former times artists, and often great artists too; but in this enlightened age of mechanics' institutes and scientific societies, if you go, he contends, to a smith with a piece of work, not of the ordinary stamp, the vacant stare of the miserable mechanic speedily convinces you, that the turning up of a horse-shoe is the extent of his knowledge in the mysteries of the smithy ; and even 'the capital hand of the establishment,' if he be sufficiently clever to comprehend your meaning, will tell you, that what you want is quite out of his line. The true Mechanics' Institute, the oldest and the best, is the Church. Under her guidance at least, he contends, the minds of the operatives were not poisoned with infidel and radical doctrines. 'The Church,' says the writer, at the conclusion of his first lecture, 'was the great and never-failing school in which all the great artists of the days of faith were formed. Under her tuition they devoted the most wonderful efforts of their skill to the glory of God ; and let our prayer ever be,' he continues, 'that the Church may again, as in days of old, cultivate the talents of her children to the advancement of religion, and the welfare of their own souls, for, without such results, talents are vain, and the greatest efforts of art sink to the level of abomination.' Such characteristic passages abound in the 'True Principles;' and if we would estimate the character of Pugin aright, and penetrate into the mainsprings of his actions, we must not overlook, or treat lightly, indications which bear more than ample testimony to the earnest mind and religious heart of the great Christian artist.

In the second lecture, after treating on decoration with regard to construction in wood, and giving beautiful specimens of wooden roofs over churches in various parts of England, and showing how a mystical and appropriate meaning was exhibited 'in the carvings on the beams, and in the vacant spaces between the rafters, painted azure and powdered with stars,' the author proceeds to the consideration of propriety in architecture; and to illustrate his meaning more fully, divides edifices under three heads—Ecclesiastical, Collegiate, and Civil. The first principle to be considered in church building is the motive or intention. It was not Pugin's habit of mind to be content with superficial and unworthy motives. A man, who builds a church, draws down a blessing on himself, both for this life and for that of the world to come, was a conviction nearest his own heart; therefore he held that religion should form a leading impulse in the mind of the man who undertakes to erect a temple for the honour and worship of the Author of all good. In the olden days, when faith had a greater hold on the minds of men than commercial speculation, each city, he shows, had its mighty cathedral, rising above all the parochial churches; then came the abbatial and collegiate churches, with their vast and solemn buildings; each street had its temple raised for the true worship of God, 'variously beautiful in design, but each a fine example of Christian art; even the bridges and approaches were not destitute of religious buildings, and many a beautiful chapel and oratory was corbelled out on massive piers over the stream that flowed beneath.' It is this oneness in principle,

this singleness of purpose, united with an infinite
variety of detail, which the author wishes to illustrate
and enforce by the examples to be found in many an
ancient city, of edifices, to use his own words, ' of
various dimensions, of various degrees of richness,
various in arrangement, yet each bearing on its very
face the stamp of Catholic—cathedral or abbey, church
or oratory, they all show that they are dedicated to the
one true faith, raised by men actuated by one great
motive, the truly Catholic principle, of dedicating the
best they possessed to God.' One principle, the author
of this magnificent treatise insists upon without qualifi-
cation or reserve,—and that is, not that all men should
build vast and splendid churches, but that all men
should render the buildings, they raise for religious purposes, more vast and beautiful than those in which
they dwell. For men, who build churches, without the
least regard to tradition, to mystical reasons, or even
common propriety, the writer has no mercy; but the
utmost vehemence of his invective is expended on the
contemptible deceptions and showy expedients, practised to disguise by artificial means the meanness of
the real building. Trick and falsehood, he urges, may
make a church appear rich and beautiful in the eyes
of men, but the deception cannot escape the all-
searching eye of God, to whom churches should be
built, and not to man. The rubble wall and oaken
rafter of antiquity impress, he says, the feelings with
reverent awe, which never could be produced by the
cement and plaster imitations of elaborate tracery and
showy designs.   z 2

The intrusion of Pagan emblems and attributes into
Christian churches, is not only, he contends, a violation
of ecclesiastical propriety, but a great inconsistency
in the admirers of classic decoration, since the Pagans
never introduced any emblem without a mystical
signification being attached to it; while great as their
enormities may be, the author does not charge the
advocates of revived Pagan decoration with an actual
belief in the mythology, of which they are such
zealous admirers. But what have we as Christians
to do with Pagan emblems in churches? How does
the owl of Minerva show our wisdom, or the club
of Hercules our strength? Still more inconsistent,
if possible, are the Pagan sepulchral monuments.
'How can we,' asks the author of 'True Principles,'
'who believe in the glorious light of the resurrection, carve the inverted torch of Pagan despair on
our tombs? Not only the details, the ornaments and
emblems, but the very plan of modern churches are
fashioned, not on the principles of Christian but of
Pagan antiquity.

The author then adduces further reasons why the
architecture of the Greek temple cannot be introduced,
or imitated with propriety by Christians, and shows
how utterly inapplicable Greek temples are to the
purpose of Christian churches. There is, indeed, no
affinity between the idolatrous rites of the Pagan and
the worship of the Christian to serve as an excuse for
such an unwarrantable and unworthy imitation. The
madness of the attempt to introduce an alien style
into a country, literally covered with beautiful models

of ecclesiastical structures, is heightened, when he shows how every portion of these buildings, from the fundamental arrangement down to the most minute detail, answers both a useful and mystical purpose. 'What indeed,' he asks, 'is more appropriate for the ancient worship than an old English parish church, with its heaven-pointing spire—the beautiful and instructive emblem of a Christian's brightest hopes— with its solemn-sounding bells to summon the people to the offices of the church, or to serve by their lofty elevation in the belfry towers as beacons to direct their footsteps to the sacred spot? How well suited, too, is the interior of such a church for the performance of Catholic rites—the spacious nave and aisles for the faithful; the oaken canopy covered with images of the heavenly host, and painted with quaint and appropriate devices; the impressive doom or judgment pictured over the great chancel arch; the fretted screen and rood-loft; the mystical separation between the sacrifice and the people, with the emblem of redemption carried on high and surrounded with glory; the great altar placed far from irreverent gaze; and all the long perspective terminating with the brilliant eastern window.'

Such, says the author of 'True Principles,' is but a faint outline of the national edifices which have been abandoned for 'pewed and galleried assembly-rooms, decorated only with gas-fittings and stoves, and without so much as one holy or soul-stirring emblem about them.'

Under the next division of his subject, architectural propriety is examined with reference to collegiate architecture, and the author shows how perfectly this principle was carried out in our old English Catholic colleges. As the celebration of the divine office, with becoming solemnity and splendour, formed a primary consideration to our Catholic forefathers, so was ample provision made for this purpose in all the old collegiate foundations; and in illustration he points to Oxford, which presents, at a distance, a complete grove of towers, spires, and pinnacled turrets, rising from the collegiate churches. After noticing how every portion of these buildings had its distinctive character, how well adapted to the purpose was the external construction, how complete the internal arrangement—the solemn quadrangle,—the studious cloister,—the turretted gate-house; he contrasts with these noble monuments of Catholic wisdom and Catholic piety the modern collegiate buildings, and the system pursued in the godless colleges. He ridicules London University with its useless dome and portico. It may, however, be urged in its defence, he adds, with equal justice and severity, that anything ecclesiastical or Christian would be very inappropriate, and that the *Pagan* exterior is much more in character with the intentions and principles of the institution.

In no place which he ever visited, did Pugin find a more scholastic architecture than in Oxford, and he expresses a hope that its glories may not exist in vain, but that learned and thinking men may be led to draw a parallel in their minds between the faith of those who founded these noble institutions and our present degraded and half infidel condition, and by this consideration be led back to Catholic faith and unity.

In the last place, the author considers architectural propriety in reference to domestic architecture, and maintains that the condition of the climate has had, in every country, a large share in the formation of architectural style. On what consideration, then, is it correct to build an Italian house in England? Another objection to Italian architecture which the author starts, is the principle of nationality. ' We are not Italians, we are Englishmen. God,' he argues, ' has implanted in our breasts the love of our country, therefore we should avoid and oppose the extraordinary amalgamation of architecture, style, and manners now in progress. We are not cosmopolitans; why, therefore, hanker after the bastard Greek nondescript style, which has ravaged so many of the most interesting cities of Europe, and forget our own land and our own national architecture, which has so many claims to our reverence and love? It is needless to remark how the great artist laments that England is losing her venerable garb, and exchanging her ancient variety for dull and monotonous uniformity. Apollo-terraces, factory-chimneys, government preaching-houses, Zion chapels, Bethel meetings, New Connections, and Socialist halls, were to him like the

seven plagues of Egypt. He ridiculed the ostentation
and vulgarity of our street architecture, where the
linendraper's shop apes the palace of the Cæsars, and
the cigar divan, with its Turkish look, is a vile bur-
lesque of Eastern architecture. The whitewasher,
the grainer, the Roman-cement men, come in for their
share of well-merited castigation. The author has
nothing but contempt for the modern castellated
mansion and the pretentious abbey style of building,
which, like Fonthill, erected at an enormous expense,
is a mere sham and unreality. Not so the old English
mansion;—it was a solid, dignified, Christian structure,
built with a due regard to the general prosperity of
the family, and to the exercise of the rites of hospitality. And in the days when Catholic England, he
urges, was merry England, at least for the humbler
classes, the almoner dealt out their share of bounty to
the poorer guests beneath the groined entrance of the
manorial gate-house; thus true architecture answered
a purpose in all its arrangements, when it was in keeping with the faith and manners of the times—at once
strong and hospitable. This original and eloquent
treatise the author closes with the following words:—
' In conclusion, Christian verity compels me,' and let
us add, the manly candour inherent in his noble
nature, ' to acknowledge that there are hardly any
defects, which I have pointed out to you, in the course
of this lecture, which would not with propriety be illustrated by my own productions at some period of my
professional career. Truth is only gradually developed

in the mind, and is the result of long experience and
deep investigation. Having, as I conceive, discovered
the true principles of Pointed architecture, I am
anxious to explain to others the errors and miscon-
ceptions into which I have fallen, that they, profiting
by my experience, may henceforward strive to revive
the glorious works of Christian art in all the ancient
and consistent principles. Let, then, the Beautiful and
the True be our watchword for future exertions in the
overthrow of modern paltry taste and Paganism, and
the revival of Catholic art and dignity.'

'An Apology for the Revival of Christian Architecture in England.'

The aim of the third work, at the head of this
chapter—'An Apology for the Revival of Christian
Architecture in England,'—is to show Gothic architecture in its true light, to vindicate its title to the appellation of Christian, and to exhibit the claims it possesses
on our veneration and obedience, as the only correct expression of the faith, wants and climate of our country.
The writer exposes also with just severity the falla-
ciousness of the arguments, used both by the advocates
and opponents of Pointed architecture, in treating it as
a mere question of abstract beauty, whereas the author
of the 'Revival' contends that fitness and congruity
is the sole criterion of architectural beauty. Not
therefore on the score of its comparative superiority
over other styles, but only because it is the most
perfect expression of the Christian idea, is the Pointed

style adopted or defended by Christian architects.
To the neglect of this principle the author ascribes
the confusion which prevails in the present most eventful
period for English art, when, after a gradual decay of
four centuries, we are just emerging from what he well
terms 'the dark ages of architecture.' Because no
fixed principle is recognised, private judgment runs
riot, and every architect adopts a theory of his own,
the result generally of the last impression of his latest
travel—a view adopted from the Alhambra, or the
Parthenon, brought from the banks of the Nile, or from
Rome—a style revelling in lotus cups and pyramids,
or in dome, basilica, or portico. What is to be said of
the taste and judgment of men, who, insensible to the
exquisite beauty and magnificence of our national
churches, borrowed their style from the heathen temple,
the Chinese pagoda, or the mosque of the Mahometan,
until the distinctive characteristic of the Christian
Church was lost in the impure emblems of Paganism?
In this carnival of architecture, as Welby Pugin termed
it, 'motley was the only wear,' 'for its professors
appear,' as he observes, 'tricked out in the guises of
all centuries and all nations; the Turk and the Christian, the Egyptian and the Greek, the Swiss and the
Hindoo march side by side, and mingle together.'
But what, however, most grieved the earnest heart of
the great Christian architect, was to behold the venerable form of our national and Catholic architecture
adopted, not on consistent principle, not as the expression of the Christian faith, but as one of the dis-

guises of the day, to be put on and off at pleasure, and used occasionally, as circumstances or private caprice might suggest; adopted, because it was a style which an architect of the day should be acquainted with, or in order to please those who admire old things, or because it was *melancholy*, and *therefore fit for religious buildings* ! ! ! With the directness of purpose which was habitual to him, the defender of the revival of Christian architecture attacked the evil in its head-quarters. Where, if not in the Royal Academy and in the Universities, had he a right to expect correct taste and Christian principles? but if he were disappointed in his expectation, he knew at least on whose head to place the cap and bells.

'A man,' he says, 'who paganizes in the Universities deserves no quarter, and it becomes a question whether the greater share of blame, attaching to such transactions, is due to the architect who could so wed himself to the bastard compositions generated in his studio, as to intrude his huge deformity, not only in the vicinity, but on the site of ancient excellence; or to the authorities of the University, who, in the very teeth of the present revival, have sanctioned so gross a violation of propriety. But their madness is paralleled at Oxford, where the same architect is erecting another unsightly pile of Pagan details stuck together to make up a show, for the University galleries, immediately facing the venerable front of St. John's, and utterly destroying this beautiful entrance to the most Catholic-looking city in England.

'The Pagan character of this edifice has however awakened the disgust of some of the most learned members of the University; and if it pleases the admirers of gin-palace design, it will draw down the indignation of every true disciple of Catholic and consistent architecture. But, although some men, by dint of name, fortune, and station, may rule for a brief space, and mock that excellence to which they can never attain, yet their day is fast drawing to a close: several of the junta who have disfigured the face of the country are already gone; and, like Bunyan's giants in the Pilgrim's Progress, the others are so enfeebled that they can only snarl at the revival of excellence. Their works will hardly be endured for the time they have to run, and the remembrance of them will be the laughing-stock of posterity; and when the ancient glories of our native land are restored, and this generation of pretenders have passed away, men will be amazed that a period could have existed when they were permitted to disfigure and destroy, unchecked and unreproved.'

If the ancient architectural glories of our country are to be revived in our time, it will be owing, in no small measure, to the labours of Welby Pugin himself, to the earnestness and ability with which he called to mind the true principles of architecture, which had, for so long and dismal a period, been forgotten or neglected, and to the unsparing vigour with which he denounced the abortions of these miserable times,—'the conceits,' as he calls them, of a Soane, or the pitiful

fancies of a Nash.' In the convulsion of the old
theories and systems of the arts, which were breaking
up at last, like the icebergs in the Atlantic after the
severity of a long winter, an inextricable confusion
ensued. On the dull uniformity which had hitherto
predominated, disorders of every description succeeded; styles of every variety were adopted and
mingled, from the most extravagant conceits of Paganism, down to the grossest caricatures of our national
architecture. At a time so favourable for a master-
mind to leave his stamp and mark upon the age Pugin
arose. He was equal to the emergency. To an originality of mind was added a profound conviction of the
truthfulness of the principles he was called upon to
defend. His love of the beautiful was surpassed by
his love of the true. His earnestness was equal to his
knowledge, and his enthusiasm was contagious. To
warn, to guide, to counsel, to recal men to the knowledge of first principles, was, to borrow a phrase so
much in vogue in the present day, the mission of
Welby Pugin. His mission was triumphant: where
pompous mediocrity had failed, and learned dulness
was forgotten, true genius succeeded. But success
was accompanied by detraction and jealousy. His
knowledge was assailed, his motives impugned, his
enthusiastic love for the olden time derided by men,
who were as incapable of judging of the extent of his
knowledge, as of appreciating the motives of his reverence for the ages of faith.

In the 'Revival of Christian Architecture,' the author

vindicates himself against the charge of being a blind
bigot, insensible to and ignorant of any beauty, but
that of the middle ages. It is indeed much to be
doubted, whether he were not better acquainted with
the principles on which the various styles of Pagan
antiquity were founded than many of their warmest
advocates. A Christian artist like Welby Pugin did
not, indeed, underrate the supreme beauty of classic
art, he only condemned it as unfit for the sublime
purposes of Christian symbolism. It was simply
incapable of expressing the divine ideas which Christianity imparted to the mind of man. 'The Pagans
wished to perpetuate human feelings, the Christians
the divine.'

'I believe,' he continues, to quote the very words of
his Apology, 'Pagan principles to be the *perfect expressions* of *imperfect systems*,—the summit of human
skill expended on human inventions; but I claim for
Christian art a merit and perfection, which it was impossible to attain even in the Mosaic dispensation,
much less in the errors of Polytheism. The former
was but the type of the great blessings we enjoy, the
latter the very antipodes of truth, and the worship of
demons.' The history of architecture, he argues, is
the history of the world. The belief and manners of
all people are embodied in the edifices they raised.
Each style was the type of their religion, customs, and
climate, and perfect in its kind. A follower of
Brahma, or Isis, a fire-worshipper of Persia, could not
have produced anything different from what they

had done, because their edifices so truly embodied
the principles and worship of their builders.   To
raise a temple, or erect a pagoda, is consistent in the
worshipper of Jupiter, or in the votary of Juggernaut.
The use of cinenary urns is necessary to them who
burn their dead, and to them who offer animals to gods
it is natural to carve sacrificial friezes of bulls and
goats.   It is right in him who denies Christ, to reject
his cross. For all these are natural consequences. But
how is it consistent in Englishmen, who profess the creed
of the Christian, to reject, in favour of a foreign and
Pagan style, an architecture, whose beauties we may
claim as our own, whose symbols have originated in our
religion and customs ? The difference, the author urges,
between the religion of England at the present day,
and the religion of those who were the founders of our
national architecture and the builders of our glorious
cathedrals, is slight, compared with the difference
which exists between our country and those nations,
from whom we have been accustomed, for the last
century, to borrow our types, as being the best suited
to our present habits.   The author then meets the objection which has so frequently been urged against
Christian architecture, namely, that the Pointed style
was not developed until several centuries after the
establishment of Christianity. The Christian faith, as
soon as it began to spread and to gain importance, had
to encounter the bitterest persecution and all the ma-
lignant hate of a tottering Paganism. Christianity
had to live in the solitude of the catacombs. It had

to be silent unless it were compelled, for God's honour, to speak. But to speak was to suffer martyrdom. This was no time for the cultivation of the material arts. But, observes the thoughtful and profound author of the 'Revival of Christian Architecture,' may we not say that the foundations of Cologne were commenced in the catacombs of the Eternal City?

There it was that the Christian idea took root, to be developed, in all directions and under all forms of expression, in its later glories. As with doctrine, so it was with art; both had their germ in the catacombs, and both found their development when the Church had liberty to speak and power to act. In his grand and elaborate argument on development, Dr. Newman has well shown how the grain of mustard-seed has gradually expanded into the greatest of all trees, until, triumphant in beauty and luxuriant foliage, it extended over the earth. Pugin is the Newman of art.

In the days of her power and triumph the Church found a voice in the material arts. And what was the language which she then spoke? Was not Gothic architecture her glorious speech, the crowning result of her earlier efforts? Byzantine, Lombard, Saxon, and Norman, were all various developments of the Christian idea, until her mind found its most perfect expression in Pointed or Christian architecture.

But why in these latter days do the material arts speak with so uncertain a sound,—why but because they do not speak the mind of the Church; if the Church have not been struck dumb, yet her voice has been paralyzed by the confusion of tongues. When all speak, there is none to listen; when all desire to lead, there is none to obey. Architecture has only shared the fate of faith, of philosophy, of literature. The change which took place in the 16th century was not a mere change of taste, it was a change of heart and mind. The illumination of faith was obscured by the darkness of Paganism, by the shadow which a pestilential heresy cast over the intellect.

'When Pagan ideas,' says the author whose argument I am pursuing, 'triumphed over Christian principles, *inconsistency* for the first time was developed in architectural designs. Previous to that period, architecture had always been a correct type of the various systems in which it was employed; but from the moment the Christians adopted this fatal mistake, of reviving classic design, the principles of architecture have been plunged into miserable confusion.'

The author then proceeds to comment on the gradual development of inconsistent design, and shows how at first it was confined to the introduction of Pagan details into the ancient buildings.

In the same manner as the 'Contrasts' this work is also enriched with plates to illustrate the arguments of the text, and to impress on the mind of the reader the gradual confusion which arose in the architecture of the 16th century. It was long indeed before the ancient plan and arrangement of buildings, either ecclesiastical or civil, were entirely forsaken, and it is only within a comparatively recent period that error

and inconsistency has reached its climax, by indulging
in unrealities of every possible description, dressing
up, as the author shows, Italian masses with pointed
details, gathered from all styles, dates, and buildings.
Illustrations of these absurd inconsistencies are given
in the numerous plates attached to the volume.

The author next treats on Sepulchral Memorials, on
the costumes of ecclesiastical and court personages,
and on sculpture, and shows how the servile imitation
of classic art, without endeavouring to embody existing principles in their works, is the great error of
modern artists, and reproaches modern sculptors and
painters with having used the Christian mysteries
as a mere vehicle for the revival of Pagan forms, and
the exhibition of the artist's anatomical skill. From this
reproach, however, he excepts the modern German
school, with the great Overbeck at their head, and
bestows on them his warmest eulogiums for their
glorious revival of Christian art and tradition.

Pugin has been often reproached, in no measured
terms, for the harshness of his judgment and the
severity of his criticisms on contemporary artists and
their immediate predecessors. But Pugin has only
anticipated the verdict which history will not fail to
pronounce on the taste and judgment of the age.
What modern monuments have we to boast of, to
illustrate the progressive march of our national greatness, to commemorate the deeds of our departed wor-
thies, or to embody and express the grandeur of our
national institutions ? The history of a mighty people

ought to be written in its public buildings; its military glories, its legislative wisdom, its religious belief, shown in triumphal arch, in palace and temple, so durable as to set even time at defiance, and so glorious and Christian as to fascinate the eye and lead captive the mind of Macaulay's celebrated 'New Zealander,' who, in ages yet to come, shall visit our shores to mourn over fallen greatness, and to study our national character. How immeasurably superior in that future traveller's eye will not appear the barbaric piles of unfashioned stone to our most elaborate productions, because they had attained the chief purpose of public buildings—a durability which had defied the ravages of ages, and remained a standing memorial of a people's greatness. Pugin is hopeful that when the principles, on which beauty in architecture depends, become more generally understood, England will once more attain to architectural excellence. He would have the architectural student learn, that the same perfection of design is to be found in the simplicity of the village steeple, as in the towering central spire of cathedral churches, and that architectural beauty consists in embodying and expressing in the structure the purposes for which it is to be used, and not in disguising, or altering its character by borrowed features. 'The peasant's hut, the yeoman's cottage, the freeman's house, the baronial hall,' he continues, 'may be each perfect in its kind; the student should visit village and town, hamlet and city; he should be a minute observer of the animal and vegetable creation, of the grand effects of nature.

2 A 2

The rocky coast, the fertile valley, the extended
plain, the wooded hills, the river's bank, are all grand
points to work upon ; and so well did the ancient
builders adapt their edifices to localities, that they
seemed as if they formed a portion of nature itself,
grappling and growing from the sites in which they
are placed.' 'The rubble stones and flinty beach,' he
argues, ' furnish stores as rich for the natural architect
as the limestone quarry or granite rock. What beautiful diversity does the face of this dear island present!
What a school for study and contemplation! Where
are to be found twenty-four cathedrals, the finest monastic buildings, thousands of parochial churches, and
interesting remains of antiquity without number, all
within a boundary of a few hundred miles? Each
county is a school, where those who run may read,
and where volumes of ancient art lie open for all
inquirers.'

England, during the last three centuries, must be
judged, Pugin contends, by the corresponding history
of surrounding nations in that period of bitter trial
and degradation, when Catholic art and traditions,
throughout Europe, were neglected and despised :
while Paganism ruled triumphant in the palace, pene-
trated the cloister, and even raised its detested head
under the vaulted cathedrals, and over the high altars
of Christendom. In the common ruin in which war
and revolution, on the countries of the Continent,
have involved abbey and cathedral, church and convent,—so reducing the most dignified clergy of France,

that not one rood of land is left for priest or altar of
all the vast estates which ancient piety had bequeathed,—he finds cause for thankfulness, that matters
are not worse than they are in our own country. Who
will not sympathise with the great Christian artist
when he says, that the sad recital alone of the sacrilegious spoliation, which demolished churches, ransacked tombs of prelates and nobles for the sake of
the lead they contained, profaned and melted the
sacred vessels of the sanctuary, and trod under foot
the images of our Divine Redeemer, moved him more
than even the record of ancient glory? ' We lament,'
he continues, ' over the prostrate pillars and scattered
fragments of some once noble pile; we raise the
fallen cross, bare the ancient legend on the wall, collect the fragments from the shattered panes, and clear
the accumulating soil from moulded vase and tomb.'
The study of Catholic antiquity, he argues, is so associated with ancient piety and holy recollections, that
the soul is insensibly drawn from the contemplation
of material objects to spiritual truths; that an Englishman needs not controversial writings to lead him
to the faith of his fathers: it is written on the wall, on
the window, on the pavement, by the highway. ' The
cross, that emblem of a Christian's hopes, still sur-
mounts,' he says, in conclusion, ' spire and gable; in
flaming red it waves from the masts of our navy, over
the towers of the sovereign's palace, and is blazoned
on London's shield. And who can look on the cross-
crowned spire, and listen to the chime of distant bells,

or stand beneath the lofty vault of cathedral choir, or
gaze on long and lessening aisles, or kneel by ancient
tomb, and yet *protest* against aught but that monstrous and unnatural system that has mutilated their
beauty, and marred their fair design?'

In these three works, which we have been attempt-
ing to analyze and digest, and in the 'Treatise on
Roodlofts,' Pugin has developed the principles of
Gothic architecture, and reduced them to a system.
No one interested in the study of mediæval art—no one
aiming at the revival of a purer taste—no one engaged
in architecture as a profession—can fail to derive benefit and pleasure of a high order from their perusal.
Pugin's works are text books in the architectural
schools of Germany. In England the name even of
Christian art was almost unknown before he commenced his labours; its revival is now associated with
his memory. He was well fitted for his task : it was no
easy one, for he had to encounter the deep-rooted prejudice against the mediæval times. 'Can any good
thing come out of Nazareth?' Was there light in
the ages of darkness? and who is he that teaches
truthfulness to Protestant England, even though it be
only in architecture? A recent convert to Rome.

He had to convict the nineteenth century of ignorance, and to twit the age of enlightenment with the
absurdity of its taste, and the obscurity of its artistic
vision. He had to lower the national pride of England. Better to face the lion in its den, or pluck its
young from the tigress, than undertake such a feat.

But Pugin was in earnest, and eloquent, and never shrunk from the conflict: he could take a blow as well as give one. He was honest and outspoken, and wrote what he felt. His criticisms, if severe, were impartial, and never sprang from personal motives. He spared no one : his denunciations fell on all alike, no matter of what age or creed. The dissolute churchman of the mediæval times, who, to the scandal of his pious clergy, squandered the vast revenues of his see, whilst the glorious cathedral was despoiled of its treasures and left to decay, met with no more mercy at the hands of this bold denouncer of abuses than he showed to the ignorant Puritan or fanatic Iconoclast. His ridicule was as frequent and as keen on the glaring absurdities of the new-fangled Catholic chapel as on the gross vulgarity of the Protestant conventicle. His writings were a key to his character ; he threw himself into his works without disguise or reticence. The thoughts which were uppermost in his mind came out; his views, often immature, often doubtful, sometimes erroneous, were spread abroad— vox scripta manet—the casual exaggeration, the incidental error, where his main position was right, were remembered against him, and brought out to his condemnation. Judged as a whole, his works, from the elaborate treatise to the dashing pamphlet, were broad in their views, vigorous in style, and original in matter and form. He avoided shallow conventionalities as he would pitch ; he was always ready to grapple with great principles, to penetrate beneath the surface, though sometimes he went beyond his depth. His writings—brilliant, impetuous, rash—were never put to an unworthy purpose—never advocated an unjust cause, or concealed an unwelcome truth : they were like the two main principles of his own Gothic style—upright and thorough.

CHAPTER II.

Pugin on Rood Screens—Tractarian criticism—' Reverence' versus the
' All-seeing Principle' of modern church builders—His controversy
with the ' Rambler,' the organ of debased Italianised principles in
art and architecture—Dr. Newman's tribute to Gothic architecture
—Pugin's denial that he would like to destroy St. Peter's, Rome—
Moorfields Chapel—Musical mass in Cologne Cathedral—Ecclesiastical
taste in France—His severe criticisms on the operative music in
English Catholic chapels—' Church-openings and religious performances'—Pugin's letter on the Catholic Church, Hereford—Legacy-
hunting—A last 'scene' described—Pugin on the English Catholic
hierarchy and its purely spiritual character—On Church government
—He is accused of advancing heretical views—Refutation of his
accusers—Episcopal opinions—Letters—Anglican orders—His advocacy of the voluntary principle—And of the complete separation of
Church and State—The abuses resulting from large endowments—
State tyranny and corruption, and consequent spread of infidelity
in Europe during the last three centuries.

ON the publication of a ' Treatise on Chancel-screens
and Rood-lofts,' in which Pugin undertook to show
their antiquity, use, and symbolic signification, a controversy arose of such a character, that if we be not
indifferent to the motives and main springs which were
at work in Pugin's mind, and to the principles which
animated his conduct in life, we cannot in justice to
him pass over in silence. It would seem, at first sight,
next to impossible, that, in an architectural treatise,
questions could be broached which should not only in-

volve the interests of religion, but arouse the spirit
of controversy. Were indeed the 'Rood-screens' a
simple architectural book, it would be unnecessary to
allude to it in this place; but like all the more important works which emanated from Pugin's hands, it
enters in a bold and searching manner into the principles which underlie modern innovation in ecclesiastical matters. It is not, he says himself, a mere question of architectural detail, but a question which in-
volves great principles connected with discipline and
even faith, for the revival of true architecture is intimately mixed up with education, and the formation of
the minds of the rising generation. It may, perhaps,
be necessary to explain here that the use of the rood-
screen has been of universal obligation, and belongs
to no particular style, or date, and that its object is to
part the people from the priest, and to set a boundary
in a church round the place of sacrifice, to teach the
faithful to reverence the seat of the holy mysteries,
and to worship in humility and awe. In the constitution of Pugin's mind reverence was the strongest element; it is therefore not surprising that his vivid
imagination should be peculiarly impressed by the
symbolism of ancient ecclesiastical architecture, in
which the doctrines of Catholicity are so reverently
figured. To him indeed the grand portals of the ancient cathedrals were ever ' *Bibles in stone.*' The preservation of the rood-screen itself, he maintained, was
a vital principle, inasmuch as it would scarcely be
possible to preserve the interior faith in the doctrine
of the holy Eucharist, if all exterior respect and re-

verence were abolished. It was not a struggle on matters of taste or ornament, but a contention for the great principles of Catholic antiquity, tradition, and reverence, against modern development and display. Rood-screens, he contended, were not only inseparable from Pointed architecture, but inseparable from Catholic arrangement in any style—Byzantine, Norman, Pointed, or Debased.

The fundamental principle of the work is the recognition of the intimate connection between the externals of religion and the faith itself, and the necessity, consequent on the sacred nature of its awful mysteries, that the Christian worship should assume a form of solemnity and reverence unknown to the Pagan, and but ill-understood in the present day.

On its first appearance, Pugin's work on chancel-screens was hailed with delight by some members of the High Church party, who strained his argument to the uttermost, in order, if possible, to twist it into a vindication of Anglicanism. One of the ablest writers, in a quondam Tractarian journal, directed the attention of the sound members of his community to this volume, ' which,' he says, ' greatly concerns the Church of England, rightly understoood, on a matter in which the great Roman Catholic architect is found on the same side as the Church of England, and in opposition to the most extreme and Ultra-montane section of his own communion.' 'Amongst the most strenuous and embittered antagonists of the said unfortunate chancel-screens,' continues the writer, with a purpose which is only too transparent, ' are to be found the " Papists "

par excellence, those members of the Roman Catholic
Church who are most Roman, most Popish, most Ultra-
montane—the believers in developments, the converts
who find their most congenial home in the oratory of
St. Philip Neri.' The writer assumes that those
Catholics who are most attached, most drawn to the
See of Rome adopted Italian as the typal architecture of ultra-montanism, whilst Pugin and another
section of Catholics, hostile, he allows it to be inferred,
to the Holy See, adopted the Pointed as the typal architecture of national Roman Catholicism. This ingenious Tractarian writer, so familiar with the doctrinal
divisions in his own community, and so wise in recon-
ciling to his own satisfaction the opposing articles of
his own creed, sets up a theory to account for the difference of opinion, which he assumes to exist, in the
Catholic Church on the subject of the Eucharist. His
theory is, that in modern ages a materialistic aspect has
been given to the doctrine of the Real Presence in the
Western Church, which 'has created, so to speak, a sen-
timental craving on the part of the ultra-Romanists for
physical proximity to the altar—annihilated in them
the conservative and repressive desire to preserve the
traditions of antiquity—the desire, for example, that
(to employ the words of our own Anglican Rubric),
the chancels shall remain as in times past.' 'These
trains of thought,' he continues, 'have created the
theory that chancels, and so forth, were all very well
for the middle ages, but that this enlightened generation had developed the necessity of the congregation
getting as near the altar as possible, as if in this bodily

approach an increase of blessing was involved. The result has therefore been a movement in a certain section of the English Roman Catholics against chancels and their screens. The controversy however,' he adds, 'is, in its most real aspect, quite distinct from any architectural differences—purely doctrinal, one might affirm without much of exaggeration, in so far as the true reasons for the maintenance of these chancel-screens were the manifestation in the first place of the awful solemnity encircling the holy Eucharist in the eyes of all the early Christian Church ; and in the second, a certain separation between those specially engaged in divine worship and the general flock—two objects conjointly accomplished by a barrier not interrupting sight or sound, and yet gently parting the *clerici* from the whole body of the faithful, and leaving them alone face to face with the "holy mysteries," as our Prayer-book calls them. Chancel-screens happen to be the battle-field, but we fancy that many things besides chancel-screens are in ambuscade behind.'

This criticism is a fair sample of the attacks which Pugin's Catholic reputation has had to endure, attacks in which more was insinuated than stated, in which impressions were intended to be left on the mind of the reader unfavourable to his character as a Catholic. It is hardly necessary to refute the confused notions which the writer entertains as to the division of opinion on matters of faith in the Catholic Church, but when he casts imputations on Pugin's orthodoxy, and on his fealty to Rome, such accusations ought not to be passed over by those who hold his Catholic name in reverence.

The facts are simply these : in his attempt to revive in England Christian architecture, Pugin was animated by no hostility to Rome, by no desire to set up a national church ; he had too great a reverence for Papal authority to be a Gallican. In his belief, which was no idle æsthetic fancy, but the rooted principle of his life, Pointed architecture was the best expression of the mind of the Church, the grandest mode of giving utterance to feelings of homage, reverence, and love. The Oratorians, so flippantly alluded to, did not cherish the bitter and inveterate hostility against Pugin and his works, imputed to them by this Tractarian writer, as appears from the subjoined letter from the Bishop of ——, and as might be expected from their character and position. The Fathers of the Oratory simply adopted, as is the custom of religious orders, the style of architecture, if one it may be called, which prevailed in the time of their founder.

'May 9th, 1851.

' DEAR MR. PUGIN,

'I saw Dr. —— this evening, and told him your declaration respecting the Oratory, and your intention to say no more regarding them. He was much pleased, expressed himself well satisfied, assumed that henceforward there would be silence on both sides in public writings from attacks, and said in a very animated tone, that he should be happy to show any civility in his power to you.

'I have also had a letter from the Cardinal in reply to one of mine, in which his Eminence says, that he will endeavour to throw oil upon the troubled waters.

'Allow me to say that I was much edified with your conversation, that is with its spirit, in a matter so personal last night, but not more than I had anticipated.

'Wishing you every blessing,

'I remain,

'Your devoted father in Christ,

'✠————'

The Tractarian writer, whose damaging patronage of Pugin's work I am noticing, and whose *Anglican* and non-natural interpretation of his views it is my purpose to rebut, introduces without the slightest warrant, and in a flippant style, the name of Dr. Newman into this controversy. There is no shadow of truth in the assertion that that eminent writer lent the high authority of his name to the assailants of Pugin, and of the revival of Gothic architecture. In a passage of a lecture, where he is pointing out how the fine arts may prejudice religion by giving the law where they should be subservient, Dr. Newman pays, in his own incomparable manner, a noble tribute to Gothic architecture, whilst he shows, at the same time, how we should be on our guard against the excesses into which all revivals have a tendency to fall. 'For myself,' he says, 'certainly I think that that style which, whatever be its origin, is called Gothic, is endowed with a profound and a commanding beauty, such as no other style possesses, 'with which we are acquainted, and which probably the Church will not see surpassed, till it attain to the Celestial City. No other architecture, now used for sacred purposes, seems to have an idea in it, whereas the Gothic style is as harmonious and as intellectual as it is graceful. But this feeling should not blind us, rather it should awaken us, to the danger, lest what is really a divine gift, be incautiously used as an end rather than as a means. It is surely quite within the bounds of possibility, that, as the *renaissance* three centuries ago, carried away its own day, in spite of the Church, into excesses in literature and art; so a revival of an almost forgotten architecture, which is at present taking place in our own countries, in France, and in Germany, may in some way or other run away with us into this or that error, unless we keep a watch over its course. I am not speaking of Ireland; to English Catholics at least it would be a serious evil, if it came as the emblem and advocate of a past ceremonial, or an extinct nationalism.'* If it be in nowise true, that the converts as a body were hostile to the Gothic revival, it is still less true that they, who were most attached to Rome, were most opposed to Pugin. It is however a fact, as this Tractarian writer alleges, that 'Pugin, from various causes, was the chief object of the attacks,' not as he supposes, of the 'ultramontane'

---

* Discourses on the Scope and Nature of University Education.

party, but of a clique of writers, whose chief organ
was the 'Rambler;' 'attacks,' he continues, 'the
bitterness of which can only be accounted for by the
fact, that those who have made them feel, in spite of
themselves, how much he has to say for his own side
of the question; and the volume before us comprises
his defence against the storm of hard words, with which
he has been unsparingly abused for these last three
years.' Pugin was not slow in retort, and when the
'Rambler' asserted that although it might be induced
to admire Gothic churches, there were three things it
could never like, and these were 'Gothic vestments,'
'Gothic letters,' and '*Gothic manners*,' and advised
the great architect to stick in future to his trowel,
Pugin replied, 'We pointed men have pointed tools,
and can contrive occasionally to cut other things
besides crockets.'

Pugin then carries the warfare into the enemy's
camp, and denounces in severe terms the modern all-
seeing principle advocated by the 'Rambler,' which,
he says, would convert ' our churches into show-rooms,'
and make them 'as barren and bare as barns, and as
hideous to look upon as the shambles of the market-
place.' If religious ceremonies are to be regarded as
spectacles, to be consistent, he argues, they should be
celebrated in regular theatres, which have been ex-
pressly invented for the purpose of accommodating
great assemblages of personages to hear and see well.
'It has been most justly said,' he continues, 'that
there is no legitimate halting-place between Catholic

2 B

doctrine and positive infidelity, and I am quite certain that there is none between a church built on Christian tradition and symbolism, and Covent Garden Theatre.' In his controversy with the writers of the 'Rambler,' Pugin, nevertheless, admits that many of the propositions advanced in its articles on church architecture and decoration are undeniable, while, at the same time, the conclusions drawn are utterly false, and that many important and evident truths are mingled with the dissemination of their debased principles. They set forth a forcible appeal for the spiritual wants of the people, and the need for a great number of moderately-sized churches; they deprecate most justly extravagant outlay on ornament in the present state of spiritual destitution; the day of combat, when every inch of ground is disputed, they argue, is not the time for triumphant display. To these propositions Pugin readily assents, but when they wish to make it appear that Pointed architecture is not adapted to meet these wants, and 'that those, who are labouring for its revival disregard these necessities, thus meriting the censure of St. Wulstan on some builders of his time—that they accumulate stones to the neglect of souls—then it becomes an absolute duty to expose the fallacy of the conclusions put forth by the "Rambler," and to explain the real views and feelings of its advocates.'

He accordingly taxes the 'Rambler,' and its supporters, with harbouring Genevan tendencies, and indulging in Methodistical cant. He repudiates its narrow and captious criticisms, and its open rupture, in the domain of architecture, church music, and ritual observances with the time-honoured customs and glorious traditions of Catholic antiquity. He finally denounces the dangerous innovations and discontented spirit which he discovers lurking in the pages of the 'Rambler,' and foretells, with an almost prophetic keenness of vision, that, sooner or later, its writers will gravely offend against Catholic judgment and wound in its dearest interests Catholic instinct.

The great restorer of mediæval architecture then defends himself against the charge advanced by his opponents, that he had treated with disrespect the most splendid examples of Catholic zeal and art, and that he had desired to pull down the church of St. Peter's at Rome. ' Is it,' he says, ' because I exclaim against the abortions of these miserable times that I am accused of being insensible, and even opposed, to the great masters of Italian art? In this country, my own bias leads me certainly to prefer and advocate the Pointed style, and while I have life left, I will protest against the caricatures of ancient temples which are daily erected, serving alike for church, dwelling, hospital, or palace. At the same time were I to withhold my just tribute of admiration for noble art of every style, were I not to ascribe to one common origin, one universal purpose, the great variety of genius, whether displayed in the Basilica of St. Peter's or in the Minsters of Strasbourg, and Cologne, whether in the massive grandeur of the Norman churches, or in the gorgeous beauties of the later periods, I should consider myself richly deserving any reproach that might be cast upon me.

' I will never believe,' he says, ' that the English Catholics as a body can be led by the hollow arguments of the writers in the " Rambler," to abandon the traditions of their ancestors in the faith, and after gaining so much, to fall back on the mongrel edifices which these men would substitute for the pure, I may say divine, architecture which was generated by Christianity in the ages of faith ; and I do say that the feeling for antiquity, which is in a manner inherent to this nation, is a more powerful lever for restoring the love and reverence for the old religion than all the controversy that has ever been preached or printed.' The traditions which clung to the old colleges of Oxford, and haunted its venerable halls and quadrangles, were to Pugin so many arguments in favour of the restoration of the ancient architecture as a help towards the revival of the ancient faith. The power of association is strong in youth, and what associations are not connected with the names of Wykeham, of Waynflete, and of Allcock ? ' England,' Pugin argues in his hopeful manner, ' must be rent to pieces before the Catholic fibres that run through her whole system can be eradicated. Links, invisible to many eyes, but strong, I may say indissoluble links, bind this country to the traditions of the past ; nor can I believe that so much has been spared and preserved without being destined to serve some great end in the hands of Divine Providence. What other nation that has departed from the faith has retained a tithe of the Catholic practices and traditions that have been preserved amongst us? I gained my knowledge of the ancient faith,' he continues, 'beneath the vaults of a Lincoln or a Westminster, and I found it indelibly marked in the venerable piles which cover the face of this land. This period of my life was one of great mental happiness. I almost lived in those great churches, and revelled in the contemplation of their ancient splendour.' How hard the struggle was for a man like Pugin to leave the spots he had held so sacred, and to worship in a room inferior to many a Wesleyan meeting-house, may well be imagined. 'I had seen,' he says, 'little or nothing of the Catholic body in England. I once had a peep into Moorfields chapel, and came out exceedingly distressed before the service, of which I had not a very clear idea, was concluded. I saw nothing that reminded me of the ancient religion, from the fabric down to the vestments of the celebrants. Everything seemed strange and new; the singing, after the solemn chants of Westminster, sounded execrable, and I returned perplexed and disappointed.' His continental journeys did not remove his perplexities. To a mind filled with the effect of the wonderful works of the Catholic Church during the middle ages, a continental journey now must always be an extreme disappointment. France he found in an execrable state, as far as regards taste and ecclesiastical propriety; but he made this just remark, that it is only those who have an opportunity of penetrating into religious houses, and of becoming personally acquainted with the ecclesiastical authorities, who can at all appreciate the amount of piety and zeal that exists even in the most worldly-looking capitals.' In Germany he found matters no better. 'I remember,' he says, 'with what extreme devotion I entered the stupendous vaults of Cologne to assist at what I expected would be a service commensurate with the majesty of the fabric. I knelt outside the choir, into which, to my astonishment, I saw a crowd of lay persons pushing or standing about the entrance. The great bell ceased.' They who knew Pugin, and have witnessed the scene of confusion and distracting noises which, at that time, used to accompany a grand musical mass in Cologne Cathedral, alone can imagine his horror and grief. The tuning of fiddles, the maestro *à la Jullien*, the women in fashionable attire, holding sheets of music and coquettish fans, the motley and moving crowd of sight-seers—tourists, infidels, bearded republicans, commissionaires in blouses, were enough to excite to indignation a calmer man than the great mediæval architect. 'An orchestral crash, commenced,' he says, 'what must have been intended for the "Kyrie." The mighty pillars, arches, vaults, all seemed to disappear ; I was no longer in a cathedral, but at a Concert Musard or a Jardin d'Hiver. I never before felt so strongly the superiority of sound over form, and, architect as I am, I would infinitely prefer solemn chants in an ugly church, than to assist in the finest cathedral of Chris-

tendom, profaned by those diabolical fiddlers. I remained in agony. Sometimes we had a sort of robbers'
chorus, sometimes the plaintive notes of a nightin-
gale.'

'Happily, at that time,' he continues, 'I did not
cross the Alps, so I escaped that severest of all trials
for the faith of the neophyte—the Eternal City. I am
quite satisfied that unless a man is able to distinguish
principles from abuses, and to separate the majesty of
the Catholic ritual from the debased externals of
modern times, he is not likely to be impressed with
the majority of the religious services at which he
assists ; and it is an indisputable fact, that out of the
thousands of travellers who annually quit this country
for the Continent, few return with feelings of reverence
for the religion of their ancestors, on account of the unfortunate garb in which it is presented to their view.
But however strongly I viewed these matters, as an
artist, my moral convictions were such as admitted of
no doubt as to my line of duty, and I felt that the only
hope of reviving the ancient solemnity was to enter in
at the gate and work on the old foundations. When
I took this important step there was little human probability of effecting anything considerable. I was not
personally acquainted with a single Catholic eccle-
siastic, without influence, and with but slender
means.'

Pugin had to contend against all kinds of hin-
drances and attacks, not only from the common enemies of religion, but from false friends, or, what is

nearly as bad, from men who take up extravagant and perverted views with good intentions, and injure what they mean to aid.

'Let me then implore,' he continues, ' those who are exciting this insane, I may almost say impious, movement against the restoration of old Catholic solemnity, to consider the mischief that may result from the course they are pursuing. They raise doubts and uncertainties among weak-minded persons; they create a spirit of division in the faithful; and, to a certain extent, they mar the erection of fitting temples to Almighty God. As to the ultimate and entire failure of their architectural principles, I do not entertain a shadow of a doubt, but, in the mean time, it is most harassing and conflicting to be obliged to turn our arms against a body of mutineers, instead of advancing on the common enemy—the Pagan and infidel principle—which requires our united exertions to subdue; and I do trust and hope that in future they will turn their talents to better account, confining themselves to subjects or questions, on which they are fully qualified to write with edification and benefit to the faithful, and leave architectural matters to those who have devoted their whole lives and energies to its study.'

The writers and supporters of the 'Rambler' were not, however, the only members of his own communion with whom Pugin came in conflict: the secular music and operatic performances which, at the time, prevailed to such an extent in the Catholic churches, as to cause a fashionable Catholic chapel in the metropolis to be popularly known as the 'Shilling Opera-house,' were Pugin's abhorrence. 'Silent contempt' was no habit of the great reformer of abuses: in an earnest appeal for the revival of the ancient plain song, the writer says: 'When chancel screens were first attacked, about three years since, I at once denounced the writer of the article as one who was opposed to the very principles of Christian architecture, and I then stated my belief, that the objection to screens was merely raised as a test of public opinion, and in order to ascertain how far the party (of which the writer was an organ) might proceed in their opposition to the whole system on which the revival of true ecclesiastical architecture was based. But although I foresaw the evil tendencies of their opinions, yet, I must confess, I was not prepared for the extent to which they have been carried in so short a period.'

What Pugin had now to complain of was, that in spite of all his noble exertions to restore a purer taste and a higher standard of Christian art among the Catholic body, not only were churches erected whose 'appearance was something between a dancing-room and a mechanics' institute,' but that the vocal entertainment of a concert-room was substituted for the solemn music of the Church. 'What!' he exclaims, 'shall the Song of Simeon, the Hymn of St. Ambrose, the Canticle of our Blessed Lady herself, give place to modern effusions? Shall we tolerate the conversion of the liturgy into a song-book?'

But his fiercest indignation is justly reserved against
the theatrical performances which too often take place
at the opening of new churches. 'Bills of performance,' he complains, 'are circulated, worded and let-
tered in the manner which a musical director with
a travelling company would put forth on arriving in
a country town. On one occasion, Madame Stock-
hausen, the star of the day, headed the bill, then the
name of some second rates and of the conductor or
leader succeeded in due order. Even the clergy,' he
says, 'were played in like soldiers to parade. Procession march! occasional overture!—so said the bills
—choruses, duets, quartets, fuges, sermon, collection,
solos, etc., succeeded in rapid succession; and what
began with an overture, ended, in true theatrical style,
with a finale.' 'This new church at Hereford,' he
adds, 'might be fitly termed the new Catholic Concert
Room; it does not possess the slightest character or
essentials of a church.'

'It is painful' (and I will quote his letter at large,
on account of its importance and of its earnestness, so
characteristic of the writer) 'to be obliged to speak
thus of a building which, in all respects, should have
been a consolation and a glory; but there are occasions when silence becomes a sin, and this is one.
The odium of this and similar transactions falls on the
whole Catholic body, and if they pass unnoticed by
any but our enemies, they disarm us of many powerful arguments against our adversaries; and as I wage
perpetual war against Protestantism and innovation

in every shape, and hope by the blessing of God to live long enough to set forth the glories of Catholic antiquity that formerly existed in this land, whenever I see Catholics truckling to the debased taste of the times and degrading their honourable title I shall not fail to reprove them, even at the cost of private benefit, or of being branded with the title of fanatic. I have, therefore, considered it necessary to make this public avowal of my horror of such proceedings as those of Hereford; in which feeling, I am happy to say, I am most heartily joined by a vast number of faithful Catholics, both ecclesiastics and laymen, who, although unwilling to incur the odium of thus publicly avowing their feelings, coincide entirely in my views. For my own part, where the truth and the interest of religion are concerned I am a stranger to fear; and all the fiddlers and organists and performers and committee-men in England, would not prevent me from exhibiting these disgraceful profanations in their true light. The usual excuse, that they are necessary to raise money, is not only false, but it shows an utter want of that confidence in God which should form the base of every Catholic's conduct. What a narrow mind and grovelling soul does it betray! with the knowledge of possessing the true faith and firm promises of God, to descend to the tricks of perambulating mountebanks, and compromise all propriety, and even common respect to holy things, for the chance of a few Protestant shillings, when a tithe of the number of real Catholic hearts, filled with true zeal and devo-

tion, would contribute more to the necessaries of the
Church, in one hour, than could be drawn from the
unwilling pockets of the heretics in twelve months.
If speculating on musical talent is to be in vogue, the
noted M. Bochsa would be a far better person to open
Catholic chapels than the most holy bishop ; but then,
let not the name of religion be mixed up with such an
exhibition. Call it by its real name—a Concert—
turn out the altar, fill the building with pit, boxes,
and gallery for the occasion, but let not the clergy
suffer the degradation of sitting in dumb show to hear
some women sing ; and, above all, let not the holy
sacrifice of the mass be made the vehicle of this horrible profanation. As for the pretence, that conver-
sions can be made by such exhibitions, I deny it *in
toto*. How was the true faith propagated in bygone
days ? Did the apostles or ministers who converted
England, lead about fiddlers to attract people to their
discourses ? No ! they held the Divine commission to
go forth, and forth they went, and God was with
them ; and the same Rock which sustained them in
difficulties ten times greater than surround us is our
foundation. Did the apostles themselves hold greater
power and authority to preach the truth and ad-
minister the sacraments, than is possessed by the most
humble of the ordained priests amongst us ? Certainly
not. Why then resort to such miserable expedients
and shallow policy, calculated to draw down a curse
instead of a blessing ? Our great object should be to
work for the love and glory of God, and do all things

in a manner calculated to please him, without regard
to worldly prejudices; and we may then expect, as in
days of old, to receive his blessing on our endeavours.
The present system of opening chapels is in complete
opposition to the intentions and regulations of the
Church. Instead of being solemn and edifying functions, they are, for the most part, scenes of irreverence
and confusion; and the building which for the first time
is sanctified by the presence of God himself, is filled
with a gazing mob and a company of noisy musicians,
who run riot in extravagant sounds, and act in direct
opposition to the decrees of Councils, and the regulations of the Pontifical.

'What I have written on the present occasion is
quite applicable to many recent openings of chapels.
I have long had it in contemplation to put forth some
observations on the subject; and as the evil seemed to
be on the increase, and the Hereford advertisement
still more outrageous than any which had previously
appeared, I could not refrain any longer from setting
forth my sentiments.

'I trust that the motives which have actuated me to
write on the present occasion will not be misunderstood.
I can solemnly appeal to God for the purity of my
intentions; and as it is only for the calumniator and
those who are actuated by private or party motives to
attack in ambush, and shelter themselves under assumed titles I most unhesitatingly affix my name,
although by so doing I shall probably expose myself
to the displeasure of many whose good opinion I

should highly value, but which I cannot purchase at the expense of sincerity, or the concealment of truth.

'A. Welby Pugin.

'Alton Towers.'

Against another obnoxious system Pugin was no less unmerciful than he was against the opening of churches with an almost theatrical display. Legacy-hunting, however disguised, he held to be as repugnant to right principles as it is destructive of true charity, and he advocated the restoration of the ancient practice of laying during life the gift on the altar as the best remedy for this evil. 'Nothing can be worse,' he contends, 'than this legacy system. However good and holy a man may be, if he expects a large reversion at the death of an individual it is almost beyond the powers of human nature to expect that he will not take considerable interest in the state of his health ; and although anything like the desire of his departure is too shocking to entertain, still, if he could be removed to a state of bliss, it would not be a very affecting occurrence.' He then in graphic terms describes a scene which, it is to be feared, has but too often been acted. 'The moment,' he says, 'a rich old fellow dies, all the relations to the ninetieth degree turn up and assemble, and if they understand his money has been left to the Church the indignation is general. Was there ever such a monstrous thing known, when he had so many relatives, and some so slenderly provided for ? One of his nephews had married on the strength of his expectations, and was now burdened with a numerous family, who would be wholly without fortunes. Another had enlarged his dining-room, and built a conservatory on the same grounds, and this money to go to the bishops; they would not allow it, they will have law. A lawyer is present and steps forward; he quite agrees; it is certainly a case for a British jury; he would be happy to conduct it himself; though a Catholic, he considers family interests should be protected. Proceedings are begun; and to prevent scandal and expense, and the glorious uncertainty of the law, half the property is made over in a compromise, and is the speedy cause of a dozen secondary suits among the relations themselves, who do not consider that they are fairly dealt with by each other. And now another bishop considers he has a prior claim or equal right on the residue. The first bishop cannot admit the justice of the premises. It must be referred to arbitration. Grave men travel up to London, put up at first-rate hotels, keep up good cheer, drive about in glass coaches, see sights, and occasionally sit in a back room round a green baize table. Portly and sinewy lawyers, with attendants bearing blue bags full of documents, read long extracts from interminable deeds. Rejoinder next day, all the preceding arguments demolished, time is up, but to-morrow the first party will again address on fresh grounds Days go by, one week gone, hotel bills running on, the cost of a small parochial church in the second pointed style swallowed up already, proceedings becoming a bore, a compromise proposed, could not two mutual friends settle it? They agree, divide again, and deduct expenses. Only one-third of the whole sum reduced by subdivision to a very moderate amount. Both bishops reported to be immensely rich, and to have received an inexhaustible fortune, no subscriptions in consequence. Pious ladies are astonished that anything should be expected from them under such circumstances. Both bishops set forth what is quite true, that the sum received was so reduced as to be comparatively small. Nobody believes it, or if they do, they pretend they do not, and excuse themselves for not giving on those grounds. Both bishops are considerably minus at the end of the year that the great benefaction fell in.

'This is no exaggeration of the evils attendant on the legacy system, and therefore I should view any legal enactment that will induce men *to be more liberal during their lives, and less relying on testamentary bequests, as a great practical blessing.* I may be considered as a visionary and enthusiast, but I am convinced that if Catholics acted practically up to the sincerity and good faith that we have a right to expect among Christian men, we could transact most important matters in the old Anglo-Saxon fashion, over shrines and before altars, and save large sums in stamps and deeds, which are no security after all, and often made the subjects of vexatious litigation. How vain are all these charters and testamentary restrictions; little better than waste wax and parchment.

What pains did the venerable founders of some of the old Oxford colleges incur to secure those institutions from change; and yet, in a comparatively few years, the whole became practically a dead letter; the altars and the very chantries pulled down, all the beautiful ornaments seized and sold by the state, and the costly foundation of Archbishop Chichele, endowed (in his remorse for the horrors of the French war, which he had instigated) for the souls of the slain, denuded of the very altars where the expiatory services were to have been offered, and the chantry priests replaced by good easy men, who say their own prayers, quite irrespectively of the memory of the brave knights and yeomen who fell on the field of Agincourt. I mention these things to show the vanity of endowments, and of providing for futurity in church matters, *when the only security consists in the succession of well-instructed and apostolic men, keeping up faith and discipline.'*

So stout a reformer of abuses was not likely to be popular except with the earnest-minded, and the earnest-minded and zealous are in every community always the few. But Pugin never courted popularity, or flattered the prevailing folly of the hour; seclusion was his choice, yet he never shrank from publicly avowing what he inwardly felt on any matter that came under his notice; his pen was never inspired by vanity or shrivelled up by an anxious regard for self-interest. His strong hand has made the first indent into many a stubborn habit of evil, or inflicted the final blow on many a time-honoured abuse. The timid and the time-

2 c

servers regarded him with equal loathing and dread. They deprecated his interference in matters which did not concern the details of his art. They would have had him leave principles to take care of themselves, and to busy himself in executing orders to suit the fancy of the day. True principles they considered inconvenient burdens ; and when Pugin insisted that all the accessories of Divine worship should be in harmony with the solemn character of the building and in keeping with the approved ritual of the church he was regarded as a man utterly given over to obsolete customs and to mediæval crotchets.

Pugin's ' Earnest Address on the Establishment of the English Catholic Hierarchy,' and its hostile reception.

We are approaching now to an important and critical period in Welby Pugin's life—we shall have to examine acts of his which have been much canvassed, and a course of conduct which has been blamed by not a few, and misunderstood by too many ; we shall have to listen with as much patience as we can command to the whispered insinuation against his good faith, as well as to encounter the graver charge brought against his orthodoxy, and we shall watch with interest and curiosity what a different effect the oblique hint had upon his mind to that produced by the open indictment. But why, it may be asked, open up the painful question again,—why enkindle anew the embers of a quarrel which has long since died out,—why awaken prejudices which have slumbered over the grave of him who had provoked them,—and why show to the world that differences in opinion have disturbed the unity of Catholics? My reason is simply this: that it is not just, for the sake of making things appear pleasant to the living, to allow the taint of imputed heresy to rest upon the name of the dead; and moreover, it seems to me unwise for Catholics to be constantly endeavouring to gloss over the differences of opinion which must arise even upon important matters, or to seek to appear before the world other from what they are. Such want of candour has neither prudence nor charity, nor any other gift of the Holy Ghost to recommend its adoption. Half-measures conciliate no one. If the life of Pugin is to be written at all it ought to be, like himself, thorough. Not a single fact of importance, even if it were painful to the feelings of others, or derogatory to his own reputation, ought to be suppressed or distorted, or receive a colouring from the bias of prejudice or from the hand of partiality. The great lover of reality, the honest-minded architect, the first and most famous principle of whose craft it was to expose the construction of his building, and to rely on truthfulness for its beauty, ought not to have his biography built up on half-concealed facts, and coloured statements that resemble nothing so much as the hidden buttresses and plastered roofs which were such an abomination to his artistic and truth-loving eye. Why indeed should there be any reticence? where is the need of concealment in the differences which arose

on the publication of 'An Earnest Address on the
Establishment of the Hierarchy?' Was there anything
really to be ashamed of in the conduct of Welby Pugin,
or to be regretted on the part of his ecclesiastical superiors? Did it not rather redound to the credit of
those most nearly concerned that so much kindness
and consideration were shown on the one hand, and
such obedience and promptitude in retracting error
on the other?

We must seek for the impugners of Welby Pugin's
orthodoxy among less noble opponents, and we shall
perhaps not be astonished to discover that they were
confined principally, as the bishop of —— indicates,
to persons not a hundred miles from ——; to the
captious writers in the 'Rambler,' and their more
immediate supporters, the ancient antagonists of the
Gothic revival, still smarting under the recent wounds
inflicted on their crude innovations by the unsparing
hand of the prime mover in the mediæval restoration,—
men, who in their ungenerous zeal to trip up an adver-
sary, did not scruple, as the bishop of ——— foresaw, to make a handle of some overstrong statements
in the 'Earnest Address,' or of some incidental errors,
to bring the writer into discredit with his ecclesiastical
superiors. The failure of their attempt was more
signal than the triumph they had vainly anticipated.
Docile and submissive to ecclesiastical authority,
Pugin was not the man to be silenced, or to be put
down, or to be turned aside from the path he had
struck out for himself, by the clamour and calumny of

those, who when beaten in argument sougnt refuge, if not revenge, in an appeal to ecclesiastical censure.

One of the first steps which Welby Pugin took to set himself right with the public, and with his fellow-Catholics, was the publication of a letter in the ' Tablet,' in which he not only maintained the ground he had taken up in the ' Earnest Address ' with his accustomed boldness and vigour of argument, but still further fortified his position by the high authority of the late Bishop Milner, while at the same time he indignantly repudiated the charge of heresy, or of holding uncatholic opinions, and denounced the dishonesty of those who dared to distort, or to misrepresent his openly-avowed principles. At the same time, however, he again in this letter fell into the error of holding the validity of English orders to be an open historical question, and one on which he was at liberty to form his own opinion.

Strangely enough this able writer seems at this time to have imagined that he was only bound or called upon to believe what the Church had solemnly defined, instead of recognising the principle that a Catholic must act and believe in unison with the mind of the Church even on trivial matters ; how much more so on matters of grave import, which she has already defined indeed by her constant practice. Schismatical Greek bishops and priests on their return to the unity of the Catholic Church she admits again into her body, but does not reconsecrate or reordain them, but Anglicans on their conversion she invariably does. This solemn act is in

itself alone a sufficient definition of the invalidity of
the English orders. It is indeed an open historical
question as to whether Barlow himself were really a
consecrated bishop, or whether Parker ever received
that form of ordination which he conferred on his
brethren, and which all the Anglican prelates received
until the middle of Charles the Second's reign, but the
dogmatic fact still remains that the 'form' of ordination out of King Edward's Ordinal was wholly invalid.

Pugin however does not appear to have allowed
this 'mere opinion' to influence his practice, nor even
to have carried it out to its logical consequences, for
if the Anglican orders be valid, so is the consecration
of 'their sacrament,' and a Catholic at their communion service would be bound to adore the real presence
which Pugin is never known to have done.

With the exception of the paragraph I have alluded
to, this outspoken letter, a sequel, as it were, or a con-
densation of a portion of his 'Earnest Address,' appears
to me to call for unqualified admiration. I know few
things more commendable than the courage he displays
in rising superior to the weakness, too common among
Catholics of the present day, of seeking to hide from the
contemptuous or hostile gaze of the world the blotches
and sores that from time to time burst out and deface
the divine beauty of the Church of God. Even if it
were possible to escape the inquisitive search of our
enemies, the attempt at concealment would in itself be
unwise, for we should soon fall into the habit, too
easily learnt, of blinding ourselves to our true condi-

tion, and be lulled into that greatest of dangers, a false security. Therefore I rejoice in the boldness of the author of this letter and of the 'Earnest Address,' in denouncing as a warning to the Catholics of the present day, and of other countries as well of those at home, the internal corruption or religious indifference of the rulers in Church and State as the primary cause of all the evils of the Reformation. Nothing to my mind shows more clearly the strength of Pugin's reliance on the divine foundations of the Church than such unreserve of conduct, and such truthfulness of utterance. The doubting mind hesitates, and want of faith makes us cowards. It is indeed but too true that long before the Reformation the subserviency of the ecclesiastical rulers to the royal authority, their jealousy of the interference of the Holy See, and their resistance to the Papal supremacy, prepared the way for the heresy and religious revolt of the 16th century.

On its appearance in the 'Tablet,' the writer forwarded his letter to a distinguished layman with whom he was in the habit of corresponding, and received a reply full of kindly counsel and advice which is worth reading, as it shows in what estimation the character and writings of Welby Pugin were held at the time by learned and religious men.

'————, March 9th, 1851.

'MY DEAR PUGIN,

'I waited for a few days before I wrote to thank you for your most acceptable present of the "*Earnest Address,*" which safely arrived; partly because the subject of which you treat is too deep an one to give an opinion off-hand, as one might on any idle question of the day. You know how fully my ideas agree with yours in the main to be prepared for my cordial concurrence with the general view of your pamphlet; and I must say I admire and approve it more than I can easily express, and heartily trust it may kindle the latent spark in very many others. Still there are one or two expressions I should have preferred altered, not because your own mind is not perfectly correct in reference to them, but because the enemy may take advantage of them; for instance, in page 12, instead of "those countries *which nominally retained the ancient faith, etc.,*" I would have put "which *continued* to *profess* the ancient faith." It would have given your meaning, and not have laid you open to the charge of looking upon the Catholic countries as only *nominally* and not *really* so, which of course you would be far from affirming. I think too you are hardly fair upon the mediæval period. You write of those ages as an "Oratorian" might write. Who ever maintained that all things were holy and perfect then? All that I would contend for them is that the *acknowledged public principle* of the period was essentially Catholic and Christian, which it never has been either before or since. That is the grand point for mediæval men like you and me to uphold, and if we cannot uphold it, we are done for. The legislative principle was truly Christian in those days as much as the architectural, and for the same reason, because the nations then made a solemn *national* acknowledgment of Christianity. The public system they upheld was perfect, sublime: the vices, the barbarism, the abuses that prevailed were in spite of it, and in flagrant opposition with it. Whereas in these days men are wicked because the public system is wicked, because

the Established Church teaches heresy, because legislation is conducted either on Protestant or *no* principles. And in degree the
same may be said of the modern Catholic countries; they are
degraded because they have admitted another principle, opponent
to the Catholic principle : they no longer make Catholicism the
basis of their legislation : there is no longer that solemn national
recognition of Christianity and Catholicism which there was in
the middle ages. This is the grand point to which I think Digby,
in his Mores Catholici, and Montalembert, in his masterly preface
to the life of S. Elizabeth, do justice and not more than justice ;
and it is upon the intimate conviction of this fact that the whole
feeling is based that would make us point to the middle ages,
whether for architecture or any other exhibition of the human
mind. And if this great fact be not admitted, the sooner we fall
in with the dull routine of the 19th century the better ; to do
otherwise in that case would be but unmeaning Quixotism. So
you see, my dear friend, I think you have been somewhat cutting
your own ground from under you.

' The *standard* of mediæval *manners*, the standard of mediæval
legislation, of mediæval *education*, of mediæval *architecture and art*,
of mediæval *literature*, were each and all eminently *Christian*, and
therefore good and worthy to be proposed by men *now* to their
fellow-men as a true type to follow in their several departments.
But for this view of the grand question I do not see how we are to
escape the charge of mere antiquarianism in seeking to revive
mediæval Church architecture. And yet if we give up what up to
now we have been so loudly vaunting—the exclusive Christian
character of those ages, I do not comprehend why we are to contend for the productions of those ages. A good tree bringeth not
forth evil fruit, neither doth a corrupt tree bring forth good fruit.
With these few criticisms I concur in all that you say most
heartily, and I earnestly wish all success to your " Appeal."

' Your truly attached friend,

' ———— '

To a mind like Pugin's, not apt in slow deliberation to weigh its conclusions, but rather impelled by the quick impulse of genius to fling them off like sparks from the anvil in rapid succession, a larger latitude of expression must be allowed than is granted under ordinary circumstances to lesser men. If, however, I confess that on more than one occasion his boldness of argument verged, to say the least, on rashness, and that his vigour of language fell, now and again, not far short of violence, I only show that I am not striving to procure his beatification; but on the other hand, when I come to examine and criticise more closely the principles laid down in the famous publication which created such a commotion* among Protestants

* On this subject Pugin received upwards of a hundred letters, many of them from persons of eminence in the literary, religious, and political world. A just tribute to his spirit of fairness was paid to him in the following letter from an eminent statesman :—

‘————, March 11, 1851.

‘ SIR,

‘ I am not aware whether I have to thank you individually for the favour of a copy of your Pamphlet on the recently instituted Roman Catholic hierarchy. If it be so, pray allow me warmly to acknowledge that favour ; but whether it be so or not, I cannot be out of place in thanking you, as one of the public, for the matter of the pamphlet itself. Among the many and varied gifts which combine to make it so interesting, I shall only particularise that spirit of enlightened and charitable appreciation of men and systems standing apart from you, which is at this moment, I grieve to say, so rare in any quarter, and which in the perusal of your work I have found refreshing and delightful in proportion.

‘ I have the honour to be, Sir,

‘ Your very faithful Servant,

‘————

‘ A. W. Pugin, Esq.’

as well as Catholics, I hope it will appear evident
that I am not in the least disposed to play the part
of devil's advocate.

The incriminated pamphlet, written with power and
manly eloquence, and bearing upon its face that
peculiar air of truthfulness which characterised all
Welby Pugin's productions, appeared at a period
when it was sure to excite attention and provoke
controversy. It was published in the beginning of
the year 1851, the year which witnessed the restoration
of our glorious English hierarchy, the revival of our
ancient faith in its perfect organization, and the futile
attack of a bigoted statesman on the liberties of the
Catholic Church in England. The outburst of popular
prejudice which accompanied this aggression on our
rights, was manfully met by our great English cardinal.
In the full vigour of his active intellect, and relying
on the soundness of his cause, and on the common
sense which in the long run seldom quite deserts the
English people, he stood almost alone against the
nation. The establishment of the hierarchy was the
turning-point of Catholicism in England, it was the
solemn inauguration of a new epoch ; and a thoughtful
mind like Pugin's could not but be alive to the dangers
which beset the birth of all great events. He was not
slow in holding up as a terrible warning the degradation which befel the ancient hierarchy in Henry the
Eighth's time, when at the bidding of the king both
bishops and clergy almost to a man forswore the
supremacy of the Pope, and fell away from Catholic

unity.   In his 'Earnest Address,' a terse but vigorous exposition of the dangers of state patronage and state interference in matters of Church government, the writer seeks to ascertain the primary cause to which all these sad changes may be traced, not only of the loss of faith in England, but of the lamentable degradation in countries where the old religion still prevails, from the standard of Catholic excellence, and of the fearful progress which indifference and infidelity have made; and he states his belief that 'we shall not fail in tracing this corruption to the common evil of state and temporal power crushing the free action of the Church, and enslaving its ministers in worse than Egyptian bondage.'

'The state of Christendom,' he urges, 'is full of matter for the serious reflection of sincere and religious men.   To begin with England—which we all know was once a Catholic country, abounding in ecclesiastical foundations, possessing all the means, all the materials, for the preservation of the faith, the instruction of the people, and support of religion in the greatest solemnity and order—how comes it to pass that it is no longer so ? that, without invasion, or conquest, or change of dynasty, the whole has been altered, transformed, the churches plundered, the country separated from Catholic unity, and, in fine, brought to its present lamentable religious position ?   Who has done this ? By whom has it been brought about ?   Is it the work of Protestantism or not ?   *I boldly answer, No !*

'It is a fearful and terrible example of a Catholic

nation betrayed by a corrupted Catholic hierarchy. Englishmen have been betrayed, and what is more, betrayed by the very power from whom, under God, they had a right to expect protection and safety. It was in a solemn convocation, when England's church-men were assembled, a reverend array of bishops and abbots and dignitaries, in orphreyed copes and jewelled mitres. Every great cathedral, every diocese, every abbey, was duly represented in that important synod; and yet the fear of a tyrant and the dread of losing a few remaining years of wealth and dignity so far pre-vailed, that they sacrificed the liberty of the English Church at one blow,—that Church whose liberties at their several consecrations they had sworn to defend, whose freedom they were bound on oath and conscience to preserve. The deed is signed. Harry is declared the *supremum caput* of England's Church: not by the *vox populi*, but *by the voice of the convocation*, the Church is sacrificed, the people are sacrificed, and the actors in this vile surrender are the true and lawful bishops and clergy of England. One venerable prelate, aged in years, and worn with fasting and discipline, alone pro-tests against this sinful surrender; his remonstrance is unsupported by his colleagues, and he is speedily brought to trial and execution. His accusers are Catholics, his judges are Catholics, his jury are Catho-lics, his executioner is a Catholic, and the bells are ringing for High Mass in the steeples of St. Paul's, as the aged bishop ascends the scaffold and receives the martyr's crown.'

None were more ready than the writer of this pamphlet, to welcome with love, and receive with reverence the new hierarchy, fresh from the hands of the common head of Christianity, and none were more eager to guard it, not so much against state hostility as against state patronage, and to keep this virgin gift, as he calls it, pure and unpolluted, free from the corrupting touch of diplomacy, from the intrigue of a minister, and from the adulation of an audience chamber. Abhorrence against interference of the temporal power in the internal concerns of the Church led the earnest and enthusiastic writer to denounce, in no measured terms, all union even with the state, unmindful that the theory of the Christian polity is, that the state, the indirect work of the Divine hand, should be the nursing father of the Church, while the Church, the direct and divine creation of the Founder of Christianity, should be in all things, and at all possible times, the guide and guardian of the Christian state. But the writer, dwelling with great force on the corruptions which were in former days introduced into the Church by the tyranny, or by the still more fatal favour and flattery, of the temporal power, advocates the complete separation of Church and State, and supports to the utmost of his power the voluntary system. This is the chief purport to which he addressed himself in writing the 'Earnest Address,' this is the main drift of his argument, and the reason why, in the manner of a man who never minced matters, or dressed up his phrases to suit delicate ears, he brought out boldly the fact 'that very many, if not all the past abuses we have been in the habit of so loudly denouncing in the Church of England, are inherited from the old Catholic times—that the ancient churchmen were notorious non-residents and pluralists, and that every synod complained of the numerous foreigners intruded into English benefices, who never visited the churches to which they were appointed, and from which they derived the revenues, while the fabrics and religion alike fell into decay. We had bishops, he says, who never saw their cathedrals, and even a bishop who ruled the diocese of Lincoln for twelve years without having been in holy orders. From these facts, gathered at chance among a mass of documents of the same import, it may be conceived there was great room for reform before the Reformation, which was in fact rather a legalization of abuse by state enactments than a remedy to their continuance.

The writer then proceeds, with just severity, to comment on the flagrant abuse descended from a very ancient period, of chapters invoking in that sublime hymn, the 'Veni Creator,' the divine illumination to guide them in the election of a man worthy to fill the office of bishop, whilst they had in their possession, during the time they were enacting this solemn farce, the name of the individual appointed by regal authority, and whose sole title to the dignity he impiously aspired to, was often the disgraceful fact of his having found favour in the eyes of a royal mistress, or in the ante-chamber of an intriguing minister.

'In a recent article, printed in the 'Times,' on the Bishop of Birmingham's letter, the editor most tauntingly asks if we consider that we are more powerful now than we were in the days of Leo X., and I,' says Pugin, 'most unhesitatingly answer—*ten times more powerful.* The days of the tenth Leo were full of corruption; it was the spring of revived paganism and heresy; the Church had just cast off her ancient traditions, and was dressing out her temples in a heathen guise; the most fearful heresies were rife on every side; abuses intolerable to Christian men existed throughout Christendom; the sacred reforms and decrees of the Tridentine fathers had not been set forth; the corruptions of centuries were drawing to a head, and the very fountain of jurisdiction itself, the Holy See, seemed poisoned with the luxury of the day; Catholicism was still wrought up with barbarisms of the nations it had converted, and which, though it had quelled, it had never extinguished. The dawn of religious freedom had not struck one ray on the dark horizon of religious persecution; if ever there was a time when a Catholic could have despaired of the promises of God to his Church, *it was then.* But now there is every cause for hope, *aye, for exultation.* The Catholic religion now exists on free principles: she has got rid of one immense element of corruption in her vast temporal wealth; her prelates have lost the temporal prince and regained the Christian bishop; we have active missionaries and preachers in lieu of lazy abbés, flirting in parks and gardens; we have no commendatory abbots, or misapplied revenues of religious houses, but active and religious orders of charity; no tonsured children holding great ecclesiastical benefices : and we have a clergy who commence to appreciate and, indeed, restore the long-neglected and despised architecture of Christendom ; Paganism is at a discount, *at a ruinous sacrifice.*'

If the preservation of the new hierarchy from the possible contamination of state influence were the main motive in the publication of the 'Earnest Address,' almost equally strong in the author's mind was the twin idea of the eventual restoration of the more Catholic-minded portion of the Anglican establishment to the bosom of Catholic unity. In the hope of bringing this union about, and in the desire to induce among Catholics generally, a more kindly consideration for the unhappy position of the more advanced Tractarians, he pointed out, to the scandal of some who were unwise in their sensitiveness, the degenerate and ungodly subservience of the Catholic bishops to the assumptions of the temporal power as the origin of the English schism, and all its consequent evils ; whilst, at the same time, he contrasted the preservation of much that was Catholic, and ancient, and grand, in the creed and ritual, and in the cathedrals of the Anglican communion, with the destructive inroads which the Paganism and infidelity of the 17th and 18th centuries

2 D

had made in many Catholic countries. But if, in the fervour of his argument, and in his joy over the surviving glories and grandeur of the old cathedrals, and out of the fulness of his gratitude towards those who had done all in their power to preserve them against the iconoclastic fury of the Puritans, he appeared, for the moment, to forget that the supremacy of St. Peter is the supreme test of the Catholicism of any community, he did not, at any rate, even in appearance, much less in reality, lay himself open to the charge of palliating the criminality of the more advanced Tractarians in remaining aloof, at the present day, from union with the Holy See. So Catholic in character, and so reverent in his demeanour towards ecclesiastical authority, it would appear almost impossible to believe that a man like Pugin could be capable of deliberately upholding heretical or condemned opinions, although it is not to be denied that he fell into the error of treating the validity of the Anglican orders as an open historical question, instead of regarding their condemnation as a settled dogmatic fact. Fortunately we have not to go far to find conclusive proof of the orthodoxy of Pugin's faith, and of his reverent attachment to the Holy See; and I am sure every Catholic will rejoice to hear that so good and great a man loyally sought the earliest opportunity to remove the imputations cast upon his faith, by publicly insisting upon submission to Rome, as in all ages a necessity of Catholicism.

'It is the fact of being in communion with the Ro-

man Church,' says the author, in a short but pithy
address to the inhabitants of Ramsgate, on the occasion
of the restoration of the English hierarchy, 'that has
formed the test of Catholicism in all ages. The manner
of celebrating the divine service, the vestments, the
ornaments, the very churches might be in perfect con-
formity with Catholic usages, and yet the worshippers
in them as far removed from a Catholic position as the
most determined Calvinist. This country was separated from the communion of Christendom by the old
Catholic bishops themselves siding with the king
against their duty and their conscience, to enable him
to contract an unlawful union; and although the
ecclesiastical rulers were unchanged, and the ancient
rites of worship were unimpaired for several years after
the separation, yet the position of the Church of
England became schismatical, and many conscientious
men suffered death rather than deny the spiritual
obedience they owed to the common head of the
Church throughout the world. I mention these circumstances to show how impossible it is for us to submit to the rule of the Anglican bishops as appointed
by the state; for if we could not have yielded obedience to the original prelates who subscribed to the
royal supremacy, of whose consecration there could
be no doubt, and who taught orthodox doctrine on all
but one point, how can we be expected to yield to the
present race of men separated above three hundred
years from the fountain of ecclesiastical jurisdiction,
of the validity of whose consecration we may enter-

tain reasonable doubts, and whose teaching is neither
conformable with the ancient belief of the English
Church, nor in many respects agreeable to their own
written formularies and articles ?'

Unnecessary as it was to those who were at all
familiar with his religious principles, yet this timely
profession of his belief on the great doctrine of the
Papal supremacy came well, and served as a just
rebuke to those who only founded their judgment of
his character from the insidious praises lavished on
his pamphlet on the hierarchy by the Tractarian or
hostile journals, or drew all their knowledge concerning his true opinion of the English establishment from
the disingenuous and distorted comments on his publication, made in no spirit of fairness, by some of
his ancient opponents among the supporters of the
'Rambler.'   It appears to me impossible to put the
conduct of Pugin in its proper light on this trying
occasion, or to elucidate the controversy which arose on
the publication of his 'Earnest Address,' if I do not
lay before the public a fragmentary portion at least of
the voluminous correspondence in reference to the
soundness of the distinguished writer's principles, or to
the seasonableness of his views.   With the tact and
consideration so consonant with the character of his
Eminence, Cardinal Wiseman intimated to Welby
Pugin, in a letter addressed to him not in his ecclesiastical capacity but in the terms of personal friendship, that grave charges had been alleged against the
orthodoxy of his recent publication, and enclosed an

extract of one of several letters of complaint which had been addressed to his Eminence.

It was intimated to Pugin that one learned priest had denounced his pamphlet as heretical, and that it was feared a more formal denunciation would be made, or even that the pamphlet itself might be sent to head-quarters. Pugin at once expressed his entire submission, and his readiness to withdraw or modify any opinion which might seem to border on heresy as soon as the incriminated passages or opinions were pointed out to his attention.

As in the 'indictment,' enclosed in the Cardinal's letter to Pugin, allusion was made to the 'sanction' which the pamphlet was said to have received from the Bishop of ——, we cannot do better than transcribe a few passages from a letter written by the bishop alluded to, and dated 20th April, 1851, in which he tells Pugin that in a long conversation he lately had with Father ——, the latter, speaking of Pugin, stated that he has always had and has the highest opinion of him and of his works and writings, bating of course some rather strong expressions against the practices (Antigothic) at the Oratory. 'This conversation,' says the Bishop, 'took place when I called upon him, some weeks ago, when there was some question of trying to get your pamphlet called "An Earnest Address" *placed on the Index* at Rome. Father —— denied all participation in any such plot against you. But I know there were parties at the time (not a hundred miles from ——) who were trying to influence the Cardinal to wage war upon you. But I trust the parties I allude to are rather ashamed of themselves. Surely *they* must see that your " Earnest Appeal " has not prevented pious Anglicans from coming over to us, though at the time they quoted some foolish and weak men of their acquaintance, who were remaining stationary in consequence of your opinion of the validity of their orders. What fools they must have been! At all events, Archdeacon Manning and the men at Leeds are not of their number. I trust we shall still see many more good Puseyites return to the bosom of Mother Church till the "Established" has no one left to be proud of.'

Numerous as were the words of advice, and the letters of encouragement, of sympathy, and of friendly correction, which Pugin received at this time from so many quarters, none manifested a truer appreciation of his services and character, or pointed out with greater precision the incidental errors into which he had fallen and the misapprehension to which certain false deductions might give rise, especially in the minds of those who were more disposed to be captious and critical than candid and fair in their judgments, than did the Bishop of —— on every occasion. The following letter will show his disposition towards Pugin, and the opinion of one so well qualified in every way to form a correct judgment on his deserts, is too valuable and important not to be recorded here.

'―――――, March 3, 1851.

' DEAR MR. PUGIN,—

' I thank you for your kind letter, your circular, and pamphlet. I think the circular excellent, and that many good things as being true are in the pamphlet. But is it correct to say that after the clergy renounced the supremacy, which they did, however they might make a clause about " *so far as the law of God permitted*," were they not then practically heretics as well as schismatics, by giving up the spiritual supremacy of Peter into the hands of Henry? I have spoken with Dr. Weedall and the Oscott people, and all think as well as myself that this statement is too strong, and may be made a great handle of.

' I much fear that the preoccupation of minds with our political position will be greatly in the way of your plan being taken up at present. Your circular has set me at work in writing out my contemplated pamphlet on the offertory, which is more than half completed; but I do not think this the moment for putting it out. There are a great many cowards amongst us, and as a body we have no surplus of spirit or generosity. There are a few exceptions, but what might we not be? And seeing how the Providence of God looks visibly for us, what ought we not to be?

' Wishing you and your family every blessing, and thanking you for your great efforts for the Church, I am,

' Dear Mr. Pugin,

'Your devoted father in Christ,

' ✠ ―――――――.'

From the statements contained in these letters we are led to conclude that the attempt to place the ' Earnest Address' on the Index originated in the indiscretion of a few intemperate men, and was in nowise supported by those who had the weight of experience on their side, or the right to judge. The Very Reverend Father——, whose name no English Catholic can mention without reverence, and towards whom our gratitude is better felt than expressed, himself assured, as we have just seen, the Bishop of —— that he had ' no participation in the plot' to arraign Pugin's orthodoxy, whose works and writings he had ever admired. The feud which was described by the Protestant, or hostile journals of the day, to be raging between the Oratorians and the promoters of Gothic art, and which was supposed or alleged to be at the bottom of this dispute, had, in fact, nothing whatever to do with the ungenerous attempt to place Pugin's name on the Index. Whatever the differences of opinion which may have arisen on the subject of mediæval architecture or Gothic art, still the collision was only on a matter of taste, and not of faith; and I am sure that on reflection Pugin would have been the first to regret that he had so far allowed himself to be carried away by the impetuosity of his argument, as to have placed a most religious and distinguished body of men in the category of those of whom the Church would be glad to be quit.

But the pamphlet which attracted so much public attention, and provoked so much controversy, as we

have already seen, contained other striking views besides those just enumerated, and propounded principles
of Church government which, especially in these eventful times, deserve, by reason of their gravity and their
boldness, the consideration of every thoughtful mind.

'Welby Pugin's "Earnest Address" will we expect,'
says the writer of an elaborate review which appeared
in the columns of the 'Morning Chronicle' on that
pamphlet, 'create quite as much astonishment among
Roman Catholics as among other readers. The name
of the writer will be very familiar as that of one of the
most distinguished architects among us, and an energetic
writer on topics connected with his profession. Those
who know no more of him than this will scarcely be
prepared for the boldness of thought, originality of
views, and vigour of language which he exhibits in
this pamphlet.'

This publication, it is quite true, 'did create much
astonishment among Roman Catholics,' but it also
succeeded in extorting approval, as much on account
of the breadth of its views, and the thoroughness of its
exposition, as from the earnestness of its tone. It
advocated the adoption of the voluntary principle, and
denounced the system of state support and of endowments, on the ground that state patronage will in the
long run, as experience has amply proved, lead to
state interference in the internal concerns of the
Church, and to the eventual supremacy of the temporal
power, while rich endowments and landed possessions
will gradually alienate from a luxurious clergy the

affections of the lower people, excite the envy of the
upper classes, and provoke the insatiable greed of the
state; if even the accumulated wealth of ages do not
always succeed in corrupting the morality, it will but
too often deaden or destroy the ecclesiastical spirit in
prince-bishop and priest.   History, indeed, affords
but too many an example of the fatal effect upon the
Church of large endowments and unbounded riches,
not to fill the reflecting mind with a wholesome abhorrence against the system which tends unduly to enlarge
ecclesiastical possessions, and not to make us receive
with a double reverence and love our new hierarchy,
free from the trammels of the state and unendowed
with the wealth óf the world.   How many a saintly
Pope, how many an ascetic writer, how many a learned
divine have not in every age urged with all the weight of
their authority, and in the respective spheres of their
influence, upon churchmen the necessity of abstention
from the pursuit of wealth, and the duty of self-denial,
and the glory of apostolic poverty.   How many a
monastic house, famous even in the world, in its reputation of austere piety, in its charity that blessed the
giver as well as the receiver, and in its intellectual productions which are even to this day our delight and
our instruction, has not in the course of time so grown
in unblessed wealth until the spirit of the place was
completely changed, and the rule of the sainted founder
so relaxed from its ancient severity by luxuriousness
of living, and lawless innovation, that the monastery
which once was a glory to the Church and an example

to the world, became a stumbling-block and a scandal to both. But the corruption of riches was not unhappily confined to isolated religious houses, but has at times spread like a canker through whole orders, and so tainted their life-blood that the strong arm of ecclesiastical authority was compelled to interpose, and to correct excesses which could not be passed over; or perhaps until, inspired by grace, some man of God arose to reform the rule, and lead the order back to the ancient austerity of its ways and to the paths of its accustomed piety. The terrible contests which St. Charles Borromeo had to endure in his attempt to reform the Church under his sway, is a signal illustration of the difficulty which even a saint has to encounter in dealing with a clergy corrupted by riches and strengthened in their insubordination out of fear of losing the benefits and privileges of their old endowments. Riches like beauty are deceitful; we are often carried away in our admiration of the outside gilding, and forget in our enchantment the snare which so often lurks beneath the hollow shows and semblances of external splendour. The ' orphreyed cope and jewelled mitre' have decked before now, but not concealed, the schismatic bishop and the rebellious heretic. The grand ritual and the gorgeous ceremonial that belonged to the ancient Church are but a delusion and a mockery when they are not informed by the spirit of faith, as the broad lands and extended sway of the magnificent abbey, and the princely dominions of the powerful bishop, though they exercise an equal fascination over

the mind, have but too often led, in the decay of the
religious spirit, to fearful abuses, such as the author
of the 'Earnest Address' has so ably pointed out, and
which brought, as he shows was the case under some
of the prince-bishops in Germany, heresy up to the
very gates of the episcopal palace, and corruption to
the threshold of the sanctuary itself.

'If the matter were not too lengthy for the space of
this pamphlet, I am quite prepared to prove,' says the
author of the 'Earnest Address,' 'that in every country
in Europe the degradation of religion has been caused
by its alliance with the temporal power, and the base
compliance of the clergy to its measures ; nay, the greatest heresies that have afflicted Christendom have been
the work of apostate monks and friars, fostered by temporal princes for their own political ends.   Even the
sacred Council of Trent was impeded and delayed in
every possible manner by the intrigues of the Emperor,
the king of France, and other potentates. All history
will prove that, for many centuries, the Church had little
or no freedom of action. Even in countries professedly
Catholic, and where it was the exclusive religion supported, or even tolerated, by the state, we find
nepotism carried to a frightful extent, and the relations of great men holding an enormous proportion of
church benefices, canonries, deaneries, and archdeacon-
ries, and even those ecclesiastical benefices most intimately connected with the salvation of souls and the
preservation of faith among the people, were considered as mere matters of revenue and property, like

temporal farms and estates; and while many of those who held these sacred offices for the most part squandered their revenues in luxury and pomp, the people were left to ill-paid and ignorant curates, whom a learned parish priest of the seventeenth century designated most justly under the appellation of *des paysans en noir.* Who can be astonished that active and zealous preachers, though teachers of false doctrines, should win the people from the religion of their fathers, when so cruelly deserted by their natural pastors? To these causes may be attributed the spread of every heresy that has torn the Catholic Church throughout Europe. They have originated in the supineness and neglect of the pastors, and the consequent ravages of the wolves on their flocks. And to resist false doctrine by temporal punishment on its propagation, is a miserable system, which, independent of its abstract cruelty and injustice, is unworthy of men professing Catholic truth. As long as the clergy instruct their people and minister to their spiritual necessities, heresies can never take root or flourish; and it is only the sad causes that I have above mentioned to which we can attribute the decay of religion on the Continent, and the extended spread of schism and error.'

Pugin then argues, in his out-spoken manner, how it behoves every English Catholic jealously to watch over the first free hierarchy created under a monarchy since the apostolic times, lest when legal restrictions fail to destroy its action, courtesy and favour be not attempted with more success. 'I should denounce,' he continues, 'any man as a traitor to the cause and to religion who would aid or contribute in any way to impede direct and free communication between the English Bishops and the Sovereign Pontiff; this is the divine constitution by which the Catholic faith is ordained by the providence of God to be preserved in unity through so many lands and people. It is a perpetual circulation, flowing from the centre to the extremities, and again returning to its source. While this circulation is free and unimpeded religion may be expected to prosper and discipline flourish; but when the channels are clogged by diplomatic impediments the faithful are sure to suffer, and if they are cut off, the faithful decay, even though all the machinery of the hierarcy remain, as I have clearly set forth in the sad but instructive history of England's schism. God forbid,' says the writer, in the concluding page of this bold and brilliant pamphlet, 'God forbid that our ecclesiastical rules should ever be again mixed up with the intrigues of a minister or the adulation of an audience chamber. In the eye of the law, our bishops will only rank as English citizens and subjects, they will bear the ordinary burdens of tax and rate; be exempt from any odious exemptions and privileges, and amenable to the common law of the land. But to us they will be the ministers of divine and ecclesiastical authority upon earth; they will receive our obedience and respect; we shall look on them as imbued with the holiest powers; they will consecrate the churches we raise for the worship of Almighty

God, and the cemeteries where we shall repose when dead; they will anoint the altars of sacrifice with the holy chrism; they will impart the Holy Spirit in the Sacrament of orders to successive generations of ecclesiastics, brought up under their guidance in their seminaries and colleges. They will be true pastors and shepherds of souls, and fathers of the poor. Denuded of their worldly magnificence, that I have shown to have been in former ages so fearful a snare, they will devote their entire lives and energies to the sacred duties of their office. And, my Catholic friends and brethren, shall not we on our side correspond to our chief pastors; thus I may say divinely established for our support and consolation? Shall we not place in their hands the temporal means to enable them to fulfil the full measure of their usefulness? God forbid: for I do not hesitate to say that if we neglect to support those whom God hath given us, he will deprive us of this great blessing. It will be vain if you agree with me in denouncing the temporal evils of rich endowments and state pensions, if you do not supply the necessities of the Church by renewing the apostolic system of *continual* and *successive offerings*. The real, the spiritual success of what the Holy Father has done for us depends *on our exertions*. I have shown that it is not in endowments, in testamentary bequests, that the true source of the Church revenues is to be found; but *in the hearts, the faithful hearts of her children*. Oh! let not this be a theory but a practice, which you would fulfil as earnestly and truly as your Easter communion. Let every man send, according to his gains and means, a reasonable sum to his diocesan for *episcopal purposes,* independent of any other duties or local works in which he may be engaged ; *let this be a distinct matter from all others.* Let every faithful man make a solemn engagement before God to do this, otherwise the *Te Deum* we have sung, the addresses of thankfulness we have signed, are a farce and a mockery. We have now an opportunity to show what the *free principle can do,* and if we carry it out nobly we shall be a beacon for Christendom. Let us show what a free hierarchy can do without pension from the state, *without endowed property, without tithes or rates, or one coercive payment from friend or foe.* Let us prove and show that Christ's Church can flourish on its own strength and the love of its children, and their free-will offerings. If you carry this out I can promise you a reign of Catholic glory to which the mediæval splendours were as nothing. Glorious as are the mighty fabrics they raised, they are often connected with men and times which detract from the fairness of the architecture, and tarnish the gilding of the sanctuary ; but if the Church, under the difficulties of such systems, could do so much, what cannot she perform when relieved from these bonds ? What ought men not to expect *under a free system and external peace?* and if we live as we ought, as Catholics *to serve God,* nothing is impossible to achieve. I fear not our enemies ; I fear not our calumniators ; I fear not the tyranny of state measures. I have but one fear ; that is, *I fear ourselves.* I fear we have been so long slumbering on under our imperfect ecclesiastical rules, that now the whole is come in all its fulness, we shall not duly appreciate the blessing, and respond to our altered circumstances. We are comparatively a small body; but we could spare many that bear our name, and yet be strengthened in our cause.

' I would we were quit of all those men, who, while retaining the name of Catholic, could betray the Church to state tyranny. I would we were quit of all those men, who, retaining the name of Catholic, afflict the pastors, and scandalise the faithful, by forsaking the holy sacraments of the Church. I would we were quit of all those men, who, while retaining the name of Catholic, exhibit no realization of its principles in their lives, but squander their revenues in every species of worldly vanity and folly, neglecting the Church and its ministers, and abandoning the temple of God to decay. I would we were quit of all those indifferent men, bearing the name of Catholic, who are almost too apathetic to try and save their own souls, and who never aid or contribute in any good work whatever; and I would we were quit of all men who degrade religion by dressing it up in Pagan and paltry externals, and who import the worst style of the most corrupt period of continental ecclesiology into a land full of the purest Catholic traditions. For all these are only drags on the wheel of the revival of faith and Catholic art and practices; and I believe, if we had only true zealous men left, like Gideon's three

2 E

hundred lappers up of water, we should be in a better position to resist the Midianites.   But this cannot be. We must trust in the arm of Almighty God to support us, and animate all with a good spirit.   If ever there was a time or occasion when we might hope for unity in the Catholic body, this is one.   If there could be imagined a moving cause so powerful as to break up local prejudices, party feelings, and unworthy division, it is this restoration of ecclesiastical government, and gathering our shattered and separated fragments into a real Church.   If there ever was a magnetic power to draw gold from misers, to make niggards liberal, and sluggards active, it is now.   If ever there was an event which was calculated to promote unity of action and unity of soul, to make men confess their past sins, and to make good resolutions for the future, to make them liberal to religion, and devout and thankful to God, animating them with a true spirit of the faith they profess, and lead them to discard for ever Paganism and its wretched incongruities, and to labour with heart and soul for the revival of the true architecture created by the Christian religion itself, it is the foundation of this English hierarchy which should be our delight and our glory, and which should now become one of the earnest objects of our lives and actions to support and maintain in all *freedom, honour, and integrity, in sæcula sæculorum*.   Amen.'

CHAPTER III.

Pugin's character as exhibited in his Writings—His originality—His thoroughness—His honesty of purpose—His strong love of the national character—His habits of activity—Pugin's incomplete and unpublished Work, entitled ' An Apology for the Separated Church of England since the Reign of Henry VIII.,' showing the general decay of the Ecclesiastical spirit and the corruptions of the Fifteenth Century—The system of endowments and large monastic possessions, and their abuses considered—The Work interrupted by Death— Conclusion.

Character and Constitution of Pugin's mind.

AFTER having traced the development of his principles in his writings, and marked the mental power he displayed in defence of the Gothic revival and of his opinions on ecclesiastical history and on matters of Church government, it may not now perhaps be altogether out of place briefly to inquire into the constitution of Pugin's mind, and examine those essential qualities which have raised him above the ordinary level of mankind. Genius, it must be remembered, has the peculiar power of bestowing vividness and variety on intellectual energy, and it freely conferred this gift on Pugin. His mind seemed to give out light. It brightened what it touched, and brought out the secret strength, the covert allusion, or the more recondite meaning of the subject of its contemplation. His creative imagination was rapid and brilliant in its conceptions. The question, however, at once arises, how came it to pass that his vast conceptions in art have realized such comparatively feeble results? Had the great mediæval-ist, indeed, sufficient grasp of mind to carry into execution the magnificence of his ideas? Was boldness as well as loftiness a quality of his mind? Or was opportunity as Pugin himself believed, and often asserted, alone wanting for the perfect realization of his designs? It appears, indeed, probable that the executive faculty, from want of the opportunity and exercise it so much needed, was somewhat weakened; whilst the energizing power was too exclusively absorbed by the imaginative faculty, which usurped the empire of the mind and luxuriated in conceptions, never destined to be realized.

If we reflect on the difficulties he had to encounter in breaking up single-handed the thraldom of a corrupt taste, and in reviving an almost defunct style of architecture, if we note the marvellous changes which have mainly resulted from the labours of his life, we must own that no man could have accomplished so vast a work, unless he possessed great originating power, as well as an inflexibility of purpose, and an enthusiatic love for his art. Pugin was no mere antiquarian, no narrow-minded bigot, as many have pictured him, wedded to a useless and impracticable theory; he was alive and alert to the necessities of the day and to the requirements of his position. He was ready to adopt and to assimilate whatever was sound in practice, though it were as new as yesterday, and all the mechanical contrivances of modern science were welcome to him as conducive to the greater perfection of his progressive art. With all the enthusiasm of his nature, and wonted energy of mind, Pugin threw himself into the revival movement, which in feebler hands had lingered so long with no positive results, and at once by the clearness of his principles and by his power in bringing them to bear, he took the lead in the movement. Had he chosen to abate one jot or tittle of his severe style in favour of foreign adaptations, had he condescended to follow a vicious fashion, he would not only have remained the master of the position and have entered upon a fine field for the exercise of his splendid talents, but have easily carried off from more compliant competitors the great national prizes which immortalize a name. But his stubborn honesty of mind was proof against the temptation. Rooted in his principles he remained immoveable like a rock, and like a rock he was left stranded by the ebbing waves of the receding tide of fashion. Such stern adherence to principle is rather out of date, and looks old-fashioned, but it well became the antique grandeur of Pugin's mind, and will be held in honour when vain applause, or the idle fame of meaner minds is forgotten.

If then we look in vain for the grand results in stone of the magnificent ideas and theories propounded in his writings, we shall know the reason of our disappointment. At the time, and under the disabling

circumstances in which he worked,—the narrow means,
—the absurd demands which he had, with the patience
of Job, to contend against,—it is perfectly marvellous
that he was able to effect so much, and proves how,
under favourable conditions, his buildings would have
corresponded in a greater degree to his vast and
glorious conceptions. In his own graphic manner he
describes the sad condition to which his buildings
were reduced. ' I can truly say,' he observes, ' that
I have been compelled to commit suicide with every
building in which I have been engaged, and I have
good proof that they are but little better than ghosts
of what they were designed; indeed, had I not been
permitted by the providence of God to have raised
the church at St. Augustine's, I must have appeared
as a man whose principles and works were strangely
at variance.' Solid, thorough, and substantial as if it
were hewn out of the live rock, St. Augustine's answers
admirably the purpose for which it was built. The
weather-beaten chapel blessing the sea, which Pugin
loved so well, and the sailor whose munificent patron
he ever was,—the Gothic-house with its unyielding
stubborn tower, enclosed by the sharp defiant wall and
obstinate gates, coped by heavy coverlids—will last as
long as the rock on which it stands shall resist the
ever encroaching wave. In building St. Augustine's
Pugin erected his monument and wrote his epitaph—
' Thorough.' The following lines I have somewhere
met with, may perhaps be inserted here :—

ST. AUGUSTINE'S BY NIGHT.

Tower and temple—built not in a day
And built to fall, but when the sea-rocks fall,
With jealous ivy on the garden wall
To bar the envious outer world away,
And turret-flag high o'er the dashing spray.
Music of waters—beauty of the night—
Here Art and Nature in one work unite,
Rear the white cliff, and crown the rock-hewn way.

If again we contemplate the mental energy exhibited by Pugin in his literary productions, we shall still find the same originality of view, the same vigour of thought and fancy as delighted us in his artistic conceptions. If a certain immaturity in judgment be sometimes apparent in the working out of his conclusions, it is mainly owing to the rapidity of his view, to his keenness in seizing upon the salient point of an argument, or the vital principle of a theory. The scaffolding of his argumentation is perfect, but the superstructure is sometimes top-heavy, since the height to which it was carried was often greater than the breadth of the base warranted. With the reality of purpose and honesty which was habitual to him, Pugin never attempted to conceal or defend an error, but at once went to work, not so much to reconstruct the principle of his argument as to widen the ground on which his operations were based. A signal instance of this habit occurs in the 'Contrasts,' and is still more apparent in the outlines and first foreshadowings of a work which Pugin projected on the English schism, and which it will perhaps be interesting to examine more closely in the course of this chapter. In the first edition of 'Contrasts' the author, namely, argues, that the decline of Gothic architecture was consequent on the rise of Protestantism; the retort was obvious, if the argument be true, how came it then to pass that in countries exclusively Catholic the degradation of art was, if possible, even greater than in England?

Pugin's argument was correct as far as it went, and in a certain sense, but to include the sweeping consequences, which were involved in the question of the decay of the true principles of art, a greater argumentative breadth of base was needed. In the second edition of 'Contrasts' Pugin, in his straightforward manner, acknowledged that he had taken too narrow a stand-point in assigning Protestant ascendancy as the primary cause of the overthrow of Christian art, since it was in itself but an effect of those Pagan principles, which at the revival of letters in the 16th century, overran Europe, and sowed corruption in literature, art, and manners.

Perhaps, however, the most marked attribute in Pugin's character was reverence. It was this quality which inspired him with so deep an affection for all that was consecrated by time, or made sacred by usage. In religion it increased the humility of his faith, it chastened in art the fervour of his imagination; and in letters it sobered the speculations of an inquisitive mind. The destructions of the sacrilegious Iconoclast, and the innovations of modern taste, so jarred against this primary principle of his nature, that he could scarcely restrain his indignation within the bounds of reason. Reverence still further developed another characteristic tendency in the constitution of Pugin's mind—love for symbolism. Nature for him was full of symbolic revelations: in the outspread wings of the bird, in the bending branches of the tree, he beheld the form of the cross; in the forest with its over-arching tops and clustering leaves, he discovered the prototype of the Gothic cathedral. The sublime symbolism of the Catholic Church in architecture and ritual first appealed to his imagination in favour of Catholicity, and at last his love for symbolism found its full satisfaction in the ancient religion, where his work was indeed worship, his buildings a perpetual prayer. There were no qualities more peculiar to Pugin than reality, thoroughness of purpose, outspoken courage. He never flinched from a principle, or shrank from a conclusion. His home-life was in keeping with his public character; he hated dissimulation or pretence in every shape. The idleness and hollow unrealities of conventional life were abhorrent to his nature. Kind, affectionate, gentle, he yet never forgot the duties of discipline or the rights of authority. And none knew better than he how, on every occasion, to enforce the respect which was his due.

In temperament sanguine and eager, active in habit, in conversation gay and agreeable, Pugin was never for an instant idle; not a moment of time escaped him. He threw his heart into the hour as it passed,

and into the present work. He lived out his days.
The close of the evening left him where the sunrise
had found him, and the toil of the livelong day made
him only the more cheerful in temper, the brighter in
mind. Labour refreshed his intellect, and made it the
more prolific, like the rain does the thirsty earth after
the noon-tide heats. But Pugin was no mere hewer
of wood or drawer of water, no mere believer in the
omnipotence of hard work. He did not forget that
the depth of wisdom lies in meditation, and that
creative power springs from the unfettered imagination. It was asserted, indeed, by many who did not
know him, that he was unfit for the work of his own
day, because he lived only in the past, and imagined
impossible things for the future. They affected to
account him, in sooth, as a mere visionary enthusiast,
and nothing more, to be pitied and passed over by the
common sense of this wise generation to which he did
not belong.

Enthusiastic indeed he was, but enthusiasm gave
him power to work as no man single-handed ever
worked before. His intense labour was all given to
his own day. In meditating on the glories of the past,
he found strength and courage to sustain him in the
thankless task of working for the good of his own time
and country. Genius, in fine, is erratic, but so long
as it does not forfeit its high calling, the errors of
genius are easily overlooked, and few men has it led
into lesser errors than Augustus Welby Pugin. The
faults of his life, though they showed him indeed to be

very human, were but the weaknesses of poor over-
burdened humanity; and as a devoted son of the Catholic Church, he found in the constant and never-failing
practices of religion, support, strength, and solace in
his day of trial.

On contemplating such a man as Pugin, we feel
with Wordsworth—

> 'That not in entire forgetfulness,
> And not in utter nakedness,
> But trailing clouds of glory do we come
> From God who is our home.'

All that now remains to do in this last chapter on
the writings and character of Welby Pugin is, if
possible, to discover the last impressions left on his
mind, and to trace in his scattered literary remains
the latest energies of his active intellect, before it was
clouded by the direst physical calamity which God
permits to befal mankind.

In the last great work which Pugin lived to complete, the following note occurs in reference to an
intended publication on the English schism:—'I
trust to be able before long to put forth an impartial
statement relative to the destruction of Catholic edifices and ornaments, consequent on the change of
religion in England.

'After the most patient investigation I have been
compelled to adopt the conclusion that the most fearful acts of spoliation were committed by men who had
not only been educated in the ancient faith, but who
were contented externally to profess its doctrines. I

had originally fallen into popular errors on these matters in some of my early publications; and it is but an act of justice to affix the odium of the sacrilege on those who were really guilty. I feel quite satisfied that one of the most urgent wants of the time is a real statement of the occurrences connected with the establishment of Protestantism and the loss of the ancient faith; of course I have to treat the subject in an architectural view, but still I trust to bring forward many facts that may lead to a better understanding and more charity on both sides, for we may all exclaim, "Patres nostri peccaverunt et non sunt et nos iniquitates eorum portavimus."'

This urgent want of the time Pugin intended to meet by his projected work, which was to have been an historical investigation into the causes that led to the Reformation, and an impartial consideration of the state of Catholicism in the century prior to that event. The ground he intended to occupy was comparatively new, or, rather, it would be more correct to say, the novelty lay in his manner of treating this debatable border-line between mediæval and modern times—this battle-field of rival Churches. The work, to judge from the brief outlines and sketches left, was no polemical work; it was no defence against the hasty and inconsiderate charge brought by ignorance or by prejudice against the Catholic Church; it was rather a confession of guilt, an acknowledgment that the general decay of the ecclesiastical spirit throughout Christendom, the loss of piety among the people, the increase of avarice and luxury among a degenerate clergy, the corruption and nepotism in the higher rulers of the Church were the chief contributing causes to the Reformation. The weight of the crimes of the preceding century broke the back of the old politico-religious system of Europe, which had so long and so nobly supported the edifice of society; and in its fall the unity of Christendom was broken, and the minds of men received a shock from which they have not yet recovered. Pugin was candid, I will not say to a fault, but to the extremest limit of candour. The ardent admirer of mediæval times had on the sudden discovered that the close of the middle ages was no period of glory of which a Catholic could well be proud, and he was forced, as it were, by the revulsion of feeling to make this public avowal.

Pugin was not only in the habit of rushing to extremes, but he often fancied that what was new to himself was unknown to all the world. This assumption sometimes gave a tone of arrogance to his censures, and led him to condemn in others a line of conduct which was often the result of prudence, and not, as he supposed, the mere effect of ignorance. It is, however, but too true that Catholics, from the necessity of defending themselves against unscrupulous attacks, have been too much in the habit of glossing over errors and evading difficulties. Polemics is the ruin of historical investigation. The period just antecedent to the Reformation, has yet to be submitted to the criticism of the candid historian. Pugin was in many respects well suited to the task he had imposed upon himself. His judgment would have ripened under the toil of long and patient research. His crude theories, his dubious or extreme views would have been modified and corrected long before he had arrived at the conclusion of his projected work; whilst his truthfulness, which was beyond question, would have won for him the popular ear. As an attempt to account for the primary causes of the defection of so large a portion of Europe from the Roman Catholic Church, and as a candid acknowledgment of the corruptions which had gradually undermined the foundations of the faith, Pugin's projected work might be fitly termed an apology for the separated Church of England. In this sense it is true that 'the glorious men the Church of England continued to produce in evil times' were not so guilty of the separation as those men who by their laxity of faith and worldly-mindedness brought about the revolt from Rome. The following is a full copy of the proposed title page of the book. 'Preparing for publication in parts at intervals, richly illustrated, An Apology for the separated Church of England since the reign of the Eighth Henry. Written with every feeling of Christian charity for her children, and honour of the glorious men she continued to produce in evil times. By A. Welby Pugin. Many years a Catholic-minded son of the Anglican Church, and still an affectionate and loving brother and servant of the true sons of England's Church.'

In consequence of the religious commotion of the times the work, by the advice of the author's ecclesiastical superiors, was delayed; he was admonished indeed 'not to go on with his promised publication without a *sound*, theological adviser, nor before he had cleared up the objections and the scandal which was feared to have resulted from his former work on the Hierarchy—a work so taken up by the hostile papers, and by whom certainly it was hoped Pugin could not wish to be considered as a friend.'

'Might I suggest,'—writes another ecclesiastical personage, the authority of whose name and position gave him a right to advise,—' Might I suggest, what possibly is already in your own mind, the caution of having your book on the Schism looked over by some grave divine before publishing it.' The work was finally interrupted by the death of the author. From the fragmentary headings and brief outline of his subject, and the scattered and unconnected sheets he has left, it is only possible to gather indications of the line of argument adopted by the writer, and of mere summaries of the results of his historical investigations. These last relics from his hand are nevertheless instructive and interesting, not only because they throw light upon his character, but because they are susceptible on many points of giving an explanation of much which has been made the groundwork of a charge against him of defection from the Church of Rome.

By connecting the stray passages and by preserving

the brief outline, or rather, headings which Pugin wrote
for his guidance, it will be possible to gain an idea, at
least, of the nature of the proposed work as a contribution to ecclesiastical history. 'May God in his
mercy,' the author commences, 'bless the work and increase the growing charity among men who see truth
and real history, and begin to throw off unfounded
prejudices on both sides and see truth face to face.'

After this appeal against unfounded prejudices the
author enters into the consideration of the English
Church in the simplicity of Saxon times, so distinguished for clearness of devotion, purity of manners,
and unwavering faith. He then enlarges on the primitive rites, and on the style, plan, and arrangement of
churches and altars. The form of vestments and ornaments were to have been reproduced in numerous
and correct illustrations as interesting to the antiquarian as to the churchman. The next subject to be
treated at large was the common ecclesiastical foundations and the possessions of the great monasteries.
The author undertakes to prove that great ecclesiastical
foundations were well suited to the wants of those ages
and were then a great blessing, but he does not accept
church endowment as a principle to be invariably observed ; on the contrary, as will be shown later on, he
is an unequivocal opponent to endowments in the
present day, and considers the accumulated wealth and
magnificence of the church at the close of the middle
ages, to have been not only the proximate cause of
the encroaching tyranny and usurpation of the state,

but also the fruitful source of the vices of the ecclesitical rulers.

In considering the period which immediately preceded the Reformation, the author points out the
general decay of the ecclesiastical spirit and the spread
of immorality and infidelity among the ecclesiastics
of the fifteenth century. 'Their pride, luxury, and
temporal pursuits had raised throughout Christendom
a general disgust against Churchmen, and had filled
the minds of men with doubts and dismay.' When
the author reflects on the religious indifference and
corruptions of Italy, and on the commotion which the
principles of Luther had awakened among the more
thoughtful and religious-minded people of Germany,
he cannot but regard the conduct of Leo X., in placing
himself at the head of the revived Paganism, as most
injurious to the true interests of the Church, and as an
evidence of his insensibility to the danger which
threatened the faith of Christendom. The mind of the
sovereign Pontiff, preoccupied with ambitious projects
and worldly pursuits, was blind to the religious necessities of the time and forgetful of the more sacred
duties of his high calling, whilst 'the cardinals of the
Roman Court,' are described by the author, as men
'puffed up with ostentation and human pride, and
many of them as disgraced by covetousness and every
degenerate vice,' whose time and thoughts were exclusively devoted to the patronage of the Classic revival
in arts and letters. The author then considers the
condition of France under what he terms its Pagan

monarch, Francis I., and describes the state of the old
religion in England under Henry VIII., and endeavours to show that the chief cause of its decay
arose from the lamentable loss of discipline in the
clergy, and from the extreme ignorance into which the
people had been allowed to sink. In consequence of
this deplorable state of things ' true religion was
often replaced by miserable superstition ' which soon
destroyed the vital energy and holiness of faith. He
next proceeds to consider the dreadful abuses connected with chantry chapels and the evils attendant
on their foundation, and treats generally on the misapplication of the great Church endowments, but shows
that these abuses were not peculiar to England, but
extended throughout Christendom, about the close of
the middle ages, when ' the fine old apostolic spirit of
serving God and him only, was changed into reliance
on kings and emperors and on mere human aid.'
The author then purposed to give a full and minute
description of these abuses in the several countries of
Europe. The state of the great monastic houses was
next to be examined, and the decay of religious zeal
was found to have paved the way for the foot of the
intruder and to have opened the door to Cardinal
Wolsey, who by his subservience to the Crown, became the herald of the Reformation, and by his rapacity in the suppression of the monasteries, anticipated in some measure its work of spoliation and
sacrilege.

The author then insists upon regarding the union of

Church and State, or rather the increasing tyranny of
the State which crushed the liberty of the Church, as
the most fruitful cause of the corruption and weakness of faith, which in the various countries of Europe
led to the overthrow of religion. He shows that the
spoliation and destruction of sacred things in England was carried on, not by Protestants, but by
men professing the Catholic religion and conforming
to its rites, by ecclesiastics and dignitaries of the
Church, who from cowardice or from the desire of
preserving their rich livings, were only too eager to
comply with the encroaching demands and usurpa-
tions of the State. The rights of the Church were
surrendered, monasteries suppressed, and even the
supremacy of the Pope impugned by men who were
the ordained ministers of God, and the corrupt servants of his Church.

'All this ruin,' the writer elsewhere remarks, 'was
brought about by the old ecclesiastical authorities, before a single professed Protestant appeared on the scene.
In many dioceses, the rector, vicar, or his curate was
compelled to read to the people four times in the year
a pastoral, dictated by the bishop, in which the
authority of the Holy See was denounced in language
scarcely less revolting, gross, insolent, and profane,
than that which has been so profusely used in the
recent Protestant demonstrations; and this poison was
infused into the minds of the people by the divinely
appointed channels of truth, their own clergy, and
soon the whole country presented a fearful scene of

destruction, carried on in the name of the old religion ; and it is a most humiliating fact that the greatest destruction of glorious churches, religious houses, shrines, and sacred places, was accomplished by men who still assisted at the holy sacrifice of the Mass and conformed to all the essential practices of the ancient religion. The great spoiler of Lincoln's glorious church was not a Protestant fanatic, but Dr. Heneage, the Catholic archdeacon ; and it was he who demolished the shrine of St. Hugh, and was, as Willis describes, very forward in defacing shrines, and delivering up the treasure of the Church into the king's hands!   The shrine of St. Thomas was plundered, and his holy relics burnt in the cathedral-yard, while the canons sang the office and Mass in the choir.   The chaplains of the chapel of old London Bridge, dedicated in honour of the same saint, broke their common seal, and petitioned for a new patron, and every Missal, gradual, antiphonal, office, or choir-book, used in England at that period, has the name of every Pope or St. Thomas either erased or defaced by ink ; and this by the hands of the priests and clergy, who read and sang, and celebrated from them in this mutilated state. Lead was stript off churches, noble pillars and arches prostrated, the tombs of venerable dead destroyed by men who concluded the despatches of their destructions to Cromwell, with hopes that the Holy Trinity and our Lady would have him in their keeping.

The lands belonging to religious houses were partly divided among courtiers who professed the old religion, and the very suppression of monasteries was carried on in a manner *secundum regulum* : the greater part of the monks resigned and were pensioned or secularized ; a few resisted and were martyred. But many of the abbots became secular dignitaries, and as was the case at Westminster and Peterburgh, bishops of their old abbatial churches created into sees by *royal authority*, and conformed to all the changes enacted by the State. As long as the ordinary ceremonial of the Church remained unaltered, and Mass was celebrated, the people, with some few exceptions, remained passive spectators of these changes. But when the innovations and destructions became apparent, there was a succession of formidable, though unsuccessful risings, in defence of the old religion. And again, in the succeeding reign of Edward the Sixth, there were several insurrections on the same ground, to quell which, and to force the new forms on the people, the Protector had recourse to the assistance of a numerous body of foreign mercenaries. I merely mention these facts to show the utter falsity of the prevailing idea that the change of religion in England was a *national* movement, or *that it was even founded on doctrinal differences*. It was a pure question of ecclesiastical power, ceded to the king by the hierarchy, and all subsequent events hang on this act.

' The people were very much better than their clergy, and had it not been that the latter were so fettered and bound by the State power as to act like machines in the hands of the civil magistrate, the

English nation never would have submitted to these
alterations in divine service and articles of faith.   But
it is very easy to conceive what difficulties attended
even a faithful people when betrayed by their own
clergy, and is a most striking example of the necessity
of *free action* for the ecclesiastical powers, for without
it a Catholic hierarchy itself offers no security to the
faithful, as the sad case of England's schism fully
shows.'

The period filled by the reigns of Henry VIII.,
Edward VI., Mary, and Elizabeth, the author intended
to consider in detail, and was to have enriched his
pages with copious illustrations.   Of the purport of
the second part of his intended volume, he has only
given the following brief sketch.   'The next part,' he
says, 'is dedicated to the history of the Church in
England from Elizabeth to our time, showing that, on
the whole, our separation as a nation from the communion of so-called Catholic countries, in the degraded
state of the continental countries and Churches in the
sixteenth, seventeenth, and eighteenth centuries, has
been a great blessing.   We have, by the mercy of God,
preserved our liberties, and ancient legal constitutions,
and the great fundamental Christian doctrines; while
continental revolutions, atheism and infidelity had, at
last, closed every church on the Continent, and in
France even exposed for worship a prostitute on the
altar of her largest cathedral.   It was impossible for
England, till the present time, to hold any sort of unity
with so-called Catholic countries, all under the severest

tyranny, and the Catholic religion little more than a mere engine of the State, to control the people and hold them in a state of ignorance and bigotry, while all free discussion and learning was suspended. But now, thank God, this state of things has passed away; religion is free in most countries; disconnected from the State it will live by the reasonable faith of men who study, and believe. Search the Holy Scriptures under holy guidance and tradition, and see those wonderful perfections and doctrines restored in the revival of ancient rites free from any superstitious abuses, and restored to their original intention and purity. Great reformers are coming everywhere. That fine work of the Ver Rongeur alone is sufficient to show the decay of Catholic faith and discipline, and the loss of all its influence on men, mis-called Catholics, for the last three centuries, and its glorious renovation by Englishmen, who, by acting up to the principles denied at the Reformation, and providentially preserved hence, to have led to assist in the restoration of pious and glorious Catholic principles and art.'

By his statement, that the separation of England as a nation from the continental countries and churches, has been a great blessing, Pugin in no wise meant that her fall from Catholic unity was a blessing, but simply that schism was preferable to infidelity and atheism. The statement as to the comparative benefit which England derived by her separation from continental countries, is as a matter of fact open to this grave objection, that the infidelity common to Europe in the eighteenth

century, was in England superadded to a chronic state
of schism; and when Pugin, perhaps in his eager
desire to palliate the defection of his country from
Catholic unity, charges the whole of the Continent
during three centuries with guilt greater than heresy,
he falls into a gross historical error, and advances facts
which, on maturer consideration and research, he
would have been totally unable to have substantiated.
His error was not in upholding false principles but in a
mistaken judgment as to matters of fact. The following letter which he received from a valued and
learned friend on the publication of his pamphlet on
the Hierarchy, and when he was engaged in preparing
his history of the English schism, was not lost on
Pugin, who was never slow in taking advice, and no
doubt, on consideration, he would have modified or
corrected many of the dubious statements and opinions
he seemed to advance in his proposed work.

'However, my dear friend, bear these things with equanimity
and offer them to God, for the great cause you uphold. Also we
must remember the old adage, "*fas est ab hoste doceri,*" and certainly it is necessary for a person like yourself, who advocate a
very grand and important work, to study extreme accuracy of expression. Of course you admit as fully as —— himself, that
neither Cranmer nor old Harry were Catholic after the year 1532,
i. e. from the moment they renounced the supremacy of St. Peter's
see. Of course after that fatal moment they became pestilent schis-
maticks, and all their sacrifices and sacraments, though far from
null, were nevertheless so many sacrileges: as holy Church sings
of the B. Eucharist "*mors* est malis, vita bonis." If you read over
the *eleventh* of Father Newman's able Lectures on Anglican Difficulties, you will find that he takes precisely the very line you

adopted in your address. I advise you to refer to it, and write again another letter making citations from it in order to strengthen your own very just and sensible view of the Anglican Church; and you may depend upon it a few sentences from Newman would have a very *tranchant* effect in your favour. See *Lecture* xi., *p.* 387, *et passim.* But in doing this, my dear friend, take care you set yourself right as to the *non*-catholicity of Cranmer and old Harry from the moment they departed from their communion with the divine centre of unity. Dr. —— is quite sound as to what he says on that head; of course they were not Catholic, no more Catholic than Blanco White or Father Gavazzi or poor ———. Cranmer was a bishop, but not a Catholic one, when he left the unity of the Church; he is a bishop now in hell, and it will increase his torment, while God is God. I perfectly understood your address in this sense from the first; all you meant to insist on was the previous Catholicity of the pseudo-Reformers, not to uphold their subsequent Catholicity; but there is no harm in setting this still more clearly before the public, and if you do it in a *dignified, temperate, charitable* reply to ——, you will gain great κυδος as we used to say in our Greek slang at Cambridge. And be sure, my dear friend, to make a strong profession of faith in the all-important principle of the supremacy of the Holy See. Every hour I live I grow more and more devoted to that great principle : it is the very life-blood of the Catholic system, and Catholic life is vigorous in proportion as this blood circulates without impediment. I owe a great debt of gratitude on this head to that admirable treatise of *the see of St. Peter* by Mr. Allies. It has made my mind so clear upon it. Let us show that *we* are the Catholics par excellence, and that it is on that ground that we are *plain chant men,* and *Christian artists.'*

The arguments which Pugin in those writings advanced against the union of Church and State it would be difficult to gainsay. The question as to the relationship of the Church to the State has much advanced since his time. Everywhere at the present

day the State is found arrayed in hostility against
ecclesiastical rights and liberties.   Kings are no longer
nursing fathers of the Church. Catholic nations in their
corporate capacity are throwing off the yoke of Christianity, and proclaiming aloud the supremacy of the
popular will in Church as well as in State. The Church,
henceforth, is at best but to occupy a subordinate position, or to become, according to the favourite theory
of revolutionary politicians, a mere department of the
State.   Nowhere, on the other hand, is the progress
of religion greater than in those lands where, un-
trammeled by State patronage, it enjoys perfect freedom of action.   The question then is how to reconcile
modern necessity with the ancient practice.   It is no
wisdom to retain an obsolete theory, sound only when
the State was Christian, or obedient to the principles of
religion. The free Church in the free State, which Montalembert desiderates, could only be obtained, in the
present condition of society, by a separation of Church
and State.   The Church itself must choose the lesser
of two evils, and divorced from the State which,
everywhere to-day upholds un-Christian principles,
leave it to the reprobation of its own choosing.   How
by advocating in the present century this necessity
Pugin could justly lay himself open to the charge of
advancing un-Catholic views, or of betraying symptoms
of incipient heresy, it is hard to perceive.   Again, it
must be remembered that in the sketch which he
gives of the second part of his projected work on
Anglicanism, some untenable arguments are broached,

some statements advanced which in the course of his investigations, or on reflection, would have been altered or modified. In the foregoing pages I have shown that it was a characteristic of Pugin's mind, if not to leap to conclusions, at least in the outset to state matters broadly which in the progress of his labours he would soften down or more accurately define. His meaning, therefore, when, as in the above sketch, it is open to a dubious interpretation, must in a spirit of fairness be judged by the principles upheld so strenuously in his completed works, which for this purpose have been fully analysed in these pages as Pugin's best justification and defence.

Again, objections have been started to Pugin's views on the subject of endowments, and to his advocacy of the voluntary system; but one cannot help acknowledging the substantial strength of his facts, and the wisdom of his deductions on this much disputed question. He had intended to devote a considerable portion of his projected work to the proof of what he elsewhere briefly states as his conviction, that the accumulation of vast ecclesiastical properties is a great evil, and that the never-failing endowment of the Church is in the succession of baptized faithful men, filled with the spirit of religion, and willing to labour like men for its support and solemn maintenance. 'This,' he continues, and we will give the passage at length, 'is an inexhaustible treasure which no Government can sequester, no law reach, no tyranny impair; this is an apostolical endowment, and while the clergy are faithful to the people and the people to the clergy, which is a corresponding natural consequence, she needs no other. Wherever, on the other hand, a richly endowed clergy exist they are no longer beloved by the people; and it is to this very cause that we may attribute the defection from the faith of so many countries in the 16th century. The ecclesiastics had become the temporal rulers and tax-receivers instead of their fathers and shepherds. Even here in England, Catholic England, Merrye England, in Richard the Second's reign, sixty thousand men were in arms to exterminate the nobles and higher order of clergy: the unfortunate and pious archbishop, Simon Sudbury, they succeeded in beheading; and had their whole plot been completed, the friars alone would have been spared in the massacre, and that, most probably, on account of their wearing a poor habit, and mingling and ministering to the lower class. When the clergy of a country is once placed above the need of the people's aid and offering, it is a state of things fraught with danger to both. There is a spirit of reciprocity under the old apostolic system that is a mutual protection, and that once gone, the wealth and endowment becomes a curse and a snare. We read an account of the death of a holy Catholic bishop, who addressed the surrounding clergy with these memorable words:—" I die, as becomes a bishop of God's Church, without money and without debts." Oh! if all the ancient bishops would have said the same, how many souls would have escaped the penalty of their avarice!

Political economists and ministers of state cannot reach the true church revenues with their artillery; the Catholic faith and practice in its purity is unassailable with the longest range they possess. *It is only when it becomes corrupt that it falls into their clutches*, but, by the blessing of God, this shall not be: with so many warnings of the past, for the future we shall avoid the old rocks of temporal wealth and endowments, which have been the cause of ruin, and scandal, and corruption in former ages.

' The closer we examine the practical result of all these large endowments, the more we shall be convinced that they were attended with far more evil than good to the foundations which possessed them. The riches of the great churches have rendered them, in all ages, objects of cupidity to the temporal rulers, who, for the sake of their revenues, deprived the dioceses of their spiritual rulers, and kept the appointments open for years, to enable them to squander the revenues on their own luxury and extravagance; and all history will show that superior piety, and learning, and ecclesiastical discipline, were by no means a certain recommendation to the high offices of the Church, connected as they were with great temporal wealth and power, and that those who were often selected to fill them were chosen from their distinguished birth, connexions, and the likelihood of a compliance with the royal will, rather than as vigilant pastors and maintainers of ecclesiastical discipline. This, as might be expected, created a class of superior clergy odious to the body of the people and unfaithful to their sacred duties, and was the occasion of some of those frightful excesses which were exercised against the episcopal order in English rebellions long before the Reformation.

' *The only dependable endowment of the Church is to be found in the zeal and devotion of the faithful.* While there is a succession of baptized persons, brought up in the true faith, there must be a succession of funds that cannot fail or be taken away. Moreover, this wealth, continually flowing in to supply the occurring wants of the Church and its ministers, present no tangible temptations, nor even the possibility of plunder, which is inseparable from great estates and standing wealth, which have been the occasion of such dreadful sacrilege and abuse in former centuries. There appears to be an internal element of corruption in the possession of great revenues, which causes the decay of that which it is intended to preserve ; and the history of every richly endowed Church presents a most lamentable succession of misapplication of its revenues, revolting abuses, and *its final dissolution, for the sake of its very wealth.* Moreover, there has been another most fatal result to religion in the irresponsible possession of rich endowments, as almost without exception, the duties have been vicariously performed, so that the very revenues have induced the evil of non-residence, while the spiritual consolations have been administered by some poor and often ignorant curate, provided at the lowest salary.

'I feel confident that while the true spirit is kept alive among the people, no investment is so certain and secure. Catholics are producers of wealth; besides so many men of noble and ancient families who still adhere to the Catholic faith, there are artists, manufacturers, merchants, traders, mechanics, labourers, all not only living but accumulating by their exertions; and is it to be supposed that any of all these classes, if animated by the spirit of their religion, will be not ready to devote a good portion of their temporal means to the support of their clergy, and, indeed, the splendour of religion? If they do not, then of course they must renounce the faith and cease to require the assistance of priests; but I maintain that all practical Catholics must, in virtue of their faith, be regular supporters of religion, though certainly up to the present time, either through a false delicacy or some other indefensible reason, *this duty of contributing has not been sufficiently urged,* and I am confident that many are deficient in this important part rather from want of reflection and instruction than good-will. But I do believe that if this duty were properly and forcibly urged by the clergy, that it will be responded to most heartily, and especially as temporal laws are in preparation to deprive the Church of other means of support.

'No human legislation can interfere with the spiritual ties that must exist between the faithful and their clergy, while the latter remain true to their sacred duties and office. As well might an act be passed to sever the husband from the wife, the parent from the child, as to disunite a faithful people from an apostolic clergy. As long as they are devoted to a faithful ministration of these sacred duties, and *serve God*, we have everything to hope and nothing to fear : serving God is the great source of all ecclesiastical strength. It was in that respect so many of the ancient bishops failed : *they did not serve God.* Was not this acknowledgment wrung from the remorse of an English prelate famous in history, a man who, though a legate and a cardinal, was in reality a greater instrument in producing the English schism than the arch-heretic Cranmer himself ; by his intolerable pride, by his worldly splendour and state, he made the highest ecclesiastical office an occasion of scandal and reproach ; by the vexatious exercise of his legantine power he caused the spiritual authority of the Roman Pontiff to become an odious and intolerable burden ; by dissolving religious houses to found institutions in his own name, he paved the way for the destruction of every great religious establishment ; and when disgraced by that Prince to whom he had sacrificed his life and his office, and abandoned by the world to die, then in anguish of heart, he exclaimed, " Had I served my God as I have served my king, he would not have thus deserted me in my old age." What a dreadful— what a fearful state of soul, for this old man when he felt himself deserted by God ! But his history and his end are but the epitome of a multitude of other celebrated ecclesiastics, who have *served the king and*

been forsaken of God; it is not only the history of men,
but it is the history of the decay of religion itself
among many of the most powerful nations of Christendom.   How very injurious must the rule of such men
as Richelieu, Mazarin, and, to come still later, the
infamous Abbé Dubois, wearing the sacred habit of
religion, engrossing the most sacred and important
offices for the sake of their revenues, and with the
externals of ministers of the God of mercy and of
justice, ruling with all the diabolical machinery of
tyranny and oppression, men who, like Talleyrand,
used language only to conceal thought, whose smile
was more dreadful than their frown, as disguising
intentions the less easy to escape ; the possession of
whose very confidence was attended with the peril of
life to the unhappy object who held it, whose sumptuous
banquets and entertainments were of so hollow a
character that the gorgeous Gobelin hangings may be
said to have only covered the dark ways which not
unfrequently conducted the guests to the dungeons
of Vincennes, or the torture chamber of the Bastile.
Such are the men who have under the name of their
ecclesiastical dignity been odious in a free country ;
and what is most unfortunate, while there were so
many truly saintly cardinals who lived in comparative
retirement, and died in the faithful discharge of their
sacred duties, scarcely known to the pages of history,
the most famous men of the order are often its disgrace.   St. Carlo Borromeo, of Milan, is indeed an
exception : his virtues and his love commanded the ad-

2 G

miration and respect of all classes of men ; but he was
detached from all temporal considerations, and we may
indeed say *he served his God.'*

The essential purport of ' An Apology for the Separated Church of England ' is no justification of schism,
but only an additional plea on behalf of those whom
the author was in the habit of terming his separated
brethren, founded on the fact which Pugin wished to
enforce, that the base compliance of the old Catholic
hierarchy itself was the first cause which brought the
English Church under the bondage of the State, and
that they should be regarded by us rather as victims
of Catholic degeneracy than the consequence of Protestant error. 'It is not for those,' as he has expressed it before, ' who have gained the ship of Peter,
and ride securely in the storm, to mock the unwearied
efforts of those good and earnest souls who yet man
the shattered bark of England's Church, brought among
Protestant shoals by its old Catholic commanders, and
who still, amid *mutiny* and *oppression*, yet labour to
guide her to a haven of safety : and I will say that,
battered as is that old hull, it is a great breakwater
between the raging waves of infidelity and Catholic
truth in this land ; that it has held so long together,
under so many disadvantages and difficulties, must be
a work of Divine Providence for some great end which
remains to be developed. It is quite true that within
her pale are arrayed the greatest opponents against
whom we have to contend ; that her pulpits are often
prostituted to the unwearied repetition of the grossest

calumnies against the Catholic faith; *but these sad anomalies are not peculiar to this age; they have existed in the Church of England ever since its separation from the communion of the Holy See.* It contains contending elements of good and evil, of Catholic faith and Protestant error that were generated at the schism and which must go on till one or the other is triumphant. Either the Catholic element will prevail, and the body of the Church return to its mother; or, which is almost too sad to imagine, the Protestant element will expel all Catholic ritual, rubric, and practices, from her ordinals, drive from her pale every faithful child, and then what remains will collapse, like an expended balloon, and go out with a stench. But we will hope for better things; and, after all, the present state of affairs is certainly not worse, if not a great deal better than they were in the sixteenth century. At that period, as I have shown, the old priests, about whose orders there is not a shadow of doubt, were actually engaged in all the measures of the State, and in the destruction of our most glorious monuments and most sacred shrines. The four most Puritan bishops of Edward the Sixth's reign had all been superiors of monastic establishments, and had broken every vow they had ever made. These old clergy were married in violation of their solemn engagements; their successors never entered into them, and consequently are free from the scandal. The great churches are no longer mutilated, but everywhere restored and protected: surely, on the whole, the Church of England

under Queen Victoria is a great advance on the
Church of England under Edward the Sixth; and, if
the truth be spoken, after the first race of Elizabethan
Puritans, the Anglican bishops have, on the whole,
been respectable tenants of the sees. Some exhibited
all the zeal of an olden time in restoring the ravages
caused by Puritan ascendancy, and preserving the
traditions of ancient architectural arrangement, when
it had been abandoned throughout Christendom. We
must not forget that many noble foundations and
works of charity and piety, worthy of the brightest
time of Catholic spirit, date from the seventeenth
century; and when we consider that the prince-bishops
of Liege and Germany were employing the vast resources of their dioceses in laying out terraces, forming artificial canals and fountains, and paganizing
their palaces, while the towers of their cathedrals were
stunted and incomplete, the names of Hacket and
Cosin may awaken a grateful remembrance in a
Catholic heart. It would be unjust to test the works
of these men by those of preceding centuries. They
lived at a period remarkable for debasement all over
Europe. Had those countries which nominally retained the ancient faith exhibited a grand exception to
the general degradation, and adhered to the noble
ecclesiastical traditions of their forefathers, then indeed
we should have a grand argument; but so far from
this, the spirit of revived paganism flourished, and
even commenced, among them, while here in England
many of the ecclesiastical erections, though debased

in detail, exhibit great traces of the old traditions. What truly edifying and reverent works have been published on Catholic antiquities by devout members of her communion—by men who appreciated and set forth in most moving and pious language the noble works and lives of the founders of our cathedrals and abbatial churches. But for the labours of these men, every English Catholic antiquity would have fallen into oblivion, and their works are the standard of information to which we all refer.

'Let us then,' says Pugin, to quote the concluding words of 'An Apology for the separated Church of England,' 'let us then always speak and think with gratitude of the old bridge that has brought us over, and lend a pious help to restore her time-worn piers, wasted by the torrents of dissent and infidelity, and what is worse, internal decay by rotten stones, but which God in his mercy, beyond our human understanding appears yet to sustain, and to make it the marvel of some of the most zealous men that have appeared since the ancient glory of the Church in the pious early times. Pax omnibus. Amen.' These were the last words which Pugin wrote. The peace of mind he wished to others was denied to his own mind. His over-exerted brain gave way beneath the pressure of labour. His words of peace, his works of charity, his efforts of genius were all paralysed at one blow. His fine intellect was gone. The malady which for a time came over his mind was the forerunner of death.

CONCLUSION.

DEATH is always a surprise, even when it comes to close with gentle hand the wearied eye of the sufferer who has lingered hopeless for years, a living corpse on the bed of sickness; it is still a surprise when with sad and strange aspect it approaches at last to gather to the grave of his fathers the time-honoured man, soldier or sage, who, full of honours, for fourscore years and more has filled the world with the renown of his name; yet to whom should death be familiar if not to him who has outlived his day and already belongs to a past generation?   But never is death so strange as when, like a thief in the night, it comes to snatch on the sudden from his incomplete work and from the unaccomplished number of his days its strong and unwilling victim.   To the young in their first disappointment death is often not so bitter as to the man in the pride of life and in the vigour of intellect; for him to be smitten down in mid-career; for the light of his genius to be extinguished; for the rich treasures of his learning, gathered from ancient lore or from modern enlightenment, to be scattered and wasted, all the labour of years to be in vain—the ripe mind, the pure taste, the correct judgment—is

indeed a loss, not to himself alone, but to mankind.
How many a noble effort to revive the glories of the
past, to dispel the ignorance or prejudice which surrounded him, and to form the mind on matters that lay
within his sphere of the future generation of his countrymen, were not rudely snapped asunder by the death
of the man whose life and works we have been contemplating!

He had accomplished much, but much remained to
be done. He had laid the foundation to the edifice of
his fame, and wished to put the coping-stone to his
own work. His fertile brain and vigorous hand were
never for an instant slack. The luminous page, preg-
nant with thought and rich in illustration, was not half
finished when the pen dropped from his hand; the
most glorious designs of his pencil were left incomplete; he was only on the threshold of his labours;
his richly-stored mind was in the act of developing its
manifold powers; his genius was on its highest tide,
when the ebb of the waters of life, which sooner or
later comes to all, came upon him at a time when he
could ill be spared by the country he adorned and the
Church he had so faithfully served. In him, as in all
vigorous and happy men, the love of life was strong;
the hopes of the future were brightening about him;
the cause to which he had attached himself with all the
ardour of his fervid nature was in the ascendant; new
prospects of usefulness were opening up to his view;
the prejudice he had to encounter from those who
ought to have stood him in good stead was on the

wane; and, in fine, domestic ties with their strong
hold bound him to life; growing sons and daughters,
the proud heirs of his name and fame, surrounded his
hearth, and the sharer of his sorrows, the best partner
of his joys, was ever near with her quick sympathy
to lessen affliction in the day of reverse, or to gladden
his heart in his hour of triumph; but in the midst
of all these delights, with a strange and a terrible
surprise, death came to still the busy brain for ever,
and to bid the full heart to beat no more.

To revive the memory of the past; to preserve the
monuments bequeathed to us by the hand of genius;
to discover the motives that impelled the men of
other days in the glorious works which still surround
us, was to him a labour of love, and the active principle of his life.   Not a spot in England consecrated
by the beauty of his noble art was unfamiliar to his
mind.   The artistic glories and the natural beauties
of France, and Germany, and Italy—the Alpine
grandeur of Switzerland, are all reproduced and perpetuated in numerous still unpublished folios by the
magic power of his pencil.   In fine, to throw light
upon an obscure period of history, to vindicate those
ages which the presumption of ignorance and the calumny of prejudice have ventured to call dark;   to
show the Church of our fathers in the grandeur of
her ritual, in the magnificence of her sublime architecture, and in the holiness of her spirit, was the work
—who shall refuse to call it the glorious work?—of
Augustus Welby Pugin.

The wondrous edifices that cover the land—the towering minster—the gorgeous cathedral—the ruined abbey, spoke to his enraptured mind of the antiquity of his faith, and of the ancient artistic glory of his country. The lofty spires, the pinnacled towers of the colleges and chapels reared by the ancestral piety of our forefathers in the most renowned seat of wisdom in the land, recalled to his memory the union which once existed between learning and religion, while the sepulchral brasses of famous churchmen, graven on the pavement of cloister and of chapel, appealed not in vain to his piety for their departed souls; though to his vision the neglected effigy of many a venerable but forgotten founder seemed to frown down from amidst the glories of the stained glass in reproach for the utter disregard that had of late befallen so many a last behest and pious petition.

An unwavering faith, a most singular piety towards bygone ages, a veneration the most profound for all that appertained to the beauty of the courts of the Lord, an imagination glowing with the glories of the past, all combined in impelling the subject of this memoir to surrender his heart and soul to the desire for the restoration of the forgotten faith and for the revival in the land of its ancient magnificence in art and architecture. He was a man not easily to be turned aside by the many obstacles he had to encounter from the purpose of his heart. Although of a retiring habit of mind he yet possessed a robust temperament and a vehement nature; and when, in spite, and almost, as it were, in

defiant outrage of the monuments and memorials of
magnificent piety which encompassed and reproached
them on all sides, he beheld every correct principle of
taste in ecclesiastical buildings, and even the bare
decency due in the public celebration of divine worship, violated, not only by the followers of an alien
creed, but even by the members of the ancient faith,
his indignant denunciations broke forth, without stint
and without reserve, upon the ignorance of church-
builders and upon the sloth and unconcern of those
who were bound to preserve the holy places of God
from all that savours of irreverence, or leads to an
ignoble association of ideas. His unsparing criticisms,
although they provoked the hostility of not a few, and
led to much unkind misrepresentation, were yet successful in quickly engaging public attention. It is
indeed true, that, owing to his absolute turn of mind,
which was ever averse to compromise, and had but
scant consideration for views opposed to his own, he
failed to conciliate many men of eminence and mark
whom a gentler treatment might have wisely won to
his side; yet it must not be forgotten that he was a
reformer of stubborn abuses, which would yield to
nothing less than a vigorous onslaught. He went like
an arrow straight to his mark, no matter how the bow
were bent in the effort. He counted not the losses
that accrued in the combat; nor did he for one instant
regard the sacrifices he made; for, thanks to an upright and generous heart, a selfish act has never yet
been coupled with his name. Even in his most ex-

aggerated statements against public opponents, or in the vehemence of private correspondence, when he was sometimes betrayed into unguarded expressions of opinion, there was yet such singleness of purpose and such truthfulness apparent that none but a prejudiced or malevolent mind could have ventured to raise on the unrestrained utterance of his thoughts the painful charges which were insinuated, rather than stated, against his orthodoxy. Great as was his love to his art, and great as his hatred to the unrealities and shams which profaned in his eyes the temples they were intended to adorn, and indignant as were his denunciations against modern innovations and irreverent familiarity in the construction of churches and in the removal of those material safeguards that had shrouded and sheltered for ages the inmost sanctuary of the house of God from the intrusive gaze of impertinent curiosity; yet he never allowed his feelings, intense and excited as they were on the subject, to interfere with the fealty and obedience he owed to ecclesiastical authority, and the homage he was ever foremost to pay to the Holy See. No truer or more docile son of the Catholic Church existed than the stern rebuker of clerical degeneracy, or than the inveterate hater of the destructive heresies which broke up the unity and destroyed the glories of the ancient Church of England. His tenderness towards the ' separated brethren ' of the Protestant Establishment arose from the hope, which he cherished to the last, that the more learned and the more pious mem-

bers of a community, which had retained in its ritual
and in its creed so much that was grand and Catholic,
could not long remain out of the pale of unity, but
must return with their flocks and with the glorious
churches which they had so nobly preserved, or so
carefully restored, to the fold of Peter. He considered,
too, with great reason, that the Protestant Establishment, with its remnants of Catholic doctrine and its
external organization, was the great bulwark in
England against the spread of more pernicious errors,
and against the onsweep of infidelity. It was not by
joining the Dissenters in the hope of destroying the
Protestant Church, but by preserving and promoting
whatever there was of good in the Establishment he
could hope to make it a bridge over the gulf which
divides the people of England from the rock of Peter.
The personal relations of Pugin with many of the
Anglican clergy were unreserved and friendly; they
shared in his desire for the revival of the ancient
ecclesiastical architecture, and they appreciated his
talents, and were not slow in availing themselves of
his advice and assistance in the restoration of many a
whitewashed church or dilapidated chapel to its pure
and pristine beauty. Although the great Reviver of
Catholic principles in the grand externals of religion,
and of the spirit which gives life and their proper meaning to the splendid ritual and rubrics of the Church
never feared or failed to denounce, in no measured
terms, the too frequent shortcomings of our own clergy
in their disregard of the outward dignity of the altar and

of the solemnity of Divine worship; yet he never in
the intimate intercourse which he cherished with many
of the High-Church members of the Anglican community, or in the long-sustained correspondence which
he carried on with many of the Tractarian clergy, gave
them reasonable ground to believe that he wavered in
his faith, or that he bestowed on Rome a divided
allegiance or a half-hearted love. Truthfulness was
to him the pillar of life. On this sure foundation
he built and rested in perfect security. Reality was
a condition of his being. The principle of truth was
the hinge on which his mind turned. It was the 'open
sesame' to his heart, and the talisman round which his
thoughts clustered and crowded. It was the eagle-
like wing whereon his genius rose and rested. All
those who knew Pugin will recognize at once that his
chief characteristic was thoroughness. He was in the
deepest sense of the word thorough. This genuineness was the source of his greatness, and the secret
of his power. All who approached him felt they were
in the presence of no ordinary man, and they who had
once enjoyed his conversation have never forgotten its
indescribable charm,—its peculiar fascination; so rich
in allusion; so suggestive of thought and so natural
in the turn it ever took. So earnest too in their tone
were the arguments on his lips that they persuaded
even before they convinced the mind of the listener.
But it was difficult to gain entrance into the charmed
circle of his home-life. He was retiring and exclusive
to a fault, almost to a weakness; he shrank from con-

tact with strangers, and would dismiss the intrusive visitor with scant courtesy. The house of an Englishman is his castle ; but the house of Welby Pugin was a fortress surrounded with a deep moat, and but seldom was the drawbridge lifted. Yet if once the gates were thrown open to the welcome guest by some secret talismanic power of association, his heart was opened with them, and his visitors were received with an overflowing hospitality and entertained with gay ceremonial and song and sprightly humour which made the Christmas revel of his sea-side home a scene of never-failing joy and of unforgotten delight. After witnessing such a festive display of mirth and jollity one would no longer be surprised to learn that the man whose mind was filled with notions of antique grandeur had the simplicity of a child, and the gaiety of heart which seems rather to belong to the dweller beneath the open and sunny skies of the south, than to the inhabitant whose character has been formed and hardened beneath the ruder pressure of a northern climate.

There was much in the character of Welby Pugin's mind which would have gone far to overcome the prejudice which Englishmen entertain against the Catholic Church. His truthfulness, the utter absence of all pretension, his outspoken boldness, his love of the national character, would have won their way by degrees into the hearts of his countrymen, and would have led them to regard with greater consideration, and to judge with greater candour, the Church which watched at the cradle of our civilization, and was the consecration of our maturer growth. His influence, indeed, was on the increase; he was conscious of power within himself to do greater things than he yet had been able to achieve; he often regretted that a larger opportunity had not offered itself; but, indeed, he had not yet arrived at the meridian of his power when he was taken down so early to the silent grave. But where then is the grave of this remarkable man? for England, if she neglect the living, never fails to honour the great dead. How shall I answer the question? Do you not know, gentle reader, how often real merit goes to the grave unrewarded, while the borrower of other men's gifts shines in false colours, and meekly assumes honours that were not his due? Pugin's tomb is in no place of public honour. No reward fell to his lot, living or dead. No troop of friends followed him to the grave to do homage to his memory, and to bear testimony to all the world that a great man had passed away from the earth. There was no solemn gathering of the brotherhood of genius, filling in grief the nave of Westminster Abbey. Against him in death the glorious temple which he loved so well in life was closed. To England's greatest architect the Gothic abbey afforded no honoured grave. No stone was raised to show to distant ages how abiding is the monument which generosity pays to greatness. *Hamlet* said of his own time, "There's hope a great man's memory may outlive his life half a year; but by 'r Lady he must build churches then, or else shall he suffer not thinking on." But to-day a

great man may build churches and yet be forgotten by
his country. I do not know who followed Pugin to his
neglected grave; we will not invade the sanctuary of
private grief, but we may be sure that the last, long
look which followed him to his resting-place, and
the treasured tears that fell, were to him of more
moment than monuments of marble and all the proud
trappings of woe. What to him in his grand simplicity
was the outward circumstance of sorrow? The pomp
and majesty of grief were our duty indeed, but not his
need. Yet while the wise men of the world drew far
off, the muse of history stood by and proclaimed over
the scanty grave of him who was indeed one of
Nature's great ones, that he had achieved immortality,
that his memory would be preserved in his country's
annals, and his name be registered in the proud
muster-roll of her great men as long as modest
worth, true genius, and genuineness of character
are loved and reverenced by the heart of man. To
such a fame the monumental marble and the elaborate epitaph can neither add nor take away. All
that now remains to do is to endeavour to stamp
the impress of his greatness on the mind of the present
generation, and, in these days of forgetfulness, when
the dim waters of Lethe are rising so fast above their
water-mark, and threatening to sweep into oblivion
all that was grand and good in bygone times, it becomes a duty, and is indeed the best memorial of
Pugin's life and labours, to keep before the public
mind that in the Gothic revival Pugin sought to

restore the fervour of faith and the self-denying spirit which were the real foundations of the artistic greatness and moral grandeur of the middle ages. Should it indeed fall to my fortunate lot to be able to recall to the memory of those who knew him a pleasant image of his life, it will be the great reward of my feeble efforts. Mine at all events shall be the honour of having paid a tribute of homage to a man of genius; and it will be a proud satisfaction if my hand shall be permitted to place the last cypress-wreath on the grave of him who lies near the murmuring sea-shore in his own monumental church of St. Augustine, awaiting in hope the glory of the final Resurrection.

MEMORIAL

TO THE LATE

Augustus N. Welby Pugin.

Ir has been resolved to do honour to the memory of the late
AUGUSTUS WELBY PUGIN, for his services in the promotion of true
principles of Mediæval Architecture, and, in furtherance of this
object, to solicit donations and devote them to the Endowment of a
Permanent Fund, to be entitled the "PUGIN TRAVELLING FUND,"
the interest arising therefrom to be awarded to an Architectural
Student in such manner and at such periods as may hereafter be
decided, and to be expended by the recipient within one year of the
time of its allotment in travelling in the United Kingdom, and in
examining and illustrating its Mediæval Architecture, Sculpture,
and Painting. To the Studentship it is proposed to add a medal.
The Royal Institute of British Architects will be asked to become
Trustees of the Fund.

This Memorial, whilst providing a lasting recognition of the services rendered to Art generally by the late AUGUSTUS WELBY PUGIN,
will be the means of promoting in a thoroughly practical manner
the PRINCIPLES so ably advocated and applied by him, and each
occasion of the award of the Fund will form a special commemora-
tion of the great Artist in whose honour it has originated.

The following words of Pugin himself at page 20 of his 'Apology
for the Revival of Christian Architecture in England,' confirm in a

2 I

peculiar manner the original opinion of the Committee that the form of memorial proposed is the most appropriate :

" God grant me the means and I would soon place Architectural Studies on such a footing that the glory of these latter days should be even greater than that of the former.   I would also have travelling students, but I would circumscribe their limits: Durham, the destination of some ; Lincolnshire's steepled fens for others ; Northampton spires, and Yorkshire's venerable piles, Suffolk and Norfolk's coasts, Oxford, Devonshire, and Warwick, each county should be indeed a school—for each is a school—where those who run may read, and where volumes of ancient art lie open for all inquirers."

Committee.

(Those marked * form the Working Committee.)

* A. J. B. BERESFORD-HOPE, Esq., *Chairman.*

T. D. ACLAND, Esq.
* CHARLES AINSLIE, Esq.
* REV. G. AINSLIE
H. G. AUSTIN, Esq.
* CHARLES BARRY, Esq.
* E. M. BARRY, Esq.
* A. W. BLOMFIELD, Esq.
M. H. BLOXAM, Esq.
REV. J. R. BLOXAM, D.D.
DE LA BARRE BODENHAM, Esq.
G. F. BODLEY, Esq.
* DAVID BRANDON, Esq.
* RAPHAEL BRANDON, Esq.
W. CUNLIFFE BROOKS, Esq.
* WILLIAM BURGES, Esq.
* TALBOT BURY, Esq.
CHARLES BUXTON, Esq., M.P.
* VISCOUNT CAMPDEN
THE DEAN OF CANTERBURY
THE EARL OF CARLISLE
R. D. CHANTRELL, Esq.
* EWAN CHRISTIAN, Esq.
* JOSEPH CLARKE, Esq.
* HENRY CLUTTON, Esq.

R. T. COCKS, Esq.
* W. C. COCKS, Esq.
* J. G. CRACE, Esq.
LIEUT.-GEN. THE HON. SIR E. CUST
* J. S. DANIEL, Esq.
E. B. DENISON, Esq., Q.C.
THE EARL OF DUNRAVEN
WILLIAM DYCE, Esq., R.A.
VISCOUNT FIELDING
* BENJAMIN FERREY, Esq.
F. J. FRANCIS, Esq.
RT. HON. W. E. GLADSTONE, M.P.
* GEORGE GODWIN, Esq.
* G. GOLDIE, Esq.
HIS EXCELLENCY G. J. R. GORDON
* J. H. HAKEWELL, Esq.
* JOHN HARDMAN, Esq.
PHILIP HARDWICK, Esq., R.A.
* P. C. HARDWICK, Esq.
JOHN HAYWARD, Esq.
LORD HERBERT OF LEA
* T. H. WASHINGTON HIBBERT, Esq.
* J. HOGARTH, Esq.
— HOLLINS, Esq.

Donations will also be received by the members of the Committee, the Honorary Local Secretaries, and at the Royal Institute of British Architects, 9, Conduit Street, W.; MESSRS. MASTERS AND CO., 33, Aldersgate Street, E.C., and 78, New Bond Street, W.; MESSRS. BURNS AND LAMBERT, 17, Portman Street, Portman Square, W.; MESSRS. BELL AND DALDY, 186, Fleet Street, E.C.; MESSRS. HOGARTH, 5, Haymarket, S.W.; MESSRS. COLNAGHI, SCOTT, AND CO., 14, Pall Mall East, S.W.; Mr. C. DOLMAN, 61, New Bond Street, W.; MESSRS. HARDMAN AND CO., 13, King William Street, Charing Cross, W.C.; 166, Great Charles Street, Birmingham; and 48, Grafton Street, Dublin; MESSRS. LAVERS AND BARRAUD, Endell Street, Long Acre, W.C.; MR. HENRY G. BOHN, 4, York Street, Covent Garden, W.C.; and MR. STANFORD, 6, Charing Cross, S.W.

Donations.

	£	s.	d.		£	s.	d.
T. D. Acland, Esq., *Sprydoncote*	2	0	0	Henry Bowman, Esq. ...	1	1	0
Rev. Geo. Ainslie	2	2	0	Mr. Samuel Brancall ...	2	0	0
„ (2nd donation) ...	1	1	0	David Brandon, Esq. ...	5	0	0
G. Aitchison, Jun., Esq. ...	1	1	0	Rev. J. R. Bloxam, D.D. ...	2	2	0
Edward Akroyd, Esq. ...	2	2	0	M. H. Bloxam, Esq. ...	2	2	0
Rev. A. Alcock	1	0	0	John Blyth, Esq.	5	5	0
T. G. D. Allason, Esq. ...	3	3	0	Henry G. Bohn, Esq. ...	5	5	0
W. Allcard, Esq.	5	0	0	Raphael Brandon, Esq. ...	1	1	0
Peter B. Alley, Esq. ...	1	0	0	W. Cunliffe Brooks, Esq. ...	5	0	0
Arthur Ashpitel, Esq. ...	2	2	0	Right Rev. Dr. Brown ...	5	0	0
C. Bruce Allen, Esq. ...	0	10	6	Mr. Joseph Browne	2	2	0
J. Lewis Andrè, Esq. ...	1	1	0	J. A. Bunker, Esq. ...	1	1	0
Edward Appleton, Esq. ...	2	2	0	A. Burges, Esq.	3	3	0
The Architectural Society				William Burges, Esq. ...	2	2	0
of the Archdeaconry of				Ven. Archdeacon Burney ...	5	5	0
Northampton	2	2	0	Rev. Henry Burney ...	1	1	0
Edward Ashworth, Esq. ...	1	1	0	Messrs. Burt and Potts ...	2	2	0
Messrs. Atchley and Co. ...	1	1	0	Decimus Burton, Esq. ...	2	2	0
H. G. Austin, Esq. ...	3	3	0	Charles Buxton, Esq., M.P.	2	2	0
Rev. and Hon. H. C. Bagot	1	1	0	Talbot Bury, Esq.	21	0	0
Charles Barry, Esq. ...	10	0	0	C. W. W. (per A. W. Blom-			
E. M. Barry, Esq. ...	5	5	0	field, Esq.)	2	2	0
R. C. Baxter, Esq. ...	1	1	0	The Dean of Canterbury ...	5	0	0
Henry Benson, Esq. ...	2	0	0	The Earl of Carlisle ...	2	2	0
A. J. B. Beresford-Hope, Esq.	25	0	0	The Carpenter Memorial Fund,			
John Billing, Esq.	2	2	0	balance (per Ecclesiological			
R. Blake-Humphrey, Esq. ...	1	1	0	Society)	4	4	6
J. G. Bland, Esq.	1	1	0	J. H. Chamberlain, Esq. ...	2	2	0
A. W. Blomfield, Esq. ...	2	2	0	R. Chamberlain, Esq. ...	0	10	0
De la Barre Bodenham, Esq.	5	0	0	R. D. Chantrell, Esq. ...	5	5	0
J. R. Botham, Esq. ...	1	1	0	Ewan Christian, Esq. ...	5	5	0

	£	s.	d.
J. A. Clark, Esq.	1	1	0
G. Somers Clarke, Esq.	3	3	0
Joseph Clarke, Esq.	10	10	0
Messrs. Clayton and Bell	2	2	0
Thomas Close, Esq.	2	2	0
Henry Clutton, Esq., *Burlington Street*	2	2	0
Henry Clutton, Esq., *Whitehall Place*	2	2	0
Professor Cockerell, R.A.	10	0	0
F. P. Cockerell, Esq.	2	2	0
Colonel Cocks	3	0	0
R. T. Cocks, Esq.	5	5	0
W. C. Cocks, Esq.	2	2	0
James K. Colling, Esq.	2	2	0
Rev. W. J. Copeland	2	2	0
R. S. Cornish, Esq.	1	1	0
W. R. Corson, Esq.	1	1	0
J. G. Crace, Esq.	5	5	0
Lewis Cubitt, Esq.	5	5	0
C. N. Cumberlidge, Esq.	5	0	0
Lieut.-Gen. the Hon. Sir Edward Cust	5	0	0
H. A. Darbishire, Esq.	5	5	0
J. S. Daniel Esq.	5	0	0
H. Dawson, Esq.	1	1	0
E. B. Denison, Esq., Q.C.	5	0	0
G. Devey, Esq.	2	2	0
F. H. Dickinson, Esq.	2	0	0
Rev. J. Downey	1	0	0
R. W. Drew, Esq.	2	2	0
Rev. J. W. Deans Dundas	0	10	6
The Earl of Dunraven	10	0	0
William Dyce, Esq., R. A.	2	2	0
E. W. P.	5	5	0
Editor of '*Building News*'	5	5	0
Francis Edwards, Esq.	1	1	0
Edward Ellis, Esq.	1	1	0
Very Rev. Mgr. Eyre	1	1	0
Mr. W. Farmer	2	2	0
Mr. W. Farmer's Carvers	1	2	6
Messrs. Farrell and Ledger	1	0	0
Viscount Fielding	5	5	0
Benjamin Ferrey, Esq.	10	0	0
Mr. W. Field	1	1	0
F. R. Fisher, Esq.	2	2	0
C. N. Foster, Esq.	2	2	0
F. J. Francis, Esq.	3	3	0
J. W. Fraser, Esq.	1	1	0
Messrs. Fulljames and Waller	2	2	0
J. Dunn Gardner, Esq.	3	3	0
Henry B. Garling, Esq.	1	1	0
Messrs. Garrett	2	2	0
Hugh Gates, Esq.	2	0	
J. Elkington Gill, Esq.	1	1	0
John Gibson, Esq.	2	2	0
C. E. Giles, Esq.	1	1	0
W. J. Gillett, Esq.	2	2	0
Rt. Hon. W. E. Gladstone, M.P.	5	0	0
George Godwin, Esq.	2	2	0
G. Goldie, Esq.	3	3	0
J. H. Good, Esq.	2	2	0
F. S. Gosling, Esq.	2	2	0
His Excellency G. J. R. Gordon	2	2	0
Right Rev. Dr. Grant	10	0	0
Messrs. Gray and Davison	2	2	0
Rev. S. S. Greatheed	5	5	0
Earl de Grey and Ripon	5	0	0
W. D. Griffin, Esq.	2	2	0
J. Griffith, Esq.	10	10	0
E. B. Gudgeon, Esq.	1	0	0
Daniel Gurney, Esq.	3	3	0
Messrs. Habershon and Pite	5	5	0
M. E. Hadfield, Esq.	5	0	0
J. H. Hakewill, Esq.	5	5	0
W. Parker Hammond, Esq.	1	1	0
John Hardman, Esq.	21	0	0
P. Hardwick, Esq., R.A.	5	5	0
P. C. Hardwick, Esq.	5	5	0
J. Battersby Harford, Esq.	1	1	0
Messrs. Harland and Fisher	2	2	0
John Harris, Esq.	2	0	0
Charles Hart, Esq.	5	5	0
Edward Haycock, Jun., Esq.	1	1	0
John D. Hayton, Esq.	1	1	0
Charles F. Hayward, Esq.	1	1	0
H. W. Hayward, Esq.	2	2	0
John Hayward, Esq.	5	0	0
Pearson Hayward, Esq.	0	10	0
William Hayward, Esq.	1	1	0
Messrs. Heaton and Butler	2	0	0
William Herbert, Esq.	5	5	0
Lord Herbert of Lea	2	2	0
George Heron, Esq.	1	0	0
T. H. Washington Hibbert, Esq.	10	10	0

	£.	s.	d.
Rev. James Hildyard ...	1	1	0
Mrs. John Hill	1	1	0
T. C. Hine, Esq.	2	2	0
J. H. Hirst, Esq.	1	1	0
J. Hogarth, Esq.	2	2	0
Messrs. Hollins, Minton,			
and Co.	50	0	0
W. Hopkinson, Esq. ...	1	1	0
Lord Edward Howard, M.P.	2	2	0
Edward Hughes, Esq. ...	1	1	0
Rev. Æneas Hutchison, B.D.	1	1	0
Edward I'Anson, Esq. ...	5	5	0
W. S. Inman, Esq.	1	1	0
J. B., *Carver, Manchester*	1	1	0
W. Jeakes, Esq.	2	2	0
Sir W. C. James, Bart. ...	2	2	0
Rev. Thomas James ...	1	1	0
Mr. George Jarrett ...	0	10	6
Rev. W. G. Jervis... ...	0	10	0
Owen Jones, Esq.	5	5	0
Henry Kennedy, Esq ...	5	5	0
Stuart Knill, Esq.	10	10	0
Mrs. Knill, *Eliot Lodge* ...	5	0	0
Mr. H. Lane	1	1	0
E. F. Law, Esq.	1	1	0
Messrs. Lavers and Barraud	2	2	0
Mr. C. J. Lea	1	1	0
In Mr. Lea's employment—			
Mr. A. Wotherspoon ...	0	5	0
Mr. West	0	5	0
Mr. S. Sharpe ...	0	5	0
Mr. R. Grimsley	0	2	6
Mr. J. Broughton ...	0	2	6
William Leigh, Esq. ...	3	0	0
T. H. Lewis, Esq.... ...	2	2	0
William Lightly, Esq. ...	1	1	0
M. J. Lomax, Esq. ...	1	1	0
Edward Low, Esq.... ...	0	5	0
Charles Luard, Esq. ...	1	1	0
Messrs. Lucas, Brothers ...	5	5	0
A. Luck, Esq, ...	5	0	0
Rev. W. C. Lukis	1	1	0
Charles Manby, Esq. ...	2	2	0
Lord John Manners, M.P.	5	0	0
J. H. Markland, Esq. ...	2	2	0
Messrs. Masters and Co. ...	2	2	0
A. Maw, Esq.	1	1	0
G. Maw, Esq., F.L.S.,F.S.A.	1	1	0

	£.	s.	d.
Mr. Mawson, *Clerk of Works,*			
(Workmen's Donations per)	0	5	6
Charles Mayhew, Esq. ...	1	1	0
Barry McMullen, Esq. ...	2	2	0
Messrs. Mears	2	2	0
George Morgan, Esq. ...	2	2	0
James Murgatroyd, Esq. ...	2	2	0
C. R. Scott Murray, Esq. ...	10	10	0
G. Myers, Esq.	21	0	0
Messrs. Myers and Sons ...	21	0	0
Rev. and Hon. H. A. Napier	1	0	0
Edwin Nash, Esq.	2	2	0
C. C. Nelson, Esq.... ...	2	2	0
W. Eden Nesfield, Esq. ...	1	1	0
W. A. Nesfield, Esq. ...	1	1	0
His Grace the Duke of New-			
castle	5	0	0
John Nicholson, Esq. ...	2	2	0
Jonathan Nield, Jun., Esq.	5	0	0
Mr. R. Norman	0	10	6
John Norton, Esq.... ...	5	5	0
A. O'Connor, Esq.... ...	2	2	0
Messrs. O'Connor's Assistants	1	0	0
Rev. R. B. O'Reilly ...	1	0	0
Mr. Osmond	1	1	0
Thomas Page, Esq.... ...	1	1	0
J. H. Parker, Esq. ...	5	5	0
Robert Parris, Esq. ...	1	1	0
T. Gambier l'arry, Esq. ...	2	2	0
Sir Joseph Paxton, M.P. ...	5	0	0
Edward Peacock, Esq. ...	1	1	0
J. L. Pearson, Esq. ...	2	2	0
R. K. Penson, Esq. ...	10	0	0
Ambrose Lisle Phillips, Esq.	5	0	0
R. M. Phipson, Esq. ...	1	1	0
Charles Poland, Esq. ...	1	1	0
Messrs. Poole and Son ...	1	1	0
F. W. Porter, Esq. ...	1	11	6
F. H. Pownall, Esq. ...	2	2	0
J. H. Powell, Esq	21	0	0
William Powell, Esq. ...	10	0	0
James Powell, Esq. ...	5	0	0
Arthur Powell, Esq. ...	2	2	0
Right Hon. the Earl of Powis	5	0	0
Messrs. Prichard and Seddon	2	2	0
G. E. Pritchett, Esq. ...	1	1	0
R. P. Pullan, Esq.... ...	2	2	0
Messrs. Randell and Saunders	5	5	0

	£.	s.	d.
Charles Ratcliff, Esq. ...	2	2	0
Mr. W. Radcliffe, *Clerk of*			
Works	2	2	0
E. T. Richards, Esq.	1	1	0
J. Richardson, Esq. ...	0	10	6
Geo. Richmond, Esq., A.R.A.	3	3	0
Mr. Ringham	2	2	0
Edward Roberts, Esq. ...	2	2	0
F. J. Robinson, Esq. ...	1	1	0
Francis Rogers, Esq. ...	1	1	0
W. R. Rogers, Esq. ...	1	1	0
R. L. Roumieu, Esq. ...	3	3	0
R. Reynolds Rowe, Esq. ...	2	2	0
T. H. Rushforth, Esq. ...	1	1	0
Lord John Russell, M.P. ...	5	0	0
Rev. C. W. Russell, D.D. ...	2	2	0
J. Watts Russell, Esq. ...	2	2	0
Anthony Salvin, Esq. ...	5	0	0
Mr. John Sanders	1	0	0
Lady Scarisbrick	20	0	0
Sir F. E. Scott, Bart. ...	5	5	0
Rev. William Scott ...	1	1	0
G. G. Scott, Esq., R.A. ...	10	10	0
Rev. W. B. Scruton ...	2	2	0
Edmund Sharpe, Esq. ...	3	3	0
R. Norman Shaw, Esq. ...	0	10	6
George Simmonds, Esq. ...	1	1	0
F. Skidmore, Esq.	2	2	0
William Slater, Esq. ...	5	5	0
Messrs. Slater and Mc Dermott	1	1	0
J. P. Smith, Esq.	1	1	0
J. G. Stapleton, Jun., Esq.	1	1	0
Messrs. Starkey and Cuffley	2	2	0
J. P. St. Aubyn, Esq. ...	2	2	0
I. H. Stevens, Esq. ...	2	2	0
T. Stirling, Esq.	1	1	0
H. L. Styleman Le Strange, Esq.	1	0	0
G. E. Street, Esq.	5	5	0
Charles Strickland, Esq. ...	2	2	0
Sir G. H. Strickland, Bart.	2	0	0
J. G. Talbot, Esq.	2	0	0
J. H. Talbot, Esq.	3	0	0
S. S. Teulon, Esq.	3	3	0
W. M. Teulon, Esq. ...	1	1	0
J. Thomson, Esq.	1	1	0

	£.	s.	d.
W. Thompson, Esq. ...	1	1	0
Mrs. Thornton	5	0	0
Archdeacon Thorp	5	0	0
W. Tite, Esq., M.P. ...	21	0	0
— Townsend, Esq... ...	1	1	0
Sir Humphrey de Trafford, Bt.	5	0	0
R. de Trafford, Esq. ...	2	0	0
R. Tress, Esq.	2	2	0
H. Tritton, Esq.	10	10	0
Mr. H. C. Tucker	1	1	0
Charles Turner, Esq. ...	1	1	0
John Turner, Esq. ...	1	1	0
Harry F. Vernon, Esq. ...	2	2	0
W. Wailes, Esq.	2	2	0
J. W. Walker, Esq. ...	1	1	0
Rev. J. Walmsley	1	1	0
Messrs. Walton and Robson	2	2	0
R. E. Egerton Warburton, Esq.	5	0	0
Messrs. Ward and Hughes...	2	2	0
Messrs. Warren and Co. ...	1	0	0
Alfred Waterhouse, Esq. ...	2	2	0
Ditto a Friend, per ...	0	5	0
C. Knight Watson, Esq., F.S.A.	5	0	0
Rev. Benjamin Webb ...	1	1	0
Julius Wegeler, Esq. ...	1	1	0
F. R. Wegg-Prosser, Esq. ...	2	2	0
Thomas Wells, Esq. ...	2	2	0
The Dean of Westminster ...	2	2	0
G. F. White, Esq.	1	1	0
William White, Esq. ...	3	3	0
Sir Gardner Wilkinson ...	2	2	0
Thomas Willement, Esq. ...	2	0	0
Rev. George Williams ...	3	0	0
James Williams, Esq. ...	2	2	0
Mr. Wm. Wilson	2	2	0
Rev. Albert M. Wilson ...	0	10	0
T. Worthington, Esq. ...	1	1	0
C. H. L. Woodd, Esq. ...	1	1	0
B. Woodward, Esq. ...	3	3	0
H. Woodyer, Esq.	2	2	0
M. Digby Wyatt, Esq. ...	3	3	0
T. H. Wyatt, Esq.	5	5	0
Hugh Yates, Esq.	2	0	0
R. Yeldham, Esq.	1	1	0
Rev. Walter Young ...	1	1	0

Total £1,074 0 0

The Committee hope to raise at least £1,500.

INDEX

compiled by Jane Wainwright